SAWDUST CAESAR

──────★──────

* *

SAWDUST CAESAR

THE UNTOLD HISTORY OF

MUSSOLINI AND FASCISM

By GEORGE SELDES

Author of "World Panorama," "The Vatican:
Yesterday—Today—Tomorrow," Etc.

*

HARPER & BROTHERS PUBLISHERS

New York and London

1935

To

HELEN SELDES

my wife and collaborator

CONTENTS

Part III—Mussolini Victorious

Appendices

Contents

With astonishing success the Fascisti have not only cut off true contemporary record of their deeds, but have invented a whole history of their past which is usurping the suppressed truth.

In another five years every scrap of material evidence of the real history of Fascism will have disappeared as thoroughly as the dossier of Mussolini from the Swiss Police Bureau.

It will be a pity, for instead of a perfectly logical and fascinating story of a human man and his ambitions, the historian will have to content himself with the false epic of romantic heroes that is being served up in every language, with photographs, today.

WILLIAM BOLITHO, December, 1925.

FOREWORD

To Americans Facing Fascism

FASCISM NOT ONLY EXISTS IN AMERICA, BUT IT HAS BECOME formidable and needs only a Duce, a Fuehrer, an organizer, and a loosening of the purse strings of those who gain materially by its victory, to become the most powerful force threatening the Republic.

Those who cannot see the growth of Fascism or deny its existence are either the many who do not know what Fascism really is or the few who prefer euphemism—a patriotic American name for a distinctly European product.

To understand Fascism it is necessary to know its suppressed history and the mind and actions of its spiritual father, and it is the purpose of this book to present documented facts, to the best of the author's ability, as objectively as possible, so that the reader can compare the origins of Fascism in Italy with the present situation in our own country, the Duce to our own demagogues, the hidden forces which subsidized the Italian movement to those just emerging in the United States.

The brilliant William Bolitho never wrote a truer word than his prediction that the real record of Mussolini's private and political life would disappear within five years. Ten years have passed, the suppressed truth has been overwhelmed by the myths created by public-relations counsel who helped float some $600,000,000 worth of Italian bonds in America, and the propaganda of such men as our late ambassador to Italy (and later Hearst writer), the Honorable Richard Washburn Child, and the ultra-Fascist Italians employed by leading American news agencies and newspapers.

There exist, it is true, some 200 volumes on Mussolini and Fascism, but reading them all, as I have done, merely confirms Bolitho's prediction. With about a dozen exceptions which are frankly anti-

Fascist but nevertheless honest in their facts and two or three which deal with specific phases or problems, there remain some 190 works, including the Duce's own autobiography, which unite in a chorus of unmitigated hero-worship while they suppress the essential story.

Many so-called important biographies are written by ladies on their knees. "Mussolini is tender and gentle. . . . He is so aristocratic and natural, and, oh, what eyes! . . . They are black and powerful and remind one of the eyes of a saint. . . . He has a wonderful sense of justice. . . . He has abolished handshaking. . . . When he receives ladies he comes around from behind his table and kisses the hand gently. . . . Mussolini is extraordinarily young to be the greatest man of the present and past. . . . All Italy adores him. . . . Forty-four million Italians pray each day and thank God for having sent them this wonderful man who has saved Italy. He is the only genius the war has produced."

This is the sort of genuflectual claptrap, romantic moonshine, and *suggestio falsi* written by hand-kissed women, but the gentlemen are little better. "Mussolini is the greatest man of our sphere and time," reports our late Hon. Mr. Child, making the inevitable comparison with Theodore Roosevelt, the Mussolini *manqué* of the generation past.

For the benefit of reviewers of a previous book I must state that I nurse no grudge against Mussolini or Fascism because of my expulsion from Italy in 1925. Quite the contrary. I believe that I owe the Duce a note of thanks. In 1923 the Soviet Cheka asked me to leave Russia for the same reason on which the Fascist Cheka acted two years later: the transmission of news items the truth of which was not denied but was held unfavorable to the ruling powers. Both expulsions were inevitable, as all writers who do not compromise and trim their sails soon learn if they defy the dictators. From the Fascist as from the Bolshevik viewpoint the expulsion was absolutely justified, although it was perhaps stupid.

In 1931 I visited Italy secretly; I have had the secret coöperation of several of the most prominent American journalists now resident in Rome who express their pleasure in smuggling news and documents to me. The materials which follow I have collected over a period of fifteen years, beginning in the days I first knew Mussolini as a fellow but rather violent journalist. The first draft, completed in 1931, was accepted by a British publisher, but suppressed at the suggestion of the Foreign Office. The Quai d'Orsay likewise asked a French publisher to "delay" publication owing to the diplomatic situation. I have tried to recount the significant facts in the belief that, although history may be "lies agreed upon," there may be some value in stating realities at a time they may be useful to those seeking a new road out of the present world dilemma.

Bandol (Var), France, 1931.
Woodstock, Vermont, 1935.

Part I

THE FORCE OF DESTINY

★ ★

CHAPTER I

Tide ... Taken at the Flood

WHEN THE EUROPEAN WAR CRISIS CAME TO ITALY, AS IT WAS to come to America two years later, all the parties of the Left, the radicals, the liberals, were joined by the Democrats, the Center, and elements of the Right in denouncing the war mongers who favored the Triple Entente or the Triple Alliance. So long as the powerful Socialist Party remained integrated, intelligent, and determined in its opposition to war, so long as its official organ, *Avanti,* and its courageous editor, Benito Mussolini, united the laboring masses to the policies of the party, the war makers dared not move.

On July 27th Mussolini wrote the decisive editorial of the time, under the startling headline, "Our Neutrality Must Be Absolute." It was more than an abrogation of Italy's contract to fight with Germany and Austro-Hungary; it was a threat of revolution at home. The government realized that *Avanti* had struck the popular tune. The Nationalists still raged patriotically about the nation's duty to Germany, and Albertini of the *Corriere della Sera* and Bergamini of the *Giornale d'Italia* coined pre-Wilsonian phrases about saving Democracy and preserving Civilization by joining the Allies, but realistic politicians knew Italy was out of the war.

Officially on the 4th of August the Socialist Party voted neutrality. Loudest and most violent of the strict neutralitarians, militant pacifists, die-hard Socialists, was the white knight of peace-at-any-price and the red internationale, the editor of *Avanti.*

Magnificently he met the challenge. His editorials were heavy with sarcasm, his phrases reeked of the Milan political gutters, he used words rarely if ever seen except on fences, but his pacifist violence was absolutely bloodthirsty. He even mocked the Belgian atroci-

3

ties which were breaking the heart of the world, and he sneered
at the pretensions of Republican France, which, he said, was born in
revolution, consecrated to the glorious future of humanity in the
bloody days of the Commune, and had now become a militaristic,
capitalistic, exploiting, and suppressing nation. Austria he hated with
a national hatred. Through his months of fury there ran this Leit-
motif: Revolt! Let the proletarians of all the nations, French, German, and Russian, and Austrian too, arise and smite the bourgeoisie
of both sides who were bathing the world in blood for their own
financial profits; smite them, destroy them, and establish the dictatorship of the working-class. Thus he echoed Lenin in nearby Switzerland.

But the German Socialists, with the exception of such men as
Liebknecht, the French with the exception of the Juarès-Rolland
group, and the liberals and radicals of many other countries, suddenly became patriots, voted war credits, and rallied round flags,
leaving for Italy and Mussolini only one honorable open road—strict
neutrality. Late in August, 1914, Mussolini was attacking the "delirium tremens of the Nationalists" whose "scandalous opportunism"
favored intervention. "Italy," reiterated the editor of *Avanti*, "must
remain neutral. We Socialists, tenacious enemies of war, are par-
tisans of neutrality."

He saw the war as the "crisis of capitalist society"; unable to
exploit it for revolt, he urged sabotage, but at least neutrality. His
old editor in Italian Austria, Cesare Battisti, who wanted Italy to
free the Trentino and Venetia Giulia, the irredenta provinces, became
his enemy. On the 4th of September, under the headline "Italian
Proletariat, Resist the War Menace," Mussolini continued: "We are
invited to weep over martyred Belgium. We are in the presence of a
sentimental farce staged by France, and Belgium herself. These two
old gossips would exploit the universal credulity. For us Belgium is
nothing but a belligerent power just like the others . . . all the powers
at war are of the same degree of guilt, and it is our right, our duty,
to cause a revolution of the working-class against them."

On the 21st of September Mussolini arose to new pacifist heights
of violence. The Socialist Party convened in Bologna under the eyes
of the belligerent world. The editor of the party organ was given

the floor. He began with an oration for neutrality, which was expected, but suddenly launched into an attack on his colleagues, the comrades of the party, saying their anti-war effort was infantile, useless, they must become revolutionary, follow him, preach and work for the new Commune in France and Belgium, in Germany and Austria and in Russia, smashing Tsardoms and republics in all the countries at war and establishing the utopian dictatorship of the proletarian masses. It was Mussolini at his best.

On the 25th of September, four days later, this same wild, impassioned pacifist issued a call for all Italy to come to arms, to join him and march to the front, to take the side of ravished France and martyred Belgium, and "to drown the war in its own blood."

What had happened in those four days between the 21st and 25th of September? Nothing short of a miracle, say all the laudatory biographers of the present Duce. He "weighed the situation," says one; "Illumination came to him," says another; and still a third informs this unbelieving world that "he miraculously changed his opinion and founded the *Popolo d'Italia* as a clarion call to all Italy to take up arms on the sides of the Allies." Mussolini himself is silent, half-hearted at best, usually mysterious and vague when this question of the miracle confronts him.

But in all the political cafés of the kingdom long-bearded ministers of state, emotional waiters and angry workingmen, discussing the situation, asked only one question: *"Chi paga?"* ("Who has paid for it?") The whispers rose; the tumult eventually reached the ears of the persons most concerned.

Mussolini was still editing the Socialist daily. On the 10th of October his leading editorial was entitled "From absolute neutrality to active and operating neutrality." The government took this as a sign that the whole Socialist movement was wavering, that it could go ahead with its plans, certain that the Mussolini wing would no longer make its promised revolutionary troubles. But Mussolini's first assistant editor, Angelica Balabanoff, said to him: "When you write as you do, it seems you go either to a madhouse or to the trenches; you must be prepared to take the consequences; there is no place in Socialism for you now."

"You will see," replied Mussolini, "that the whole executive committee will declare its solidarity with me."

He spoke in such a grandiloquent, theatrical voice that Dr. Balabanoff had the feeling he was suffering either from delusions of grandeur or actual insanity. She informed him of the table talk in all the cafés, asking him for a straight answer. All she got were shouts of denial and threats of revenge.

Then suddenly, early in November, Mussolini resigned as editor of *Avanti.* His associate had begged him to stay and asked him how he would make his living.

"Five lire a day are enough for me," he replied, "and I can earn them as a mason.

"I will never write another word.

"And of this you can be assured: it is that I will never write a word against the Socialist Party."

Just eight days later, on the 15th of November, 1914, there appeared a new journal on the streets of Milan. It was called *Il Popolo d'Italia* and underneath the title were the words: *Quotidiano Socialista* (Socialist Daily). In its right ear appeared the quotation *"La rivoluzione è un'idea che ha trovato delel baionette*: Napoleone" ("Revolution is an idea which has obtained bayonets"). In the left ear of this new "Socialist" newspaper was the quotation from the rebel leader, Blanqui, *"Chi ha del ferro ha del pane"* ("Whoever has a weapon has bread").

The feature of the first issue was a large editorial with the heading "Audacia." It concluded:

"I shall produce a daily which shall be independent, liberal in the extreme, personal. My own. . . . For I shall be answerable to my own conscience and nothing else. I have no aggressive intentions towards the Socialist Party, in which I propose to remain. . . .

"Continuing my march after a brief respite, I fling to you my call, O Youth, Youth of Italy, youth of the workshops and universities, who have your heart and soul young, who belong to the generation which has to make the future according to the command of destiny—my call, which will resound into History.

"This appeal, this cry, is a word that I would never have uttered in normal times, but which I give out today clearly and vigorously, without reservation, and I give it with full confidence—that one rebellious and terrifying word, W A R!"

The leading pacifist of Italy now essayed the rôle of leading interventionist. But he still called his a Socialist newspaper and proclaimed his adherence to the Socialist Party and its major doctrines.

Led by Serrati, Mussolini's boyhood friend and teacher, the Socialist Party now took action. A general assembly was called in Bologna for November 25th, at which the former editor accepted the invitation to defend himself.

As Mussolini entered the excited hall the congress shouted as one man: "Chi paga?"

The general assembly became a trial for treason. Mussolini accepted the challenge. Immediately Serrati and the remaining editorial board of *Avanti* demanded Mussolini's political life. (In time to come all men and newspapers which now attacked him were to feel the clubs, the bullets, and the flames of an old-fashioned Italian blood vendetta.)

"Chi paga?" thousands of voices shouted, "Traditore! Venduto! Sicario!"

The assembly, members who participated recount, was tumultuous and bellicose. There was difficulty in finding a president, a personality strong enough to calm the angry accusers and permit the defendant to speak, explain. It seemed impossible. The assembly became unruly, infuriated, vociferous in its insults. Judging by the shouting, one would have believed it wanted to beat the accused to death. Serrati arose, begging that he be allowed to speak in perfect quiet. Utopia! For a minute the pacifists were pacific. Mussolini was called to the platform. Suddenly all his enemies decided to hear him. "Louder! Louder!" The orator's voice was lost in the uproar.

But it was none the less stirring. "You are more implacable," Mussolini cried, "than the bourgeois judges who leave the right to the defense. If you have decided that I am unworthy of fighting amongst you . . ."

"Yes, yes!" shrieked the audience.

"Expel me, then, but I have the right of demanding an act of accusation in good form. . . . I will not be guillotined with a motion that doesn't mean anything. As far as the moral question is concerned, I repeat once more that I am ready to submit to any commission of inquiry whatsoever.

"You think you are destroying me, but I tell you that you are mistaken. *Voi mi odiate perchè ancora mi amate!* You hate me today, because you still love me. But you will not ruin me. . . . My twelve years of party life are or should be a sufficient guarantee of my Socialist faith. Socialism is something which is rooted in the blood. . . . What separated me from you now is not a petty matter; it is a question which is dividing all of Socialism. Amilcare Cipriani himself has declared in speech and in writing, that if his seventy-five years would permit it, he would be in the trenches today, fighting against the European militaristic reaction which is stifling our revolution.

"But I tell you," continued Mussolini, "that from now on I shall have no mercy, no pity for all those who in this tragic moment do not speak their minds, for fear of being either hissed or cried down. I shall have no mercy, no pity, for those who are reticent, hypocritical, vile. . . . And you shall yet see me at your side. You will not have to believe that the bourgeoisie are enthusiastic for our intervention. They are gnashing their teeth, they are accusing us of temerity and are afraid that the proletariat, armed with the bayonet, may use it for its own purpose.

"Don't think that by tearing up my card you will deprive me of my Socialist faith, and that you will keep me from fighting for the cause of Socialism and the revolution."

In spite of this stirring self-vindication, Mussolini was struck from the party. Thus it is recorded that "the first responsibility for Fascism falls to Socialism."

Mussolini, raging, ran to his paper, the *Popolo d'Italia,* and between shouting and waving his arms wrote the following reply:

"EXPELLED

"If I wanted to stand on a question of procedure, I would have the right of putting in doubt the legitimacy of the vote, in demanding even whether a true and proper vote had taken place, given the manner in which this discussion evolved from the beginning to the end, directed by the shameless partiality of the assessor Schiavi. But I accept the *fait accompli.* I consider myself expelled. The history of

Italian Socialism does not have in its more or less glorious pages a more summary execution, more Inquisition-like, more bestial than the one that trapped me. De Marinis, Bissolati, and the others were submitted to exclusion from the big debates of the congress, and were accorded very broadly the right of defense; and their accusation was carried to the tribune, documented, exhausting its object.

"For me, nothing of the sort. The trial was conducted in the shortest possible way. Some one presented the most radical motion without even sustaining it; after much hesitation, I was allowed to expose my thought; then Lazzari [a Socialist], instead of bringing up an act of accusation, repeated the usual low insinuation. The political question was not even touched, the moral question not examined. If that is Socialist justice, truly one should prefer that of Magistrate Allara. But the breed which dominates the party wished to conquer, and conquer it did.

"I am expelled, but not tamed. If they think me dead, they will have the terrible surprise of finding me alive, implacable, intent upon combating them with all my strength. That is why I have forged for myself the weapon with which to enlighten the proletariat and to remove it from the sad influence of these false preachers. And I hope that in the proletariat of the simple and upright soul, the light will be seen promptly.

"It is not against the proletariat—it is not against the sacred principles of the proletariat—that I am fighting. The proletarians know well that when it was a matter of assuming responsibility for the uprisings, for the lawsuits in the Court of Assizes, for the campaigns of the party, I gave freely of myself out of an incoercible need of action, without worrying about the danger, without measuring my fatigue. But you, gentlemen, who form the directing élite of the party, you who speak when you should be silent, or who are silent when you should speak; you with the medals, you who have preferred to hide your votes in the amorphous and tempestuous hand-raising, you who, however, owe something to the 'Barbarossa' of June, you will have to pass under the Caudine forks. I understand the hatred, the exasperation of the proletarians, but your reticences constitute a document of a baseness which dishonors Italian Socialism to the extreme point. But I am precisely here to spoil your little party.

"*The Mussolini case is not over, as you think. It is just beginning. It is becoming complicated. It is taking on vaster proportions. I am openly raising the flag of schism.* I am not becoming appeased—I am crying out. I do not bend; I am revolting.

"All the Socialists who claim for themselves the right to live, and to think; the proletarians who refuse to bend to the wishes of a coterie which pretends stupidly to stay the course of history and to dictate an eternal and universal law, must gather around this paper, a free arena for free minds, a pure standard which the infamous insinuation of a damaged breed will never succeed in soiling. A party which 'carries on' in this fashion is a party into which men worthy of the name cannot enter—or, once inscribed, cannot, must not remain. I invite them to leave, to seek more liberty, more air, more light, more humanity, and more Socialism.

"And now, driving into the depths of my soul all sadness and all complaint, I gather together my weapons, all my weapons. For Socialism! and against the obvious enemies, and the occult enemies of Socialism!"

Looking back to that great crisis which was to lead so quickly to Fascism and to dictatorship, Mussolini says of his expulsion and of his raising the banner of schism: "I felt lighter, fresher, I was free."

He was free.

The turn in his life had been taken. Our Caesar had crossed his Rubicon. He was now editor and owner of a paper; he was becoming feared and respected and followed; moreover, he was no longer held by party lines and rules and the ideas of dead men. He was free!

This was the moment for which he had waited. Out of biographies and histories he had made a pattern for his own life and built a world-empire for himself, which he ruled with appropriate magic words. Denying in childhood and youth the power of men and gods, he had spoken always of his Star of Destiny, repeating Napoleon's favorite phrase until he believed he was its author, and always he had cultivated not only the historical but the Shakespearean Julius Caesar in word and look.

In his youth he had announced sententiously his belief in both

Free Will and Predestination, and unlike his fellow men who drifted where tide and wind fantastically veered, the young editor of the Socialist *Avanti* felt that a situation would one day arise, that he would master it, and then achieve that satisfaction which a magnificent egotism, chained in childhood by poverty and misfortune, in youth by the dead hand of Karl Marx and the pressure of political organization, had made inevitable for him.

Good European that he was, he realized early in life that the road to power led directly through the doors of a newspaper office. He had before him the picture of the first and third Napoleons, the later Bismarck, the contemporary Northcliffe. He had already tasted the surprise and satisfaction in the effects of his amateur writings on the mass mind, both in Switzerland and in his native province, and the elevation to *Avanti* had confirmed every thought about the power of the press. He was free. He was independent.

And yet, there was that childhood in Socialism and that manhood suffering for "the cause" which could never be forgotten. "Socialism is something which is rooted in the blood." It was to appear time and time again in the black blood stream of Fascism.

He had raised the flag of schism, but the old ideals which he had absorbed with his mother's milk and his father's sweaty bread were still beneath the banner. He had been horribly wounded, but he still believed it was he who was the great hero, the noble patriot, and although the Italian world shouted "Traitor" for many years, he tried more than once to return to that paternal heaven under which he was born and raised to leadership.

And again the cry "Chi Paga?" would be raised, the charge of betrayal, the charge that he had sold the Socialist Party and peace for a handful of silver from a foreign country.

★ ★

CHAPTER II

The Romantic Rebel

BY DESERTING THE POLICY OF NEUTRALITY AND PACIFISM OF HIS
Socialist colleagues, young Benito Mussolini earned the immediate enmity of many million compatriots who, naturally accusing
him of treason, suspected that the Allies had invested large sums in
this secret business. Even today, reviewing the entire political career
of the Duce, there are some who say that "he has raised betrayal to
a mode of life" and who offer documentary proof of this appraisal.

As an action, of course, Mussolini's was not without parallels in
past history, and it recurs in the lives of other notable living men.
If, however, we accept the philosophy of the Gautama Buddha, if
we desire to understand all so that we may forgive all, it is necessary
first to review for a moment the childhood and youth of the man who
has risen to such worldly eminence by following a course which to
some may appear nothing but zigzags, retreats, and changes of face,
but to others the straight and narrow path of a fierce and victorious
will to power.

The great students of human behavior agree that a human pattern
is "set" before the fifth year; the child grows to be a hero or a
traitor, a racketeer or a statesman; he becomes an artist, a leader, a
neurotic, a madman, because of his treatment by his parents, his
brothers and sisters, his companions; because of his youthful sex
life; because of these and many other events or influences, and the
environment of childhood.

Violence is the keynote of Mussolini's youth. He was whipped and
bullied by his father, pampered and kissed too much by his mother.
It was a hard childhood spent largely near a blacksmith's forge and
in a dirty country saloon. The blows he got from the fist and the
belt of Alessandro, that towering bulk of a blacksmith, the boy gave

in turn to weaker boys. The affection of his mother he kept for himself, repaid it only to her; he never loved deeply and he never had a true friend. He was *condemned*, says one who knew him in his youth, to either great good or great evil.

"I was not a good boy." "I was a restless and pugnacious child." "I was an audacious *ladro campestre*," he writes at various times, the third confession translatable as "rural thief" according to the dictionary, but "young buccaneer" by romantic lady biographers. He fought with his hands and with stones, sometimes sharpened, and there was blood spilled when young Benito engaged in battle with peasant lads and schoolboys. When his younger brother, Arnaldo, began to grow up he too was bullied and hit by his senior. "I was a little rogue, restless, exacting, passionate, pugnacious, and ever ready to fight. Often I came home with my head broken with stones, but I knew how to revenge myself."

The vendetta motif comes early. Life in that hard countryside around Varano da Costa, where he was born on July 29, 1883, was for children and men a constant struggle amidst great poverty, and where there is poverty and desperation there is always vendetta and betrayal and feuds and bloodshed and a more violent outlook on life. No wonder, then, that father Alessandro, an excellent man, an honest man who lived and suffered for his socialistic principles and who had spent three years in prison for having associated with the revolutionist Bakunin, when it came to teaching his own son the rules for getting along in a mean world, inculcated the policy of revenge, blow for blow, blood for blood. It was the philosophy of survival.

In his passionate Socialist days when he published his own little weekly, *La Lotte di Classe* (The Class Struggle), Benito wrote of Papa Alessandro:

"My father was born in 1854 in Predappio. . . . He became an apprentice in a smithy at Dovadola. Then he went to Dovia and there opened a forge. I do not know at what time and under what influences he became a follower of the Internationale. But it is certain that when he arrived at Dovia he was already carrying on a great propaganda, and had formed the first organization of the Internationale. He was thrown into prison. When he returned he remained under police supervision for forty-two weeks.

"His house always offered shelter and friendship to those pursued by the authorities. Later, when the Socialists had come to take part in municipal politics, my father became mayor of Predappio. In 1892 he formed in Predappio the first labor union. . . . In 1902 he was again arrested. . . . The clergy, the police, and the moderates persecuted him ceaselessly. . . .

"He left me no material heritage, but he left me a moral one—his treasure: the Ideal. . . .

"And after this sorrowful burial, I pursue my way, following in his footsteps."

The boy was named after Benito Juàrez, liberator of Mexico. Papa Alessandro chose the name for two reasons—anti-clericalism and rebellion; he taught his firstborn to hate the Catholic Church and the Royal State, calling both the oppressors of the human spirit.

From his father Benito learned that intelligence and subtlety must be employed by the minority if it was not to be forever suppressed by those in power. In his father's fate Mussolini saw that failure came to those who knew and spoke intelligent plans for the remaking of the world but who were weak in action. With every year of his childhood his confidence in himself increased.

Most characteristic of all the incidents which Mussolini himself recalled in the first days of his success, concerns his early oratory. His mother, terrified by tremendous noises and a locked door, said to him one day:

"Are you mad, my son? Only lunatics talk to themselves. What is ailing you?"

"Do not worry, dear mother," Benito replied, simply. "I was practicing oratory. Believe me, mother, the time will come when all Italy will tremble before me."

Friends and enemies alike have also drawn many morals from another youthful incident. Fear, betrayal, perfidy, treason, revenge, blows, bloodshed, all enter into it and all are remembered throughout a lifetime, and satisfaction comes over the face of the dictator as he recounts, time after time, how on his father's advice he sharpened a stone, ambushed his enemy, cut open his face, and cursed him. He had earlier that day come naïvely forward to accept the other boy's invitation and, if one is to believe the narrator, the neighbor lad, without provocation or warning, had smacked his face. That night he had had his revenge. But in the young mind the blow on the face remained forever imprinted, warning the coming leader never to trust another man, never to surround himself with friends, never to put his trust in humanity, but to rely on the ethics of Schopenhauer, Nietzsche, and above all that Machiavelli who despised the mass of human beings.

He was sent to the cloister of the Salesian Friars at Faenza, his mother hoping that the atmosphere of order and piety and the companionship of a better class of children would have some effect in curbing that violent nature. But the boy continued to seek quarrels, to insult those smaller and weaker than himself, and to give the monks many uneasy moments.

"Your father is a rebel," they once said to him, "and you, you are turning into a young anarchist." If he did not change he would be expelled. Then another schoolboy fight and more punishment. "Mussolini," the friar said, "your soul is black as hell. Confess your sins. Repent before it is too late. Confess or we expel you."

He fled from the school. He roamed, afraid of shadows, through the night, only to be caught and whipped and taken to confession. But instead of that being a lesson to him it only hardened him. The next time he got into a fight it was with an older boy. But young Mussolini knew now how to fight those physically stronger than himself. The world was civilized and there were weapons to be used. Mussolini gave his enemy what the Italians call a *temperinata*: he got out his penknife and stabbed the older boy.

Although, fortunately, the wound was not serious, the action was. The Salesian monks would stand for much; they would preach and they would use the rod, but they would not have bloodshed in their quiet walls. So Benito was sent home.

He had been a rebel. He had been a solitary. From the first days he could not mingle with others, could not accept orders, could not follow. He walked alone. He sought trouble and it always led to more loneliness. "Who in my whole life" he burst out one day, years later, "has shown me tenderness? Nobody! Poor, dreadfully poor, was my home, poor and bitter my life. Where could I have learned tenderness? Perhaps at school, in the cloister, or in the world? Nowhere. Then why do people wonder that I am reserved, solitary, harsh, and stern?"

At his next school at Forlimpopoli it is recorded by one named Bonavita that Mussolini "got into a fight with three fellow students; he went beyond legitimate defense and he had to flee from the college." The weapon used is not named. But it was always the same. From the first days when he pulled the hair of little girls, climbed about on the floor pinching bare feet, or bullying the children on the playgrounds, to the days he drew a knife, it was always the same rebellion to discipline, the rebellion of a spoiled child, a beaten child revenging himself upon others for youthful sufferings at home.

The father passed from blacksmith to tavern-keeper, from tavern-keeper to mayor of the district. In the forge he had pounded society as his anvil; his saloon, "l'Agnello," became a political center of the countryside, and Alessandro himself was always a politician. The young Benito, who had been whipped for not minding the bellows, was now to receive another sort of education. For now he lived in a political café. Here was the place men came to drink and talk, and to drink more and talk more wildly of the coming revolution which would assert the rights of man. Socialism, Karl Marx, the First Internationale, the Communist Manifesto, syndicalism, direct action, and anarchism, those were the subjects over which men drank and fought and fought over again, night after night, while children stood around in adenoidal astonishment.

Young Mussolini grew up a soap-box orator and a sturdy brawler. Throughout his province there are many alive today who fought with him, drank with him, gambled with him and sometimes engaged in bouts which led to police interference. At Tolmezzo and later at Pieve Saliceto, province of Reggio Emilia, where he taught in the elementary schools, there are strange tales about the youth with the furious eyes and black temperament. In a quarrel at Tolmezzo with his landlady and her lover who accused Mussolini of replacing him, there were blows and a knife wound. Mussolini was hit by the lover. The landlady was stabbed.

At Caneva, where he taught in 1905, an attempt was made to discharge him on the ground of blasphemy in the schoolroom; the teacher escaped the charge by protesting he was using the names of Oriental gods only; the reason, however, of the town's dissatisfaction was the terror that ruled the children who were the innocent victims of Mussolini's hatred of the teaching profession. His eyes, his hands, his voice were continually in a state of violence; he was impatient, would strike the children and so thoroughly scare them they would run home weeping and trembling.

In a Zürich beer restaurant, his admirers relate with joy, Mussolini, in an altercation with a waitress over a franc, became so angry when some one placed a hand upon his shoulder that he called out that now was the time for all good men to come to the aid of a compatriot, and accordingly three Italians arose and the four thoroughly wrecked the place.

In Berne there was another case of the boarding-house mistress and the handsome black-eyed boarder. "Was it owing to political feeling or was it lovers' jealousy. Was it the outcome of theoretical conflict or of mere male rivalry?" asks the devoted Signora Sarfatti. Two pistol shots. No bloodshed.

In Italy Mussolini's first arrest occurred in Oneglia in 1908 when he marched at the head of a group of workingmen who insisted on their right to work and to strike and who got into a fight with the authorities. The sentence was ten days in jail. In his home district, in Forli, Mussolini led a mob into the mayor's office: the price of milk was too high and the way to cure that was to throw the mayor and his staff through the window, to injury or perhaps to death, it did not matter; those were moments of direct action for the young man who had absorbed so many of his ideas around the wine-dripping tables of his father's saloon. The mayor capitulated and the man of action was lionized.

No other leader of violence has led so violent a life. Lenin, Trotsky, Kemal Pasha, Pilsudski, in fact most of the modern dictators, have a long police record, but no history of stabbings, shootings, barroom brawls, jealous battles with fellow boarders for the affections of a landlady, street fights, as well as political adventures, make up the youth of Mussolini's prominent colleagues. It was the same in his birthplace, his Swiss exile, his first sojourn in Austria, his return to Italy, his editorship in Italia Irredenta, and finally his years of power as member of the directorate of the Socialist

Party in Italy, immediately preceding the war. Almost every year is marked with a deed of violence.

It was shortly after his second visit to Austria that Benito, a rare visitor at home, noticed the pretty servant whom his father had employed for more than a year. Papa Alessandro, lonely widower, had found it difficult to manage his café. Fortunately, there had arrived in town a handsome buxom widow with a pretty growing child. They were glad to find employment, the former as housekeeper, the latter as scullery maid of the "Agnello," and eventually the widow became Alessandro's mistress, while the girl, Rachele Guidi, waited on table, washed the wine-glasses, and worshiped the achievements of her master's elder son.

She was young and blond and sweet and innocent. Without coquetry and pretensions, she fell in love with the handsome youth with the soulful eyes. But she was only a servant girl, while Benito was a man of the world, a man of book learning who had already established himself as a person of importance, and who spoke of his "will to power" and other things she could not understand.

In the atmosphere of that political café all was rebellion. The workingmen who shouted there accepted Papa Alessandro and his mistress without a comment or a raised eyebrow. Everyone was anti-clerical. Although the majority were legally married, marriage itself was frequently discussed and denounced as part of the conventional, narrow-minded bourgeois social system which all intelligent men hated.

To young Mussolini, returned from several years of work and travel, with the memory of one love-affair indistinguishable from that of many others, the idea of marriage was non-existent when he beheld the child he had seen several years before grown into a startlingly attractive young woman. He did not fall in love with her, but he desired her. And she, who worshiped him and could not hope for marriage with such a great personality, believed that "love was the pardon for any sin of the flesh," as Mme. Jeanne Bordeux, who alone among Mussolini's worshipful admirers mentions the romantic episode, says in explanation.

But Papa Mussolini, learning soon enough that his son was the lover of the sweet girl whose mother was his own mistress, shook his head, and said to Rachele Guidi: "Do not let yourself think of that young man. Better for you to throw yourself under a train. If you marry him you will have neither peace nor happiness."

But Rachele never regretted her passionate surrender to Benito.

When they moved from the village to Milan, Rachele and their daughter Edda accompanied him and they lived as signor and signora. In all those years Rachele was content to love and remain a servant; she never spoke a word of advice or reproach, she sank into oblivion when the leading radicals came to the house to discuss the proletarian revolution, she waited on table, was grateful for a kind word sometimes, refused to listen to tales of other women in her common-law husband's life, and never poisoned it by nagging for a few words mumbled by a clerk which would legalize her position.

At first, it is recorded, Benito had the idea "of transforming her, of making her into other than a kind and gentle home body; but in every sense of the word she had been a good wife to him and she was the mother of his two children, Edda and Vittorio. He had recognized her position by living with her, but, unfortunately, before the law a common-law wife in Italy is not a wife, and in all countries the children of such a liberal union are illegitimate. . . ."

Although no record has been found of a marriage between Benito and Rachele, some admirers of the Duce declare that it took place during the war, while others place it much later, on the eve of the signature of the treaty with the Pope, and quite a theory of statesmanship and diplomacy has been built upon this supposedly later incident. Mme. Bordeux is authority for the statement that there was a marriage, and in explanation of its lateness quotes Mussolini saying:

"Perhaps I never thought of it in the rush of my outside work, but I guess I have always had a conscience-stricken feeling regarding la mia signora, for now that she is my legitimate wife a great weight has been lifted from here," and he placed his hand over his heart.

From the earliest days of his life with Rachele Guidi, Mussolini engaged in his most violent political activities. Frequently he went to jail. And it is in this record, perhaps, that the key will be found to his decisive action during the war, because it becomes obvious that it was a will to power, and not an idealism disciplined within party barriers, that animated the fiery revolutionary in his youth.

His *Lotta di Classe* pretended to be a Socialist organ at the time. Social Democracy in Italy was about as radical as the Socialist Party in the United States is now, and even less so than the British Labor Party, or the Social Democrats of Germany in the early days of the Republic. But Mussolini's paper advocated syndicalism and direct action. "I understood now," the editor wrote, "that the Gordian knot of Italian political life could only be undone by an' act of violence." And sadly, "The man who still cherishes ideals in his heart is rated an imbecile or a lunatic." It did not matter what the world called him, he still chose to belong to the Socialist Party and to proclaim ideals which the majority denounced as violent or called childish and Utopian.

The Socialist Party, however, did not know what to make of this super-enthusiastic adherent who preached and practiced things it could never harbor nor endorse. Mussolini was for direct action and sabotage. "When I declare myself in favor of sabotage," he declared himself, "I mean in accordance with my theories, economic sabotage, which is not to be confused with *vandalismo*. . . . Sabotage according to me ought to have a moral bearing"—and this led to the July, ¹)10, arrest. When Italy made war in Tripoli, Mussolini was leader not only of those who opposed that war, but of the pacifists who were willing to spill blood in the name of peace at all costs.

An attempt was made to call a general strike. For three days in Romagna the proletariat became master of the streets. At Forli they occupied the railroad station, hindered the sending of troops, sabotaged the government in every way. Cavalry was sent. Mussolini and Nenni, destined later to be his successor on the *Avanti*, led the mob. Sticks and stones. A fence was destroyed. The strikers armed themselves with staves and the women shook them in the face of the sabers.

The cavalry charged. The women threw stones or placed themselves in front of the men, daring the horsemen to run them down or cut them with their swords. The cavalry charged again. There was confusion. The cavalry charged a third time and there was the moaning of the wounded, the weeping of women, and the curses of Mussolini and his men followers. But they won. The strikers marched to the railroad station and tore up the tracks. A train had just arrived with soldiers, but they would not let it proceed.

The next day, martial law. Arrests everywhere. The hastily constructed barricades became again nothing but a lot of junk and the might of law and order was felt. Mussolini sat in his prison cell meditating on the injustice of this world and planning the liberation of mankind when he had risen to power. But with that feeling there was that other view, gained from his books, that distrust and disgust with his fellow men. "Only twelve of us here," he said to Nenni amidst the dirt and vermin of the prison, "and the cowards, they are not going out on a general strike."

He stayed in jail from that 16th of October to the 23rd of the next month, when he was tried on eight serious charges:

"Opposition to the supreme power and defiance of authorities.

"Attempt to prevent recruiting.

"Inciting to strikes and stopping of work at war factories.

"Violence in stopping street-car communications and damaging tracks.

"Cutting telegraph lines.

"Destroying a telegraph office.

"Violent seizure of a railroad locomotive.

"Laying telegraph poles across railroad to derail an express."

On November 23, 1911, he was sentenced to seven months' imprisonment, which term was reduced to five on appeal. His opposition to the war, during the war, was almost treasonable. "Every honest Socialist must disapprove of this Libyan adventure," he had declared. "It means only useless and stupid bloodshed," and thousands had agreed with him. Were it not for this fact of public support his sentence would have been more severe. At the trial he denied only those acts which might have resulted in the deaths of innocent persons, such as the laying of telegraph poles on the railroad track. Before sentence, he said to the judge:

"Honorable Court, if you acquit me you make me rejoice; for then I can return to work and the community of human society. If you sentence me you honor me, for then you will be condemning not a criminal, but a follower of the Ideal, an agitator according to his conscience, a Soldier of the Truth."

This Soldier of the Truth came out of prison the Hero of the Truth with the halo of a Socialist martyr about him. He had been the leader of a small branch of the party, the editor of only a local little weekly, but he had been remarked by the national leaders and his trial, related to a war which was going badly and which was unpopular, brought him some fame; he stepped out of prison into the midst of an intense political campaign which came to a climax at the congress of his party in July, 1912, at Reggio Emilia. It was this meeting which made Mussolini nationally known as a leader.

Some months before there had been an unsuccessful attempt on the life of the King. Congratulations were in order. Other crowned heads sent telegrams and ambassadors; the President of the United States offered his felicitations; the Senate of Italy and the Chamber of Deputies expressed their joy, and among those who subscribed to these sentiments were three Socialist leaders, Bonomi, Bissolati, and Cabrini.

It was the action of these three deputies which caused a crisis in the affairs of the Socialist Party: was it to remain Right and loyal and pacifist, or go Left, use violence, prepare for that blood-bath of the proletariat which the editor of *The Class War* was advocating? Bissolati was for evolutionary legal progress; Mussolini leaped into the discussion, demanding action.

"On the 14th of March," cried the boyish demagogue, "a Roman mason fired a revolver against Victor Savoia"—there was a shout of joyful laughter when the orator thus labeled the King. "There have been precedents which ought to indicate the line of conduct for us Socialists. There has already been strong criticism of the indescribable spectacle offered by subversive Italy after the *attentat* of Bresci at Monza. We had reason to hope that after ten years we would not again see the flags hung in mourning and the Socialist mayors sending telegrams of condolences and congratulations and all democratic Italy subversively on its knees at a given moment before the throne.

"It is very difficult to separate the political from the human question. It is very difficult to separate the man and the king. To avoid pernicious misunderstanding the Socialists have but one duty after the *attentat* of March 14th: to keep away.

"Attempted assassinations are the accidents of kings, just as falling chimneys are the accidents of masons. If we must weep, let us weep for the masons.

"Why weep for the King? Why this sentiment, hysterical, excessive, when it concerns crowned heads? Who is the King? He is by definition a useless citizen. There are peoples who have sent their kings for a walk when they did not want to safeguard themselves better by sending them to the guillotine, and these peoples are the advance guard of civil progress.

"For us Socialists an *attentat* is a historical act or it pertains to the daily news according to the case. Socialists cannot associate themselves in mourning or in deprecation or in monarchist festivities."

The Socialist congress became a maddened crowd. Mussolini called for the expulsion of the three leaders of the moderate, pacifist, anti-violence Right wing of the party. Bissolati stood as their spokesman, a Socialist of the old school, an intellectual, a thinker, a man of the finest moral fiber and highest ideals of humanitarian philosophy—and like many others of like character, a victim later of the universal war mania which engulfed Europe.

The Reggio Emilia congress was the prelude to the Milan meeting which decided Mussolini's lifetime direction. Here, as later, he felt *la forza del destino*, he played opportunism to its utmost, using the appeal to emotion to overcome the appeal to reason.

Ivanoe Bonomi was forced out of the party because he was not radical enough. Claudio Treves was dismissed from the editorship of *Avanti*, and his successor, Giovanni Bacci, six months later made way for that same Benito Mussolini who had defeated Leonida Bissolati at the Reggio Emilia meeting and who had become, in addition to director of the Socialist Party, one of its accepted leaders.

Direct action, sabotage, revolutionary tactics, the use of violence to establish philosophical ideas, in other words, the Mussolini program, was victorious. He became not only the head of the party, but one of the men in control of Italian politics. Bonomi said of him, he is "a revolutionary in whom the spirit of the barricades is stronger than Marxist discipline," and Georges Sorel, whose disciple Mussolini had declared himself, wrote[1] from Paris: "Our Mussolini is not an ordinary Socialist. It is my belief that some day we shall see him at the head of a mighty legion saluting the Italian flag with his sword. He is a fifteenth-century Italian, a condottiere."

The Sorel prediction appears in all the early Fascist biographies, and in one instance was used as a triumphant book blurb, the publishers evidently being unaware that in the days of the free republican cities of Italy, in the time of the Renaissance, the condottieri were captains who bought and sold themselves and their soldiers to princes and were hired for pay to wage the battles of other people.

Apocryphal or holographic, the Sorel letter and the judgment of Bonomi help explain the character of the man and the force driving him into a career of power; they forecast the decision of 1914 and illuminate the historical events of Mussolini's rule as a dictator.

In 1912, when Bonomi spoke and Sorel prophesied, Mussolini was one of the directors of the Socialist Party and all the signs pointed toward a Revolution, and towards the editor of the *Avanti* as a duce, or leader, of a victorious proletarian uprising.

---

[1] No proof that the letter is genuine has ever been produced by the Fascist biographers, but the contents read more like an accusation than an endorsement.

★ ★

CHAPTER III

"Dieu n'existe pas"[1]

IF THE EPISODES OF HIS CHILDHOOD FURNISH A CLUE TO THE MAN'S
behavior in the critical year 1914, the *emigré* years in Switzerland provide the key to all actions and decisions of a whole lifetime.

The little violences of youth were now to be followed by violence
in the political field, the little treacheries of boyhood, of which proud
parents had boasted, were now to become a pattern of living, while
the will to power, demonstrated at first by merely oral declarations,
drove through opportunities in dynamic fashion.

Although we are told that love and hate are the opposite poles
of the same emotion, we find evidences of the second, the harder
impulse, in this period of the hero's existence. We see him now as
a complete rebel, but that which has driven him into that position
was not the usual humanitarian reaction. It was almost purely hatred.
Mussolini hated the church, religion, the rich; he hated society and
he hated the State, but his was not the class hatred shared with
socialist, proletarian friends, it was a personal hatred, a desire for
revenge, the result of what he himself, not his people, had suffered. He was not "class" conscious. Whenever he spoke of his
childhood it was with bitterness; of his hunger years in Switzerland it was with a desire for revenge.

He joined and passed through anarchist, socialist, republican, and
other groups which opposed the state of things as they are, not
with the ideal of hastening the day of Utopia, but for a vendetta
against elements and persons, the Church, society, individuals he
believed had wronged him. For the same reason he opposed Freemasonry, first as a Socialist and later as a Fascist, because its policy
was incompatible with his personal program of retaliation. He never

[1] See appendix with same title.

acted from social consciousness, as other radicals, but from individual necessity.

Now the State, which he had fought with the same fury which later was to mark his exaltation of it, was reaching out inexorably to subdue him as it for generations had subdued all rebels. The time for compulsory military service was coming and the eyes of the police were upon him; as in all conscript countries where the military age is twenty, the authorities began their watch a year or more before. Mussolini fled to Switzerland. Officially, on the 10th of April, 1904, in his home judicial district, he was accordingly listed as *renitente di leva*—one who deserts before being called to the colors.

Switzerland was the second choice, the choice of economic necessity. He desperately wanted America, the still unrestricted land of opportunity where all his countrymen had relatives, where success was easy, opportunity more equal, gold and success to be had, where class barriers were more easily broken, where liberty and Italian dreams came true. Frequently during the exile years he thought of America with longing.

"Yes," he once said to the present writer, "I came very close to that decision on several occasions. Once it was in fact a fifty-percent chance. I was a political exile then, you know, and for us there were but two lands of freedom. Times were hard in Switzerland; I thought I would try my fortune in America as so many Italians did at that time.

"I knew I could get work in my line. I was a mason. Well, I tossed a coin." He was silent, meditating; he seemed to follow that coin spinning in the air, falling, sending him to America, where he would have been swallowed, obliterated in the regiments of labor-union masons in New York.

"Youth, youth," he sighed, "a dream. A dream. I wonder what would have become of me in America. Had I gone over as an emigrant in 1904 what would I be now?"

"Why did you go to Switzerland?" I asked.

"Because my views conflicted with that of the Italian government. I was the victim of a love of freedom and individualism."

He hated the "cramped, confining atmosphere" of Italy; he yielded to "his restless wanderlust"; he decided "to seek his fortune in

Switzerland, as it was the easiest country to be reached"; say the biographers, and he himself declares in writing that "I did not want to go back to my family. There was a narrow world for me . . . one could neither move nor think without feeling at the end of a short rope. I became conscious of myself, sensitive to my future. I felt the urge to escape. . . . Courage was my asset. I would be an exile. I crossed the frontier. . . . It was the milestone which marked my maturity."

He telegraphed home and got the equivalent of nine dollars. At the frontier station he read in a Milan newspaper that his father, accused with others of smashing ballot-boxes to prevent the Catholics from winning the local elections from the Socialists, had been arrested. "This piece of news placed me in a dilemma. Was I to return or go on?" He did not hesitate long. He had made his decision to escape the army and he took the first train, arriving at Yverdon, Switzerland, with just forty-two cents in his pockets and the address of some one who might give him a job.

But it was neither fear nor cowardice, as his political enemies say, which drove Mussolini to Switzerland; it was rather a deep belief in pacifism and individual defiance of the power of the State which he detested. It is only the fact that later he was to outpatrioteer all patriots in militaristic passion, which makes the escape noteworthy. At that time thousands of Italians, pacifists who believed in sabotaging militarism, from principle and idealism, were refusing to train as soldiers and accepting the refuge which America and Switzerland offered them.

In those terrible and glorious years of his Swiss exile, those honest years of his life, he often boasted of his desertion. That act had been his passport into the hearts and homes of all the exiles and rebels of all the world, who were grouped in Geneva and Basle and Lausanne, reading Karl Marx and plotting revolution and liberty for Russia and Finland and for Czechoslovakia, for suppressed nations and persecuted races. Men starved and struggled in those days, but kept alight the red beacon of revolutionary hope.

Young Benito went to Lausanne. Eyewitness accounts of his arrival present a human picture of almost irreconcilable contrast. We have already seen the violent child bending to the blows of his father's leather belt and attacking a weaker youth with a knife; we have on more than one occasion had a view of that future leader of men, that burning orator who could scatter his fire into weaker vessels, that proud, domineering boyish ego. How different he looks when hunger and poverty hold him a prisoner.

It was evening. At the Italian Socialist club of Lausanne which housed also the coöperative stores and the communal restaurant, many men, all of them rebels, some republicans, a few anarchists, a majority revolutionary Socialists and most of them refugees from the army and from the law, sat at their coffee and gesticulated about the future.

A colleague entered. "I want to introduce a compatriot who has left Italy to escape military service." He indicated a new face, a face sad and humble and somewhat starved.

Serrati, that same Serrati who was later to befriend more passionately and to forgive and aid more frequently the young Radical Mussolini, and who was afterwards to feel more fully the power of the Duce's retaliation to the comrades of his youth, Serrati as secretary of the club arose, went to the stranger, gave him his hand, made him welcome.

Mussolini was modestly but somewhat flamboyantly dressed; with his plain, commonplace iron-gray suit he wore an artist's hat of wide brim and an artist's large black tie, knotted at his throat, the wide silk ends flowing romantically over his bosom.

"My name is Benito Mussolini," he said in a low voice. "I am a school-teacher. Born in Predappio. My father you may know, a pure Socialist, councilor of the Socialist minority of our commune." He was ingratiating.

"You may feel yourself at home here," replied Serrati. "Speak without shame and fear nothing. You are among your friends. Tell me frankly, first of all, have you eaten today, do you want food?"

Everyone had turned towards the new young man. He was agitated, embarrassed, he murmured something about hunger.

"*Allons!* Do not blush. We are among comrades," said Serrati, smiling encouragingly and taking Mussolini by the arm and calling on Francesco Capassi, director of the coöperative restaurant, conducted the former to the dining-room on the second floor and ordered a plate of spaghetti. . . .

"When you've eaten, descend," said Serrati, "and we will talk. We will find a roof for you. We will find something for you."

To Capassi, Serrati gave the order that the meal should be paid for out of the Socialist Party funds. While the hungry man, the future Duce who had exactly one cent in his pocket that night, gorged himself on spaghetti and bread, the good comrades listened to the one who had found the wanderer at the Place Pepinette, where he had come after sleeping under a bridge of Lausanne. It was an unwritten law of the club that everyone who flew to Switzerland to escape military service must be aided because there was perhaps no better proof of class solidarity.

Mussolini descended with a full stomach. He was welcomed to a table, offered coffee, a glass of wine; he asked advice about work and something to live on until he found it. Serrati, a sweet and sentimental soul, adopted him as a friend. He called on one Marzetto to give him a bed or a blanket on the floor, and that night when Karl Marx had been exhausted for the hundredth time, the leading old radical and the beginner of nineteen went out arm in arm to find their roofs.

What a different man he became when the dictates of his belly were satisfied. Within a week from his hesitating entrance into the club young Mussolini was arguing theories with other members, almost as loud, as cocksure, as vehement as the rest, and in another week he was intimidating them with his non-conformist attitude. He had claimed he was a Socialist, but now, they said, he had proven either that he knew very little about Socialism or that, if he did, he was already too individualistic to be a good party member, to belong to either the left or the right wing, both of which contending for the approval of the masses, agreed, however, on the main Marxian tenets.

So long as Mussolini argued Karl Marx they could understand him. But the newcomer had new views almost every week. If the book he happened to be reading was by Nietzsche, he was a Nietzschean that week, full of phrases about the will to power, the revaluation of all values, and the whipping of women; if, on the other hand, he became interested in Sorel, why, it was all syndicalism that week and the devil take more timid social philosophy. Sometimes it was Schopenhauer, when he would enjoy a week of misogyny, and again it would be Stirner, when the Ego and its Own set him on fire with faith in himself.

He had a sick man's, a weakling's, belief in strength. (He had not yet come upon Machiavelli, who, four or five years later, was to make such an impression on him as to rule his thoughts forever after.) For him there never arose the question which has troubled philosophers from Athens to Harvard, the question of Free Will. "I have willed this," "It is my will," are his favorite expressions. In his childhood he had not been allowed any freedom, yet he speaks of carrying out his "will" on certain occasions, while in Switzerland his daily reference to his own strength, his courage, his power, his "clear will" so impressed his colleagues that, not seeking the psychological reasons which force a sick, unhappy, suppressed individual to resort almost daily to such terms, they accepted him at his own estimation, as his party and the nation later were to accept him, and as propaganda later was to exhibit him to all the weak-willed people of a mediocre world.

New revolutionary vistas opened to Mussolini with every book he found in Switzerland. After he had studied Karl Marx's Communist Manifesto he became interested in Babeuf, whose ideas Marx had studied, and in Blanqui, the political heir of Babeuf, absorbing but not digesting all these violent views, one after another. He accepted Babeuf's statement that the French Revolution "is only a forerunner of another, a greater, a more majestic revolution which will be the last" and "it is our duty to set up a dictatorship of the poor." Babeuf "conceived of revolution as an insurrection on the part of well-organized and armed plotters,"[2] and Mussolini, at Socialist gatherings, where all spoke of peaceful changes, of philosophic progress, of the education of the masses in preparation for taking over power, advocated activity, not talk. He was young and he was headstrong. Blanquism, "a synonym for revolutionary adventuring," was seized upon by Mussolini and made his guide; Blanqui's motto, *Chi ha del ferro ha del pane,* became his motto.

[2] Isaac Don Levine, *Stalin.*

Mussolini was developing into a fine soap-box orator. Although he knew little about Socialism, and despite his lack of orthodoxy, he had frequent opportunity to exhibit himself on the stage and in public squares. He seemed destined to sway people by words, and just as he had astonished his own mother with his speeches to himself and the schoolchildren of Forlimpopoli with his extraordinary gestures, he now began to lead in debates. Once he had a serious rebuff. Vandervelde had come to Geneva. It was at the time the Socialists had discovered that Jesus Christ had preached the rights of the weak and the suppressed, of the under dog against the masters, and Vandervelde, the leading Belgian Socialist, was just the type to expound Christian morality as Socialist practice, while Mussolini, brought up in an anti-clerical atmosphere, took it upon himself to denounce "the milk-and-water revolutionary ideas of Christianity." But when Vandervelde, after listening to the youth's diatribe, remarked that Jesus, "this milk-and-water Revolutionist," had preached enough Socialism to alarm Rome with such fears of a proletarian rebellion that the Crucifixion had been ordered, the disciple of violence, amidst the crowd's laughter, fled from the hall.

He continued to make speeches, mocking the King of Italy, defying the ruling powers everywhere, deriding parliaments, and at times defying God. Because work was scarce, he had to go from canton to canton, and there was no job too humble for him. There were times when extreme hunger drove him into the streets to accost some well-dressed stranger, to beg for bread and money, and there were grand days when he had enough to fill his stomach, and his mind at one of the liberal universities. He worked chiefly as a mason's assistant, but he was also a porter once and a butcher boy, delivering packages to the neighboring bourgeoisie and envying their litres of wine and their kilos of fresh meat.

He hated the rich. A murderous hatred. One hungry day he crouched outside the iron railing of the Beau Rivage Hotel—which later was to be the headquarters of dictators and prime ministers of a League of Nations conference—and listened to the orchestra. "The music comforts my brain and my stomach. But the intervals are terrible, the cramp stabbing into my entrails like red-hot pins. . . . The rustle of silks may be heard and the murmur of languages which I do not understand. An elderly couple pass me by. They look English. I would like to ask them to give me money for a bed that night, but the words die on my lips. The lady glitters with gold and precious stones. I have not a cent, I have no bed, I have had no bread. I make off, cursing. Ah, that blessed idea of anarchy of thought and action. Is it not the right of the man lying on the ground to murder him who crushes him?"

He went again to his dirty resting-place under the Grand Pont, that main bridge which breaks the cold wind and shelters other beggars, where he met a man he recognized as an Italian. He hailed him in the native tongue, asking for alms. "He laughs at me. I curse him. He puts his hand in his pocket and gives me ten centimes. I thank him. I hasten to the shop of a baker and buy a piece of bread. . . . For twenty-six hours I had not eaten."

Occasionally the police clean out the beggars. One morning he opened his eyes to find the helmeted face of a policeman with a cynical stare. He is not beaten on the shins nor clubbed on the head, his sure fate in the same circumstances had the coin fallen otherwise and had the bridge been Brooklyn. In Europe even policemen are men. Instead there is a conversation.

The policeman says, "What are you doing here?"

Mussolini replies, "I was just thinking of getting up."

"Then get up quickly, for I have been waiting for you."

"Very kind of you. Please tell my valet to bring me my clothes and toilet requisites."

"Get up quickly or I'll help you up."

"Precisely what I want. Give me your hand."

The policeman gave the beggar his hand: "You are an Italian?"

"Yes. Of the extradition department" (army refugee).

"Follow me."

In this way Mussolini was taken to jail for the first time in his life, and locked up for vagabondage.

Everything he did got him into difficulty with the police. It could not be otherwise. With that anomalous upbringing, of whipping and pampering and the teaching of violent individualism, he had become a complete rebel. He accepted nothing. The gendarmes were forever on the trail; he was always denouncing the law and the petty agents who served as club-bearing symbols—he who could never conform and who was afterwards to organize next to the Russian Cheka and Hitler's Gestapo, the most all-invading police force of modern times, to destroy all non-conformity in the nation.

The Protestant evangelist, Alfredo Tagliatela, came to Lausanne preaching the goodness of God. But Christianity, too, with its vast organization of popes and tikhons and bishops and ceremonials and parades, Mussolini placed with all things bourgeois, like the military, the gendarmerie, the regimented passive minds of the masses who were not brave enough to accept his style of paradoxical individual Socialism. The evangelist challenged one and all to refute him.

Mussolini, who with a few workingmen friends was sitting in the back of the hall, accepted the challenge. But not for debate. He arose and his friends with him. Five or six in number, they rushed up the aisle, stormed the platform, and grappled with the speaker.

"God does not exist," shouted Mussolini. "Religion! In science it is an absurdity; in practice it is an immorality; among men it is a malady."

The good Christian crowd now raised angry fists. While some howled down the blasphemers, others ran to the aid of the evangelist. Tagliatela was rescued. Turning to Mussolini, he said:

"You are the sort of atheistic fanatic who at the age of forty will turn reactionary and be a lickspittle of the Vatican."

Mussolini shouted back: "Bourgeois! Renegade! Slave!"

A few days later, making an atheistic oration, Mussolini drew his watch from his pocket, placed it on the table, and defied God to strike him dead within five minutes.

No thunderbolt came.

This was the proof, the orator told his followers, that there was no God.

When this meeting ended, another Italian radical, Carlo Tresca by name, protested this exhibition. He thought it unfair. Mussolini began an argument which lasted all night, and in the morning, when the two parted, one to return to demagoguery, the other to try his fortune in the United States, the former said:

"Well, Comrade Tresca, I hope America will make you over into a real revolutionary."

"I hope," replied Tresca, "that you will quit posing and learn how to fight, Comrade Mussolini."

Commenting recently on this episode, Tresca said he had left Italy because he had been sentenced to eighteen months in jail or ten years in exile for an article he had published in his paper, *Il Germe* (The Seed). He found Mussolini "weak-tempered and vain, a man who would poosh himself forward so people applaud. He says he is very radical man, extreme Socialist, that I am not radical enough.

"Can you imagine? I am an anarchist now and what is Mussolini, who was so radical? A traitor. He remembers that incident; if I go anywhere near Italy now I don't live long."

Within a few months after the Tagliatela encounter Mussolini published his first work. It is a pamphlet entitled *Dieu n'existe pas*, and its preface states:

"Besought by certain comrades, I publish today the development of my thesis, 'God does not exist,' and refute the principle arguments of the evangelist Tagliatela.

"The struggle against religious absurdity is more than ever a necessity today. Religion has revealed its soul in the full glare of the sun. To be still deluded would be cowardice. No matter what the adaptations of the Church to the new and inexorable necessities of the times may be—alas, it is to weep!—they are attempts, generally vain, to resuscitate the titles of the 'divine bank' which already is on the road to failure.

"Confronted with the spread of free thought, Pope Sarto,[3] fearful of the destinies of his domination, cried out:

" 'Faithful, the Antichrist is born!'

"The Antichrist is human reason which rebels against dogma and a beaten god."

Switzerland is a Christian country but it grants religious liberty. Mussolini was safe in his heresies. But in June, 1903, Mussolini

---

[3] In those days Mussolini's sense of denunciation found satisfaction in calling kings and popes by their born names; he here refers to Pius X.

organized a strike of some stoneworkers, and the authorities of the canton of Berne expelled him with promptness and smug satisfaction.

"My stay in Switzerland was a welter of difficulties. . . . I did whatever came to hand. . . . I knew hunger, stark hunger, in those days. . . . I took part in political gatherings. I made speeches. Some intemperance in my words made me undesirable to the Swiss authorities. They expelled me from two cantons. . . ."

They did more than that. They expelled him, as is the custom of the country, from canton after canton for violation of "State rights," but finally they expelled him from all of Switzerland.

When that order came the Socialist Party of the confederated republic thought it time to protest the persecution of one of its least important but loudest and most active personalities. In the Grand Council of Geneva,[4] the Socialist deputy Wyss denounced the government.

He demanded to know, first of all, why the government's order of expulsion indicated Chiasso obligatory as the frontier station; Chiasso was an Italian town and Mussolini would find himself in the hands of the Italian police—but had the authorities forgotten that Switzerland was an asylum for deserters as well as for political rebels? Why did the government act with cruelty even if its charge was just? Why not send the victim to France or Austria?

But that was all secondary. Why were the bloodhounds of the government driving from canton to canton and finally out of the country a man who had committed no crime except that of being a Socialist? True, he was more radical than most, he had spoken a little too freely, perhaps, he had in moments carried away by his own oratory used some violent words, but no laws had been broken and the serenity of Swiss existence was untouched. Yet because he was a Socialist . . .

When M. Wyss had emptied himself of all invective, the Minister of State, M. Odier, responded to the interpellation:

"Mussolini had presented himself on the 9th of March at the office where the *permis de sejour* [residence permit] is granted and demanded an authorization.

"He supplemented his request with a French matriculation receipt

[4] Parliamentary reports, session of May 11, 1904.

which indicated that he had previously used a passport. The officials replied that the matriculation was not enough and Mussolini was requested to present his passport, which he did and which at first sight seemed to be in order.

"It bore the date December 31, 1905; but traces were visible of a modification, and it related to the changing of a 3 into a 5."

Minister of State Odier further declared that while a provisional *permis de sejour* had been granted Mussolini, a request for information had been made to the Italian consul at Bellinzona, who confirmed the fact that the passport had been forged. On the 9th of April, therefore, when Mussolini presented himself to receive the permanent card, he was arrested. Interrogated, Mussolini replied:

"I know that the date 1903 has been falsified into 1905, but I am not the author of this falsification. I admit that knowingly I have made use of a falsified passport."

In conclusion M. Odier said:

"Mussolini was a school-teacher in Italy; here he has occupied himself with social-revolutionary propaganda. He was arrested in Lausanne for vagabondage. In Berne for a political crime. He was detained and expelled from the canton of Berne on the 19th of June. He has been published by the federal authorities as an anarchist. I believe, however, that he would protest against this qualification as an anarchist and content himself with that of social-revolutionary. It is in effect in that quality that he has been presented to us.

"But can anyone make a complaint against the State for having asked Mussolini to recross the frontier, when on the one hand, to remain among us he seeks to serve himself of dishonest means in falsifying an *acte de légitimation* which has been asked of him, and on the other hand he has used words and developed his activity in a milieu essentially revolutionary and seeks with all his means to destroy the institutions of our Republic?"

M. Odier said he understood quite well the purpose of the altered passport. Born in 1883, Mussolini would have had in his twentieth year to present himself for military service, and this he had not done, therefore he could never have had a passport legitimately prolonged after 1902—"except by a false act, which has now been discovered, to his dishonor."

In Germany, France, and Austria Mussolini saw the inside of prisons; in Italy and Switzerland many times. "These bars and railings, I can't stand them. They torture me. I can't stand the feeling of being suffocated. Oh, yes, you others, you may laugh but you have never known what it is to have been in prison—eleven times in prison, my friends! It is a feeling you can never get rid of."

In January 1925 the *Popolo d'Italia* attacked the "dirty lies of the Aventino" which was spreading the report that "Benito Mussolini, chief of the Italian government, and Duce of Fascism, had been condemned in Switzerland for a common crime." The paper defied Senator Luigi Albertini, owner and editor of the *Corriere della Sera* to produce the evidence of the sentence. One report said that the letter which Mussolini had written asking pardon for the theft of a gold watch had been given to a friend of the Premier Giolitti who dared not publish it for fear of meeting the same fate (assassination) as Matteotti.

Eugene Chiesa in his book, "The Political, Financial and Economic Situation in Italy," Paris, 1929, says:

"At the police station of Zurich there exists the record of this gentleman (Mussolini) with fingerprint chart used only for infamous persons. It deals with theft of a watch. The facts are: Mussolini took a coat from a comrade; there was a watch in the coat. Afterwards the coat was returned, the watch never. The original document is at Lausanne, a copy at Geneva and one at Zurich. Naturally at present, conforming to orders given by the former president of Switzerland, all these have become invisible."

Of course nothing of this documented history appears in either the autobiography or the histories written by the admirers. Mussolini has only this to say: "To remain in Switzerland became impossible. There was the yearning for home which blossoms in the hearts of all Italians. Furthermore, the compulsory service in the army was calling me. I came back . . . I joined the regiment. . . ."

But not so fast as all that.

M. Wyss and the comrades were not without power. They could not maintain their request for Mussolini's freedom in the face of the charges against him, but they did insist that the Swiss law regarding Italian deserters apply to Comrade Benito and that the government must not deport the undesirable to his own country. Thus the frontier to Austria was opened.

Mussolini went to Tessin. At the frontier he was cheered as a Socialist hero and a martyr.

CHAPTER IV

Comrade Angelica and Comrade Benito

IN SWITZERLAND MUSSOLINI MET A WOMAN WHO MORE THAN any other, except his mother, shaped his life. If at one time the hero could quote Abraham Lincoln, as he did, that all he was he owed to his mother, so at another moment he could have said "and all I hope to be I owe to Comrade Angelica."

She was not the fair-haired, light-eyed goddess, the romantic inspiration of youth, which the writers for the popular magazines have found in one or another of Mussolini's mistresses of a later period and to whom in turn they have given the title "Joan of Arc of Fascism," or the more commonplace "the woman who made Mussolini." Angelica Balabanoff was and remains today a true Marxian Socialist who naturally enough looks upon her collaboration with the Fascist Duce as a regrettable waste of time.

And yet it was she who picked him out of a dark corner and made a man of him. For just ten years she ruled his life. There is no mention of her in the Duce's autobiography.

Described by all as the "soul" and "the moving force" of the Russian revolutionary movement in Switzerland, which was in reality the mind and spirit of the Russian revolution of 1917, this woman, whose life is a book of amazement, occupied the unique position of. comrade, associate, fellow worker, with the two most contradictory dictators of this modern world, Lenin and Mussolini.

With Lenin and with Trotsky, and with other Red leaders, Dr. Balabanoff sat as an equal, sometimes even occupying a higher elected position, at conferences, internationales, public meetings. She was part of the conspiracy to win freedom in Russia. With the Black leader the situation was different, for it was she who took him in

39

hand and began his education as a Red, teaching him the first principles of Karl Marx, whose follower she has always been.

The contrast between Balabanoff and Mussolini was extreme. He was the plainest of proletarians, she the daughter of a rich bourgeois merchant, brought up in a house of twenty rooms, surrounded by servants and luxury. But she too was born with the soul of a rebel, and in that they were alike. As a child Angelica fought her mother for mistreating the servants; sometimes she would take her belongings and run down the street to give them to beggars who had been denied food or money at her home. From childhood her heart was filled with a flood of sympathy and pity for the poor and weak and oppressed throughout the world, and when she grew up she gave away all she inherited and to this day whatever she has above her needs, which are plain food and plain clothes, she gives away. A hater of property. A lover of humanity.

Lenin, Trotsky, Liebknecht, Rosa Luxemburg, idealists, radicals, exiles, revolutionaries from all of Europe, worked with Comrade Balabanoff and loved her. Mussolini could hardly believe his good fortune when she offered to help him. She was already famous as an international leader, a brilliant mind, a marvelous orator, a great force in all movements for freedom and liberation which at that time centered in Switzerland, and he was the lowest of nobodies. Little did he know the depths of that human heart which his misery had sounded. There was terror in his eyes when Balabanoff first saw him, that night in the small meeting-room of the Italians of Lausanne, more than thirty years ago. There were quite a few there, workingmen and workingwomen, all very poor, all eager for the riches of a Socialist paradise, all at least washed and clean. But in the corner sat a man in filth. His face was unwashed, his clothes, which had been slept in, bore the traces of the sand and dirt of the little projections of land under the Grand Pont. He had flashing black eyes, a bulging jaw as well as bulging eyes, a bellicose bearing with a timid, cringing demeanor, nervous and inquiet. It was the first time he had come to hear the famous Russian speaker.

"Who is that strange creature?" Dr. Balabanoff asked a mason after she has finished speaking.[1]

---

[1] The episode as here related was written by Dr. Balabanoff for this book.

"The most miserable being I ever met," the mason replied. "He is an Italian, like us, and at home was supposed to be a school-teacher, but he was always getting into a scrape, and he drank too much. Then when the time came to do his military service he fled to Switzerland, and now he is a tramp. But he says he is a Socialist and I think he means well."

"A tramp? Is he so poor?"

"He sleeps under the bridge. Except when I take him in and give him my bed when I am out at work. I feed him when I can."

Another club member, also a mason, came up to Balabanoff. "I have asked my wife to make him a shirt and a pair of pants out of some old cloth," he said; "next time perhaps he will be better dressed."

Others came up and shook the speaker's hands, as was the custom, then drifted out. Dr. Balabanoff went to the unhappy vagabond and took his hand.

"I hear you have no job," she said, kindly. "Can I help you in any way?" She had given away her fortune; she was always giving away every cent she had.

"No, nobody can help me," Mussolini replied, somewhat dramatically, and most tragically and without lifting his eyes, "I am condemned to remain a wretched vagabond all my life."

"Do not despair. Look at these men here. They are all proletarians like you, but when they became Socialists they found they had a great deal to live for, a great ideal."

"But *I* can't. My father was a drunkard, and besides I have a congenital sickness for which I have to thank him. I can't work and I can't be militant. I will have to die as miserably as I am living."

"No, no," replied the woman, "I will see that something is done for you."

The man never looked up, never changed his black expression, but fidgeted endlessly, twisting his dirty black cap in his hands. Later he said, timidly:

"I have just had an opportunity to earn fifty francs, but I lost it, of course. I was not able to do the work. A Socialist editor offered me fifty francs if I would translate Kautsky's pamphlet, *The*

Coming Revolution. But how could I? I do not know German and I do not know the Marxian terminology."

Dr. Balabanoff offered to help.

"You, help me?" he exclaimed, surprised, but still not looking up.

"Why not? I am a Socialist and I find it quite natural. When I was young I had opportunities and privileges, while you lived in misery and could not study. It is not your fault."

This was the episode, a stepping-stone which became a turning-point. Dr. Balabanoff took the unkempt vagabond in hand and made a man, a radical, a revolutionary, out of him. She who had associated with Lenin and Trotsky as an equal leader, who was intellectually miles above the youth of twenty with his weeping self-pity and his lackadaisical despair, his gauche manners, his embarrassed attitude, his masochistic satisfaction in proclaiming himself a lost soul.

Dr. Balabanoff resided at that time in Lugano, in the Italian-speaking part of Switzerland, but came often to Zürich and Berne, now more frequently, not so much for the purpose of helping a man earn ten dollars, but to rehabilitate his character. They would meet at the railroad station or at the club. "He worked very hard, and although I was young at that time," says Dr. Balabanoff,[2] "I at once realized that the man's nature was very susceptible to the influence of suggestion. I felt that I had given him confidence in himself. I noticed that during the time I worked with him he did not again speak of his inability to earn his living. He showed strong ambition to complete the task and it seemed to me that his efforts were due to a desire for personal success rather than an enthusiasm for our cause.

"But what surprised me most in him at that epoch was his great helplessness; it was that which had inspired my pity for him. Later I had occasion to observe very closely his psychological and political development, while he was assimilating some literary culture, initiating himself into Socialist doctrine, taking part little by little in political action. I was able to follow attentively his anti-militarist and anti-clerical expressions. He had set himself to propagate by word and by writing the doctrines which came from the depths of

[2] Angelica Balabanoff, *Erinnerungen und Erlebnisse.*

his moral and material misery. I never lost sight of him until the moment he betrayed us all."

After Mussolini's expulsion from Switzerland he wrote to Comrade Angelica frequently from Trento, telling of his activities and success as a journalist. He was meeting notable *irredenta* patriots who were to influence his actions in 1914, and a young woman named Irene Desler, who was to play a dramatic episode in his life. He was also aiming to write a history of philosophy.

One day in 1905 the King of Italy issued a birthday amnesty. Political refugees, provided they had committed no civil crime at home, were free to return to the fatherland and so were deserters who had fled to escape army service; the latter must, however, come back to the colors.

Mussolini came back.

He went to Austria again after he had completed his military duty. Again he got into trouble with his political expressions which offended the authorities, and again he returned to Italy. He was now noted as both journalist and orator. In 1912, after the Reggio Emilia congress, a committee of directors of the Socialist Party, which included Comrades Balabanoff, Serrati, Vella, and Mussolini, was appointed to name a new editor for the party's organ, the *Avanti*. Most of Italy's leading journalists lived in Rome; they sought a man from the industrial north. One of the central committee members mentioned Mussolini, and Balabanoff seconded the motion. With the exception of Vella the committee of directors voted for him. Mussolini at first objected, saying he lacked the ability, the information on politics, the knowledge of Marxism, the necessary background and culture of an editor, and above all he did not want to assume such a great responsibility.

Comrade Balabanoff took Comrade Mussolini to lunch. There were hours of talk, argument, persuasion. The woman insisted it was the opportunity of a lifetime, and that the man must take it now or lose his chance forever. The man wavered. He could not accept such a responsibility. Comrade Balabanoff insisted. She said she would help.

In the afternoon Mussolini conferred with other members of the committee. They too urged his acceptance.

"I agree, but with one condition," Mussolini said, that evening. "That Comrade Balabanoff must work with me on the newspaper as my assistant editor."

It was then almost ten years from the day Dr. Balabanoff had picked the vagabond out of his dark corner and started him on the road to dictatorship. She, of course, had meant to do nothing of the kind. If there was any dictatorship idea in her mind, it was that of a class, the mass, the proletariat, the common people, the workers, the suppressed, the suffering, the miserable have-nots of this world. For ten years she taught Mussolini the doctrines of Karl Marx, hoping he would some day join with many others, with her colleagues in another part of Switzerland, Lenin and Trotsky, in a world-wide economic and political war of the classes. She never suspected that this fledgling would one day become the instrument and the leader of the very class against which all the revolutionary forces everywhere were lifting their voices and their hearts.

When she won him over to taking the editorship she believed she had achieved something of importance for him, and when he replied by making her his assistant she was pleased because she believed this coöperation would have large results. The entire Socialist Party was pleased. The records exist and there is the testimony of tens of thousands. Strange it is, therefore (unless due to the jealousy and rivalry and hatred which women alone can hold for other women and which is beyond strangeness), to find that the ladies who recount this so well-known and historic incident fill it with such hatred. Balabanoff "forced herself upon him" after "presenting her card at the office." "She imposed herself upon him; he decided to make use of her by handing over the less important subjects for her to work on. . . . She had no sense of humor." "This was the woman who with her perfervid mystic's temperament and with the deficiencies, the lack of balance, the excesses that go with it, imposed herself upon young Benito Mussolini."

So some women[3] write history.

It is true that Dr. Balabanoff was surprised when Mussolini made her taking the assistant editorship the one condition of his acceptance, because during the lunch he had made no conditions. It was only

[3] Signora Sarfatti and Mme. Bordeux.

later that she realized the significance of his behavior. He was young and afraid of responsibility; all that he knew he got from books and from association with her; she was internationally known, the equal associate of the great radical leaders everywhere, and if she would stand by him he would have the best chance of success. He had not asked her directly, fearing a refusal, but he knew that when he made his proposal to Serrati and other directors of the party, and the Socialist Party requested it, Balabanoff could not refuse.

They collaborated for about a year and a half, the greater part of which they had desks side by side and worked their editorials together. Not a single decision of importance was taken by him without consulting his guiding star; to every objection she made he quickly acquiesced, recognizing her intellectual and moral superiority. Frequently the situation was complicated or dangerous, whereupon he would ask her, as one of the oldest and most trusted of socialistic comrades, to write the editorial in his stead and to accept full responsibility for it. Which she did.

"Rarely in my life," she records, "have I seen a human being depend on others as much as Mussolini did. His characteristics at that time were lack of independent courage and incredible physical fear. When leaving the headquarters of *Avanti* at night, or rather in the early morning, he would always ask me to accompany him. After my own work was finished, I had to wait for him.

"When he learned that we lived in the same street, he asked me to take him to his very door. I was surprised. I asked him what was the matter.

" 'It bores me to go home alone,' he replied. 'One never knows
. . .'

" 'What are you afraid of?'

" 'What am I afraid of? Myself. A dog. A tree. My own shadow.'

"He could not ask one of the men of the *Avanti* to take him home because he was proud; he could not confess his disease to a fellow male.

"In the office he would frequently burst out weeping over the trouble his disease was causing him, and the treatment he was going through, which required him to visit a specialist at exactly the same hour every day.

"He had a pathological need to call attention to himself at all times, and frequently this took the form of exhibitionism; he spoke openly of a malady which is generally kept secret, thinking he was making himself interesting by telling.

"Seeing him so downcast, and in order to cut short his almost daily time of tears, I advised him to visit one of our comrades, a renowned doctor, who would make a diagnosis and prescribe a régime. He hastened to follow my advice.

"In my whole life I have never seen a being so lamentable, so destroyed, as the man who entered our office some time later, his face pale and defeated, his eyes more haggard than usual. Without saying a word he cast himself into a chair, hid his face in his hands and began sobbing. His Wassermann test had proved unfavorable. Accustomed as I was to his excessive impressionability and to his exhibitions, I was nevertheless moved by a sentiment of profound pity, seeing this unfortunate man who was crying.

" 'You do not know what has happened to me,' he said in the midst of his sobs; 'the doctor made a blood test. He anæsthetized my thumb with ether. The odor of ether follows me. It is in the air. Oh! I beg you do not leave me alone. I am afraid. I am haunted by that odor.'

"And in truth he passed a whole week under the terror of that impression. Every day when the hour approached which reminded him of the injection, he was carried away by emotion. He could not work.

" 'It is going to kill me,' he said.

"To calm him I had the clock secretly advanced an hour.

" 'It is five o'clock, the hour is passed; calm yourself,' I said to him. He looked at the clock, became quiet immediately, and began working as if nothing had happened."

Comrade Balabanoff recounts scores of incidents, from small events in the office to large episodes in public squares, from personal and domestic difficulties which had a strange way of airing themselves in the *Avanti* headquarters, to disputes over party policies in which Mussolini, who now stands as a symbol of national strength, a symbol for the youth of the land, the living superman who appeals to all the mentally groveling and enslaved of the world, was not altogether the brave, bold, unhesitating hero which accumulated biographies and myths have made him out to be. According to the associate editor her chief kept a revolver on his desk, a sharpened stiletto handy, was scared when voices were raised in political dispute, and led the mob only when it was overwhelming in number, and stayed discreetly behind when physical danger threatened.

"Of course," Comrade Angelica recounts today, "I never suspected that Mussolini, whom I taught radicalism from his youth to his rise to power, would or could betray our ideals. I never in all the years of our collaboration was blind to some of his inherent traits, his fundamental weaknesses, to his physical cowardice in personal encounters as contrasted with his heroic gestures when surrounded by numbers, to his inability to resist temptation for personal power, to his unbridled egotism.

"Naturally he was a strong pacifist in 1914. At one of our editorial conferences, however, he told us he favored the German cause and ridiculed France. But when he was offered the opportunity of personal power which a newspaper was sure to give him, it was a temptation which a weak will could not resist. We did not know then why he went over to the enemy. We could only suspect that an offer had been made him by French representatives."

CHAPTER V[1]

A Miracle Is Explained

THERE WERE RIOTS IN THE VINEYARDS OF FRANCE AND MME.
Caillaux shot M. Calmette, the editor of *Figaro*. In Ireland
seven hundred years of strife were again accented in a civil war;
patriots fell in the streets of Dublin and British soldiery prepared
for fire and blood. The Balkans were enjoying temporary peace,
armed peace, reeking with plans of revolt and assassination. And
in Italy there occurred a revolutionary outbreak of national importance. All these facts the German general staff noted with utmost
satisfaction. The omens were good. The Central Powers, whose
policy was Discipline, Order, Hierarchy, goose-stepped to world
empire.

The Settimana Rossa, or Red Week, of 1914, was Italy's prelude
to battle. A decade of strife between workers and employers was
to have its test in a general strike which began that 7th of June.
All the elements which were anti-government or anti-ruling-class,
from the Liberals and Democrats to the Socialists and Radical-
Socialists, and even the anarchists, were joined against the forces
of law and order—and oppression.

This general strike, like the World War, was held inevitable, and
a simple incident which paralleled the assassination of the Austrian
archduke at Sarajevo ignited the spirit of Italy. A conscript soldier
had fired at his colonel. The case became national, a symbol. When
the government sought the easy way out by declaring the would-be
assassin insane, condemned to prison for life, the masses screamed
for his freedom, and Mussolini, in the *Avanti*, joined. At first it
was decided that there should be one day of national protest in
honor of Masetti; later a general strike was declared. Mussolini

[1] See appendix "Mussolini's Money," for documentation.

48

not only participated, but suggested revolution. One of his collaborators and admirers, Rossato, calls him "the Lenin of the Red Week, the originator of the idea of a Romagnole Republic." Mussolini hoped to turn the general strike into a national uprising. He made speeches, wrote articles, and one day, the 10th of June, led his followers into the Cathedral Square of Milan as the first move to occupy the town and eventually seize power in all of Italy.

There are two versions of what followed. One, the later Fascist, has Mussolini first to arrive and last to go; he stood his ground, "heedless of cavalry charges," as his passionate biographer, Mme. Sarfatti, more recently has it, "erect, motionless, his arms folded, hurling forth his invectives with eyes ablaze," but all contemporary reports state merely that "when the mounted police arrived the demonstration was broken up" while still other testimony, from an eyewitness participant, is that "we acted like human beings, we fled."

It is of little importance. The Settimana Rossa was a fiasco. What is important is that it confirmed Mussolini as a revolutionary Socialist, taught him that without violent leadership and organized violence there would be no success, and inspired him with the idea of armed leadership.

"The attempt at revolution—the Red Week—was not revolution as much as it was chaos. No leaders! The middle class and the bourgeoisie gave us another picture of their insipid spirit." But the idea itself he defended, likening the event to the French Commune, "a magnificent insurrection of the Paris populace presenting all the characteristics of a revolutionary movement . . . but when the Commune was crushed by the bayonets of Thiers, a man, an immortal master for us all, arose to defend it. Karl Marx justified all the measures taken by the Commune and also many measures initiated by persons unknown. He justified the incendiarism and also the shooting of hostages; he celebrated the flame and the blood and the deaths; he raised on high the cry, 'Long Live the Commune!' in the face of that European bourgeoisie which with a ferocity made hundredfold by fear, prepared itself for its great revenge." Prophetic words!

The World War came almost immediately after this attempt at

Italian revolution. The Socialist Party on July 29, 1914, issued its proclamation:

"It is to the interest of the proletariat of all nations to impede, circumscribe, and limit as much as possible the armed conflict, useful only for the triumph of militarism and parasitical business affairs of the bourgeoisie.

"You, the proletariat of Italy, who, in the painful period of crisis and unemployment of the recent general strike have given proof of your class consciousness, of your spirit of sacrifice, must now be ready and not let Italy go down into the abyss of this terrible adventure."

The phrasing of the proclamation was Mussolini's; his name was signed with that of other leaders. One day earlier, he had written in *Avanti*, "The proletariat must no longer temporize, it must express immediately its desire for peace. If the government does not heed unanimous public opinion but enters into the new adventure, the 'truce of arms' declared by us at the close of the Red Week will be ended." And another day: "In the case of a European conflagration Italy does not want to precipitate itself into the ultimate ruin, but has one attitude to take—neutrality."

Thus July, 1914, passed into history and August finds all the pledged nations of both armed camps, with the exception of Italy, at war.

The Nationalist Party, under Federzoni, who later sat symbolically at Mussolini's right hand in the first Fascist triumvirate, demanded that the government join Germany and Austria. The patriotic Socialists under the expelled leader, Bissolati, tried to drag the party towards the Allies. Mussolini and Bissolati met in furious debates which always ended in the triumph of the former.

Then came the mysterious September when Mussolini made the decision of his life and, as first payment on it, surrendered his membership in the party. In the new freedom which began for him he was better prepared, he wrote later, "to fight my battles than when I was bound by the dogmas of any political organization. But I understood that I could not use with efficient strength my convictions if I was without that modern weapon, capable of all possibili-

ties, ready to arm and to help, good for offense and defense—
the newspaper.

"I needed a daily paper, I hungered for one. I gathered together
a few of my political friends who had followed me in the last hard
struggle, and we held a war council. When money alone is concerned, I am anything but a wizard. When it is a question of means
or of capital to start a project, or how to finance a newspaper, I
grasp only the abstract side, the political value, the spiritual essence
of the thing. To me money is detestable; what it may do is sometimes beautiful and sometimes noble."

While Mussolini sat in the office of the *Popolo*, writing his
harangues in favor of the noble Allied cause, the whispers of the
cafés and the rumors throughout the land were investigated by the
party he had left.

It was soon learned that many elements were buying public
opinion in Italy. The Germans were represented by Prince von
Bülow, ambassador to Rome, from whose immune offices agents
operated in much the same manner as they did in neutral America
at the same time. In New York, it will be remembered, the Germans succeeded in buying up only one important newspaper, the
Evening Mail, whose unfortunate Dr. Rumeley went to prison when
the United States some time later decided to join the war, but on
the side opposed to Rumeley's masters.

In America, in Italy, in Spain, in Switzerland, Holland and Scandinavian countries the subsidization and purchase of public opinion
was largely a Franco-British enterprise. In fact, a large part of the
world was divided into so-called spheres of influence. Despite *The
Secrets of Crewe House* and the French *Behind the Scenes in Wartime Journalism*, the world still knows little of an effort which compares relatively with the slaughter at the front. The poisoning of
the world mind is just as necessary for a successful war as the
murder of millions of deluded subjects.

Lord Northcliffe was active in both the French and British spheres.
Between November, 1914, and May, 1915, when the declaration of
war abolished the free press of Italy, the Socialist newspapers published considerable news of the efforts of this British publisher in

converting, by promises and money, a large number of bourgeois journals to the cause of intervention.

Meantime the charge had been made on the floor of the House of Representatives[2] in Washington that in March, 1915, the banking interests, "the steel, shipbuilding, and powder interests and their subsidiary organizations, got together twelve men high up in the newspaper world and employed them to select the most influential newspapers in the United States. . . . These twelve men worked the problem out by selecting 179 newspapers, and then began, by an elimination process, to retain only those necessary for the purpose of controlling the general policy of the daily press throughout the country. They found it was only necessary to purchase the policy, national and international, of these newspapers; an agreement was reached; the policy of the papers was bought, to be paid for by the month. . . . The effectiveness of this scheme has been conclusively demonstrated by the character of stuff carried in the daily press since March, 1915. . . ."

The charge was also made that while the United States was nominally neutral but actually preparing to join the Allies, no less than 1,400 British agents were active in propaganda work under supervision of Lord Northcliffe. Certainly there is evidence today that Allied agents were at work in every country, and Italy was no exception. There is evidence that editors and newspapers were bought everywhere. Sir Basil Zaharoff bought up practically the entire press of Athens at this time and founded additional newspapers to support Greek coöperation with the British.

Secret as these efforts were, a few facts became known and were published in Italy in 1914 and 1915. The Socialist press began to answer the ominous question of the cafés and the party congresses—*Chi paga?* Without fear of libel suits or contradiction, the secret of Mussolini's change from advocate of proletarian revolution against the French government to ally of the French army, was soon known throughout Italy.

The "miracle" of the days between the 21st and 25th of September, 1914, was manipulated by Filippo Naldi, publisher and editor of the *Resto del Carlino*, who from the first days of the war was

[2] *Congressional Record*, February 7, 1915.

publicly charged with having been subsidized by the French government along with dozens of smaller publishers.

Naldi prepared the populace for the "conversion" of Mussolini with the publication of two articles by Libero Tancredi (Massimo Rocca), the first headed *Un Uomo di Ferro* (A Man of Iron), the other *Un Uomo di Paglia* (A Man of Straw). There was no secrecy in the *Resto del Carlino* office about its being an agency for Italian intervention on the side of France.

Among that nation's foremost agents in this patriotic business was a member of the Chamber of Deputies, Marcel Cachin, one of that considerable group of Socialist deputies who had been pacifist until the first shot was heard on the Alsace-Lorraine frontier, and who from that moment became enthusiasts for war, calling upon enemies of bloody conflict to support it under the banner of The Sacred Union (*l'Union Sacrée*). This is the same Marcel Cachin who was later to edit *l'Humanité*, to become the leader and the inspiration and the occasional martyr of the extensive French postbellum Communism. To Naldi, Cachin confessed his desire to win many political leaders and journalists for the French side. He was especially anxious to gain the support of men like himself, Socialists who had seen the light of nationalist patriotism. Mussolini fitted all his requirements.

In Bologna, one of those mysterious miraculous days, Mussolini confessed to Naldi his aforementioned "mortal desire" to edit his own newspaper. A newspaper, he said, was a fulcrum on which to rest a lever to move the world. He must have his own press. On its quick wheels one rode to power. One had to force ideas upon the masses; they were so stupid, such cowards, and the Nationalists, the bourgeoisie as well as the Socialists, all of them were doing one thing or another, and everything wrong, because one and all they were afraid to listen to a bright new intelligence. Yes, the Socialists, too, his own people, they restrained him, they bossed him, possessed him; they overpowered him in the central committee, issuing orders which he had to carry out in his newspaper office, which was their office, and every time he swerved, every time he changed a comma, there would be uproar; his associate editors would shout he was betraying the Socialist cause, they would expose him, drive him out of the party. He was a man born to live and act independently; he hated restraint of any kind; he needed a newspaper to show the world what he could do.

Naldi did not quite understand. He himself had no such ambitions. He was the typical continental European newspaper owner, living daily in trepidation that no one would try to corrupt him. He was, however, ethically on a par with the great Havas news agency and the greatest of all French newspapers, *Le Temps,* and twenty other French newspapers, all of which received several millions of gold francs from the Tsar for the purpose of propaganda and news suppression from the time of revolution, 1905, to the Russian collapse of 1917.[3] Now it was France paying money to editors. Naldi knew where the French funds were and the man to be "seen"; when Mussolini was through talking, Naldi made him a promise. But in return he demanded of Mussolini an earnest of good faith.

Returning to Milan, the editor startled Italy with the leading article, sensational for the official Socialist paper, the first appeal against neutrality.

Quite sure of his future, no longer caring whether or not the party would accuse him of betrayal, nor fearing the criticism of fellow editors, Mussolini did not hesitate to gain his end by using as a means the very official organ of the pacifist party, and in it proclaiming a policy which the paper, the fellow editors, and the party stood pledged to denounce with all their strength. The office became an uproar. There were angry scenes. Day and night fists were shaken and loud voices penetrated into the streets to the amazement of strangers. What was "relative neutrality"? Nothing but a step to "no neutrality, to war." "Who authorized the editorial?" "How dare you publish it without consulting?" But Mussolini had made his bid to the French representatives, sitting lightly on their moneybags, in the hotels of Geneva. He had shown them he was willing to be approached. He had taken the first step.

Then news came from Naldi that the financial negotiations were satisfactory.

Mussolini rushed from the *Avanti,* traveled the short distance to

---

[3] Documents from the Russian War Archives published in France as *L'Abominable Vénalité de la Presse.*

Switzerland secretly, came back quickly, and just fifteen days later, "starting with empty hands," as his admirers so quaintly put it, he produced the first number of the *Popolo d'Italia*, a French newspaper organ, a long but strong finger of the Quai d'Orsay. Polemic after polemic against the Socialist Party, against last month's friends on the *Avanti*, against the atrocities committed by the Central Empires, filled the new journal.

A complete *volte face*. But Mussolini's feet were now on wheels, and the wheels were turning out newspapers, and every edition was a challenge for power. It filled his own ears, leaving no room for the cries of protest. He did not hear, because he did not want to hear, the accusation of a former colleague—"if the Kaiser had offered you a double sum you would have defended neutrality." He immediately made his newspaper the organ of the Fasci, a little interventionist group which had been founded in July, 1914, months before his "conversion," and which had from its origin been his enemy. He became the patron of the Fasci Nazionali per l'Intervento.

Returning from Geneva, several weeks later, Marcel Cachin took into confidence the Chamber of Deputies[4] and, burning with pure passionate patriotism, he spoke of glorious achievements for the French cause.

"*Voyez*," he cried, "that which has happened in the Italian section. *Voilà* Mussolini who in the *Popolo d'Italia*, today in its fortieth number, has had a great success, declaring that the revolution is an idea which has found bayonets. We register with joy the happy and concordant symptoms. Everything presages the inevitable intervention of Italy. She will help us finish the war, assuring victory against the militarist reactionaries, the Hapsburgs and the Hohenzollerns." France applauded Mussolini and Cachin.

To this very day France remembers, even in times of crisis when the Fascist cohorts stand beside their Duce, crying "*Abbasso la Francia*," that among the many subsidized by the Foreign Office there is one who can never be paid in full. To the good patriots, French politicians and journalists, there is nothing but honor in what happened, for that handful of silver also bought historic importance. Thus, for instance, Louis Roya, remarking the sudden

[4] *Journal Officiel.*

founding of the *Popolo*, asks "What were his means, who aided him?" and replies, "Let us admit that France aided Mussolini. . . . She did so and he accepted for the purpose of making triumph the Cause of Right," while a lady biographer,[5] French patriot but passionate devotee of the Italian, reasons that "Admit, then, that France had offered Mussolini help. What would the next move be? She might have offered and he might have accepted in order to see the triumph of right and justice. Certainly not for himself would he have made such a move." The cause of right. Right and justice. Paul Ronin,[6] a Frenchman less given to national patriotism, says bluntly that in quitting the *Avanti* Mussolini was not without resources, "no matter if he pretends to the contrary. He had in his pockets the funds furnished by Filippo Naldi, agent of shady affairs; by the Italian industrialists who manufactured arms, munitions, military equipment; by Marcel Cachin in the name of the French government," and Deputy Renaudel in writing an editorial in the *Quotidien* on the aid which Mussolini had given to France remarks that "Many of us well remember that the first issues of the *Popolo d'Italia* were published, thanks to French money; Cachin knows all this, but he does not like it to be talked about."

The miracle of Mussolini's acceptance of Allied patriotism[7] was finally explained in a famous case in the courts of Paris in 1926. The name of Charles Dumas, secretary to Minister Guesdes, as the actual bearer of the money was given and the sums specified. It was during the trial of one Bonomini for the murder of Buonservizi, friend and colleague of Mussolini on the *Popolo*. Maître Torrès, a French lawyer of renown, always the defender of victims of injustice, personal and political, pleaded for Bonomini. Maître Gautrand represented the *partie civile*, in the pay of the Italian embassy. The Italian government and its newspapers were demanding the guillotining of Bonomini and were bringing intimidating pressure upon France.

Maître Gautrand resorted to that commonest of all commodities, wartime patriotism. Italy, "blood sister of France," had stood by

[5] Jeanne Bordeux.
[6] L'Ombre sur Rome.
[7] Complete documentation has been made by Professor Salvemini.

her; Italy had helped win the war. Fascism was the patriot of Italy.
Mussolini was the chief of Fascism. Buonservizi was the colleague
of Mussolini. It was all very simple. A political crime had been committed. The victim was a great patriot. Patriotic France and Patriotic
Italy demanded the death of Bonomini!

Maître Torrès arose.

Italy, he said, it was true, had entered the war on the side of
the Allies. Italy had done so because the Allies had made a financial
and territorial deal with Italy. And as for Mussolini, it was the
pure result of a plain business transaction on the part of the French
government. It was a matter of dollars and cents, not sentiment.

Maître Gautrand was outraged. He demanded instructions from
the Italian embassy in Paris. The embassy cabled to Rome. But to
this very day no action has been taken against the accusation. In
fact, Maître Torrès was willing to amplify his charges in print. In
Stockholm, and in the Italian newspapers published in Paris, he tells
the story of how the Allies won Mussolini:

"There had been a moment, the first moment, in which the
Italian Socialist Party was unanimous against the intervention of
Italy in the war. The situation preoccupied the French government.
The problem was examined at a council of the Ministers. The question was taken up, how to convert some one leader for the war, with
the aid of money, and the name of Mussolini was suggested. The
first sum was 15,000 francs ($3,000) and it was followed by monthly
payments of 10,000 francs. The man who actually carried the money
was M. Charles Dumas, secretary of the Department of War Propaganda to Minister Guesdes. Thus was born *Il Popolo d'Italia,* immediately interventionist. This is the precise history to which no one
could dare bring any denial for fear of a documentation more
crushing."

There was a time when the history of the "miracle" was common
knowledge, when the opposition press referred to it as merely one
of hundreds of similar wartime episodes which fill many a dossier
in the British and French foreign offices. Today all the documents,
the books, pamphlets, and the newspapers dealing with this subject,
have disappeared.

In 1924, when they were still in circulation, the present writer asked Mussolini a question touching on this dramatic and decisive moment of his life. The Duce replied:

"The turning-point in my life was the war. The war showed the world plainly, I think, the utter bankruptcy of internationalism. We had been fighting for a hollow fraud. I had fought for internationalism all my life, preached it, gone to prison for that same cause, and suddenly the war came and I realized first that internationalism was dead because it had never really lived, and that I had a real duty in life, and that was to my country."

But if a man's life story, his childhood, the making of his behavior pattern and the evidences of its fulfillment in youth, mean anything at all, they indicate that beyond patriotism and duty, there is a stronger force tugging at his vitals.

Mussolini was "condemned" to march towards power. As he so readily admits, he needed most of all a daily newspaper. To the shouts of treason and betrayal he can always reply he did no more or less than hundreds of other highly respected gentlemen, the leading patriots, the numerous editors and publishers throughout the world who took up either the side of France and England, or that of Germany and Austria, because in some way or another, it paid.

Luckily for him, he had chosen the winning side. In America, in a similar situation, Dr. Rumeley, the editor who chose the loser, paid for his error by a term in prison.

CHAPTER VI

A Politician Goes to War

THE PURCHASE OF NEWSPAPERS AND EDITORS IS A SMALL THING compared with the purchase of nations. Usually the first is the necessary prelude. And so it proved in Italy. That nation officially renounced the Triple Alliance on the 30th of April, 1915, and amidst the applause of half the world joined the forces of Democracy, Humanity, Liberty and commercial penetration on the following 15th of May. It was not until the days of the peace-making in Versailles that the secret of Italy's noble act became known.

In April, 1915, according to the treaty signed by France, Britain, Russia, and Italy and presented to an incredulous and angry world by the Russian Soviet government, which had opened the Tsarist archives in 1917, Italy was bribed by the Allies with a promise of plunder equal to that which they themselves as victors had planned to share. Italy, too, was to receive lands and populations over which she had no moral, ethical, geographical, or ethnological claim.

In that same April of 1915 Benito Mussolini was arrested in Rome for violation of law and order in his activities in the interventionist movement. Thus was the spectacle of strict neutrality maintained publicly. Incidentally, on the 29th of the month, Mussolini fought a duel with the pacifist anti-interventionalist Socialist leader, Claudio Treves, the latter wounding the patriot, but not severely.

When war was declared amidst public rejoicing the elderly Socialist leader Bissolati joined the immediately created volunteer corps. Mussolini remained in his office, writing enormous editorials urging those who through age or youth or other reasons might expect exemption, to step forward. He did not reply to the ensuing personal taunts of his enemies.

In September, when Mussolini was called up, there occurred an event of personal and emotional significance, but not unlike the experience of many other soldiers in many other countries. Cast-off wives, cast-off mistresses, forgotten children, doubtful children, began to appear in various parts of the country. The call to arms had revealed many men leading double or triple lives, under many names in many cities and strange ports. Mussolini the rebel had never believed in the sacredness of marriage. But now because he was famous as an editor and war-maker, and leaving for the front, several women came forward to ask him for a marriage ceremony, or to safeguard their common children, or to provide themselves with financial security in the form of a pension should the soldier fall. It was a matter of finances.

At the office of the *Avanti*, these women presented their cases and offered their documents, but the Socialist paper refused to give them publicity. These were personal, not political, matters in which the journal did not care to interest itself. The two most important cases brought to the attention of the *Avanti* editors were those of Signorina Rachele Guidi and Signora Irene Desler-Albini, each seeking the soldiers' remittance because each was the mother of one or more children of whom Mussolini was the common parent.

"I have seen Irene Desler and read her letters and documents," Dr. Balabanoff, associate editor of the *Avanti*, writes me, "but neither Serrati nor I thought it fair at that time, despite Mussolini's betrayal of our paper and our cause, to take up her case. Mussolini was still claiming to be a Socialist and Fascism still did not exist."

The widow Desler-Albini, with her son, Benito Mussolini, Jr., according to her sworn statement of birth registration, were soon interned in a little village near Florence, awaiting deportation to the south of Italy as enemy aliens. The camp was full of persons of foreign birth and Italian pacifists or subversives. Many of them were border people from the irredenta country and therefore suspect by both sides. Some, however, were victims of a vendetta, of a whisper from a personal enemy, for it was easy in those days to utter the word "Austrian" and have your revenge on some one you had hated many peaceful years. Rivals got rid of rivals that way. It was a time of successful enmity.

One day a rumor reached a group of relief workers that among the refugees was an important lady with a sick child. A committee was organized by Armando Borghi, who with some companions at great risk broke the regulations in the military zone and came to Florence. In a small hotel in the Via Nazionale the victims were found. To the great surprise of the four men, the "important lady" was the common-law wife of Mussolini. The child bore the unmistakable traits of his father, the jaws which in unhappy times were called protruding but are now called Roman, those wide-open black eyes, bulging, sparkling eyes of the father, overemphasized in the young large head.

With Borghi on this visit were Di Vagno, who later became a member of the Chamber of Deputies and was one of the first Opposition politicians murdered by the Fascisti; the lawyer Mario Trozzi and the journalist Armando Aspettati of Florence. Irene Desler, widow of Signor Albini, told the committee her story. She had lived with Mussolini for several years and was the mother of his child. They had been happy together for a little more than a year, when her dowry of ten thousand lire was exhausted and quarrels became frequent. The child was a burden. But foremost, she told the committee, was Mussolini's fear that she might reveal all the political secrets of the famous editor and easily ruin his reputation and his career. She had pleaded with Mussolini for a legal marriage, but he had refused. She had then visited the editors of the *Avanti* with her documents, but they would not listen to her; neither would Claudio Treves, who said to her that he did not hate any man alive so much as Mussolini, but nevertheless he would not interfere in personal affairs.

The police chief of Milan, she continued, was a close friend of Mussolini's. One night, shortly after Mussolini had placed her in a separate apartment, carabinieri came and arrested her. She and her child were taken to prison. She did not know who had denounced her as an enemy alien, so she begged the police to inform her "husband." She sent word and letters. But she never received a reply. Several days later a convoy of political prisoners was sent to a concentration camp near Florence and told to prepare for a long journey to southern Italy. She was penniless and her child was stricken with fever. The committee gave her money, sent a doctor, and Borghi never saw or heard of the unfortunates again.

The political secret to which Signora Desler refers is most likely the following legal document[1] signed "Irene Desler del fu Albini, nata a Trento e diplomata in Parigi":

"I declare that I have lived as the wife of Signor Benito Mussolini for about two years and that I have a son with him legally recognized by his father and inscribed in the office of the *Stato Civile* of Milan and under my signature.

"I certify that at the time when Mussolini resigned from the newspaper *Avanti* we were in such poverty that we had planned to leave for America, a project which was abandoned on account of what followed. In this period I placed at the disposition of our menage the little I possessed to suffice our needs. After the foundation of the *Popolo d'Italia* our situation did not change much and our difficulties continued. But suddenly after the return of Mussolini from a voyage made to Geneva, our economic situation changed completely. This happened during the month of January, 1914, or 1915, I cannot say more precisely." (Note: It could not have been 1914, inasmuch as the war did not begin until August of that year.) "Mussolini then told me he possessed considerable money and I remember that I saw much pass through his hands.

"After his return from Geneva, Mussolini spoke to me of an offer of a million which a French person had made to him, and gave me the name, which I have forgotten, on condition that his newspaper take up a strong campaign for the intervention of Italy into the war and against the enemies of this intervention. On his return I asked him if the money he showed me came from the person of whom he had spoken. He replied that it came from France. He wanted to make me a present of a diamond, which I refused.

"I remember that Mussolini was much worried over the commentaries which his voyage to Geneva had occasioned in the Socialist circles of Milan. He said to me, 'I am lost if they find out anything about it.' For that reason Mussolini decided never to go to a foreign country

---

[1] Registered in the archives of the city of Turin by the notary Camillo Tappati; numbered 51413; visible for several years. Copied by Armando Borghi. Document now destroyed by Fascist officials.

again, because his trips were too much noticed. He sent in his place Clerici and Morgagni. Clerici replaced him for the trips to foreign countries and Morgagni for exchanging money and other operations. I remember that Clerici and Morgagni, who were almost poor before knowing Mussolini, at the end of these trips abroad began to live in luxury. And Clerici, so Mussolini confided in me, had bought a villa in Varese.

"I repeat that several times Mussolini spoke to me of the French origin of the money. I am ready to repeat the declarations at any time and before everyone, also under the legal oath."

The fate of this mysterious woman is known to very few. At various times before 1925 American and British journalists were able to trace her movements. John Bond learned that in February, 1923, Signora Desler, accompanied by her son, appeared at the offices of the archiepiscopal palace at Trento. Mr. Bond (who gives her name as Delsier) describes her as comely and in her thirties, and the child unmistakably a Mussolini: . . . "a pair of blazing black eyes, large and round," which "made the pallid features all the more conspicuous." To the princely clerk she made the claim that she had been married to Mussolini in the diocese of Trento and that she wanted a copy of her marriage certificate. She knew the name of the priest, which she gave, and the year, 1910, the season, which was early spring, but not the day or month.

This claim was investigated by the Archbishop Celestino Endrici. He ascertained easily that Mussolini had spent almost all of 1909 in Trento, that he had been a frequent speaker at Socialist meetings, at one of which Irene Desler claimed she had met him, and that he had disappeared as suddenly as he arrived. Signora Desler had stated that they had been married just before her son, whom she had baptized as Benito Jr., was born and she had letters regarding the payment of money to support herself and the child.

The archbishop had the statement written out by his chancellor and the woman signed it, then departed after being cautioned to remain silent. Mother and son knelt and kissed the archbishop's ring.

Within a week, according to Mr. Bond, Signora Desler was visited by the prefect of police, who advised her to move to a small house on the outskirts of the city. It was on the Verona road. There was no secret about that. Mr. Bond is also authority for the statement that the marriage records were found and that they bore the signature of the present Duce, and that the child, born four months after the marriage, is registered on the baptismal record of 1911, a year after his birth.

The common knowledge of Signora Desler's whereabouts, however, led to considerable embarrassment for the authorities. Although a relay of carabinieri guarded the house night and day, refusing to permit the woman to do even her marketing unaccompanied, she was able to communicate her complaint to all she met. Then, in midsummer, 1927, the police chief Tamburini and several aides arrived with the request that this Mussolini family accompany them to another town. Signora Desler refused. Neighbors, alarmed by her calls for aid, were driven off by the guards. They say they saw the woman beaten. At all events, she was forcibly ejected from the house and taken to Pergine, where, for all the public knows, she is still an inmate of the insane asylum. Benito Mussolini, Jr., when last heard of, which was in the same year, 1927, was living in a parochial school at Moncalieri.

The Desler episode,[2] however, did not disturb the leading patriot of 1915 very much. He left for the front to the accompaniment of journalistic fireworks. He was himself made into a patriotic symbol for a nation which needed enthusiasm badly.

Early in December we find him in a hospital suffering from gastroenteritis. In 1916 there is a period of intensive training, another trip to the hospital, recovery, a duel with General Count Spingardi, a series of articles in his newspaper telling about life near the front, a brief period in the trenches.

[2] There is a reference to "my unfortunate family" in one of Mussolini's letters of the Trento period which has been interpreted to mean Signora Desler and his son. Sarfatti, without mentioning names, tells of a jealous Austrian woman apparently living with Mussolini who destroyed his notes for the history of philosophy believing they were letters to another sweetheart. Domenico Gasparini, labor leader of Trento, writes in the Paris *Avanti*, June 7, 1931, that it was he who wrote to Serrati to ask Mussolini to accept the secretaryship of the Trento Chamber of Labor; he describes a scene at a banquet on June 19, 1926, when Signora Desler, accompanied by Benito Jr., broke into the banquet room where Fedele, a cabinet minister, was entertaining. The scandal of her arrest and confinement in an insane asylum, concludes Gasparini, was so great that Mussolini never visited Trento.

It was a quiet sector where the enemies had by a routine of action established a code of ethics. Every soldier who has ever kept his head down in the trenches knew and respected it. It was simply a live-and-let-live system by which firing was done at certain known intervals and a large part of the training-time was devoted to strictly human civilized activities. It made life possible—for a little longer for some men, the allotted peaceful span for others.

The leading editorial warrior came to the trenches full of the fury he had preached in print. He demanded, first of all, why the sector was so quiet, why the Italian army didn't advance, why the war was not being fought as it should be. The replies did not satisfy him. One night of his first week at the front he was looking over the trenches, himself an easy mark for any Austrian sniper, when he beheld a soldier in the enemy line lighting a match. In a flash Corporal Mussolini had removed the pin from a hand grenade and thrown it in the direction of the smoker opposite him. The crack-boom and a small flame broke the quiet monotony of the sector.

"Why did you do that, my son," the captain, who was making his rounds, asked of his corporal. "They were sitting peacefully and not doing us any harm. They were smoking their pipes in silence and perhaps talking of their brides. Have you no heart? Why was it necessary to send them to death?"

"If that is so, my captain," replied Mussolini, in the account which his worshiping admirers tell to emphasize his patriotism, "then perhaps we had all better go for a little promenade on the Milanese Corso, a more agreeable occupation, certainly."

With great satisfaction the corporal learned the next day that his lucky grenade had killed two men and wounded five. But the established code also had been broken, and in retaliation the Austrian snipers picked off many Italians during food-delivery time and other previously peaceful hours, and the act of heroism resulted in useless deaths on both sides.

Fortunately for our hero, he had little time in the front line, although many months at the front. He frequently had his photograph taken sitting or standing on top of a parapet which he sent back for publication in the illustrated weeklies. They were marked by him "front-line trenches." No British, French, or American soldier in the Great War was able to equal this photographic feat.

In December, 1916, Mussolini recorded in his diary that a cat was scratching about in the Italian wire and that, taking advantage of the first rainless evening, "I wandered about the battlefield a little." Again, no Allied or American soldier can boast of such a deed. A few days later he is visited by Fasciolo of the staff of his *Popolo*, now a captain of artillery, and de Ambris, a naval officer, and he reports seeing them walking on the road. It must have been indeed a strange front when men photographed each other on parapets, strolled for their health in No Man's Land, and could see friends coming and going on a public road.

New Year's day our hero was marching; from the 10th to the 20th of January, 1917, he "rested in the hutments of Santo Stefano." In February he notes the formation of a second section of the Bettica trench mortars of which he has been placed in command, then "practice in the Polygon of Ronchi."

On the afternoon of February 23rd "we were engaged in trial-firing with a trench mortar on Hill 144. . . . The firing went off without the least incident until the last round but one. But this round—and we had fired two casefuls—exploded in the barrel. I was hit by a shower of splinters and hurled several yards away. I cannot say any more. . . ."

Thus ended the war career of the hero.

But not the history of myth and oratory.

When the senior corporal was taken to the hospital it was found that the mortar splinters were imbedded in what the Germans unromantically call the *Sitzfleish*. From the bed of pain, on which Mussolini lay on his stomach, rose the deep cry:

"I shall not die, because I *will* not to die.

"I shall not die even if all the doctors explode with fury.

"No doubt medical science says that I cannot remain alive, but I snap my fingers at medical science."

Thus, and thus only, can a man of destiny speak.

Many years later journalists seeking biographical details of the career of the Duce obtained from the press department of the Italian Foreign Office, notably from Baron Valentino and Barone Russo, stories which made of Mussolini the bravest soldier in all the Allied and enemy armies. He had been wounded in battle, and no less than thirty times. Thirty wound stripes! This was indeed a record few if any soldiers could surpass. Nungesser, the aviator, shot down time after time, alone could equal it.

But in the war histories published before the advent of censorship there are other pictures of the event. For instance, there is the story written by de Ambris, who later became premier of Fiume, which is simply this: "Mussolini preferred to wait until his class was called. Once at the front, he passed almost all his time in the special school, the school for officers, and in the hospital. In the trenches he stayed a total of thirty-eight days, and never took part in action. The wounds on which he prides himself, thanks to which there was an end to the brilliant career as warrior, were received during grenade practice, in a training-school, miles to the rear. It was an accident, nothing heroic. The gravity of the wounds was due to the fact that a disease had poisoned his blood. When healed, this thundering warrior stayed in Milan until all danger of a return to the front had passed. This is the entire glorious history of the participation in the war of Mussolini who had preached intervention with fervor inspired by the money of the French government."

It is really amazing how facts known to so many men can be blurred, romanticized, mystified, turned into propaganda in this enlightened age of a free press and free opinion. This epiphenomenal Mussolini myth has grown so quickly. We find the *London Morning Post* saying: "Signor Mussolini fell on the Italian front with as many wounds as Caesar"; the *English Review*: "He received forty-two wounds"; G. M. Godden's biography: "Mussolini, on leaving his hospital bed at Ronchi after he had been wounded, literally with a hundred wounds"; Jeanne Bordeux: "On the hills of Monte Nero they at last took their stand. In the hell-fire of the fighting Mussolini was always in the first line, ready and willing to face any and all danger. On February 23, 1917, about two o'clock, he was wounded. There were forty splinters in his body"; Vladimir Poliakoff in the *Fortnightly Review*: "After months of hard campaigning he was dangerously wounded, and carries unto this day in his body splinters of an Austrian shell"; Sir Percival Phillips, K.B.E., of the *London Daily Mail*: "Mussolini fought with conspicuous bravery, was hit by shrapnel which made, literally, a hundred wounds."

The sweetest of all worshipers, Mme. Sarfatti, declares that "he took part in a terrific bombardment, overwhelming the enemy with a rain of bombs. The trench-mortars became almost red-hot. [The mortar burst.] Those around were killed or maimed. Mussolini, terribly lacerated, was hurled some distance away and stunned. I remember the terrible shock when the news that he was wounded reached Milan. What fearful details! Forty-two wounds. He seemed like San Sebastian, his flesh pierced as with arrows, scarred with wounds and bathed in blood."

And finally there is the soldier's own story:

"Almost at once I was, to my great relief, dispatched to the thick of the fighting on the high Alps. For a few months I underwent the hardest trials of my life in mountain trenches. I amused myself by joining the most dangerous reconnoitering expeditions. It was my Will and my wish. After one week of leave I went back to the trenches, where I remained for months. We lived only a few dozen yards from the enemy, in a perpetual and, it sometimes seemed, an eternal atmosphere of shell-fire and mortal danger that would be our life forever. I was compelled from time to time to give out in the newspapers news concerning myself. This was in order to smash the suspicions of those persons who thought me hidden in some office, distributing mail and entertaining in my mind doubts of the possibility of our winning the war. I was then corporal of the Bersaglieri and had been in the front line trenches from the beginning of the war up to February, 1917, always under arms, always facing the enemy without my faith being shaken or my convictions wavering an inch. From time to time I sent articles to the *Popolo d'Italia* exhorting endless resistance. On the morning of February 22, 1917, during a bombardment of the enemy trenches in Sector 144—the sector of the hardpressed Carso under the heaviest shell-fire—there happened one of those incidents which was a daily occurrence in trench life. One of our own grenades burst in our trench among about twenty of us soldiers. We were covered with dirt and smoke and torn by metal. Four died. Various others were fatally wounded. My wounds were serious. The patience and ability of the physicians succeeded in taking out of my body forty-four pieces of grenade. Flesh was torn, bones broken. I faced atrocious pain; my suffering was indescribable. I underwent practically all my operations without the aid of an anæsthetic. I had twenty-seven operations in one month; all except two were without anæsthetics."

There is, it is evident, less myth in Mussolini's own story than in those of his admirers. And no less honor for a soldier in being wounded by one of his own shells. How many of our own dead were victims of our own guns no one can tell, and an accident at the front is no less painful than a sniper's well-directed bullet. The number of wounds was forty-four, not thirty, and not an even hundred, and a soldier hit by one shell or bullet or burst of gas is entitled to *one*, not forty-four wound stripes. There is no evidence, however, that the corporal was ever in a real battle, but that too is of no serious importance; he was a soldier and he was wounded at the front.

Mussolini, however, was a politician gone to war. When he left Milan he was already well known as a rabid patriot and his officers were told to keep him out of real danger, since he was more valuable as a journalist writing propaganda good for civilian morale, than as a common soldier. In a much smaller degree Mussolini was in the position of ex-President Theodore Roosevelt had President Wilson permitted him to go to France. The American military establishment, it was revealed after the war, had asked Wilson to refuse the request because it feared Roosevelt would play the politician in the trenches. It thought he would be running for President while fighting the Germans, and for like reason General Leonard Wood, another strenuous militarist with political ambitions, was also kept at home.

When Mussolini was wounded, considerable propaganda was made of this unforeseen accident. It is true that his own newspaper, the *Popolo*, on the 24th of February was able to print the comforting announcement that the wounds were not serious, but the process of creating a hero was well begun. When Mussolini wrote from his hospital that "I am proud in the fulfillment of duty, perilous duty, to have contributed to the opening of the road to Trieste with my own blood," the noble if not quite truthful but nevertheless magical words caused a considerable burst of patriotic hysteria to be felt in newspaper offices, and the time of the singing of hymns had come.

The importance of hero-making in war time cannot be over-estimated. From a purely military viewpoint it must be said that Mussolini's wounds, accidental as they were, had a moral value surpassing perhaps the capture of a large section of enemy trenches or several hundred prisoners. In a manner it was like the battle of Cantigny which the American First Division fought, a minor episode in military history, but a tremendously invigorating force throughout France because it was the first appearance of Yankee soldiers in a successful action.

While Mussolini lay in hospital the King of Italy came to visit the little corporal.

He progressed to crutches, to a cane. He then "asked exemption from further military service as being indispensable in the management of the *Popolo*."

Returning to Milan, he records, "I took my place as a fighter in my newspaper office."

After Caporetto, that defeat of defeats of the Allies, Mussolini, who had played a small part in bringing Italy into the war, exerted himself to maintain her there. And so long as the Allies and the Associated Power, which is the United States of America, can believe that the World War was justified slaughter, that it helped civilization, that it was blessed by Almighty God, as thousands of preachers once declared, so long must they confess their gratitude to Benito Mussolini for his work in helping the victory.

General Cadorna did not think the corporal rated elevation to a sub-lieutenancy. As for himself, he records in his autobiography, "I was a good soldier."

CHAPTER VII

Fiume or Death!

Il Generale Cadorna
Scrive alla Regina:
Se vuol veder Trieste,
Compra la cartolina!

IT WAS TREASON TO SING THIS SONG: "GENERAL CADORNA WROTE
to the queen: If you want to see Trieste, buy a picture postcard,"
but the soldiers sang it and a volunteer ambulance driver named
Ernest Hemingway composed another stanza about the regiment
being decimated, the colonel being decorated, hurrah for the can-
nonade. The soldiers sang and shouted, "We want peace," and, "Long
live the Pope," who on the 1st of August, 1917, had sent a peace
plan to all the nations.

October 17, 1917: Caporetto. The retreat. The Germans announced
the collapse of Italy.

Gabriele d'Annunzio suggested to Editor Mussolini that he form
an organization of all patriots whose work would be to restore
civilian and military morale. Mussolini and many other patriots did
so. It was called the Fascio di Resistenza.

From that day on, through the Vittorio Veneto of the following
year when Italy triumphed, and in time of armistice and peace conferences, the two men were joined in many activities. One was the
leading politician, the other the leading poet. They came back two
of a triumvirate of acclaimed heroes. Benito Mussolini, Gabriele
d'Annunzio and Raffaele Rossetti shared many honors. The politician had played his part well, even if he was not long at the front;
the poet had flown in the back seat of an airplane which bombarded
Vienna with leaflets of warning, and the third was an engineer who

71

had, single-handed, ridden a torpedo into an Austrian harbor and destroyed the flagship of the navy. Rossetti was Italy's Sergeant York. Of the three, one rules, another does strange mystic rites on a battleship fastened down in his front yard, wearing the collar of the Annunziata and answering to the title of Prince, while the third is a workingman in Paris, a refugee, a rebel.

All three were participants in the Fiume adventure. D'Annunzio led it; Mussolini gathered the funds, and Rossetti one day, overcome by Mussolini's editorials, went into the office of the *Popolo* and presented to the sacred cause a small fortune which the nation had given him for his exploits. In exile he has time to think and regret.

D'Annunzio marched on the 12th of September, 1919, a time of chaos and peace conferences. "We had won the war," wrote Mussolini, "but were utterly defeated in the diplomatic battle. We were losing—except Zara—the whole of Dalmatia, our land by tradition and history, by manners and costumes [*sic*], by language spoken and by the ardent and constant aspirations of the Dalmatians towards the mother country. Fiume, most Italian of cities, was contested."

Mussolini had been appointed "consul-general" by d'Annunzio, who gathered about him the Arditi, the ardent young veterans, many officers, some peasants, many socialists, some roustabout boys and adventurers. The march on Fiume was the forerunner of the march on Rome. Both were the poet's ideas. He marched, and he was met by General Pittaluga, commander of the port, peacemaker for the Allies.

"Thus you ruin Italy," he declared.

"It is you who ruin Italy by opposing Fiume's destiny," replied d'Annunzio.

"I must obey military orders," countered the general.

"What? You would fire upon your brothers?" cried the poet. "Then fire first upon me."

With a noble gesture d'Annunzio tore open his military tunic, exposing his undershirt.

Pittaluga was overcome.

"With you I cry, 'Viva Fiume,' " he cried.

"Evviva Pittaluga," cried d'Annunzio.

So they embraced and, crying together, led the march into Fiume. The forty trucks started their motors. The general advanced very militarily. D'Annunzio did his best in a bow-legged way. The next morning he put on a field-marshal's uniform.

Comic opera as this may seem today, the attack and its success led directly to the making of the Fascist movement and the advent of Mussolini in Rome. The poet had supplied the black shirts, the black fezzes, the slogans, the spirit of armed adventure, the ideal of force triumphant and the salutes, yells, and claptrap of Rome of the time of the Caesars. A shrewder man knew how to employ them on a national scale.

Italy, the people of Italy, cheered the coup d'état as an act of justice. Mussolini editorially proclaimed that "the government of Italy is not in Rome, but in Fiume. It is that government which we must obey," a declaration of pure patriotic treason which Premier Nitti promptly denounced. He also saw with alarm that sedition for the first time had entered the Italian army.

Every evening the victorious poet held an oration and listened to the cheers of his men; several times a week he led parades, and again listened to shouts, watched the waving of stilettos, the shaking of muskets, and found it all magnificent. He gave Fiume a charter full of romantic poetry . . . "to instil into the daily life a sense of that virtuous joy which ought to revive the spirits of a people liberated at last from the yoke of restraint and falsehood." He also created ten classes of men, in ten corporations, the ninth for seafaring men, the tenth for the intelligentsia. "Its coming is expected like that of the Tenth Muse. It is reserved to the mysterious forces of the people in toil and attainment. It is almost a votive figure . . . to the complete liberation of the spirit over pain and agony, over blood and sweat." The corporations, circumcised of poetry, remain in the present Fascist state.

To the people of Fiume the poet said: "I shall not leave here alive nor shall I leave here when I am dead, for I shall be buried here, to become one with the sacred soil."

Always d'Annunzio dramatized himself. One day he strutted about like Napoleon, a bow-legged Napoleon it is true; another day he was Lenin; and again he would become Captain Kidd and organize expeditions to raid the main, board ships, steal cargoes of food. Twice his men raided and annexed islands. Frequently they brought prize ships and much booty into port. Sometimes d'Annunzio would play the part of field-marshal in resplendent uniform. Frequently he assumed his favorite rôle, which was that of Prince of the Renaissance.

Every day he held a ceremony of the Arditi. He concluded by asking: "To whom does Italy belong?"

"*A noi* (To us)!" shouted the trained Arditi.

"Who are our enemies?"

"They disgust us," replied the Black Shirts, and with a superior smile the commandante, field-marshal, Napoleon, and Prince would dismiss his cohorts.

Frequently he called for the Socialists and Communists to come to the governor's palace to discuss revolution. In a strange muddled way be believed himself a rebel, therefore akin to the Bolsheviki, who in those days were enjoying the hatred of the universe. In that, too, he felt himself a kindred victim and flooded his emotions with self-pity while he made a grandiose gesture of dictatorship. I can still hear him talking in dactylic hexameters in answer to my simple journalistic questions.

"Our cause is the greatest and the most beautiful that today is opposed to the dementia and to the vileness of the world," he said. "It extends from Ireland to Egypt, from Russia to America, from Rumania to India; it gathers together the white races and colored races, reconciles the Gospel and the Koran, Christianity and Islam, rivets in one sole will as many peoples as possess in their bones and in their arteries salt and iron sufficient to feed action. We shall be victorious. All the rebels of all races of mankind will gather under our banners. And the weaponless shall be armed. And violence shall oppose violence. There shall be a new crusade of all the poor and impoverished nations, of all poor men and all free men against the nations, against the caste of usurers which yesterday made the profits of the war and today profit by the peace; and we shall reëstablish the true justice which a cold and foolish man with a hammer borrowed from a former German chancellor, crucified with fourteen nails."

He demanded an insurrection of the spirit, "against the devourers of raw flesh, and against the exploiters of weaponless peoples," and he called upon all the victims of their or foreign governments to come to him in Fiume and conspire with him for revolt and rebellion and violence and insurrection everywhere and at once. As for himself, he intended to march on Rome. He had already arranged for that with his close associate, Benito Mussolini, the patriotic journalist who in Milan was acting as his "envoy to Italy," and collecting three million lire from sympathizers. He would await the troops which Mussolini was arming for him, join them to the Arditi, land at Rimini or Ravenna, receive the acclaim of liberated Italy, and with thousands upon thousands joining him at every footstep, march victoriously into the streets of Rome, dissolve parliament and declare the dictatorship of the patriots.

Every evening he made an oration. He spoke with poetry and fire and beauty against the wrongs of Versailles; with irony and fire he lashed Clemenceau and Woodrow Wilson and all the betrayers of the cause of Fiume, the Fiume of Italy and d'Annunzio. He spoke as if he were not merely the governor of a seized seaport, but Messiah of all the downtrodden of the earth, a Messiah in a military uniform, but holding aloft a flag which all the unhappy and idealistic could see from their unfortunate parts of the world.

At the end of every evening's oration the same ceremony:

"For Gabriele d'Annunzio!"

"Ayah! ayah! ayah! Alala!"

"For the people of Fiume!"

"Ayah! ayah! ayah! Alala!"

"What is our slogan?"

"*Me ne frego!* [We don't give a damn!]"

The Arditi in unison lifted their stilettos and the Prince smiled.

Twice or three times a week, depending upon the state of morale of his own troops, who were not getting enough to eat, and the Yugoslav population, who were enemies, there would be a full-dress parade of the Fiumian Legion which the commandante would lead up to the main square, where he would mount a tribune and review. There would be fanfares and loud and continued "Ayahs" and "Alalas." Salutes and poses. Frequently there were ceremonials and always there were new ribbons, new medals for bravery, new victories to be celebrated. It was, in short, a carnival which was to end in bloodshed.

Among the important factors contributing to the final slaughter were the arrangements which the government was able to make with Mussolini, which resulted in his withdrawal of support, moral, financial, military, and commissary. Starvation and lack of new troops defeated d'Annunzio.

Almost from the first days trouble arose. The thousands of lire for Fiume came from all over Italy, but the big sums outside Rossetti's contribution, were sent by Italian-Americans; it is estimated that $50,000 came from the United States in the first three months following Mussolini's appeal for funds "to feed the starving babies of Fiume" and to aid the poet in other ways. In November, 1919, after Mussolini had run for parliament and received almost no votes, he was publicly accused and tried by the journalists' association for using the starving babies of Fiume fund to run his own election campaign.

This charge Mussolini denied, but admitted "diverting" some of d'Annunzio's money.[1] He admitted that two of his assistant editors resigned after accusing him of helping himself to Fiume money for political purposes, he admits he appeared for "trial," and adds that "my justification was ample and precise. The board was forced by the acts to do me justice. As for the disposition of the funds for the Fiume campaign and other unworthy calumnies, I published in my newspaper documents and testimony which could never be refuted. The conclusion arrived at then has been and always will be the same until I cease to exist: on the score of integrity there is no assault to be made upon me. My political work may be valued more or less, this way or that, and people may shout me up or howl me down, but in the moral field it is another matter. Men must live in harmony with the faith by which they are pushed on; they must be inspired by the most absolute disinterestedness. I am proud to know myself as one not to be suspected—even by myself—and feeling that my inmost moral fiber is invincible."

Against these lovely and noble words we have the testimony of the prime minister of Fiume, Alceste De Ambris, the man who was the practical strategist of the adventure, who was one of the original legionaries of d'Annunzio, who marched and fought, held the highest

[1] *Popolo d'Italia,* February 20, 1920.

political office, and who later at the risk of his life came to Milan as the poet's personal representative to negotiate Mussolini's aid.

"I was at that time," states De Ambris, "chief of the cabinet of the provisional government of Fiume and I recall with what repugnance d'Annunzio received Mussolini's request for aid.

"D'Annunzio had large ideas, but at that moment the legionaries who occupied Fiume suffered literally from hunger and d'Annunzio found it strange that Mussolini was taking the bread from the mouths of the soldiers and inhabitants of Fiume for the purpose of electoral ambitions, and for personal expenses.

"Nevertheless, d'Annunzio did send a letter which would serve Mussolini in making a public denial of the grave charges made against him by the *Avanti*. Later, d'Annunzio was to learn with what gratitude Mussolini would repay."

The two editors of the *Popolo* who resigned and brought charges against their duce were Capodivacca and Rossato; the trial was begun on February 3, 1920; Mussolini wrote:

"The Fascist election bloc fought with its own money, exclusively its own and not that of Fiume. Of the sums received, several thousands of lire were used to pay the salaries of legionaries coming to Milan from Fiume and other Italian towns and which formed the armed bands, at my orders."

The accusation declared that these "armed bands" were in fact the beginnings of the Fascisti, or Mussolini's private militia, which were armed and outfitted by him, to be used by him to help in the election, and never to be sent as reinforcements to Fiume. Mussolini replied:

"We must distinguish two periods, the period of 15 April to 15 May, and that which is truly the period of the 'bands' of the *Popolo d'Italia*. It concerns the group of twenty to twenty-five Arditi who stood guard of my papers. Now we come to the other 'bands.' The fact is, as I have told the judge, during the most important week of the election campaign, several dozens of Arditi, officers and sailors, came from Fiume. There were in all several hundred men divided into squadrons commanded by officers and naturally all obedient to me. It is perfectly true that they were paid; they were given 20 to 25 lire a day."

It was this confession, incidentally, which caused Premier Nitti to act, because obviously the arming of several hundred men to use in an election was the formation of a small professional army by a candidate for parliament, was a breach of the constitution; it was no concern of the government's whether the men were paid out of the Fiume fund or not. It was at this moment that Mussolini was taken to the prison of San Fedele for a short sojourn when Nitti feared a coup d'état.

When Giolitti came into power he devoted himself to two problems, the industrial revolution in the north, and the Fiume question. At Rapallo, September 20, 1920, he signed a treaty renouncing all Dalmatia except Zara, and returned to Yugoslavia a part of the port of Fiume. Premier Giolitti and Count Sforza, Minister of Foreign Affairs, heard from Mussolini that he would accept this arrangement although d'Annunzio refused. Mussolini again had turned his coat.

Moreover, d'Annunzio informed Mussolini he knew of a letter containing a secret codicil giving the Yugoslavs portuary rights in Fiume, but the agent sent with this news to Milan came back to say that Mussolini, who was now writing editorials praising the peaceful conclusion of the affair, had refused to change his attitude.

De Ambris then invited Mussolini to visit Fiume at the end of October, where a definitive meeting with d'Annunzio was arranged, but at the last hour Mussolini refused, going to Rome instead on political errands of his own. D'Annunzio at last began to suspect treason. Early in December it was apparent that the loyal royal Italian troops were concentrating for a march on Fiume. It was then, according to De Ambris, that d'Annunzio sent his ultimatum to Mussolini, asking for "an act of solidarity," and for money and more troops which Mussolini had promised for just this emergency. Mussolini replied:

"The commandante wants me to start a revolution. But can he be sure that the workmen will work again, twelve hours a day?"

D'Annunzio's representative did not understand.

It is true that the question of a revolution in Italy had been discussed by the two leaders of the Fiume adventure. Much later, in self-defense, accused of betraying d'Annunzio, Mussolini in a public speech declared:

"Let no one reproach me because I have not made that little, easy, cheerful, pleasant thing called a revolution. The Fascisti have never promised to make a revolution in Italy in the event of Fiume being attacked. I personally have never written to d'Annunzio to make him believe that a revolution in Italy depended on my inclinations. I do not bluff or talk hot air.

"Revolution is not a surprise packet which can be opened by all. I do not carry it in my pocket. Revolution will be accomplished with the army, not against the army; with arms, not without them; with trained forces, not with undisciplined mobs called together in the streets. It will succeed when it is surrounded by a halo of sympathy or by the majority, and if it has not all that, it will fail."

A fine prediction, the confession of a plan, as we shall see afterwards. At present the Machiavellian Mussolini, the practical gentleman who had collected the funds and had armed his own bands in Milan, was making cryptic remarks to d'Annunzio, who, however, replied he was not asking that the revolution begin at once, but that troops and money for food be sent as promised. To this Mussolini did not reply.

Left alone in Fiume, the poet heard the government troops were on the march. General di Caviglia surrounded Fiume and sent an ultimatum to d'Annunzio. This fact was communicated to Mussolini, who, however, just before the ultimatum expired and the bombardment began, was able to write:

"In the hour in which we find ourselves we cannot know what reply Gabriele d'Annunzio has given to the ultimatum sent by General di Caviglia which expired yesterday at 18 o'clock. On the other hand, a declaration made by the Honorable Giolitti to the Honorable De Nava, president of the parliamentary commission on foreign affairs, signifies that the affair will not have a tragic end. The Honorable Giolitti has declared that the Fiume situation is such as to give no one any worry.

"This optimism, veritably olympic, contrasts with the tone of the note sent by di Caviglia and with the ultimatum which has already expired at this hour."

No neutral could have written a more suitable editorial. This was from the pen of the man who was the principal backer of the movement.

On the night of December 24th the bombardment began. From Christmas Eve through four nights and four days there was small but effective shooting from land and sea and blood was spilled in the houses and streets of Fiume, while in the *Popolo* not even a cry of indignation was raised by Mussolini.

When d'Annunzio gave up his command to a committee of citizens and left Fiume, only then did the Fascist chief utter a valedictory, which he proudly recounts today:

"Beneath all the verbosity and the shuttle of mere words, the drama is perfect; horrible if you choose, but perfect. On one side is the cold Reason of the State determined to the very bottom; on the other the warm Reason of the Ideal ready to make desperate, supreme sacrifices. Invited to make our choice, we, the uneasy and precocious minority, choose calmly the Reason of the Ideal."

"The Reason of the Ideal," according to De Ambris and to thousands of other politicians and leaders, was soon apparent: the government and Mussolini had come to an agreement by which Mussolini, in return for withdrawing his support from Fiume, would be allowed free hand with the arming and organizing of the entire Fascist movement.

"We know now," states the former premier of Fiume, "that the new phase of the political fortune of Mussolini, and especially of Fascism, dates from the treason to the cause of Fiume, after his negotiations with Giolitti. From that moment dates a different attitude of the government vis-à-vis with Fascism and the rapid transformation of it into a reactionary movement. From the end of 1920 the Fascisti were in effect armed by Giolitti and largely paid by him.

"Giolitti had been called into power to solve two problems, Fiume and Bolshevism. To solve the former he obtained Mussolini's passive consent to the fratricidal aggression of Christmas 1920; to solve the latter Giolitti obtained Mussolini's active consent and engaged himself to furnish arms and other material means for the guerilla warfare against Socialism.

"Giolitti believed himself powerful enough to suppress the Fascisti after he had used them as an anti-Socialist reactionary force, without compromising the liberal state directly in the civil strife. But the old fox fooled himself and lived to regret it bitterly.

"Mussolini turned his treason into profit. I do not know what thirty pieces of silver the Fascist Judas got from Giolitti (as he had once before gotten from France by becoming an interventionist), but it is certain that between Giolitti and Mussolini, after the Treaty of Rapallo, there was a pact whereby Mussolini, abandoning Fiume to Giolitti, received in compensation the government's aid for the Fascist enterprise. And the treason was doubly completed by Mussolini, who, on coming into power, annexed Fiume, instead of letting it remain free as specified in the Treaty of Rapallo. Moreover, the Treaty of Nettuno which Mussolini later signed with the Yugoslavs, surrendered more than specified in the secret letter of Count Sforza. When Mussolini was confronted with this fact in the Chamber of Deputies, he replied by calling Sforza a 'traitor' and a 'liar.'

"But Count Sforza did not lie to anyone and betrayed no one; he merely executed his program which was inspired by the idea of a peaceful understanding with Yugoslavia, even at the cost of grave sacrifices.

"If there is a traitor and a liar in this affair, it is uniquely Mussolini. That is the truth which I, a legionary of Fiume, can repeat even if the other legionaries, now in the service of the traitor, have forgotten."

(In January 1924, Italy and Yugoslavia in the hall of victory of the Chigi Palace, signed their peace pact. It was announced as a great Fascist victory. The terms are almost identical with those proposed years before by Sforza; the organization of the port, the division of the harbor and docks, the free-port part as designated in 1921, were approved by Mussolini and remain so to this day. But in 1921 he had said to Sforza:

"You are placing a knife at the throat of Fiume.")

Both d'Annunzio and Mussolini had floated the banner *"Fiume o Morte,"* over their ambition and their followers for more than a year. D'Annunzio had said: "Until that day when there are only three men left standing up there will be one less shame in this world," but he had marched out peacefully at the head of thousands.

To the new commander, the podestà of Fiume, he said: "I confide to you my dead, my sorrow, and my victory. Italy is not worth dying for."

There was only one victor at Fiume. It was the man who built Fascism upon its sorrow, its ruins, and its dead.

★ ★

CHAPTER VIII

The Secret of 1920

GABRIELE D'ANNUNZIO, LIKE MANY ANOTHER PARENT, SOON EX-
perienced the disillusioning sensation of not knowing his own
child. Born of his furious poetic brain in Fiume, it was a mad, reckless, violent, but romantic and idealistic infant given to heroic pos-
turings, intriguing clothes, Roman gestures, and semi-communistic
dialectics. A year later, in Milan, he found it brandishing blackjacks
and revolvers and castor oil.

Mussolini, the new foster parent, as well as d'Annunzio, united
in admitting Fascismo to be the stepchild of still another leader of
that time. That man was Woodrow Wilson. It was the President
of the United States who had journeyed to Rome at Christmas time,
1918, and who in Milan had been worshiped in the streets because
Italy believed him to be the man who would grant the nation its
political demands and the people the same "new deal" which Lloyd
George had just proclaimed in Great Britain.

But when the Allied nations exposed their secret treaties and asked
President Wilson to agree to them, he compromised on some, accepted others, and remained steadfast in his decision against Italy
in Fiume.

It was then that Mussolini in his paper and d'Annunzio among
the soldiers began the campaign against Wilson. In Rome crowds
demonstrated against the American embassy crying, *"Ridacci la lupa*
(Give back our wolf)," the gold wolf of Rome which had been
Italy's contribution to the trunkloads of presents given the man
who had saved the world for democracy and the Allied politicians.
The police charged the mob. D'Annunzio exploited the spirit of the
nation. He organized the march on Fiume.

More recently still another stepfather has been added to Mussolini's Fascismo. Granting that the idea was d'Annunzio's, that the inspiration was inversely Wilson's, and that the leadership was successfully Mussolini's, the astute politicians in Rome knew that the movement was deathly sick with the loss of blood at Fiume and that nothing but a transfusion would save it. And this was supplied by the government itself, and more particularly by the "sly fox" of the generation, the premier Giolitti who as de Ambris has stated at one and the same time liquidated the uprising at Fiume and the uprising in the factories in the north, ending social agitation and radicalism and the revolutionary strikes and, as he believed, bringing about a permanent era of good will in Italy in 1920.

From the end of the war until the seizure of the factories in August of that year, things went from bad to worse in Italy, and Mussolini vigorously approved this turn of affairs.

Every day or every week there was a new strike. There occurred the greatest horror which the American tourist has ever experienced and about which to this very day he speaks with emotion, thanking God and Mussolini—the horror of tourist trains not running on time. That Mussolini himself backed the railroad strikers[1] and that he urged them to seize the railroads are historical facts of no interest to those who, armed with a rapid schedule, see the Sistine Chapel on Monday, the Pitti and Uffizi on Tuesday morning, St. Mark's Wednesday, get romantic in a gondola that night and make the 10:15 Thursday for somewhere else, as per orders of the clerk in the express company office in Paris. The railroad strikes had something to do with the social revolution? The Americans did not care to hear such things discussed.

Besides the railroad workers, the ironworkers of Genoa, the post-office employees, foundry workers, agricultural workers of Novara, street-car men of Genoa and others struck. Soldiers were spat upon and officers were followed by crowds who insulted them because they still wore the uniform. They were sometimes attacked, forced to run, barricade themselves. Honorable wound stripes were torn off and even the medals of bravery ripped from brave breasts and trampled. The government could do nothing. Parliament was a big talking-affair but law and order were paralyzed while in a sort of

[1] See Appendix, "Mussolini and the Bolshevik Era."

nebulous and oratorical chaos various elements, aiming to restore liberty and justice to the masses, muddled around helplessly.

More strikes. Metal workers, bread workers, waiters, teachers. On May 4, 1919, Mussolini wrote: "Convinced that the strikers are right and have justice on their side, we are lending them our disinterested support." On June 7, he added: "The nation follows with sympathy the strike of the teachers." Almost every day Mussolini commented favorably on the moves of the unionists, insulted the government, cursed the employers. (Later, on taking office, one of the first things this man, great enough to change his mind and political party, said of the strikes was that "they were the low acts of the Socialists against which the Fascist patriots had to fight," but before, during and after the strike Mussolini not only supported it, but urged the semi-Bolshevik idea that the railroad and other unionists seize and operate their own industries.)

Prologue to the seizure of the factories in 1920 was the episode at Dalmine, March, 1919, when Fascist agitators caused a strike at the Franchi-Gregorini plant, the workers raising the national, instead of the red, flag, and demanding participation in the operation of the factory which they had seized and refused to leave.

Mussolini called this a "creative strike." He rushed there to aid the Bolsheviki, addressed them, saying: "To protect the interest of your class you could have called a strike in the old style, the negative and destructive strike; on the contrary, thinking of the interests of the people, you have inaugurated the creative strike which does not interrupt production." In another exhortation he exclaimed: "You have proven your Will, and I say to you you are on the right road. . . . I say to you that your gesture is new and dignified, by the motives which inspired them, worthy of sympathy. Your rights are sacred, and I am with you."

Meanwhile back in Milan his associate editors wrote: "Today the masses at Dalmine have shown a significant action, they have reaffirmed their rights, they have vibrated to the impetuous and incisive words of Benito Mussolini."

"At Dalmine," wrote one of Mussolini's colleagues, "he was the Lenin of Italy."

On March 23 the Fascisti organizing, sent their salutations to the men who had seized the factory, and to the workers of Pavia who had gone on a general strike. Said the future Duce: "Historically we are on the grounds of the revolution begun by us in 1915. We must go ahead of the workers. We must accept the postulates of the working-class. Do they demand the eight-hour day? And the control of the industries? We must support all these demands especially because we want little by little to make the working-class capable of directing the works. Economic Democracy! That is our banner.

"The Senate must be abolished. We want to erase from our constitutional organization this feudal organism. We demand proportional representation. We want a national assembly which will have to decide whether Italy is to be a monarchy or a republic.

"We reply now: Republic!

"We are absolutely against all forms of dictatorship."

Employers associations and the trades unions kept up the war for another year. Italian money fell; the cost of living mounted; wages were never raised, except once in a while when a strike was successful. The war profiteers held on to their money. The workers were exploited. All the promises of better times which the government at war had made to the people were studiously forgotten. But eventually there were revisions of salaries made individually. Then the metal workers association decided for a general revision of wages based on the cost of living. The employers objected. On July 29, 1920, they issued the statement "We cannot admit the possibility of fixing salaries in relation to the rising cost of living."

But public opinion forced the employers to agree to a conference. Mussolini backed it. Yet on August 12th the owners crushed the conference with the statement: "All discussion is useless. We make no concessions."

This challenge to battle was accepted. A few days later the program of the trades union was announced. It was "Obstructionism." But it was not violence, nor was it sabotage. It did mean slowing up. There was to be no "good will" in the work; the men were to work mechanically, to do just what they were told, never to use their judgment, even if work done in accordance with orders from the bosses led to the spoiling of goods and tools. The letter of the law was obeyed.

The employers did not like that at all. But they could do nothing to obtain healthy coöperation, enthusiasm, good will, from underpaid and sometimes starving employees. So they threatened the lock-out. The Alfa-Romeo automobile works was the first to drive out its workers. The manufacturers association agreed to follow. In reply the trades unions then ordered the occupation of the factory and the continuance of work, or the "Creative strike" of Dalmine which Mussolini had favored, on a large scale. There was no sabotage. On August 30, 500,000 men were ordered to occupy factories and they did so without any troubles worth recording. Two men were killed in Turin. About a million men joined in the movement, which, when it reached the bottom of Sicily, was turned into the seizure of land by dispossessed peasants. Not a safe was cracked. Nor a skull.

But from Paris the word was flashed around the world that Italy had "gone Bolshevik." The workers had seized the factories. The peasants had taken the land. The red flag was flying and the people were shouting, "Viva Lenin." If there were no dead, well, there should be. So all the journalists of Europe came to Milan and Turin to participate in the revolution.

The excitement in Europe and America was unbounded. Russia and Hungary were red, there were communist troubles in the Balkans, Germany trembling on the verge—(the German "verge" lasted more than a decade and became a Fascist verge in the end)—and now Italy was gone, and who knows, perhaps all of Europe would soon be engulfed. Foreign offices kept open nights and newspapers clamored for lists of dead and wounded.

Commotion everywhere except in Italy. It is true that day by day more and more factories were being occupied by the workers. Soon the 500,000 "strikers" were at work building automobiles, steamships, forging tools, manufacturing a thousand useful things, but there was not a shop or factory owner to boss them or to dictate letters in the vacant offices. Peace reigned.

A feeling spread throughout Italy that the great day of liberation had arrived.

It was holiday. Crowds came in automobiles and wagons or walked by the thousands to see the great sight. What they saw was pure normality, but they got a thrill out of it. Tourists, caught in the midst of the revolution, when their first fears were over, and not a rifle-shot disturbed the sunny calm, ventured out, too, and saw nothing unusual.

For us of the press it was a terrible disillusion. There was simply no story. We did see the red flag waving from the chimneys, but there was smoke issuing from them, too, and all the sounds from within were those of ordinary industry and progress. Occasionally someone shouted, "Viva Lenin," or, "Long live the revolution," and sometimes a patrol of workingmen would go by. The police let them alone even when they bore arms. There was much joyful singing.

The nation awaited the outcome hopefully. Everyone was pleased that things were going so well. Labriola, Minister of Labor, was the first to attempt a conciliation, but it did not succeed. The state did nothing. The press was fair. Mussolini's paper applauded. To satisfy our own newspapers, which were demanding that something happen to justify our presence during the "revolution," we rushed around from Milan to Turin and from Turin to Genoa, chasing rumors, that some Fascist spies had been caught and burned alive in a furnace or that "Mr. Fiat" had been murdered by his employees, and other timely lies.[2] In order to get Bolshevik pictures we had to persuade the workingmen and women to erect barricades, arm themselves, take up menacing positions, and act in a revolutionary manner, which they did with laughter and smiles, much to the chagrin of the newsreel men.

From our journalistic point of view the Italian Bolshevik revolution was such a complete fiasco that we looked for other news. I had arrived with Harry Greenwall of the *London Express* who had a tip that Emir Feisul, later King of Iraq, was stopping incognito in the Villa d'Este near Milan, en route for London, where he wanted to see Lloyd George about a throne. Accordingly, we went to inter-

---

[2] Charles H. Sherrill, general, sportsman, author and diplomat, wrote: "At Turin a Red Tribunal, composed partly of women, caused men to be thrown alive into the blast-furnaces. . . . Some sailors . . . were ambushed by a band of Socialists, men and women, and literally torn to pieces, every last one of them, with all the excesses of the French revolution—the women ripping off ears with their teeth . . ." etc. In addition to being hysterical this account, typical of reports of the time, is absolutely untrue.

view the dark lord and he told us he had made a secret treaty, thanks to Lawrence of Arabia, whereby the British government promised him a kingdom in return for his aid against the Turks. That was a fine news item. Then, journalistically opportune, there was an earthquake in Fivizzano, somewhere north of Pisa, and off I went with Lieutenant Cleveland, U. S. N., to help pull men and women and children out of fallen houses and debris in wrecked towns on the vine-clad hillsides. That was a three-day story, too. All these news happenings were much more sensational than the peaceful occupation of the factories which Mussolini then supported and which years later, for political purposes, he was to denounce.

The whole nation also approved the seizure of the land. Agrarian reform had long been promised. When Nitti was Premier he had a law passed giving land, paid for by the government, to ex-soldiers. During the war the troops were fed on the propaganda all wrongs would be righted when they came home victorious, and the land workers, who were little better than Russian serfs, would be given farms. Now they were taking them. In every instance the revolutionaries who were dividing up the huge estates in the south were led by former soldiers, some of whom were Fascists, Mussolini having in 1919 declared for land seizure. (In fact, in 1923, nineteen months after he came into power, he let the Fascist syndicates seize ten properties in the province of Novare for division among war veterans.)

Despite the fact that one big bank had offered capital for employers and employees to try a communal collective experiment with the factories, despite the fact the railroad men refused to transport troops when the government one day thought it would end the situation by force and bloodshed, what happened in September was stagnation and compromise. On the 10th and 11th the Socialist congress considered two proposals, one to retain the original character of the occupation, the other to turn it into a movement for political power— *i.e.,* to capture the government in Rome. The vote was 591,241 against 409,569 in favor of the former plan. Syndical control of the factories was endorsed.

Premier Giolitti then called a meeting of both sides, asking the employers to recognize the principle of the workers participation in industry. Again there was compromise. Labor accepted a small wage rise and employers agreed to the government's plan that henceforth labor was to share with capital in the manufacture of the nation's goods. Mussolini, declaring himself happy with this ending, said he had always favored such a plan, said it was the beginning of a new era in social evolution.

The State triumphed. The revolutionary spirit of the workmen, which first flamed under Mussolini at Dalmine, was now smothered in compromises and political deals. Dictatorship of the proletariat was shown to bè a dream. Although there never had been a burst of real Bolshevism, it was now recognized that there never would or could be a really Russian revolutionary uprising in Italy.

With the peaceful failure of the occupation movement, called Bolshevism abroad, but in fact a real attempt to establish a peaceful coöperative industrial commonwealth, came the gradual disintegration of radical labor hopes in Italy. This double movement, the building up of discipline, the restoration of confidence, reconciliation and pacification on one side, and the war against violence on the other, was the work of the liberal, democratic parties. It was the crowning effort of Premier Giolitti. At least it was so heralded in those forgotten days.

But time reveals many secrets.

In the middle of the great crisis of 1920 there was a meeting in the Hotel Lombardia, in Milan, between the Honorable Bruno Buozzi, secretary-general of the Federazione Italiani Operai Metallurgica, or Italian federation of metal workers, and the editor of the *Popolo d'Italia*. Signor Buozzi occupied a place and a reputation equal if not superior to that of Samuel Gompers in the American Federation of Labor, and the revelations which follow were made by him to the present writer and have been confirmed by other Italian leaders.

"I remember," Signor Buozzi says in a statement signed and authorized by him for publication in this book, "the social revolutionary Mussolini studiously and transcendentally dressed the part, with his large black hat and his artistic necktie. When we met to talk politics in the old days he was always the one to assume studious attitudes of mystery, of a conspirator or of an agitator; at a café table he would speak as if from a tribune haranguing the crowd of thousands of listeners, although we sat there four or five. I remember an evening in Turin in 1913 where we held a conference on 'The Commune of Paris' in the hall of the syndicates. Mussolini even then spoke as a consummate actor; his histrionism carried away the least intelligent part of the auditors. He had a marvelous mobility in his face, he rolled his black eyes, his shoulders were agitated energetically, he modulated his voice, made long pauses, then suddenly burst out in the loudest tones, sweeping the crowd with him. He exalted to hyperbole the heroism of the Paris communards, but did not spare with his acid criticism their leaders. He denounced, for example, the stupidity which ordered the leaders of the armed patrols to defend the Banque de France.

"'Money makes war,' cried Mussolini. 'If the communards had appropriated the gold contained in the vaults of the Bank and utilized it for their ends, history might have had another face.'

"We all went to the hotel then and sat around a table discussing the social revolution. It was lively. Some one suggested that the social revolution presupposes a knowledge and a mastery of formidable political and economic problems. Mussolini replied that for the true revolutionist such problems were unimportant. To solve all problems, 'down with the bureaucracy'. The real political leader, he said, needed nothing but action. He had studied the essentials of romantic revolution and its prophet, Blanqui.

"At one turn of the conversation, attacking our social-democracy, Mussolini arose, pointing his index finger at us and speaking in a cavernous voice, accenting each syllable:

"'Italy is the only country,' he said, 'in all Europe which in the past hundred years has not had a revolution. *L'Italia ha bisogno di un bagno di sangue* [Italy has need of a bath of blood], and you, social democrats and leaders of the syndicalists, are the major obstacle against the accomplishment of such a fact. We ought to barricade for ten years the doors of your organizations.'

"Mussolini had always said and printed in the paper which he directed, that programs are obstacles under the feet which impede the man who would go forward. He said and wrote that the syndicates and the coöperatives were developing among the people an unhealthy sense of responsibility, they were checking the people from dedicating themselves to the fight on the barricades and to the conquest of power. It was for this reason that he participated in every strike, trying to turn each into a general strike.

"At the end of the war he organized the Fascio with an extreme radical program, supported strikes and agitation among workingmen, denouncing the Socialists for not being sufficiently revolutionary. He gave his sympathy to the occupation of the factories by the workmen.

"The history of that movement is almost unknown. The Federazione Italiana Operai Metallurgici, the F. I. O. M., of which I was secretary-general, had requested the owners to augment wages in proportion to the increased cost of living. The request was fully justified and many industrialists realized this and willingly raised wages. But at a certain moment the industrialists' association denied the assurances previously given and refused in a bloc to accede to the demands of the laborers. The F. I. O. M. replied by ordering obstructionism.

"In one of the days which followed, I do not remember whether it was the 6th or 7th of September 1920, Mussolini's secretary, a certain Manlio Morgagni, came to the headquarters of the Confederazione Generale del Lavoro (the general federation of labor). I was busy then. Morgagni sent in his card on which was written 'My director, Mussolini, desires a conference with you; please let me know when and where he can be received.' I replied that by day I was almost always at the Confederazione and that I lived at the Hotel Lombardia in the via dell' Agnello.

"The next morning, while I was in my hotel room, washing, a waiter came to inform me that two gentlemen were waiting to speak to me. I said for them to send up their names and to wait in the hall a few minutes. I had hardly finished speaking when the door opened and Mussolini entered my room, followed by his secretary. There was also present a functionary of the F. I. O. M., Mario Guarnieri.

"Before the war, as I have said, Mussolini and I were on very good terms despite the fact that he belonged to the ultra-revolutionary left wing of the Socialist Party, and I to the right. For five years, however, we had not met and therefore the salutations which we now exchanged were naturally somewhat cold.

"Mussolini in his usual histrionic voice opened the conversation with these words:

" 'You have seen that my newspaper, the *Popolo d'Italia*, while not building itself up as the organ of the occupation of the factories, desires to give an objective chronicle and has already published an editorial stating it was more favorable to the workers than the industrialists.'

" 'That is true,' I replied, 'and we acknowledge it.'

" 'But,' continued Mussolini, 'your movement has assumed a great national and international importance and that is why I wish to follow it personally and to comment on it in the columns of my journal. I desire to have all the information possible on the march of events and of the intentions of the F. I. O. M.'

"I replied that the ideas of the directors of the committee of the movement were expressed in the communiques issued daily to the press, but that I was ready at all times to reply to special questions which he might put to me. Questions and replies followed. But the interview remained cold.

"Now Mussolini tried to animate the conversation in a semi-dramatic tone. 'The industrialists,' he said, 'are in a state of imbecile intransigence but I recognize that the workers are right. The situation in the country verges on the revolutionary, and I am asking if you have thought of an eventual political turn to your movement?'

"I replied coldly with a simple monosyllable, 'Yes.'

"Mussolini sensed from this interview that he was not just the right man to whom to confide such plans, and calming his tone, becoming more insinuating, thought it opportune to close the conversation with these words:

" 'Listen. To me it is no difference that the factories belong more to the workers than to the operators. It is important that work goes on. But if it concerns a revolutionary movement, serious, socialistic, for the profound transformation of the country, know that you can count on my support and that of my friends.' "

This was Mussolini's offer to return to Socialism. He was willing to make Fascism, its newspaper and its armed militia, a part of the workers' revolutionary movement to capture the country.

The Socialists had torn up his red card in 1914; they had called him traitor, "hired assassin of the bourgeoisie," expelled him from the party, and he had replied that "you will not deprive me of my socialist faith . . . you will not keep me from fighting for the cause of Socialism and the revolution." He had cried out that "Socialism is something that is rooted in the blood," and now he was to prove it by returning to the fold after six years' absence. He believed he would be accepted as a hero.

But although he still called himself a Socialist, he was really more of a Bolshevik and a revolutionary opportunist, ready to engage in a civil war, to shed any amount of blood, for the establishment of a proletarian dictatorship which the occupation of the factories seemed to make imminent. He frightened the Socialists and the trades unionists. The Honorable Buozzi, realising how useless his mission, took the proposals of Mussolini's return and the incorporation of the Fascist bands, to a congress of the metal workers which, on hearing the plan to use an illegal militia, to wage a war, to use violence, to burn and to seize, in short to continue the campaign which the Fascisti were waging independently, refused indignantly to traffic with bloodshed. They, they replied to Mussolini, intended to conquer legally; they, they said, had no use for a condottiere or a modern captain of racketeers.

They did not know at that time, however, that Mussolini was merely offering Fascism for sale to the best bidder.

With the same proposal offered to Buozzi, Mussolini approached the metal-works owners, the Milan bankers, the large landed proprietors, the Lega Industriale of Turin, the Associazione fra Industriale Generale dell' Industria, or the entire ruling industrial and financial class of Italy.

"Several months after our interview," states Buozzi, "speaking to one of the captains of industry, Signor Agnelli, head of the F. I. A. T. automobile works, I referred to the fact that Mussolini had offered to come over to our side. Signor Agnelli informed me that Mussolini, at the same time he was making me this offer, had been dealing with Signor Olivetti, secretary-general of the Confederazione dell' Industria.

"This is the secret: animated by an unhampered ambition, Mussolini sought to keep one door open, be it the Right or Left, so that no matter what would happen after the occupation of the factories, he would always be able to emerge, be it at the head of a revolutionary movement or of a reactionary movement. If the seizure of the factories ended with a victory of the workers in the economic field, a prelude to the conquest of power by the Socialist Party, Mussolini would be on the Left. Otherwise, on the Right. When he saw that the Socialist Party was torn by internal dissensions, that it could not march towards power, Mussolini threw into the sea his offer and his Left program and dedicated himself to the arms of reaction. There was now no longer a question of a proletarian revolution—leadership would be too difficult and dangerous for him; he realized how much easier it would be to arrive in power if he served the ultra-nationalistic banner, renounced his past, and betrayed his old companions."

The industrial and agrarian bourgeoisie, still scared and distrustful, desperate before the menace of the seizure of factories, and failing to realize that the collapse of that movement meant the end of radical danger, immediately accepted the Fascisti as its military weapon. The Confederazione Generale dell' Industria openly began paying money, and other organizations secretly subventioned Mussolini and his militia.

Immediately the deal was made, Mussolini turned the threat of the Fascisti away from the warehouses, the factories and the lives of the war profiteers, the industrialists, the big-business men whom he had been threatening with hanging on lamp-posts, and directed them against the Socialists, the workingmen, the coöperatives, the clubs, and the newspapers of the proletariat. Just as in 1914 he took his revenge on those who did not follow him, so now he began on a large scale to accomplish his vendetta. From that day on bloodshed increased throughout Italy. The very same boys and men who had been attacking the bourgeoisie were used a day or a week later to attack the working-class.

"The victory of Fascism over the Socialist movement," says the pro-Fascist Prezzolini, "is due to the Fascists not fearing to employ violence which the extremist preached but had never succeeded in putting into action, and because the Fascists' offensive coincided with the disruption of the Socialist Party which began about this time. It was an ill-matched contest. . . .

"Mussolini realised . . . strikes were no longer a weapon. The Russian revolution had proved that armed force alone could secure the reins of power. And in this lay the novelty of Fascism—in the military organization of a political party."

So now Mussolini, his militia sold to the ruling class, moral support and financial security arranged, marched forward on the road to power with an army behind him.

CHAPTER IX

Fascism Conquers Mussolini

THIS NEW ARMY'S TACTICS BECAME KNOWN AS SQUADRISMO. Flying detachments of Black Shirts, aided by the military supplies, guns, and transportation of the regularly constituted authorities, concentrated secretly, rode to given destinations and wrecked the Socialist and labor movement in villages or towns by destroying its newspapers, coöperative stores, headquarters and meeting-halls. Frequently they killed.

In America the first mention of Fascismo occurs on the 18th of October, 1920, when "armed radicals in black shirts" were reported attacking the offices of the newspaper *Il Lavoratore* in Trieste with bombs, hand grenades, and bludgeons; it was an item worthy of publication because it affected the lives of two American citizens. Twenty shots were fired at Joseph Emerson Haven, the American consul who had his office in the newspaper building, and Lincoln Eyre, the representative of the *New York World*.

Consul Haven sent an indignant report to the State Department, while even more indignant Mr. Eyre cabled that "this outrage is one of a long series committed by these bandits, these nationalist hoodlums, Fascisti as they call themselves, the word meaning 'nearly leaders' (sic) or perhaps with greater precision 'gangsters' who pretend to be inspired with patriotic devotion to Italian ideals. This sentiment translates itself in their strangely warped minds into systematic oppression by the most brutal and cowardly means, of all who venture to disagree with them. Militaristic nationalism is their creed and d'Annunzio (sic) is their prophet."

In November occurred the first large-scale military action of the newly armed illegal forces of the monarchy—the sack of Bologna—when the Socialist town council was driven out, the Chamber of

97

Labor wrecked, the trades unions and coöperatives burned to the ground, the newspaper presses smashed and workingmen found on the premises beaten or murdered.

Between January and May, 1921, the Fascist squads destroyed 120 labor union headquarters and invaded 243 Socialist centers, killing 202 workingmen and wounding 1,144. In 1921 and 1922 they burned 500 labor centers and coöperatives and forcibly dissolved 900 Socialist municipalities. In almost all instances the military, the national and the local representatives of law and order, were confederates of the Black Shirts. For 162 Fascisti arrested in the first six months of 1921 the authorities jailed 2,240 workingmen. Of this period of violence Prezzolini, who at the time was neutral, wrote:

"They [the Fascisti] could organize themselves in armed camps and kill right and left, with the certainty of impunity and with the complicity of the police. It is thus no overstatement to recognize that the Fascists fought with 99 chances out of 100 of gaining the victory."

This guerilla warfare was waged chiefly against the coöperative movement, the labor unions, the Social Democrats, and the Catholics. It was not a war against Bolshevism, because whatever remained of Bolshevism after the 1920 factory-occupation episode was unimportant. Despite a million repetitions made since 1925, the year public relations counsel were engaged to help float Italian loans, it is a historic fact that there was no Bolshevik danger in Italy, and final proof can be found in the *Popolo d'Italia* of June 2, 1921, when Mussolini himself wrote:

"The Italy of 1921 is fundamentally different from that of 1919. . . . To say that the Bolshevik danger still exists in Italy is equivalent of trying to exchange, for reasons of self-interest, fear against the truth. Bolshevism is conquered. More than that, it has been disowned by the leaders and the people."

Trains, which had not been running on time, improved their schedules. Strikes, which had been daily occurrences, became less frequent. Wages went up a bit. The cost of living went down. Exports and imports showed some satisfactory figures, and slowly Italy began lifting itself out of its despair. The best proof in the world is the rate of exchange. The dollar which had gone from 18 to 23 in 1920 came back to 20.15 for the first half of 1922.

Throughout Europe a rumor of optimism was spreading. For the first time since the war there was a small restoration of good feeling. In Italy the end of 1920 marking the liquidation of the insurrection of Fiume was followed by the famous January, 1921, Socialist Party congress in Leghorn which drove out the Communists, emancipating itself from a program of retaliatory violence and earning the support of organized labor throughout the world. Italy felt it was now convalescent from the wounds of the war and after-war.

With Bolshevism officially exiled and actually dying, there was now no reason for the continuance of the Fascist movement. But the price of the surrender of Fiume had been the semi-official recognition of the Black Shirts as collaborators of the forces of the State. Fascisti now carried arms openly. Meanwhile the country had grown so quiet that a general election was fought bloodlessly. It gave Italy a new parliament constituted as follows:

Democrats 195
Socialists 126
Catholics 91
Nationalists 40
Fascists 32
Communists 18

For the Communists it marked a significant defeat. The Fascisti, who in 1919 had fared so badly, got some satisfaction out of their 32 delegates in 1921, and the Popolari, organized in 1919, with 91 members, became a national force to be reckoned with in any future struggle for the maintenance of the middle road. Most important of all is the great victory of the Democrats and the moderate Socialists. The election showed the world that Italy was getting well politically and would remain a peaceful democratic constitutional nation.

It was at this moment that Mussolini, as usual without a platform, but with many promises to draw the sympathy of the masses whose psychology he knew so well, began his republican movement. But it did not go far. Immediately he played still another trick from his inexhaustible sleeve. To the astonishment of his followers,

on the 23rd of July, 1921, he announced a proposed truce between
the Fascist Party and militia and all of its enemies, also close co-
operation between himself and the Socialist and Catholic Parties,
both of which represented the working-classes.

In August this truce was signed "for the realization of the return
of normal conditions" and for the renunciation of violence. The
simple yet amazing text of this document, which, if made in good
faith and capable of being carried out without opposition to Mussolini, would have changed the course of Italian history, is given in
full in the Appendix. The signatories pledged themselves to end "all
menaces, all reprisals, all punishments, all vengeances, all personal
violence"; they were to respect the political insignias and economic
organizations and to submit all violations to a college of arbitration,
and to coöperate for the restoration of peace in the nation.

The treaty was signed by Mussolini, De Vecchi, and Giuriati for
the parliamentary Fascist group, by Cesare Rossi and three others
for the Fasci di Combattimento, by the Socialist Party, the Socialist
parliamentary group, the General Federation of Labor, and by Enrico
de Nicola, president of the Chamber of Deputies.

It may be noted that the first man to sign for the "Fighting
Fascisti" was Cesare Rossi, he who was later to become head of
the Cheka, carry out all orders against opposition leaders, finally to
be implicated in the assassination which almost destroyed Fascism,
a blow unforeseen by the disciple of Machiavelli.

With the ink hardly dry on the peace pact, Mussolini, who had, I
must be truly admitted, initiated the conference, went to his desk and
wrote the following declaration of reaffirmation and defiance to his
own followers:

"I will defend with all my forces this treaty of peace which to
my view attains the importance of a historic event on account of its
'singularity' without precedent.

"For this purpose I will attempt to apply the old and very wise
proverb, 'Whoever does not employ the rod hates his son.' Well!
If Fascism is my son—that which everyone has always known—I
swear with the rods of my oath, of my courage, of my passion, I
will either correct him or I will make his life impossible."

Can anyone doubt the courage, the passion, with which these words are written? Are they the expression of an honest man or can they possibly be those of the deepest hypocrite and villain? History alone can tell. Certain it was that in the August of 1921 the nation believed whole-heartedly that Mussolini with an outburst of frankness and honesty and fearlessness had done a great thing, had accomplished more than parliament and the polemics of the party press. This was the real peace of the people!

August passed in tranquillity. But there were signs of trouble. All the forces of reaction, of private property, the bankers, the proprietors of the factories which had once been seized, the ship companies, the hotel keepers, and certain large landowners, who had once seen the menacing specter of Bolshevism, now determined that Socialism, liberalism, democracy, despite their legality, their pacifism, their disorganization, and their weaknesses, must also be banished. These elements were the employers of Mussolini the condottiere. On the other hand there were liberals of the same propertied classes who expressed their support of the Black Shirt leader orally.

With tremendous enthusiasm Mussolini, who again saw himself as a popular figure, attempted to curb the forces he had originated or encouraged. He thundered against the "hot heads," the "irresponsibles," the "violent elements," and he withdrew the radical pledges he had made. But it was useless. The times were out of joint for that sort of leadership. Tuscany, Emilia, and his own beloved Romagna refused to ratify the peace treaty.

Within the Fascist Party the movement against its duce grew in the cities and in the country. One of the most noteworthy breaches of the treaty occurred at Modena September 24th. The Po Valley Fascisti, who had refused all attempts at pacification, not only kept their squadristi on a war footing, but used their newly acquired guns to terrorize the Socialist coöperatives, the Catholic clubs, the labor organizations. The prefect of police of Modena had adopted measures to insure public order. The Fascisti protested this action. They marched into the public square opposite the prefecture and began their orations. Everyone who passed was forced, with clubs, to take off his hat during the speaking. The prefect, hearing the orators urge their followers to invade the police station, called for extra police, who, however, refused to obey the order.

Several excited persons rushed the commissaire of police and his men, striking about with clubs. Soon the whole Fascist group in excitement turned against the police, who, believing themselves in danger, fired into the crowd. There were seven dead and twenty wounded.

In the same month the Fascisti organized the assassination of the Deputy Di Vagno and the anti-French demonstrations of Venice.

In Bologna the Fascisti sang anti-Mussolini songs. During a meeting of the local committee practically everyone attacked the leader and soon printed signs appeared on the streets: "Who has betrayed once will betray again." It was ominous.

Old friends, leaders, founders of Fascism, deserted. Strangely enough, the one who stood steadfast was Cesare Rossi. Mussolini, seeing his followers in arms against him, said again: "If Fascism does not follow me, no one obliges me to follow Fascism. I am duce, a leader, a word which does not especially please me but which pleases others. We are numerous: schism is fatal. Let it come. The peace pact will have the reaction of precipitating the cleaning out of the party."

Bologna then voted against Mussolini.

Mussolini resigned.[1]

For a moment a great change came over Fascism. In all the industrial towns now and wherever there were large estates, the owners of land and factories became more active, disregarded Mussolini, organized their own clubs, rented headquarters, subsidized new branches about which Mussolini himself knew nothing. Among the more than 100,000 army officers that peace had thrown out of work

---

[1] He wrote: "The nation turned to us when our movement appeared as a liberator from a tyranny; the nation will turn against us if our movement takes on the guise of a fresh tyranny. . . . The nation needs peace in order to recover, to restore itself, to fulfill its highest destinies. You do not understand, you do not wish to understand, that the country wishes to work without being disturbed. I would enter into an alliance at this moment with the devil himself, with Anti-Christ, if that would give this poor country five years of tranquillity, of restoration, of peace.

"From my point of view, the situation is absolutely clear: if Fascism will not follow me, no one can oblige me to follow Fascism. I understand and sympathize a little with those Fascisti who cannot get away from their own surroundings. . . . I am a leader who leads, not a leader who follows. I go—now and above all—against the current and never abandon myself to it and I watch always, above all, for the changing winds to swell the sails of my destiny."

many found employment in this new business. Arms were bought by the manufacturers and landowners; when military supplies arrived, it was the duty of the officers to drill and train and finally to lead the Fascist squadristi who were receiving money, guns, and orders from their new masters.

Thus it came about that Mussolini, seeing his life work disintegrating, himself disappearing as a national figure, reconsidered his resignation, and at the congress of the Fascisti in Rome, November, 1921, made a complete *volte face* again.

The pacifist of August who had sworn to whip Fascism into shape as a peaceful legal weapon, was himself whipped by Fascism. At the congress of Rome, Mussolini accepted the incorrigibility of his "son" and became Fascism's follower, not leader. He declared publicly that the peace treaty was dead and buried. Suddenly he announced himself for violence as a holy crusade against the Socialists and liberals. He even included the Catholics and Democrats in his speech demanding reprisals, renewal of bloodshed, supremacy of the Fascisti, and for the first time in history shouts of "Down with parliament," and, "Long live the dictatorship," were heard, shouts which were to lead within a year to just the event they presaged.

Thus passed another great crisis in the life of the child of Destiny. He had meant to conquer, had been conquered, and knew how to rise again even if his new leadership was for a cause, a program, an idea entirely opposed to the one for which he had a few weeks earlier announced himself prepared to risk his position, perhaps his life. The honest and sincere man of August who swore with "the rods of his courage and his passion" became in November an instrument for ruthlessness, violence, bloodshed—the program which the proprietors of Fascism demanded and which he humbly accepted, suddenly trying to make himself appear their leader again by being more extremist than the rest.

Mussolini was conquered by Fascism because more powerful forces had taken possession of his movement. In 1920 he had placed his forces at the disposal of certain industrialists without realizing that in saving them he would make them his masters.

Shortly after Mussolini's lieutenant (and later ambassador to the Vatican) De Vecchi had burned the Rome offices of the *Avanti*,

he, a Torinese, was taken up by Com. de Benedetti and Avv. Ugo
Codogni of the Lega Industriale of Turin. Benni and Gino Olivetti,
the directors of the Confederazione Generale dell'Industria, and
Director Mazzini of the Associazione fra Industriali Metallurgici
Meccanici ed Affini who was later to succeed de Benedetti as chair-
man of the Lega Industriale, were not only collaborating with Mussolini but with more trusted lieutenants who had less radical minds.
These associations, corresponding to the various manufacturers' associations in America and the Stahlverein and other organizations
which subsidized the Nazi movement in Germany, not only supplied
the money for the Black Shirts, but succeeded easily in organizing
the rebellion against Mussolini.

Whether or not he was previously aware of all the facts, he
learned, at the Rome congress which ended the schism, that he could
no longer defy the financial forces of which he was merely the political and military spearhead.

He now was given orders to destroy the labor movement. As the
correspondent of the *Manchester Guardian* and *New York World*
wrote at the time, "the enemy was not, however, the Communists,"
because they were unimportant: the enemy was the federation of
labor, social democracy, and the newly arisen Catholic party of
workingmen and peasants who were led by a priest, Don Sturzo, and
who were demanding agrarian reform, social justice, and a share in
the wealth of the nation.

★ ★

CHAPTER X

Priest versus Politician

AT ARGENTINA ALTABELLA REBELLIOUS PEASANTS, MARCHING BE-
hind a priest who held a crucifix above their heads, occupied
the fields of the wealthy landowners in the name of Christ and Christian Communism. The soil, rich and poor, was equitably divided
among workingmen who, like their ancestors for a thousand years,
had tilled it and built up the fortunes of the landlords while they
themselves slaved and hungered. To each man was given land according to his ability; from each was expected a contribution to the
commonwealth according to his capacity.

> *"Avanti o popolo! Con fede franca*
> *Bandiera bianca trionferà,"*

sang the rebel peasants, substituting only one word for the common
song of the Bolsheviki, the word "bianca" for "rosso" ("white" for
"red"); the "white flag of Catholicism will triumph." Throughout
the south of Italy and notably in Calabria the emancipation of the
peasantry gained enormously. The masses "hailed Don Sturzo as an
apostle, obeyed him as a dictator."

Thus, rudely, Italy's attention was called to a new force in its
national life, the marching Partito Popolare Italiano, the party organized January 18, 1919, by the priest Don Luigi Sturzo for perpetuating the ideals of Christian democracy. This was his stirring
proclamation:

"To all men free and strong, who, in this grave hour, feel
the high duty of coöperation for the supreme ends of the Fatherland. . . .

". . . We uphold the political and moral program, the patrimony
of the Christian people. . . .

". . . As the soul of the new society, the true sense of liberty responding to the civil maturity of our people and the highest development of its energies; religious liberty not only for the individual, but also for the Church, for the unfolding of her spiritual mission in the world; liberty of teaching without a state monopoly; liberty of class organization without preference or privilege for any party; communal and local liberties in accordance with the glorious Italian traditions."

The men who joined the Popolari were mostly peasants and urban members of the Azione Cattolica, so it became known as the Catholic Party, although it was no more affiliated with the Vatican than the Centrum in Germany and Catholic parties in many other nations. Significant, however, is the fact that the *non expedit* of February, 1868, which withdrew good Catholics from participation in elections, was canceled ten months after Don Sturzo organized his party.

The leader in every way, character, appearance, action, appeared to be the opposite of Mussolini. He was a man from the south, a pacifist, fanatic in his belief in human liberty, a radical social reformer like Savonarola, candid and frank and incapable of making compromises, and lacking entirely in the urge to self-advancement. He was truly the shepherd of his flock and his flock was all the poor and oppressed of the country. He loved them like brothers. Don Sturzo is an almost emaciated figure, the picture of asceticism, his gaunt eager passionate sincere face distinguished by a long narrow nose set between deep brown eyes which seem to be afire with his great idea of Christian brotherhood.

He was forty just after the war when he made his first political step by permitting his election as sindaco or mayor of his home town, Caltagirone, in Sicily. Here he collected a sum of money, bought 2,000 acres of land, divided it among the poorest, and demanded that the agrarian reform, promised for decades, be accomplished without violent seizure and illegal confiscation.

> *"Vogliamo le fabricke, vogliamo la terra,*
> *Ma senza guerra, ma senza guerra,"*

sang Sturzo's adherents at the time the workingmen had seized the factories. "We want the factories; we want the land; but without war," was their song and their policy. On the occasion of the railroad, telegraph and telephone strike, Mussolini urging the men to use violent methods, came face to face with Sturzo's party for the first time. Sturzo denounced the strike because of its violence, and helped the government to win.

In 1921, 1922, and 1923, as radicalism receded in Italy, the Catholic Party grew in strength in parliament and eventually replaced Social Democracy as the chief opponent of Fascism.

In these years Mussolini was still the anti-clerical of his exile in Switzerland. In his public speeches he ridiculed the Pope and made jokes about the size of Sturzo's nose. In April, 1921, he wrote: "Fascism is the strongest of all the heresies that strike at the doors of the churches. Tell the priests, who are more or less whimpering old maids: Away with these temples that are doomed to destruction; for our triumphant heresy is destined to illuminate all brains and hearts."

Don Sturzo, on the other hand, wrote of his chief opponent: "Of mediocre culture and meager political experience, Mussolini has the brilliant qualities of the extemporizer and none of the scruples of those who, convinced of an idea, fear to be false to it. . . . He can pass from theory to theory, from position to position, rapidly, even inconsistently, with neither remorse or regret. . . .

"Another quality which he possesses is his constant ability to seize the moment, to profit by circumstances. . . .

"His friends and companions he holds in esteem so long as they are useful to him; he fears them when he cannot do without them; he abandons them to their fate when they are in his way."

In February, 1922, Don Sturzo was the leader of the most powerful party in the Italian parliament. He was also a great influence in the Church. In the conclave for the election of a Pope in that month it was commonly said in Rome that "Don Sturzo might in one day name his Prime Minister and his Pope." But the priest had no such ambitions. Recounting the accomplishments of his party early in 1922, he summarizes them in this way:

1. Entry of the Catholic masses into political life after half a century of abstention.

2. Adoption of proportional representation in parliament.

3. Opposition to the Socialists, and to general political strikes.

4. Collaboration with the Liberals and Democratic-Liberals.

5. Brought question of freedom of schools to public and parliament.

6. Contribution to solution agricultural and economic problems.

7. Support of administrative decentralization.

8. Support of solutions of Yugoslav problem.

9. Early realisation of the Fascist peril and stand against armed violence.

On the debit side Don Sturzo wrote: strength wasted in compromises with opposition and in collaboration with the government; lack of courage to take office when a crisis arose.

The political war of 1922 was over proportional representation. "Here," commented Don Sturzo, "was a source of friction between the old oligarchic currents and the new wave of democratic life. The latter was therefore labeled demagogy, or even, with the Russian term, Bolshevism and much was written against the Red Bolshevism of the Socialists and the White Bolshevism of the Popolari, and against their possible union.

"Therefore both Democratic Liberals and industrialists and agrarians turned to Fascism as the force that could save them. Thus was invented the fable that Fascism in 1922 saved Italy from Bolshevism. There was no peril of Bolshevism in Italy nor did Fascism save her from it. If by Bolshevism is meant the agitations and disorders of 1919-20, up till the occupation of the factories, these were already past history, and the general elections of May, 1921, were evidence of the state of mind of the country and of its constitutional normality.

"There does not exist in Italian political life a more insincere phenomenon than the fear of Bolshevism on the part of the wealthy class in 1922; the latter had taken the offensive against the State by the Fascist acts of violence, and had to justify both offensive and violence: this they could only do by crying out that there was peril of a Bolshevization of Italy in the near future."

In 1922 the Fascist squads attacked Catholic institutions with the same enthusiasm with which they wrecked labor unions and cooperatives. The squadristi of Fascism stormed Catholic institutions and murdered more than one parish priest, but the Catholic leader insisted that violence should not be answered with violence.

To conclude the tragic story of Don Sturzo it is necessary here to disregard the chronology of the history of Fascism and its Duce. In April, 1923, when clubs and headquarters of the Popolari again were being looted and wrecked and burned, the party held its fourth congress in Turin where it reaffirmed "its will to continue the fundamental battle for Liberty and against any centralizing perversion in the name of the pantheistic State or deified nation"; it asserted its "solidarity with those who suffer for the idea and for internal peace, and invokes for the welfare of Italy respect for human personality and the spirit of Christian brotherhood." The party decided to remain independent, to protect individual liberty in Italy, to defend religion and the church.

Shortly afterwards Mussolini proposed a new election law. The "reform" as he so brilliantly called it, would give the party which obtained 25 per cent of the total votes cast 66 2/3 per cent of the seats in the Chamber of Deputies, while the remaining 33 1/3 per cent would be divided among all other parties proportionately, thus making it possible for the Fascist minority to rule the anti-Fascist majority "legally."

Into the final struggle Don Sturzo put all his force; while other parties still proclaimed liberty, his was the only one which dared, in the face of Black Shirts armed with rifles, bludgeons, and castor oil, openly to resist. But his was passive resistance and his weapon chiefly an appeal to reason and Christian morals.

His followers in hot-headed Calabria got out of control. For every Catholic institution attacked they attacked a Fascist institution, and in Naples and less important centers the Catholics found that the employment of retaliatory violence was the one and only way to victory. They beat Fascismo at its own game.

It was at this moment that Mussolini's envoys went to the Vatican with a message which was also a threat. The attention of the Pope was called to the fact that St. Peter's and the Vatican were surrounded by Fascist bayonets and yet had not suffered harm. Unless pressure was brought against Don Sturzo the Catholic churches and the Catholic religion would suffer great harm.

On the 9th of June, 1923, Don Sturzo sent his resignation to the Pope, and on the 10th he departed for the monastery of Montecassino and retirement. Some time later, unsure of his safety, he went to London, where he is living today, "recommended by Fascist newspapers to the special attention of any assassin who happens to be idle in England," according to Professor Gilbert Murray, who befriended him.

That the Pope and the Catholic Church have been threatened with attack by Mussolini was admitted more recently when Don Sturzo wrote that "at the critical moment the man who was believed by the Fascisti and philo-Fascisti alike to be the pivot of the situation, the convinced adversary of Mussolini [meaning himself], left the leadership of his party because of obscure Fascist threats of armed reprisals against the Church. . . ."

In this way the last and most important political party to dispute Mussolini's claim to dictatorship was eliminated from public life. The epitaph was written by Don Sturzo: "Fascismo came forward as an anti-constitutional and revolutionary movement based on violence and direct action. Popolarismo was law-abiding, constitutional, and moral. Fascismo considers itself as the absolute and sole manifestation of political life. Popolarismo looks on itself as a political party with rights and duties like any other party functioning in the plane of the modern state. Fascismo is against liberty, against democracy, against the parliamentary State. Popolarismo is for liberty, for democracy, for the parliamentary State. Fascismo upholds the nationalist, plutocratic and imperialist State. Popolarismo upholds free trade, international coöperation and peace. . . .

"The Popolari arose in the name of liberty. In the administrative and educational, in the social and religious, fields they fought for liberty in the teeth of the Democrats, the Liberals and the Socialists . . . for liberty, based on the rights of human personality, is unalienable and cannot be surrendered for any material prosperity or alleged national right. . . ."

The unarmed prophet had failed, and the armed prophet again had won, as Machiavelli had informed Mussolini in his exile years.

Part II

THE CONQUEST OF POWER

CHAPTER XI

The Glorious March on Rome

AFTER THE BATTLE OF ARQUES, WHICH WAS FOUGHT THROUGH
September and October of the year 1589, Henry, King of
France, wrote to the Duke of Crillon: "Hang yourself, brave Cril-
lon; we have conquered at Arques and you were not there."

Just three hundred and thirty-three years later, almost to a day,
occurred another great event, the glorious Fascist march on Rome,
which has now become in the black-shirted minds of Italy the noblest
victory in all its history. Only a few years past, and in the memory
of most men now living, this episode has become a marvelous myth.
National hymns, popular songs, millions of photographs, hundreds
of paintings, new sagas, and at least one made-to-order epic tell us
how Mussolini led the Fascisti into Rome and conquered Bolshevism.

The books of history are being rewritten. In Russia, Trotsky, the
hero of the Bolshevik revolution, the military genius of the war with
Poland, becomes in a decade a minor figure of no importance if not
an actual villain, while in Germany a similar decade is wiped from
the public mind to leave room for the inscription of the record of a
new man. And so it has been done in Italy.

But if history has any value for the people who are its inheritors,
it is indeed a simple task to right the record of which we ourselves
are the witnesses and at times the participants. Was Trotsky a nobody? Are a dozen years of the German Republic to be regarded
solely as the story of Hitler's rise? Did Mussolini really slay the Red
Dragon, and was he even present at the Arques of 1922?

That year opened for the European world with another of its
supplementary conferences which, despite a denial to Russia's claim
to participation and America's refusal to do so, was hopeful of accomplishing something in righting the wrongs of the Versailles con-

gress. Here in Cannes, on the French Riviera, hundreds of journalists of many lands were almost as important as the diplomats of the great nations.

Here Benito Mussolini came as the representative of his own newspaper. But neither he nor Fascism were at the time interesting enough to warrant attention from the American, British, or other noted journalists who had accompanied Lloyd George and Briand and the premiers of Belgium and Italy and Czechoslovakia and the sensational delegation from Germany under Walther Rathenau.

Among the Italians, however, Mussolini had an imposing reputation. The press conferences which the diplomats of this country held were marked by Mussolini's violent outbursts of oratory which would divide the assembly into hostile camps, the majority shouting the disturber into silence.

Notable among Italy's journalistic representatives was Pietro Nenni, Mussolini's successor as editor of the *Avanti*. The two had not only worked together but, it will be remembered, during the anti-Tripoli war demonstration in Forli had spent nights in the same prison jointly cursing the government which had placed them there.

They were friends; they could talk with extreme frankness, and this is their conversation during a walk on the seashore as Nenni records it:

MUSSOLINI: Civil war has become a tragic menace. I do not fear the responsibility. The kindliness of the State forces the formation of a party to smash the Bolshevik menace, reëstablish authority, save the victory.

NENNI: To the class of which you have become the instrument, the right of the workingmen to organize themselves for the defense of their social interest and for the conquest of power, that is now called Bolshevism. The police personifies authority and as for victory it is conceived only as a form for the survival of the military spirit over the civil spirit.

MUSSOLINI: I know everything about the sentiments of the class about which you speak. I am not their instrument. At a given hour I have not hesitated to proclaim that one must escape from the bloody circle of violence.

NENNI: Your individualism always strays. I do not care what you have become. I am certain that lacking a sentiment of justice, everything that you will do will be marked with the red iron of arbitrariness. The peace which you offer from time to time to my friends is for them a renunciation of their ideal. At that price the bourgeoisie is always ready to act. Moreover, you forget many things.

MUSSOLINI: What?

NENNI: You forget the dead; you forget that you were the chief of the Socialist Party; you forget perhaps the workingmen fallen under the clubs and the stilettos of the Black Shirts.

MUSSOLINI: There must be no sentimentalism in life. I know that the dead hang heavily. I frequently think about my past with a profound melancholy. But it is more than a few dozen deaths in a civil war. There were hundreds of thousands dead in the war. We must also defend them.

NENNI: The proletariat against whom you now direct your offensive, defends the dead by fighting against war and against militarism. Frequently they are mistaken in details, but they never mistake their ideal.

MUSSOLINI: Your friends must understand. I am as ready for war as for peace.

NENNI: You have lost the possibility of choosing.

MUSSOLINI: In that case, it will be war.

NENNI: For the past two years it has been war.

This dialogue occurred just eight months before the guerilla warfare which Fascism had been waging throughout Italy, was ordered turned into a civil war by Mussolini at the national congress which the party held in Naples in October.

"All armed prophets have conquered and the unarmed have been destroyed," Mussolini had read and underlined in his Machiavelli. He had no intention of marching on Rome with the few bayonets of his own illegal Fascisti. He was not that foolish.

To take over the Italian government required not only the leadership of the Fascist squadristi, but the violation of the oath of fidelity to the crown on the part of many generals in the regular army, because it is quite evident that a regiment or two with their usual rifles, a few hand grenades, and machine guns, not to mention some gas bombs or perhaps one battery of three-inch guns firing shrapnel, could have, in five minutes, made of the "march on Rome" what the cautious Mussolini, safe in Milan, feared it would be, a bloody fiasco. But not a regular soldier moved.

The scheming Duke of Aosta, cousin of Victor Emmanuel III, was another important part of the Fascist plot. He was a man of great ambition who believed himself the most capable of the House of Savoy to rule the country. He had great influence in the army. It was one of his followers, General Vaccari, who succeeded General Badoglio as chief of staff after the latter, who under Giolitti's régime had armed the Fascisti, had resigned. It was Badoglio who had from time to time made the declaration that the Fascisti were not to be feared by the King because he would destroy their pretensions with one regiment in a few hours.

While the Fascisti were holding their congress in Naples, on October 24th, a secret conference was being held in Florence, where Black Shirt leaders, chiefs of the regular army, representatives of the nationalists and the imperialists in parliament and a representative of the Duke of Aosta, decided that the time had come to take over the Facta government. Even at this late date the man chosen as representative of the "New Italy" was not Mussolini, but the man of heroics, Gabriele d'Annunzio. But the poet refused. The second choice was not Mussolini, but General Peppino Garibaldi, who had led an Italian legion on the French front from the first days of the war. Garibaldi refused. Then it was that Mussolini was chosen, and that the Duke of Aosta's intervention with the army was promised on the basis of his receiving the regentship.

The Duke went to Spoleto and put new oil into his motor-car, filled up the gasoline-tank, and waited the word to ride into Rome and take his cousin's throne.

Mussolini, on the 24th, made his big speech to the congress at Naples. It was a thundering speech. The time had come. The country had had enough. It must be saved despite itself. But from what? From Bolshevism? From Communism? There is no mention of these terrible forces. Mussolini had thundered against them in 1920. Now Jove was sending his thunderbolts against—Democracy.

Under that vague term the following forces were joined: the several liberal parties, including the Catholics, Socialists, and Republicans (but not the Communists who had split from the Socialists and drifted weakly away); the labor unions with some 2,000,000 members; and the coöperatives which, despite Fascist fire and sword, were flourishing remarkably in city and country.

The nation in 1922 had recovered from the economic and political chaos of 1920. When, some time later, the distinguished journalist, Hiram Kelly Motherwell, had charts and graphs prepared of the standard of living, exports and imports, rate of exchange, wages, unemployment, etc., from figures officially supplied by the Fascist government, these showed without exception that every line going up or down, all favorable to Italy, had the crucial favorable angle sometime between the end of 1921 and the first months of 1922.

Even the wartime national budget, which caused deficits of scores of billions of lire in the first post-bellum years, was now about to balance. In fact, the deficit which the liberal premiers cut down to about half a billion was to be replaced, thanks to the program of economy outlined, with a flattering surplus.

So much for facts and figures. But the effects of these changes were as far reaching. If, as figures prove, the standard of living of the Italian masses had gone up, if wages had gone up, if the coöperatives were flourishing, it is evident that some one had to pay for all these magnificent national achievements. These wages had been won by that series of strikes which so disgusted American tourists and bankers; but they disgusted even more the Italian employers who were forced by this demonstration of power and solidarity among the workingmen to disgorge some of their war profits. Wages increased and the chambers of commerce, the association of metal factory owners, the national industrial associations, the industrial banks and the employers' organizations which were sorely hit in their financial plexus, and whose thousands of newspapers could no longer raise the shout of "Bolshevism" because this red herring was now a dead herring, turned in their last extremity to the use of violence to alter an economic situation.

The coöperatives were destroying private profits. Therefore the coöperatives must be destroyed. The labor unions were becoming arrogant. Therefore the unions must go. The liberal-socialistic régime in Rome was nothing but a school of gossips. . . .

It was to the financial interest of the big-business men of the north to encourage the squadristi to plunder and destroy the coöperatives, the labor unions, the Socialist, and the Catholic institutions. But for the condottiere of the squadristi, Mussolini, it was the weak bombastic parliamentary system which became the objective of attack.

Italy was recovering. In a little while, perhaps only a few months, it would be too late to act. In August armed Fascist bands indulged in a general campaign of terror in the large cities, and the labor unions, demanding that the government use armed force to smash Fascism, called a general strike. This labor union strike, which had not one glint of red in its spectrum, was a miserable failure. Times were so much better, progress was so rapid, that few heeded the call to protest.

It was then that opportunity, which had knocked at Mussolini's door with the noise of cannon in 1914, and practically smashed in his door in 1919, again visited him. That same Will to Power of which he spoke daily, that same "star of destiny" which he says guided him always, informed him that unless he made his bid immediately the situation would be forever changed and locked against him.

"I take a solemn oath," roared Mussolini, "that either the government of the country must be given peacefully to the Fascisti or we will take it by force."

Again, as at Reggio Emilia and in the Socialist congress of Milan, the violent enthusiasm of the speaker communicated itself to the mass.

"*A Roma! A Roma!*" the Black Shirts shouted, hysterically.

And again Mussolini became the master.

He had, as is well known, had no intention of marching on Rome in October, 1922. He did not know at first, as did d'Annunzio and later Garibaldi, that the military forces were conspiring for a *coup d'état* and needed a leader. Although the Naples congress was intended by him to be a test of his power, it surprised him by its readiness to risk a civil war.

On the 19th of the month he had written to his good friend De Santo, Italian, Fascist, and Rome correspondent of the *Chicago*

Tribune—in fact the predecessor of the present writer—the following letter:

> Caro De Santo:
>
> I thank you for your many kindnesses in presenting the Fascist cause to America. I regret deeply that the American ambassador, Signor Washburn-Child, does not seem very sympathetic to Fascismo and I would esteem it greatly if you would take me and introduce me to him.
>
> I am going to Naples in a few days. I do not think that anything of consequence will occur there, and on my way back to Milan I will stop in Rome, and hope you will make the appointment for me.
>
> Cordially,
>
> MUSSOLINI

But instead of stopping in Rome to see the American ambassador, Richard Washburn Child, Mussolini went from the Naples congress directly to Milan to lead his "revolution."

The secret of this action was a series of telegrams from Florence, where the military heads who planned the overthrow had made Mussolini their third choice. Among the generals who had betrayed their oath to the King and the royal constitution were De Bono, Fara, Magiotto, Zamboni, and Tiby. And when they had been informed from Naples that Mussolini had accepted leadership they sent him the following telegram:

> VENITE. LA PAPPA È PRONTA. LE MENSE SONO IMBANDITE. NON AVRETE CHE A SEDERVI A TAVOLA.
>
> (Come. The gruel is ready. The dinner is served. You have only to seat yourself at the table.)

Thus revolution began.

On the 26th the Fascisti had sent an ultimatum to the government demanding the premiership for their party. Facta, the Prime Minister, replied by handing his resignation to the King. On the 27th Mussolini went back to his newspaper office in Milan and the Fascist *squadristi* got their orders to move.

Under the command of many generals, they "marched" on Rome

in three columns. From Umbria, Romagna, and Tuscany the Black Shirts came to Foligno, where General Fara took command and led them to Monterotondo, north of Rome. The men from d'Annunzio's Abruzzi assembled at Tivoli, under Bottai. Genoa, Milan, Bologna, and western seaboard cities and towns, north and south, sent delegations to meet at Santa Marinella, and as their open trucks went slowly along the dusty roads the Fascist civilians praised the adventure as friendly, while opponents said simply it was child's play.

But when the concentration began the city of Rome was alarmed and the garrison was put to work stringing wartime barbed wire around some of the gates. On the morning of the 28th the general staff officers had reports there were no more than 8,000 Fascists in the neighborhood of Rome, scattered, ill-clad, and ill-fed and listless. Premier Facta, who could have sent a few machine-guns against them, or who could merely have surrounded them and starved them into jail or dissolution, did what was typically in the character of the parliament of that day and in himself—he did nothing but run around excitedly, talking, gesturing.

The King had returned from Pisa on the evening of the 27th. Angry with the cabinet and particularly with the weakness of Facta, he threatened, "Before I'll give in to them I'll take my wife and children and leave." However, the King agreed to declare martial law. Facta drew up the proclamation. Certain of the King's promise, he informed the prefects everywhere to take the necessary measures to crush Fascism.

Meanwhile the Fascisti who were not "marching" were "storming" the public buildings of doubtful cities, occupying and holding the railroad stations, post offices, telegraph offices, armories, all upon the invitation of the authorities.

Facta arrived early on the morning of the 28th with the decree of martial law. The King weakened. It might cause revolutionary bloodshed. Facta, who had a consummate will to surrender, was caught in the emotions of the King and did not insist. But when Facta tried to spread the emotional contagion to the cabinet, it stood firm, and at a few minutes after ten that morning the official news agency announced to the papers that the King had declared martial law.

With this *fait accompli*, Facta ran back to the King, who now firmly refused to sign. While Facta had been trembling, the King had been acting. He had received members of the Nationalist Party, and other imperialists, who made two declarations, one of which was untrue and the other doubtful: they told the King that the Duke of Aosta was among the Fascisti outside the walls of Rome, and that he had 80,000 men ready to seize the crown, and that the army had refused to fight against the Fascisti. The King was frightened. He believed. He surrendered.

At noon the decree of martial law was declared null. The King telegraphed to Mussolini in Milan to come form a government.

With shouts of joy men who had been scared put on black shirts and, jumping into railroad trains, refused to buy tickets, but shouted "To Rome! To Rome!" so that by the 31st of October about 20,000 were assembled outside the walls of the Eternal City.

But where was our hero all this time? He was at the head of the revolution. While the Black Shirts were riding in crowded railroad coaches, much to the indignation of American tourists, and commandeering trucks and even peasant carts, Mussolini spent anxious moments waiting for reports from headquarters which the generals had established in Perugia.

One of the generals, Mussolini relates proudly, then appeared in Milan with the news that the "offensive" was proceeding excellently and that there would be no opposition from the Royal army or in fact from any of the forces of law and order. "We know from very faithful unforgettable friends," he repeated, "that the army, unless exceptional circumstances arise, will maintain itself on the ground of amiable neutrality." There was no other organized armed force in Italy. The liberals and the radicals had no weapons.

But the leader knew that there must be bloodshed to have a revolution. Somehow or other there must be the blood bath Mussolini had asked first for the proletariat, now for the Fascisti, if the thing were to be done properly, successfully, and impressively. But not one report that came in of all the street cars occupied and all the railroad coaches filled with "marching" Black Shirts, spoke of anybody getting killed.

Well, if there was going to be no revolution in the open country-side, perhaps there would be one in Rome or Milan.

"To the barricades! On to the barricades!" shouted the future Duce, but there being nobody making an attack, and no barricades anywhere to defend, he proposed building them around the *Popolo* office in Milan.

Soon the whole staff, including the women, were busy. Boxes, wood, the little carts which had been used for distributing the paper, trash of every description, were piled into the street, the silent unrevolutionary street, and the barricades arose as in once glorious Paris.

"I put on the black shirt. I barricaded the *Popolo d'Italia*. In the livid and grey morning, Milan had a new and fantastic appear-ance. Pauses and sudden silences gave one the sensation of great hours that come and go in the course of history. Frowning battalions of royal guards scouted the city and the monotonous rhythm of their feet sounded ominous echoes in the almost deserted streets."

Almost deserted. The police kept away. The enemy kept far away. Only the Fascisti were busy running about, building up, moving around, shouting instructions, warnings, greetings, getting their guns ready, peering about for trace or smell of an enemy. The barricades were beehives and bedlam, but on the other side there was nothing but sunshine and dead quiet, dead sunshine and pale quiet. Mussolini had protected his offices "with everything needful for defense." He knew that "if the government authorities desired to give a proof of their strength they would have directed their first violent assault at the *Popolo d'Italia*." One morning he looked out and saw machine-guns pointed at him.

"I had my rifle charged and went down to defend the doors. The neighbors had barricaded entrances and windows and were begging for protection. During the firing bullets whistled around my ears," reports Mussolini.

The bullets that whistled so melodramatically around the heroic ears of "the Duce who precedes" came from behind. All the con-fusion, all the hurly-burly of a revolution, was behind the barricades. All the shooting was there, too. The entire personnel of the news-paper, including the editors, among them Signora Sarfatti, the devoted, the hero-worshiping one, were behind the barricades making a noise of revolution. It was midday of the 28th of October when the first firing was heard, when Mussolini, according to the eye-witness lady editor, seized his rifle and rushed down to the barricade: "At that moment he ran the greatest risk of his life. One of the young men who followed behind him, seeing him mount the barricade, leveled his rifle in the direction of the enemy and fired, the bullet grazing the head of the Chief and whistling through his hair just above his ear."

A frightened Mussolini did not at first know whether the bullet which "whistled around my ears" came from the enemy or from one of his ardent followers. That shooting, the most memorable of the Fascist revolution, which almost caused the death of its leader-in-chief, resulted in a terrific uproar behind the barricade. With savage anger the staff of the *Popolo* threw itself upon the unfortunate Fascist who had fired with good intention and bad aim. It was bent on a lynching. For a minute it did look as if there was to be some blood in this revolution, after all, as if there was actually to be blood upon a revolutionary barricade.

But Mussolini himself said, No.

He stepped down from the barricade, rubbing his head. He mixed into the fray, shouting down the would-be lynchers, extricating his zealous follower and pacifying the others. There was no more shooting.

At midday on the 29th the telephone rang and Mussolini was offered the place of Prime Minister of Italy. He had conquered.

The last attempt to keep him from his goal of power was made by some politicians. Just after the horrible episode on the barricades, the royal guard had made a peaceful arrangement, a truce, which provided for the removal of the machine-guns. "With that sort of armistice began for me the day of October 28th." That night the politicians proposed a truce and armistice with the government itself. Salandra, a nationalist, one time premier, would take the job again and conduct Italian policies more to the liking of the Fascisti. Mussolini replied:

"War is declared. We will carry it to the bitter end. The struggle is blazing all over Italy. Youth is in arms. I am rated as a leader who precedes and not one who follows. I will not humiliate with arbitration this page of the resurrection of Italian youth. I tell you it is the last chapter. It will fulfill the traditions of our country. It cannot die in compromise."

Then came the telephone call. Guido Barella, of the *Secolo*, and also correspondent for my newspaper in Milan, thus vividly describes the scene in the office that afternoon. Mussolini still had the receiver to his ear. About him was grouped the staff of the paper.

"I will come to Rome," he replied without a tremor in his voice, "when the charge to form a Ministry is official." He hung up.

He stood still a second, his expression serene, his eyes far away. Then:

"My Ministry . . . !"—a hard dry sound like a sob was in his voice. "My Ministry will be thus . . . ;" half closing his eyes contemplatively, he added:

"If they will not accept my proposition and allow me to put in the men I consider suitable for office, then I will have a Ministry that is entirely Fascist, from the president to the last office boy."

That evening he was still at his post in the newspaper office, a gray raincoat over the black shirt and uniform, a soft grey hat, as usual, down over his eyes.

More telephoning, more excitement, and we are only a few hours before his departure for Rome, in answer to a confirmatory telegram received from the King's aide-de-camp:

> His Majesty King Victor Emmanuel begs you to come to Rome at once. He wishes to offer you the task of forming a new ministry. GENERAL CITTADINI.

(Such was the lamentable state of communications of the execrable Facta régime that the urgent message from the King had taken hours to reach Mussolini, who had not trusted the telephone and who had remained torn between doubt and hope and wonder.)

Notified by telegrams and telephone messages, the legionaries cheered and shouted:

"To Rome! To Rome!"

Time seemed to pass with uncanny swiftness. Of a sudden Mussolini was running down the stairs and had disappeared in a waiting car.

Thousands of people had gathered in and about the station, as he slowly passed through the throng, alone, in his gray raincoat, hands deep in his pockets, his hat down over his eyes; the shouting and applause increased until it was a mad delirium.

He was pale, paler than usual.

Flowers were showered upon him as, tranquil and serene, he slowly advanced through the dense crowd to the platform and the train.

He arrived at the steps of the special car reserved for him. The presidential train was on its way to Rome. The son of the blacksmith had become the Duce, and he was going forth to his unending fight.

Just before he left for the station, Mussolini turned over the barricaded *Popolo* to his brother Arnaldo. He then "asked the assistance of God." Still earlier in the day he had gone to the Fascist main barracks, where he met his faithful friend and henchman, Cesare Rossi, and told him the "boys" could now go ahead and burn down his old enemy newspaper, the *Avanti*. "I was in a terrible state of nervous tension. Night after night I had been kept awake, giving orders, following the compact columns of the Fascisti, restricting the battle to the knightly practices of Fascism."

As the train took him to Rome and power, the *Avanti* went up in flames, the first knightly act of victorious Fascism.

The Duke of Aosta was kept waiting at Spoleto. He had been used as a pawn, and now he was forgotten.

The Vatican had remained neutral but fearful. It knew that the young atheist of Lausanne was coming into power and anything might happen to the Church—bloodshed, fire, annihilation. The Pope sent emissaries to General De Vecchi, member of the quadrumvirate, and to Dino Grandi, one of the ruthless politicians who had become a power in the north. De Vecchi and Grandi sent back word that the Catholic Church had nothing to fear, that, on the other hand, Mussolini had realized the necessity of having the coöperation of the Vatican in order to establish a successful régime in a country almost wholly Catholic. Mussolini gave orders to respect the Church and its property.

The Fascisti piled out of their trucks, street cars, and trains and occupied Monterotondo, not far from Rome. Mussolini speaks of 100,000, but other reports say there were but 8,000 of them. Both may be right. Only a few Black Shirts came to Monterotondo, yet when the triumphal parade was reviewed by Mussolini several days later, their number had swelled to many tens of thousands.

Mussolini, some time afterwards, in one of his speeches, when he had worked himself up into a fury, mentioned "three thousand dead" as the cost of the glorious victory, but James Murphy of the British diplomatic service, and Carlton Beals, the author, who were both in Rome reporting, say there were no dead. Murphy speaks of one boy who succumbed to fatigue as the full casualty list. It is most likely that Mussolini was thinking of the Fascist claims that they had lost several thousand members in all the years of street fighting from the time of first organization until the glorious March on Rome.

As his train approached the Eternal City, Mussolini got out his black shirt and put it on. The fog lay thin and cold over the land and the thin notes of a military cornet announced the arrival of *il duce che precede* (the leader who precedes) at Civita Vecchia. Thousands sang Giovinezza as the engine groaned its last.

"Where is he," shouted the frenzied multitude.

Pale, "his large eyes reflecting a soul on fire," he stood in the last car, "silently surveying the mob." In the raising of his hand for silence "there was a feeling of history."

"The Naples Congress," he said, "has its logical conclusion in the irresistible march on Rome. Friends, his majesty the King has called me to Rome to form a government. I will form it. But I demand calm, order, discipline. It is necessary that nothing corrupts my victory.

"Princes, Triaires, Fascists! Our movement is victorious. We have conquered without firing a shot because Fascism has been more than ever stirring to the depths the strict and generous interpreter of the national conscience.

"Italy is in your hands, and we swear to place it on the road of its ancient glory.

"Viva Fascismo! Viva l'Italia!"

The crowd: "For Benito Mussolini. Ayah, ayah, ayah. Alala!"

Fascists, officers, regular soldiers, station hands, women and children cheered.

Mussolini got off the train, motored to the Quirinal in his black shirt, was introduced "without formalities" to the King. "I beg your Majesty to forgive me for appearing in your presence in uniform," he said after kissing the royal hand. "I have just come from a bloodless battle which had to be fought." The King smiled. The next day some twenty thousand Fascisti who had arrived by train, truck, and horse-carriage, and the many thousands who had arrived after the "capture," were reviewed by Premier Mussolini and King Victor Emmanuel together.

The photographs of this event to this very day are labeled "Mussolini leading the March on Rome." But like the Duke of Crillon at Arques, the Duce of Fascismo had not been there.

There was no revolution. No blood was shed. It was a military conspiracy[1] to which the generals and the government were party and the industrialists in the north the financial backers. Nevertheless, it was a great victory for the student of Machiavelli. "I was triumphant in Rome," he wrote, triumphantly.

[1] On September 29th, writes the historian Salvemini, the Fascisti had been assured that the army would remain neutral. "This essential fact was divulged by Alessandro Chiavolini, Mussolini's private secretary, in the *Popolo d'Italia* for October 27, 1923. Mussolini himself in a speech on October 30, 1923, declared that he knew that 'at the opportune moment the government machine guns would not fire on the revolutionaries.' " Richard Washburn Child, the American ambassador, wrote that he had it on good authority that the army secretly favored the movement.

Two weeks before the coup d'état Mussolini, replying to General Badoglio's exclamation, "At the first fire, all of Fascism will collapse," said, "General Badoglio fools himself. . . . The national army will not go against the army of the Black Shirts. . . ." (Beals, *Rome or Death*, page 264.)

Wilbur Forrest, correspondent in Rome and now editor of the *New York Herald Tribune*, was at Civitavecchia during the "march." The commanding regular army general informed him he had received orders from Rome not to fire on the Fascisti but to place the railroads and other transportation at their disposal. Forrest was given a truck; a dozen Fascisti barged in, and so the American journalist also led the march on Rome.

★ ★

CHAPTER XII

The Victor in Search of a Program

THE FIRST FASCIST DICTATORSHIP WAS ESTABLISHED WITHOUT the loss of a drop of blood. It was a sort of palace revolution, a conspiracy within the army—whole regiments wore the black shirts under their uniforms—at first a mere change in premiership brought about through armed intimidation instead of a plebescite at the polls.

But a frightened Europe pounded on Mussolini's door, demanding whether he intended to suppress the labor unions; whether he would respect Italy's obligations to the Allies; if his policy was peace or war; and if he would pay the debts to the United States.

Much to everyone's surprise, Premier Mussolini announced the formation of the conventional parliamentary coalition government. Immediately the world breathed regularly again. Then, being a professional journalist and knowing that the press made and unmade all the political beds in Europe, the Premier, whose first act had been to proclaim a censorship, issued the following statement: "When conditions are settled I will restore liberty of the press, but the press must prove itself worthy of liberty. Liberty is not only a right, it is a duty."

To the Allies he said: "France is dissatisfied with the peace and she is right. It is a bad peace. The war was not pushed to its natural conclusion. We should have finished it, you at Berlin, we at Vienna and Budapest. It is necessary to take the enemy by the throat. You have little chance of getting what is owed you. You were deceived. Germany has the will not to pay. She is dangerous."

To the masses he said: "The Fascist movement which began as bourgeois, now has become syndicalist, but of national syndicalism, taking into account the interest of workingmen and those of employers and producers. Please emphasize we are not anti-proletariat."

To the American journalists he gave a special session in the Hotel Savoia: "Nothing but good can be said about the United States. One always speaks well of his creditor—and we all owe the United States money."

The great day of the new parliament came. In his hand Mussolini held the scepter of .semi-legal power. As all the trains out of Rome carried the Black Shirt army which had not fired a shot in its victory nor enjoyed the delirium of a revolution, back to its homes, the new Prime Minister stood at the head of a government in just the same relation as his predecessors, the "cowards," "traitors," "incompetents," and "gossips" whom he had denounced. The cabinet was a coalition, continuing many democratic and liberal elements and policies. There was no dictatorship, only a faint rattling of a sword.

"Gentlemen," the new Premier said on his first day in parliament, "that which I have done today, in this room is a formal act of deference towards you for which I do not ask any testimony or particular recognition.

"A revolution has its rights. I am here to defend and to strengthen to the highest degree the revolution of the Black Shirts in introducing profoundly, like a force of evolution, progress and equilibrium in the history of the nation. [Applause, Right.]

"I could abuse my victory, but I refuse to. I am imposing limits. With my three hundred thousand young men, armed in every way, decided for anything, and so to speak mystically ready to carry out my orders, I could chastise all those who have defamed and attempted to throw Fascism into the mud.

"I could make of this hall, low and gray, a bivouac of corpses. . . ."

Applause interrupted from the Right benches, where sat all the new parliamentarians who had won their seats by knife and gun. Murmurs of discontent from the Center. Protests shouted from the Left. "Long live parliament. Long live parliament," cried Modigliani to the cheers of his followers. The speaker's face grew darker.

"I could close this parliament and establish a government composed exclusively of Fascists. I could do it, but I have not willed it; at least not for the present moment."

The Right benches remained silent, but the tumult of the Center and Left increased.

"My adversaries have remained in their hiding-places; some have tranquilly come out and obtained free circulation, profiting thereby already by spitting their venom and by attempting their ambushes.

"I have established a coalition government, not with the intention of obtaining a majority in parliament, which today I can very well dispense with [Applause, extreme Right], but to unite—to aid this suffering nation—all of the shades and parties who would save the nation.

"Before arriving here we were asked what was our program. Alas! it is not programs which are lacking in Italy; it is men and the will to apply the programs. All the problems of life in Italy, all, I say, have already been solved on paper, but the will to translate them into facts is missing. The government, today, represents this will, firm and resolved."

But within a few days the old parliamentary game began. Having arrived in power without a program—the ragged ends of several old and frequently changed programs having proved inadequate— and unable to produce anything new except such words as "discipline" and "work" and "patriotism," the new Premier found himself the object of attack of all the Opposition and the neutral. The great newspapers kept asking him for a program, and the humorous weeklies made him ridiculous. A dog doctor had a big sign painted over his clinic with an English bull in the center, a growling likeness of Mussolini, who, as a punster later put it, "hounded" the veterinarian out of town. A leading comic sheet published a series of articles on a modern, humorless, impotent, bellicose, weak, threatening, vascillating, furious, unvictorious Napoleon. In Turin a journalist, Gobetti, launched irony and sarcasm upon the theatrical conqueror. The entire independent as well as the liberal and opposition press, still untouched by draconic suppression, joined in exposing the falsity of claims, the failure of action, the lack of definite aims, the foolishness and fatuity and frustration of the new régime and its blundering leader. The Fascist honeymoon was over and again disillusion gripped the nation.

Fascism had come into power. It was powerless. So long as legality remained, it was still possible to overthrow the government by a vote; if the Black Shirt militia were to be mobilized again, it was possible that the second time it would be met by armed force, now that its régime was proving the same weak and ineffectual debating society as its predecessors, and losing the confidence of neutral leaders and the vast mass which had hoped for a miracle in a few months. The lire, moreover, had continued to fall and the economic situation, which for three years of liberal governments had grown better daily despite the enormous payment of war debts amounting upwards to 25,000,000,000 lire in one year, now became worse, approached desperation. Perhaps a second "march within Rome" would be a failure.

From all sides came criticisms and criticism was one thing this journalist, who above all others should have realized and appreciated and valued, refused to hear. He knew the power of the press and feared it. Criticism can crush empires. He decided to smash it. Then there was a stream of irony from the speakers of the Opposition and from the comic press. This Mussolini could not understand and therefore could not forgive. He began planning revenge. In 1923 he organized the Cheka.

The chief enemy, of course, was his old party, the Socialist. "Skillful and astute in every political art, they protracted without end all the annoyances they could devise. It was a game played with the deliberate aim to destroy and tear down. In this subtle work of exasperation Matteotti, the deputy, distinguished himself above all others—he reached a degree of absurdity even beyond that attained by any other Socialist."

What Matteotti did was to settle upon Mussolini like a gadfly, a gadfly armed with two stings, irony and humor. The wounds left were incurable because they required, in the blood of the dictator, a prophylactic, a lymph, an antitoxin which he did not possess, and unable to heal himself he found he must destroy his adversary.

Day after day Matteotti would hurl at Mussolini the planks of the Fascist program of 1919, the written and signed pledges of

1920, and conclude with, "Well, what are you going to do about
it?" "You have written that 'the Italian revolution of 1920 [the
seizure of the factories by the proletariat] is a phase of the Fascist
revolution begun by Fascists in May, 1915,'" Matteotti would say,
holding aloft the *Popolo d'Italia* of September 28, 1920. "Do you
deny it now?" and Mussolini would frown and double his fist and
keep silent because he could not answer.

"I see by your own admission that 'Bolshevism is dead,'" Matteotti would say, "and now you declare that the chief object of your
party is to fight Bolshevism—you would not whip a corpse, would
you?" and Mussolini would not answer except by a threat and one
of his favorite words, "coward" or "scoundrel" or "traitor."

"If, as you said, Italy has saved itself, when the Socialist Party
expelled, in 1920, all the Communists and the violent enemies, how
do you intend to save her again, how do you explain the civil war
which the Fascists have inaugurated, their destructions, their burn-
ings, their assassinations? How do you explain it?

"How do you explain that Fascism, playing the adulteress, has
passed from the bed of the working-class to the bed of the capitalist
class, betraying turn in turn, at its wish, at its fantasy?

"You have declared publicly and in writing that 'Fascism will
never throw itself at the foot of the King because the King has no
identity with the idea of Fatherland,' and you were the first to throw
yourself at the foot of the King, you who announced for a Republic.
How do you explain it?

"You have proclaimed the moral right of the regicide, you have
denounced financiers as brigands, you have fought the army, you
have attacked the clergy, you have denied that God exists, and today
you are the chief defender of these persons and ideas. How do you
explain yourself?"

Mussolini refused to reply publicly. But as he left for Lausanne
to attend the Allied annual peacemaking congress, he gave Cesare
Rossi, the one person to whom the word "friend" might be applied
with any considerable correctness, the order to increase the Black
Shirt squads to 500,000, a strength superior to the regular army of
the King, and to organize within it a powerful secret political police

which he called the "Ceca" and whose counterpart was then known in Russia as the Cheka, and now as the Gaypayoo.

Much to the amusement of those diplomats who knew the secret, was the tardy act of the Swiss government which had some seventeen years before expelled an undesirable Italian emigrant, placed his name on the consular black list maintained at frontier towns, and now was forced to expunge it and change all the police records of the new Premier of Italy, about to enter its peaceful borders.

"What is your foreign program?" asked Lord Curzon.

"My foreign policy is 'Nothing for nothing.'"

"Indeed," replied Curzon in his cold British Foreign Office way, "very interesting. Very interesting. And what has Italy to offer Great Britain?"

Silence.

From that day on, for many years, Mussolini trailed Curzon like a good little boy and Britain had a lot to say in Fascist diplomacy.

Returning to Rome, he found parliament protesting, playing the old game of talk, and the Italian press, about 80 per cent non-Fascist, exposing the assaults and violences the Black Shirts, now victoriously ruling, were committing in all parts of the country against Socialists, Liberals, Laborites, and Catholics alike.

All these Opposition parties, their leaders and the press, united in shouting one question to the new Premier, "What is your program." Never was a nation more puzzled over the supposed policies of a new régime. Fascism, the Opposition said, repeating Matteotti's words, had passed from bed to bed, like an adulteress, stopping a few months with the Communists, a little while with the Republicans, a long time with the syndicalists; it had been liberal and anti-liberal; it had proclaimed itself anti-Catholic and apparently had made a treaty with the Vatican; it had supported the monarchists and the reactionaries, and had at last again proclaimed itself in favor of the proletariat. What was its program? What did it intend to do?

On the eve of the 1919 elections Mussolini had written for campaign purposes the first program of the Fascio di Combattimento,[1] helping himself liberally to the ideas of Karl Marx, as the following parallel will show:

[1] *Vide* Appendix 1.

Communist Manifesto of 1848	*Original Fascist Program 1919*
Abolition of property in land and application of all rent of land to public purposes.	Extraordinary tax on capital, progressive, causing partial expropriation of all riches.
A heavy progressive or graduated income tax.	Seizure of all property of the religious associations.
Abolition of all right of inheritance.	Seizure up to 85 per cent of the war profits.
Confiscation of property of emigrants and rebels.	Formation of technical councils for industry, communications.
Centralization of the means of communications and transport in the hands of the State.	Proletarian organizations to manage public services.
Extension of factories and the instruments of production in the hands of the State.	Realization of the rights of the railroad workers. ("The railroads for the railroad workers.")
Equal obligation of all to work.	Participation of the workingmen in the management of industry.

And if this original Fascist program was not Karl Marxian enough, its author elaborated it in the fall of 1919[2] adding:

The creation of an Italian national assembly to be part of an International Assembly of All Peoples (*i.e.*, the equivalent of the Communist Internationale).

Freedom of thought, conscience, religion, association, press, propaganda, individual and collective agitation.

Creation of a national financial institution (*vide* Karl Marx, point 5, the national bank).

Confiscation of unproductive revenues.

All landed estates given to the peasants.

These two Radical-Communistic programs explain the possibility of Mussolini's negotiations with Buozzi, the head of the labor unions at the time Mussolini planned to make himself theirs and not the condottiere of the industrial associations of the North. It was Comrade Angelica who first opened the books of Karl Marx for the future Duce and taught him the ten points of the Communist Manifesto of 1848; it was Mussolini who remembered and rewrote them in 1919; and today in Italy it costs five years of a man's life to reprint the two programs given above. The Liparian Islands give the living proof.

On the 10th of November of the same year of the revised pro-

[2] *Vide* Appendix 1.

gram Mussolini wrote, "We are preparing not against the working-class, but in its favor.

"We are so little kindly towards the bourgeoisie that we have placed at the head of our program expropriation of riches, confiscation of super profits of the war, heavy levy on capital. *We will accept no dictatorship.*"

On the following day, "We are for liberty and against all tyranny."

And two days later, "The most sacred thing in the world—Liberty!

"In Italy there is no one who would be governed by anyone who arises in the name of the Messiah, or a Tsar, or God the Father. We want liberty for all. We demand that the Universal Will governs us and not the will of any group, or of any man."

Marching to victory, the Fascisti sang their now famous "Giovinezza,"

> *"Youth, Youth, thou lovely thing,*
> *Time of springtime's blossoming.*
> *Fascismo brings the promise*
> *Of Liberty to the People."*

But amidst the shouts of Liberty there were also mingled the sounds of the slogan inherited from d'Annunzio of Fiume, "Me ne frego (I don't give a damn)." Not a damn for anything but power.

"They ask us what is our program," exclaimed Mussolini in a speech a month before the "march"; "our program is very simple. We want to govern Italy."

More specifically, on the 4th of October he wrote in his *Popolo*: "The imbeciles, Jesuits and Democrats, incessantly demand a program of us. The Democrats of *il Mondo*, do they desire to know our program? To break the bones of the Democrats of *il Mondo*. And the sooner the better."

It was not until March, 1923, that the new Prime Minister delivered himself of the famous blast against liberalism and liberty and announced the first idea of the present Fascism program. He wrote:[3]

"Know then, once for all, that Fascism recognizes no idols, adores

[3] Appendix, "Fascism: 'Reactionary,' 'Anti-Liberal.'"

no fetishes; it has already passed over the more or less decayed body of the Goddess of Liberty, and is prepared, if necessary, to do so again."

Order, Discipline, Hierarchy! These three words were Mussolini's new program, the substitute for Liberty.

"Hierarchy," he wrote a little later, "must culminate in a pinpoint," meaning, of course, without any intention to belittle, no other than himself, the Duce.

Of the original 1919 program, which consists of seventeen points, but one or two have been remembered. The rest were immediately forgotten. Thus the Commission for Inquiry into the Expenses of the War (similar to the Congressional investigation in Washington into war profits) which the liberals had created and which would have recommended a confiscation of those profits which Mussolini demanded, was immediately dissolved by Decree 487. Moreover, Mussolini threatened to punish severely anyone who dared publish any information of the previous results obtained by the commission which had already forced the return of several hundred million lire to the Italian treasury.

"Another *volte face*," cried the Duce's enemies; "he is now the condottiere of the war profiteers."

There was no expropriation of the war profiteers, no expropriation of riches, no seizure of the property of the Catholic Church or other radical fulfillments of the program; there was no proletarian participation in industry, no abolition of the Senate, no proclamation of free speech and press, no division of land among the peasants. Yet the chief official biographer, Signora Sarfatti, writes that "in less than two years these demands (quoting the 1919 program, but omitting the final third) had been translated into action by the Fascist government."

Chivalry alone prevents comment.

From Rome the unimpeachable authority, William Bolitho, wrote: "The whole baggage of Fascist theory, its nationalism, its royalism, its gospel of violence, its anti-parliamentarianism and its denunciations of the liberty of the press, its hierarchy and its history of the Pelasgian stock [the forerunner of the Hitlerian Aryan myth], are not clauses in a social theory, but a sophisticated word-spinning around the incidents of an energetic and unscrupulous man's march to power."

But powerful as Mussolini was, he was still not so strong as those who made his career possible; he could not yet throw his financial backers overboard, nor could he defy the dangerous element which both had used—the army.

What thoughts were clashing in that egotistical mind in those days, what conflicts in his emotions, we can only guess; but we know that all those plans for justice for the common people, the distribution of land to the enserfed peasantry, the expropriation of the universally hated war profiteers, and all the Communistic plans out of Karl Marx, were in the early days of Fascism no mere word-spinning, no sham demagogic banners to attract the masses. In his own muddled way Mussolini had made a compromise between Karl Marx and his own Ego, between humanitarianism learned out of a book and the inborn Will to Power, a compromise which made explanation and program announcement difficult if not impossible. He temporized.

Much less difficult was the answer he made years afterwards when an interviewer asked him, "What is the chief problem of Fascism today?"

"Its duration," he replied.

CHAPTER XIII

Personal Vendetta

EVEN BEFORE HE TOOK HIS FIRST DICTATORIAL STEPS, THE COALItion Premier dispersed his enemies. It was good political tactics and it also provided the outlet for that powerful spirit of vendetta which had ruled his life from childhood.

He had been taught to trust nobody and he trusts nobody today. "If the Eternal Father were to say to me 'I am your friend,' I would put up my fists against Him," one of his closest associates sympathetically quotes the Duce saying, and again, "If my own father were to come back to the world I would not place my faith in him." It is the confession of a man who has gone through life friendless and alone. Mussolini never forgives, never forgets.

In 1923 he began his personal vendetta.

It will be remembered that the first to befriend young Benito in Switzerland was the Socialist Serrati—Giacinto Menotti Serrati, a native of Oneglia in Italy, an ardent syndicalist and, like Mussolini, an extremist of the Left wing at a time Communism was merely a theory.

So closely allied were the two that Serrati made Mussolini welcome at his home. There the latter was treated as a child by the mother of the former. Signora Serrati not only gave him that motherly sympathy which the young man so intensely needed, but she fed him and washed his clothes.

All went well until one day Serrati's sister and her husband arrived for a visit. Then an unfortunate drunken event occurred. After a violent scene, Comrade Benito was asked to leave the house. Whatever happened was apparently important enough to be reported in the press, where it is stated that "Mussolini played the villain with the sister of his benefactor, and the brother-in-law tried to strangle him."

Comrade Benito apologized. He wrote the following letter which Signora Serrati years later made public: "I beseech you to have pity on me and not to forget that I am the son of an alcoholic." The Serratis, however, were not impressed, because they knew that Papa Alessandro, the café-keeper, although a hard drinker, as were many in Forli, was not a drunkard. They did not forgive Mussolini and he never forgave Serrati.

The latter had drifted easily into extreme Socialism, had at one time been an envoy to Moscow, and at all times true to his radical up-bringing. Mussolini had become the archenemy of his own past and every man connected with it. Some time after his arrival in power the new Cheka spies brought word that there was a radical con-spiracy against the régime and that among the leaders was his old friend Serrati. Serrati was arrested. But the trial for treason and "inciting class hatred" failed and Serrati was freed. Mussolini greeted the news with fury. Turning to Cesare Rossi,[1] official of both the press bureau and the Cheka, he said:

"The next time an affair like this comes along I will send a patrol of national militia to San Vittore to await the liberated prisoners. The judicial authorities may liberate him, but I will shoot him. Each to his functions." But instead of shooting Serrati, Mussolini set his police agents on him, so that his old benefactor spent his remaining Italian years in misery.

The vendetta Mussolini-Nitti began in 1919 when d'Annunzio occupied Fiume and when the first conspiracy to seize Rome was being organized. With Mussolini, the Futurist revolutionary poet Marinetti, and several others were arrested on Nitti's warrants, which charged "armed plotting against the security of the nation."

Mussolini never forgave Nitti for the one night he spent in jail.

Explaining his action to parliament, Nitti had said:

"Those who inflame the public betray the interests of the country. Italy at present ought to inspire the utmost confidence abroad in order to obtain the credits she needs. A policy of adventurers would have us fall into anarchy. Workmen and peasants should check this

---

[1] *Vide* Rossi memoranda.

dangerous adventure; they should warn us and Italy should push forward upon the road of renunciation and duty."

Mussolini's newspaper replied with broadsides of the most vulgar and insulting words outside the dictionary. There was freedom of the press in those days. Then one day a Nitti newspaper published the report that of the first million lire Mussolini had raised for Fiume he had used a third for his own armed bands. Mussolini added this insult to his memory. In all his writings, including the recent Autobiography, he turns again and again to denunciation of the former Liberal Premier:

"Nitti . . . was and remains a personality that is a negation of any ideal of life and of manly conflict. He has a fairly good knowledge of finances. He is impudent in his assertions. He is intensely egocentric. . . . He never would face Bolshevism . . . (*re* Fiume) he summoned up the dangerous idea of protest by a general strike. . . . Nitti thought and acted only as a consequence of physical fear. Attacked full front and exasperated in his mad and miserable dream, he plotted with every means to overcome the resistance of the Fiumean legionaries. . . . The whole tone of his speech is vile, dreadfully vile. . . . One must not forget when considering aviation that Nitti had forbidden flight . . . his command was to demobilize the nation. . . . It was a kind of premeditated murder of a nation which really did not want to be strangled. . . ."

In the autumn of 1923 the Cheka informed Mussolini that Nitti had returned to Rome and that Opposition deputies and journalists from New York and Manchester were callers at his house. Rossi, head of the Cheka, was consulted. According to him, Mussolini said:

"It looks as if the Rome Fascio does not exist, but remains inert as regarding men of the Opposition, otherwise it would make the presence of Nitti impossible in the capital."

Rossi admits he called upon Polverelli and Foschi, directors of the Rome unit, and told them the wishes of the Duce. The three then decided to call out some university men and others of the squadristi to visit Nitti and sing "Giovinezza" under his windows.

But the small group soon attracted several hundred more Fascisti, and once the mob spirit prevailed it was determined to murder Nitti.

The house was entered. But Nitti happened to be hidden in an upper chamber. Everything in the villa was destroyed, including the former Premier's archives and the manuscript of a book on which he was working.

Nitti fled to France. But Mussolini's vendetta did not end at the frontier lines. For several years not a month has gone by without spies and agents of the Cheka coming to Nitti to attempt involving him in an anti-Fascist plot. The purpose is to prove to the French government that the former Premier is conspiring while in asylum; it is hoped that France will expel him.

How one of the latest Cheka plots turned out was told me the other day by Vincenzo Nitti, son of the Premier.

"Among the spies who come to our house," said he, "are several persons we knew well in Rome and whom we trusted. One of them proposed to us that we finance a revolution. Another brought us complete plans for large-scale bomb manufacture; if father would supply the funds and give his approval, he would make enough infernal machines to blow up the Fascisti, etc.

"But the best case is that of Signora B——, who arrived with clippings from the Rome newspapers saying she had been expelled from Italy because she was too anti-Fascist. She was a well-known actress, a young and beautiful and talented woman, and a friend of Mussolini's. I suspected at once that she was his agent.

"However, she and I became quite good friends. It was only when I noticed that she had a habit of taking papers—from coat pockets, too—that I became certain she was a Chekist. So I began planting all sorts of letters and documents, all of which she stole. In this way I was able to send directly to Signor Mussolini all communications I could not otherwise have made.

"But all the time I knew Signora B—— she pestered me about our underground press system. As you may know, we publish the *Becco Giallo*, the old satirical paper which Mussolini never could abide, here in Paris; we photograph it from the big sheets and print the miniature plates on India paper, so that we can send thousands in a small package.

"Well, one day, at a café, I pretended I was very drunk and the dear lady took advantage of that to ask me again to tell her in deepest confidence how we smuggled the propaganda into Italy. I told her we had two ways: whenever one saw a priest with an extraordinarily large stomach, crossing the frontier, you may be sure that under that black cassock there were several thousand copies of our publication. But our best way was in sardine-tins. In fact, the next day, when she confronted me with my 'confession' and I could not deny it, I had a workingman bring me a sample sardine-tin with a cover, and in it I placed ten copies of the *Becco Giallo*. I showed this to Signora.

"What happened? First of all, every fat priest crossing the frontier was hit across the stomach with the club of a Fascist militiaman, and believe me that did not further relations with the Vatican any. But afterwards there was a diplomatic incident you might have read about. It seems that at least many thousands of cans of sardines were opened at the frontier. And every can contained sardines, and all were spoiled, and the French and Italian governments got to making nasty remarks to each other about this wastage.

"Then Signora B—— arrived one day and told me she had been severely admonished by Mussolini and was going away to Buenos Aires. 'You've betrayed ME' were the last words of this spy. And away she sailed to ply her spying trade in the Argentine Italian colony. Of course I cabled our friends to beware. But new Cheka agents arrive weekly, trying to provoke my father and myself into doing something illegal so Mussolini can report it to the French Foreign Office and thereby revenge himself on our family."

Vengeance against his old newspaper and old colleagues on the *Avanti* was carried out through many years. Mussolini's last words to Mme. Balabanoff and others of the staff were words of faith in Socialism and in its journalistic organ; he would never forget them, the theory was part of his blood, he could never betray them, never write against them, always love them.

But the *Avanti*, restored to anti-militarist editors, turned against Mussolini, calling him every vile name from traitor to "hired assassin of the bourgeoisie," the latter phrase being attributed to the woman who had picked him out of a dark corner and made him a great man. After a short campaign of vilification the *Avanti* decided upon another course: it would ignore him completely, and a rule was posted that his name should never be mentioned in the columns.

This rule was kept until November 18, 1919, when the Fascisti were completely whipped at the general elections and their political death, as well as that of its leader, generally (but prematurely) conceded. Said the *Avanti*:

"A corpse in an advanced state of putrefaction was dragged out of the Naviglio yesterday. It was identified as that of Benito Mussolini."

It was meant to be an obituary.

Ironic as this incident is, its sequel is tragic. For Mussolini never forgives and never forgets. He cannot survive irony. Writing of his parliamentary defeat of 1919 he said later:

"The *Avanti* wrote on that occasion a short notice about me. 'A dead body has been fished up from the Naviglio.' It was said in this note that in the night in the modest Naviglio canal which cuts Milan in two, a dead body had been picked up. According to the document they said it had been identified as the dead body of Benito Mussolini—his political corpse. They did not say that its eyes were gazing ahead."

What Mussolini never forgot was the mock funeral which the Socialists and the *Avanti* crowd held that day. "The procession passed under the windows of my house . . . I have not forgotten the episode, but I always see it. . . ."

The crowds had gathered in the streets. The Socialist victory had been impressive. Placards were printed with just these words: "Turati 180,000; Mussolini 4000," and given away, to be waved under the eyes of the landowners and the factory-owners and the gentlemen looking out of big offices and big club windows. Francesco Zanardi, mayor of Bologna, came out to salute the masses with a wave of his arms. Speeches were not necessary. There was no hatred, because the election had proved there was no enemy worth hating.

The funeral notice of the *Avanti* thrilled the crowd. Some one proposed a funeral procession, and soon a hack was found, a wooden coffin-like box placed on it, black drapings and funereal flowers. A man climbed on the shoulders of another and was carried ahead of the coffin, imitating a priest, singing a ribald litany, concluding always with his "Requiem æternam," to which the mob joyously responded "Amen, Amen." Psalms were parodied amidst laughter and applause. Numerous candles were lighted and relighted and a sort of carmagnole atmosphere filled the city as vast crowds mocking Mussolini paraded before his house, calling, "Come on out to see your own funeral," and, "At last we honor you."

(It was two days later that the Fascisti threw a bomb at another Socialist march and the government, searching the Arditi clubrooms, found a lot of war material, all of which resulted in Nitti's order for many arrests, including Mussolini's.)

He always saw that ribald funeral. It rankled in his mind, it penetrated his subconscious the moment he received the telegram from General Cittadini confirming the telephone call from Rome to take over the government. The first thing Mussolini did was to fulfill his vendetta. Rossi describes what happened that day. "The new president of the council, the Honorable Mussolini, in this wise began his mission for the restoration of national discipline in October, 1922:

"Meeting me at eleven o'clock in the morning at a school situated on the bastions of Piazza Nuova and employed those days as a barracks by the Fascist mobilization, he gave to several of his brigades news and an order. The news was that he had received a royal telegram charging him to form a new Ministry; the order was 'to proceed during the day with the scientific destruction of the buildings of the *Avanti* and the *Giustizia*, on the San Gregorio road.'"

The two newspapers were partly destroyed by bands led by Negrini and Forni, the latter a Deputy of the national parliament. The interiors were wrecked. The men of the Black Shirts, armed with guns, clubs, and fire, smashed everything, tore up the books, broke the furniture, and becoming frightened that the picture they left behind them would be used against them, poured gasoline over everything and set the buildings on fire. One old man found in hiding was murdered.

Neither the militia nor the police, who were informed that the building was being pillaged, made any effort to stop the squadristi and the firemen received an order not to intervene until the vandalism was complete and there was danger of fire spreading to other houses.

To the destruction of the *Avanti*, Mussolini's assistant editor, Signora Sarfatti, points with pride; she recalls the racketeers marching four abreast, carrying a blood-stained helmet, charred pieces of wood of the building, other souvenirs of vandalism. "We had begun our offensive," Mrs. Sarfatti bursts out rapturously.

Mussolini himself defends it: "As an answer to the anti-Fascist provocation I ordered another general mobilization of the Fascisti. . . . The Fascist technicians were to be brought together to continue the work in the public services. The squadristi were to disperse subversive organizations. The Fascisti of Milan assaulted the *Avanti*, which was considered the lair of our opponents. They burned the offices."

Another newspaper which Mussolini hated for its fairness, its honesty, and its liberalism was the *Corriere della Sera*. It stood in Italy as the leading honest newspaper, much like the *Manchester Guardian* in England, the *Frankfurter Zeitung* in pre-Hitler Germany, and the late lamented *New York World*. One day Mussolini denounced it.

"The *Corriere della Sera*," said the *Popolo*, "should be treated as a Jesuit and as a scoundrel, and above all as a coward."

The same evening at eleven o'clock a bomb was thrown at the *Corriere*. Similarly when the Fascist Minister Giuriati delivered a violent speech in Milan, attacking opposition newspapers, the Fascio again invaded and devastated the offices of the socialist *Giustizia*.

Mussolini first expressed his hatred for the *Corriere* on the day he founded his Fascisti, when, he admits, only fifty-four persons signed "our program which was necessary to lay the foundations for a new civilization." The meeting passed almost unnoticed. The *Corriere*, however, did in fact mention it, but "that great liberal newspaper dedicated to this news about twenty lines in its columns!" The exclamation mark, Mussolini's, is the expression of his chagrin and disgust.

It turned into fury when the *Corriere* accepted Woodrow Wilson's proposal for arbitration of the Fiume boundaries. Treason, shouted d'Annunzio's consul in Milan.

In 1923 the *Corriere* joined with Don Sturzo and all liberal elements in supporting the proportional-representation law and opposing the Fascist proposal which gave this minority party two-thirds of the Chamber of Deputies. As Fascism could not hope for a majority and yet desired to appear legal, such opposition was extremely dangerous to it. Finally, in 1924, the *Corriere* published the documents implicating Mussolini in political assassination, and since the Duce could not suppress his enemy legally, as he had no ground for libel and feared popular reaction if he used violence, as in the case of the *Avanti* or the *Giustizia*, he smashed the great free liberal newspaper through an intrigue among the intimidated stockholders. When the *Corriere* passed into Fascist hands the London *Times* said that Mussolini had made Italy suspected and incomprehensible; the disappearance of the independent *Corriere della Sera*, it continued, editorially, was "a serious loss to European civilization."

★ ★

CHAPTER XIV

The Assassination of Matteotti

BUT HOW WAS IT POSSIBLE FOR FASCISM TO RULE A NATION WHICH was strongly anti-Fascist? Five political parties representing a majority of the people, the best part of the press including all the great newspapers, the labor unions with their millions of adherents, the best minds, including Croce and Ferrero, in fact all Italy except the associations of industrialists, the bankers, their commercial allies and their Black Shirt militia, opposed the new régime whose military conspiracy they had been unable to frustrate.

The only road from the dilemma was suppression of the press and elimination of Opposition political parties. It was the road Moscow took after the attempted assassination of Lenin in 1918, but Mussolini, envious of Russian success, was still afraid to emulate its methods.

Meanwhile he was being attacked by internal enemies. The financial backers were demanding payment on their investment.

One day in the Chamber of Deputies the now acknowledged speaker of the five Opposition parties, Matteotti, informed the nation that the Fascist State was paying its debts to big business in many ways; it had secretly used public funds to refloat the Ansaldo enterprise, which was near bankruptcy; it had purchased 18,000 shares of the Mineral Oil Refinery of Fiume; it had rescued the Banca di Roma and it had permitted the heavy industry Consortium to draw upon the banks of issue for credit, in addition to obtaining secret subventions. Moreover, the Fascist régime was engaged in a deal by which the Sinclair Oil Company of America would obtain a monopoly in Italy; although the American corporation was acting legitimately, several of the highest members of Mussolini's staff were attempting to make millions in graft out of this enterprise.

Matteotti's second point of attack was the corruption of academic liberty in the universities.

His third was an exposure of the violence by which the Fascist victory at the April 6th elections had been achieved.

With a hint of these scandals which he intended to document in ensuing speeches, Matteotti on the 30th of May, 1924, began his campaign against the régime while Italy listened breathlessly and with secret satisfaction.

"In the last election," said Matteotti, "the government, having declared it intended to remain in power no matter what the result, nevertheless implemented this declaration by employing its armed militia. . . ."

Mussolini interrupted. "Enough. Stick to the question."

MATTEOTTI: The honorable president perhaps did not hear me. I am speaking of the elections. There exists an armed militia whose fundamental purpose is to sustain a certain chief of government, well known to you, a certain duce of Fascism, and not, as with the army, the head of a state. Now while the law says that the militia must abstain from all political functions, we saw throughout Italy that this militia . . .

FARINACCI: You must have seen the Balilla (the Fascist boy scouts).

MATTEOTTI: In truth, Honorable Farinacci, it was the Balilla which in many districts did the voting.

The orator then began the list of violences. As each shout of "liar" and "falsifier" and "prove it" arose from the Fascist benches, Matteotti brought out the sworn statements, the Fascist newspapers, the Fascist orders for violence. Mussolini squirmed and scowled.

MATTEOTTI: And at Genoa, when the Honorable Gonzales [member of parliament] came to address a meeting, the hall was invaded by Fascisti who blackjacked . . .

Voice from Fascist benches: "Liar."

MATTEOTTI: Well, then I will correct myself. If the Honorable Gonzales spent eight days in the hospital it means that he had wounded himself, that he had not been blackjacked. The Honorable Gonzales is a disciple of Saint Francis—perhaps he had flagellated himself. . . .

MUSSOLINI· Honorable colleagues, I deplore what is happening. Honorable Matteotti, be brief; conclude.

MATTEOTTI: I will limit myself to nude and crude exposition of facts. . . ." He cited case after case in which members of parliament as well as other speakers had been assaulted by Fascist racketeers. As each new name was added the tumult increased.

MUSSOLINI: Conclude. Honorable Matteotti, do not provoke scenes.

MATTEOTTI: I protest. If you cannot see that it is the others who are stopping me, who are making scenes . . .

MUSSOLINI: Well, you've finished! Let the Honorable Rossi speak.

MATTEOTTI: What's the idea? It is your duty to protect my right to speak, I am merely reciting a list of facts. I have the right to be respected.

MUSSOLINI: Let the Honorable Casertano speak.

MATTEOTTI: I protest.

MUSSOLINI: Well, then, speak, but prudently. . . .

MATTEOTTI: I do not desire to speak prudently nor imprudently, only parliamentarily.

MUSSOLINI (with a gesture of disdain): Well, speak.

MATTEOTTI: The Honorable Piccinini was assassinated in his home for having accepted candidature against the Fascist list. . . .

The list of murders and assaults was continued.

There followed a description of election-day terror—assaults, stuffed ballot-boxes, forcible prevention, threats of death to every elector not a Fascist.

"And so," continued Matteotti, with smiling sarcasm, "only a small minority of the Italian people was allowed to vote, and these citizens can hardly be suspected of being Socialists."

In a previous speech Mussolini had listed many political crimes and acts of violence. He repeated the Fascist propaganda claim that Fascist crime was always in self-defense against the criminal provocation of the Socialists. Matteotti took up the crimes one by one; in every case he quoted Mussolini's own newspaper or the impartial *Corriere della Sera*, the findings of the courts, and the police records; in every case Matteotti proved from Fascist or neutral sources that the aggressors were always the police or the Fascist squadristi.

Mussolini could not conceal his hatred or his raging anger. Matteotti, like a young apostle, spoke "with inexhaustible energy, indomitable tenacity, with inspired fervor, obstinate, implacable, accomplishing his sacred mission at all costs."

When the Deputies walked out of the Chamber that evening and all the liberal elements clustered around Matteotti, congratulating him, he said, laughingly, "And now, my colleagues, you may prepare my funeral oration for the Chamber."

It is a fact that it was that very day that the Fascist Cheka discussed the case. On the morning of the 1st of June appeared a front-page editorial in the *Popolo d'Italia*, unsigned but written by Mussolini,[1] demanding physical violence against Matteotti. The epithets and threats in the Chamber were not enough, said the editorial; what was needed was a more tangible acknowledgment.

But the first speech of Matteotti's concerning the fraudulent election and the facts known throughout the country of the two forthcoming speeches were having tremendous political reaction. Mussolini felt it necessary to defend himself, and did so with amazing Machiavellianism. Suppose it were established, he said, that a million and a half votes cast for the Fascist list were fraudulent, the Fascist Party would still remain in power as rightful representative of the nation.

"You of the Opposition," he continued, "complain that you were restrained from holding free election meetings. What of it? Such meetings are of no use, anyway."

But the damning climax came a few days later. Mussolini lost his head completely. On the 6th of that crucial June, with Matteotti scheduled to make his most dangerous revelations of Fascist violence and financial corruption on the 10th, when the atmosphere throughout Italy had become evidently hostile, the other Opposition leaders continued the Matteotti policy of irony and iron facts, Mussolini became almost hysterical with hatred. When one member drew a parallel of Fascism and Bolshevism, Mussolini shouted:

"In Russia they are great masters. We have only to imitate what is being done in Russia."

---

[1] The original holograph was kept by Fasciolo, the Duce's secretary.

Uproar followed. Approval. Disapproval. Shouts. Waving of fists, the Right and Left benches threatening blows.

"They are magnificent masters," Mussolini repeated. "And we are wrong not to imitate them in full, so you would not now be here—you would be in jail."

Uproar. Applause. "We've just come from there," shouted a Communist.

"You would have a bullet through your spine," roared Mussolini. Another interruption. "We have the courage. We will prove it." Applause from the Fascisti. "We are always in time," continued Mussolini "and it will be done sooner than you think."

That same evening a journalist named Carlo Silvestri met Cesare Rossi, co-director of the Cheka. Rossi, as Silvestri later at the risk of his life testified under oath, said to him:

"With people like Matteotti the only thing to do is let the revolver speak. . . .

"If they knew what passes through Mussolini's head at times they would lay low.

"Mussolini is fully determined to carry out his threats. Anyone who knows him must know that every now and then Mussolini needs bloodshed—and counsels of moderation will not always prevail."

A boy of twelve, to whom Matteotti had been pointed out frequently as a "great man" since he was a member of parliament, and an old woman dozing in her doorway but suspicious over the actions of five men and their automobile, were the two accidental witnesses who betrayed the murderers and almost caused the downfall of Fascism. The woman noted the number of the automobile.

"Porca Madonna! Bastava avessero pisciato sulla targa," Mussolini exclaimed to his secretary, Fasciolo, when he heard about this old woman.

The boy testified:

"I was playing with my companions. Near us was a motor-car which had stopped just by Via Antonio Scialoja. Five men got out and began walking up and down, up and down. Then I saw Signor Matteotti come out. One of the men went forward and when near him gave him a violent push, making him fall to the ground. Signor Matteotti cried out. Then the other four men came up and one of them struck him a hard blow in the face. Then they took him by his head and feet and carried him into the car which came by us. So we were able to see that Signor Matteotti was struggling. We saw nothing more afterwards, as they rode away."

Of the five men in the car the ringleader was Amerigo Dumini, Rossi's colleague in the Cheka and "household friend" of Mussolini. He is American born, his father having emigrated from Italy and settled in St. Louis, where he married an American woman, Jessie Williams. Returning to Italy, Amerigo followed the calling for which he had been trained in American slums; he was a common gangster. In Italy he is first heard of as coming and going in Mussolini's office in Milan and in Mussolini's home. After he had committed his first murder and the Milan Fascisti under Mussolini's guidance had saved him from punishment, Mussolini began to use him for various purposes. Several times a week Dumini called to receive the "suggestions" of Mussolini and Rossi.

Like a bad man in the bad days of the American Wild West, Dumini made notches on his revolver for each mortal crime. Just before the Matteotti assassination he got into the habit of introducing himself boastfully as "Amerigo Dumini—Eleven murders." Confident he would be freed, he boasted of the death of Matteotti.

Kidnapped, beaten, stabbed, mutilated, burned, parts of the body of Mussolini's great political enemy were buried, disinterred, left for the foxes and pariah dogs to worry, then buried again. There is no evidence to the report that a part of the body had been sent to Mussolini as proof of the death, but there are confessions that bloodstained garments, the passport, and other identity papers of the murdered man were sent to him. With blood on their hands and joy in their voices high officials of the Fascist Cheka came immediately to Mussolini's office to tell him that the enemy was dead.

Parliament had waited, some members angrily, some anxiously, for Matteotti to deliver the last and most dangerous of his accusations; he had already proven that the election was a fraud; now he was to prove that most of the Fascist mandates were obtained by fraud or violence, were invalid, that the Fascist Party, in fact, had no right to occupy the majority benches in the Chamber. Such an exposure at a time the nation was pretty tired of Fascist pretensions and Fascist violence and the failure of the régime to redeem its radical promises, could have brought on a new election, with the probable defeat of Fascism.

As the hours passed and Matteotti did not appear it became rumored that he had been killed. In fact there were such whispers hours before the murder had been completed. Because that was the mood and circumstance of the nation in those days: when a prominent liberal somehow failed to keep an appointment, to arrive for dinner in time, to show up in his office at his usual hour, it was taken for granted that he must have fallen in with some of Mussolini's glorified squadristi, beaten up, forced to take castor oil, or murdered. Therefore the Left benches whispered tragedy.

The next day the whispers became loud. They penetrated the inner circle. Turning to faithful Rossi on their way back from Montecitorio, Mussolini said with that heavy sarcasm which his admirers call a sense of humor: "The Socialists are disturbed because they cannot find Matteotti—he must have gone to a brothel."

On the morning of the 12th, Rossi not only informed Mussolini that Matteotti had been assassinated, but that "the murder can only have been the work of people belonging to the Fascist Party Cheka."[2] Later in the day Filippelli rushed in frantically with the same news: Matteotti was dead, the Dumini gang had killed him and buried him.

That afternoon Signora Matteotti came to parliament seeking news from her husband's friends. Mussolini sent a messenger asking her to the Foreign Office.

When the widow arrived in the magnificent hall of the Palazzo Chigi, Mussolini sprang to his feet and stood at attention, as before a high officer. The effect of this gesture was to cause Madame Matteotti's collapse in tears.

"Signora, I should like to restore your husband alive to you. You may be assured that the government will do its utmost duty. We know nothing for certain, but there is still some hope."

The murderers had confessed. The hired assassins had come with their proofs, the blood-stained passport and blood-stained clothes; the body had been hacked to pieces, burned, buried; the chief of

---

[2] Rossi's memorandum, Salvemini's translation,

police had been informed and he had told Mussolini. But, there was still hope!

The widow of Matteotti was led to the door by the Duce himself. He bowed her out. Returning to his desk, he immediately sent for Rossi.

"There is nothing to be done," he said; "the boys have made too many mistakes. I am powerless. De Bono is good for nothing. All under suspicion must be patient. I must have my hands free to make the counter-attack. The hour of revenge will come."

At 7.30 that evening Mussolini, addressing the Chamber, concluded: "I hope that Honorable Matteotti will shortly be able to resume his place in parliament."

That night Dumini was arrested.

The next morning there was panic in Italy.

Mussolini ordered his militia mobilized. In Rome itself only half its strength responded; in Milan, birthplace of Fascism, the Duce's own bailiwick, only a quarter responded, and no one answered the call to the black colors in the industrial city of Turin.

On that day and following days the pictures of the most photographed man in the world were torn from the walls of Italy or smeared with the word "Assassin" or "Morte a Mussolini." From the liberal printing-presses came a flood of pictures of Matteotti which were pasted over that of the Duce with "Viva Matteotti" in red paint. The black shirt and the black cap disappeared from the streets, the leaders of Fascism were in tremulous hiding, and a cry for freedom and liberty arose in the land.

Cardinal Maffi of Pisa, the most brilliant mind, the most liberal thinker in the Catholic Church, telegraphed to Mussolini: "As a priest I weep; as an Italian I am ashamed."

The King considered calling the loyal army, proclaiming martial law, abolishing the illegal Fascist militia, restoring democratic government. But he was afraid. The Opposition parties had only to take one decisive action, but for four days they talked and talked because they foresaw two or three hundred men killed in the rioting which must ensue before Fascism was abolished; despite the fact they had already lost four thousand men, dead in fighting with the

Black Shirts, they decided not to shed more blood but hope for peaceful evolution without action.

Those four days Fascism was a living corpse. But there was no one willing to kick it into oblivion.

The day of the panic Mussolini addressed the Chamber. That brave man of the twenty feminine biographies, that soldier-hero who loved to taunt the Austrian army by perching himself on the parapet of the front-line trenches, that demigod of power who never knew fear, the implacable, the pitiless Mussolini, arose, but his body slumped; he spoke, but his words trembled, his gestures were pale, ineffectual. He was a whipped man.

"If there is anyone in this hall who, more than any person, should be heart-broken, even exasperated," he said in a voice no one recognized as Mussolini's, "that person is me. Only one of my enemies who would during the long nights consider such a diabolical action could have committed the crime which today strikes with horror and makes us cry out in indignation. . . .

"The situation, gentlemen, is extremely delicate . . . one must deplore, one must condemn, one must push the inquest for the search of all the guilty and all those responsible, and we are here to repeat that all this will be done, tranquilly, inexorably. . . .

"The law will be executed. The police will deliver the guilty to the judicial authorities. . . . One must be calm and refuse to amplify the terrible and stupid incident into a question of general politics and the policy of the government. . . .

"Justice will be done, must be done, because the crime is a crime which is anti-Fascist and anti-nation. It is more than horrible, it is of a bestial humanity. One must not hesitate before such an act to separate crime from politics."

Justice, of course, was never done. Dumini, it is true, was in prison, but Dumini was a household friend and could be relied upon to keep his mouth shut. That very day agents went to the other four murderers and gave them money to flee the country. And years later Mussolini was able to comment in his autobiography:

"One day Matteotti disappeared from Rome. Immediately it was whispered about that a political crime had been committed. The Socialists were looking for a martyr who might be of use for purposes of oratory, and at once, before anything definite could possibly be known, they accused Fascism. By my orders we began a most painstaking and complete investigation. The government was determined to act with the greatest energy, not only for the sake of justice, but also to stop, from the very first moment, the spread of any kind of calumny. I threw the prefect and police chief of Rome, the Secretary of the Interior, Finzi, and the chief of the press office, Cesare Rossi,.into the task of clearing up the mystery. Activity on the part of the police for the discovery of the guilty persons was ordered without stint. Very soon it was possible to identify the guilty. They were of high station. They came from the Fascist group, but they were completely outside our responsible elements.

". . . It seemed hardly possible that only a few days after the opening of the twenty-sixth legislature a group of men of position could carry through an enterprise which, begun as a jest, was to conclude in a tragedy. I always have had harsh and severe words for what happened. . . ."

To this same Cesare Rossi, Mussolini's right-hand man, his most intimate friend from Socialist days and the writer of eulogistic prefaces to innumerable biographies of Mussolini in days of Fascist triumph, all the acts of violence of the two years of Mussolini's rule were not jests, they were the bloody realities of successful government. Now on the 14th of June he saw himself made the sacrificial goat of the hierarchy. He went into hiding. But before he did so he wrote a confession, which he intrusted to his friend Virgili, saying it was to be published only if Mussolini betrayed him, and he sent a similar threat to Mussolini.

The Rossi "memoriale" lists criminal acts Rossi charges against the dictator in addition to complicity in the Matteotti murder. Rossi concludes:

"All this happened according to the direct will or complicity of the Duce. I allude to the clubbing of Deputy Amendola, the order given De Bono, commanding general of the Fascist militia and director of the police, by Mussolini, unknown to me and executed by Candelori, console of the militia; the beating of Deputy Misuri carried out by Balbo, generalissimo of the militia, at the suggestion of Mussolini; the aggression upon Forni, candidate in the April elections, for which the order was given me personally by Mussolini and carried out in agreement with Giunta, secretary-general of the Fascist Party; the attack on the villa of ex-Premier Nitti; the recent demonstrations against the Opposition parties ordered by Mussolini to be undertaken by Foschi, secretary of the party for the province of Rome; the proposal advanced by Mussolini to the Quadrumvirato, the central assembly of the party, in order that the Honorable Ravazolo, Fascist Deputy, should be given a well-earned lesson in consequence to his insubordination; the destruction of the Catholic clubs in Brianza ordered by Mussolini, carried out by the Fascist Deputy Maggi and then complacently repeated to me. I add that daily Commendatore Fasciolo, Mussolini's secretary, had the order, at the suggestion of Mussolini, to forward to the Fascist locals the names of subscribers of the *Voce Republicana, Avanti, Giustizia, Unitá, Italia Libera,* et cetera, so that the subscribers might be dosed with castor oil and clubbed."

In a second memorandum Rossi lists thirty-seven murder and clubbing orders or suggestions from Mussolini. Number 13: "Mussolini expressed his regret that we did not succeed in beating up Matteotti on his way home from a convention." Number 21: "Mussolini ordered the murder of several radicals who had succeeded in worming their way into the Milan Fascist local." Number 32: "Mussolini ordered the founding of the Cheka." Number 36: "Mussolini's ambiguous relation to the assassination of Matteotti.

"I, Cesare Rossi," he concludes, "who on his order have been left in the lurch, accused, vilified, and made out a liar, have no longer any duty to remain faithful to Mussolini or to conceal the truth.

"I have also lost all faith in the régime and the Fascist Party which accepts and approves not only these acts of violence, but also all terrible crimes. Mussolini, the government and the party, in June made a political crime out of a tragic crime; it is due to the blind egotism of the Duce, the perfidy of General De Bono, the apathy of the party, and the panicky anxiety of the masses.

"I publish this memorandum to protect my honor. I feel also that I am taking a wise and necessary step in the service of my fatherland. With a firm hand and a clear conscience, I sign, Cesare Rossi."

But clear as that conscience may be, this same Rossi, as head of the Cheka, stands accused by all parties in Italy, Fascists, anti-Fascists, Catholics, and Republicans, in many of the crimes he himself lists, including that against Matteotti.

Other leaders of Fascism were going into hiding, fleeing the country, or protecting themselves against Mussolini by writing out confessions to be intrusted to friends or journalists. Filippo Filippelli, director of the Fascist Rome organ, *Corriere Italiano*, in his memorandum given to the journalist Naldi and attested by him later before a magistrate, accuses not only Mussolini and the assassin Dumini, but also Rossi; he speaks of the agreement for the murder by these three leading gentlemen and details their complicity. Filippelli relates the events of the Wednesday, June 11, when, alarmed by the news of the disappearance of Matteotti and the rumors that the Cheka had acted, he went to Rossi, who, he testifies, related to him:

"That Dumini had told him that he had used the car which in all good faith I had lent him;

"That the matter was serious;

"That Mussolini knew everything;

"That Marinelli and he [Rossi] had given the orders after previously agreeing with Mussolini;

"That the thing must be hushed up, otherwise Mussolini himself would be smashed."

The Filippelli memorandum continues:

"I thought it expedient to inform De Bono, Finzi, Marinelli, and others. From Finzi and others I learned that:

"The victim of Dumini's outrage was Matteotti;

"That the order to suppress him had been given by the Cheka of the National Fascist Party, of which the executioners were Dumini and others well known to Mussolini, who knew also of this special mission;

"That they had had an interview with Mussolini that day [June 11th] and that they had handed to Mussolini the papers and the passport of Matteotti as proof of his disappearance."

Filippelli fled. Mussolini sent his secretary, Fasciolo, to Rossi to make terms with him and to ask him to leave Rome. Finzi, seized with the same panic which had driven Rossi and Filippelli to write confessions, made a testament which he gave to his friend, Schiff-Giorgini, and the journalist Silvestri. Finzi's brother told Guglielmo Emmanuel, correspondent of the *Corriere della Sera*, the Hearst International News Service, and the *New York American*, the contents of the confession.

The search for scapegoats continued; the panic continued, and still the Opposition talked and refused to ask the King to outlaw the outlaw party. Mussolini had Filippelli dragged out of hiding and taken to prison; he ordered General De Bono to resign as chief of police, and he himself made one of the grandiose gestures of his career: he gave up one of the many portfolios he, as dictator, had accumulated for himself; he resigned as Home Secretary, and as a sop to the monarchy and the Vatican, both unfriendly now, he named Federzoni, head of the old Nationalist Party, Royalist and Catholic, in his place. Throughout Italy members of the Fascist Cheka were placed in jail. Rossi was finally arrested.

Humbly, very humbly, Mussolini began to make amends. To the Chamber he said on the 24th: "The crime against the person of the Honorable Matteotti has wounded and moved profoundly the Italian public opinion which loudly demands justice.

"The voice has been and will be heard.

". . . Out of this crime, which has had profound repercussions in the national conscience, there may be born a period of concord and peace among the Italian people."

On the 26th of June Mussolini abandoned the dictatorship!

With tears in his eyes.

He had in his pocket the letter from Rossi calling him a doomed man—the letter smuggled out of jail, saying, "If during the coming days you fail to furnish me proof of solidarity, not so much for the past and for my position as your collaborator and executor of our sometime illegal orders, but of your solidarity for essentially governmental reasons, I shall put into effect what I told you. I deem it superfluous to warn you that if the revolting cynicism which you have displayed up to now, complicated by fear that has seized you just at the time you should dominate a situation created exclusively by you, should advise you to order free violence, while I am in jail or in the unfortunate case of my arrest, you will equally be a doomed man, and with you will be destroyed the régime. . . ."

With tears in his eyes the "doomed man" addressed the leaders of Fascism in the magnificent gold and brocaded Palazzo Venezia.

"There is no longer a question that Matteotti was assassinated," said Mussolini; "it is no longer a question whether six or fifteen or twenty or thirty individuals are in prison, it is no longer a question whether the Ministry is to remain or to be transformed, if the party is to be cleaned: one sees now clearly the goal of the Opposition, it is the régime itself. They propose to annul all that it signifies, from the point of view of morals and politics. So you see the game become most attenuated. I declare to you I do not propose to see annihilated a state of things which we have created with grand efforts, with much pain, with, indeed, much bloodshed. . . .

"I admit that the militia should be promptly included in the armed forces of the State.

"And because I have been reproached for not having let it take the oath of allegiance to the King, I engage myself to have that formality executed now.

"What will be my program?

"What I have said before, I repeat. I propose to have the Chamber, the parliament, function. I repeat: it is my intention in the future not to issue decrees, because if the government makes its own laws, then the Chamber has nothing to do.

"We will enter into legality, absolute, and repress illegality; clean out the party. . . . I am disposed to follow a policy of conciliation and to forget the past, to forget all the battles of the past."

The abolition of the illegal militia, the one element upon which Fascism rested, forcing itself upon a mass now no longer willing to give it a chance or to accept it at any price, would have meant the collapse of dictatorship. "Enter into legality" would have meant the collapse of the dictatorship. The moment the five Opposition parties could be assured a legal election they would have obtained a legal majority reducing Fascism to a third or fourth party. The abolition of rule by decrees would have meant the end of dictatorship.

All this Mussolini promised the day he was a doomed man and had tears in his eyes.

This abnegation of dictatorship was due to the reaction of the press. After two years of Fascism the total number of readers of the party papers was 400,000 while the anti-Fascists with their great and popular journals and their support by the great majority of Italians had at least 4,000,000 readers.

Scared by the press, Mussolini had, in accordance with its demands, resigned one office, and rid himself of members of the Quadrumvirate, the Pentarchy, the men who made him and his party. Among the founders of Fascism who were driven out were General De Bono, Undersecretary of the Interior Finzi, Chief of the Press Bureau Rossi, Administrative Secretary of the Fascist Party Marinelli, Editor of the Fascist Organ Filippelli, Chief Assassin Dumini, and "six or fifteen or twenty or thirty individuals," all in prison.

The press almost brought about a revolution. It did in fact inflame the mass mind to the point of rebelling. A word from the King or an order from Amendola, the new leader of the five Opposition parties, would have ended by small violence the dictatorship Mussolini himself had declared abandoned. But no word or order ever came.

The morning after the Premier's confession of a return to legality the Opposition parties met at Montecitorio and unanimously voted a motion. They talked a lot, and what they did was to sign a paper. The document is important because it is the accusation not only of Matteotti's party, but also the Republican Party, the Catholic Party, and two other non-liberal or non-radical parties, that Mussolini is the responsible accomplice of the assassination.

The resolutions called international attention to the existence of the Fascist Cheka, "grafted on the very organization of the government and by the confidants of the Chief of Government [Mussolini]"; it placed the blame for the assassinations upon the President of the Council [Mussolini]; and it concluded by announcing the abstention of the Opposition parties from parliamentary participation.

In America not a line appeared about the Matteotti case because the newspapers were filled to overflowing with news of another

murder, that committed in Chicago by two young neurotic million-
aires, named Loeb and Leopold. But in England Premier MacDonald
attended a meeting of the Labor Party at which a resolution was
passed condemning the assassination and sending the sympathy of
British labor to the Socialist Party of Italy.

Pope Pius was terribly shocked. Finzi, whose complicity was
generally admitted, had married a niece of Cardinal Vannutelli,
dean of the Sacred College and one of the closest associates of the
Pope. Cardinal Gasparri made visits to both the mother and widow
of Matteotti, expressing his sympathy and horror.

From New York Luigi Barzini, editor of the *Corriere d'America*,
cabled Mussolini, advising him to purge the Fascist Party, drive
out the Black Hand, see that justice was done and that Fascist
prestige was restored.

Italy's leading intellectual, the philosopher Croce, passed the following verdict upon the régime: "The Fascist movement is incapable
of setting up a new type of State despite the ostentatious utterances
of its supporters; therefore Fascism in my judgment could not and
should not be anything more than a bridge to lead to the restoration
of a more strictly liberal régime in the frame of a stronger State.
. . . Because Fascism cannot create a new constitutional and judicial
organization as a substitute for that of Liberalism, it finds itself
forced to move along by the same violent means that accompanied
its birth, and so it perpetuates what should have been occasional
and transitory. In this series of violent actions we cannot exactly
see at what point we are to stop."

Weeks passed. The five Opposition parties became known as the
Aventine. They met. They talked. Their one great gesture was
to withdraw from parliament; after which they did nothing. They
were socialists and reformists who did not believe in direct action,
in arms, in violence, legal or illegal.

Not so Farinacci. "Farinacci the Sadist," as he was frequently
called, was unaffected by bloodshed or murder or revolutionary
hysteria. He sneered at weakness. He despised the Socialist pacifists
and he jeered at Mussolini for acting as timidly as they did. The
Duce became the meek follower of his assistant; the desperate, sick
man accepted the doctor Farinacci's violent remedy, and between

July 29 and September 30, 1924, he instructed the Cheka and the squadron leaders in metropolitan centers to revive the 1922 terror. Sixteen anti-Fascists were murdered, 36 seriously wounded, 172 assaulted; 46 homes and clubs of Socialists, Catholics, and labor organizations were destroyed.[3]

Most important of all was the decree abolishing freedom of the press. (Freedom here is underlined to distinguish it from a later decree abolishing the opposition press; the first placed it in the hands of censors, the latter ended its existence.) Newspapers were burned, presses smashed, buildings destroyed.

As the voices of opposition were stilled in fire and blood, the hero-conqueror found his own. He forgot his promise of justice, he forgot the "return to legality," he issued nothing but decrees, and the militia which he had sworn to disband he used for the purpose of destroying his political enemies. And when the time came for him to write his autobiography for the *Saturday Evening Post* he forgot even the fact that Matteotti had been murdered.

"The course of Italian public life from June to December, 1924," he wrote, "offered a spectacle absolutely unparalleled in the political struggle in any country. It was a mark of shame and infamy which would dishonor any political group. The press, the meetings, the subversive and anti-Fascist parties of every sort, the false intellectuals, the defeated candidates, the soft-brained cowards, the rabble, the parasites, threw themselves like ravens on the corpse [of Matteotti]. The arrest of the guilty was not enough. The discovery of the corpse and the sworn statement of surgeons that death had not been due to crime but had been produced by a trauma, was not enough. . . .

"I did not have a moment of doubt or discouragement . . . the swelled frogs waited for their triumph . . . this base and pernicious crew. . . . The contemptible game lasted six months. . . .

"I held the Fascist Party firmly in my hand during this period," comments the later-day Napoleon. "I curbed the impulse of some Fascist who wanted violent reprisals, with a clear order: 'Hands in your pockets! I am the only one who must have his hands free.'

---

[3] The complete documentation for these figures, which apply to North Italy only, has been published by Bolitho.

In Florence and Bologna, however, there occurred episodes of extreme violence. I understood then that it was time to speak and act."

The speech came on the 3rd of January, 1925, when the situation had so completely reversed itself that Mussolini at last was able to accept and to glorify the assassination of his chief rival.

"On June 10," said Mussolini, addressing the Black Shirts, "there was sequestered in Rome the Honorable Matteotti, who during a ride succumbed.

"This event was singularly enveloped in a certain mystery for the purpose of shocking public opinion. The Fascist revolution had been very gentle. . . . Just the same, the Honorable Matteotti, who during the war had affirmed the most dangerous principles of defeatism, after having always and everywhere offended Fascism, pronounced in the Chamber a terrible and vicious attack upon the régime. . . .

"Sentimentalism in Latin countries is very dangerous. . . .

"The sequestration of Matteotti, with its consequences, belongs morally, politically, historically to Fascism. It is useless and stupid to search for the guilty at the moment when the fact arrives. This, only this, can be the language of revolution."

When the Fascist Deputy Cesare Misuri stepped out of the party traces to declare that "Mussolini fell among bad companions," and named Rossi, Luigi Freddi, Finzi, Francesco Giunta (to which list the press added De Bono and Marinelli, four of these six being under charge of complicity in the assassination), Mussolini took cognizance and for once—that is, for a while at least—stood by his colleagues. "The men denounced as 'the bad counselors of the good tyrant,' " he said, "are five or six men who reported to me in person every morning. I herewith make distinct avowal that I look upon them as my closest collaborators and fellow burden-bearers, who share with me the salt bread of direct responsibility for the acts of the Fascist administration. I declare in your presence that I owe them the deepest sentiments of gratitude and affection."

These early days of 1925 ended the crisis. When the Rossi memorandum was published and there was a last wave of antagonism, Mussolini replied by threatening to mobilize the Fascist militia. This time it was too late for the King to mobilize the army; it would have meant civil war, and Amendola and the other leaders again talked about a general strike, which well could have been called were it not for the fear that Mussolini would use the militia against the workingmen. It became apparent that a psychological moment, that of June, could never be revived. From January, 1925, on, Fascism grew stronger than ever and its course seemed certain so long as economic pressure (which shares with violence in shaping history) did not militate against it.

The atmosphere was now clear for the Matteotti trial.

CHAPTER XV

Blood and Irony

ALTHOUGH THE DUCE HIMSELF SAID, "IT WAS WORSE THAN A crime, it was a blunder," the assassination of Matteotti was in fact a necessary step in the consolidation of power. With Matteotti alive Mussolini could not be certain of success. The man who sentenced the leader of the Opposition to death obeyed literally the rules for guidance of princely power as written and expounded many years ago.

The Machiavellian Prince was bitter in his victory. Above all else it was being spoiled by the wit, the humor, the irony of that other young man who, although born bourgeois and grown wealthy, stood up as a leader of the proletariat and jested over the story of the Socialist blacksmith's son who had become the champion of the steamship lines and automobile manufacturers of Milan and Turin and the tourist-promotion society of Rome.

"Remember, Razumof," says one of Conrad's characters in *Under Western Eyes*, "that women, children, and revolutionists hate irony, which is the negation of all saving instincts, of all devotion, of all action."

Matteotti the revolutionist loved irony; Mussolini the revolutionist had neither irony nor humor. Matteotti smiled; Mussolini frowned. Matteotti was irony's gadfly, nipping the dictator, bringing up deeply felt hatred and rage in his black glowing eyes.

He was two years younger than Mussolini. His well-to-do family sent him to Rovigo to be educated, then to the University of Bologna, where he obtained a doctorate in jurisprudence. His interest in Socialism at first was academic. Unlike Mussolini, he suffered from no inferiority complex, no minority complex, no "suppression" by family or circumstance.

He was careful, precise, logical; he had an ordered mind and was not swayed easily by emotions. His brother, a physician and Socialist, and he discussed liberal ideas as philosophy, not as a course of action.

In 1914 Matteotti, like Mussolini, spoke for absolute neutrality. It was the duty of the proletariat, of all independent minds, of all persons having ideals, to oppose this war, any war. For several months these two men in far-removed centers preached the same thought. But Matteotti never sold out—for wealth or power or a seat in congress or a newspaper. He was arrested in June, 1916, for a speech denouncing war. After his acquittal he was drafted and remained in the army three years. Most of that time, however, he was interned in a British camp on account of his pacifist views. In 1919 and again in 1921 he was elected to the Chamber of Deputies, where he became an expert in finance and economics.

He had a fiery face, like Mussolini's, but a cold mind. His appearance was cold but flashing; he had a sensitive nature which his passionate eyes betrayed.

"Every time I saw Matteotti," says his friend, Giovanni Zibordi, "his face and figure full of energy, his movement agile, I would think of an 'espada,' a Spanish matador, one with every part of his body alert and his muscles of iron, his nerves taut and his heart unmoved, who plays with a fine blade, conquering the huge and blinded fury of the bull. . . . Such was Matteotti in the parliamentary arena, alive, prepared, vigilant, a fencer, direct and valiant, always armed with documents and with facts, with reason and with opportune blows and adequate replies.

"Irritating? Yes. He had a thin sharp voice which was not checked by sweet inflections, but a manner of speaking in a flow of irony, of logical irony—an audacious fighter."

Matteotti stood in the way of Fascist progress. His words, his pen, his activity were a daily reproach to tyranny. He had no fear of the Fascisti; the Fascisti were afraid of him. They could not answer him. They assassinated him.

Mussolini had no moral or intellectual arms to equal Matteotti's. And he simply could not live under irony. So he nodded yes to the Fascist Cheka plan of assassination.

But even after death, tragic irony played its part. The trial of

Dumini and the other four confessed assassins became a trial of the dead.

It was held in March of 1926, almost two years after the murder, at a time when Fascism had so intrenched itself that nothing could shake it; it controlled the army as well as the militia now, had suppressed all the newspapers and corrupted the entire judiciary. Judge Giuseppe Danza presided. Chieti was chosen because it was an out-of-the-way village where the secret service could control the journalists and the proceedings easily. Co-accused with Dumini were: Albino Volpi, Amleto Poveromo, August Malacria, and Giuseppe Viola, all members of the service and all present in the automobile during the murder. Malacria had served a prison term for swindling. Poveromo had been sentenced once for robbery. Viola had a record of bankruptcy, desertion, and rape.

Roberto Farinacci, secretary-general of the Fascist Party, was appointed by Mussolini to defend the murderers. If there was one man in Italy who more than Mussolini himself was an advocate of violence in the achievement of power, that man was Farinacci, the so-called "left" or extreme hand of the Duce. The trial began with Farinacci's attack upon Matteotti. In opposing Fascism, said Farinacci, Matteotti had proven himself plainly a traitor to his country and therefore his death was justifiable. After this declaration the trial became a tragic farce.

One murderer testified that because Matteotti refused to sit quietly in the car it became necessary to subdue him. "I kneeled on his chest," he testified, "but he kept on resisting. So I pressed my knees into his chest until the arteries broke and the blood came out of his mouth."

Dumini, the American gangster, was the star witness, despite his numerous contradictions.

"When we had Matteotti in the car," he testified, "he made us all very sore by the way he thrashed about, and as we did not want to attract any attention and had determined to take him far away in the campagna, I hit him several times with the butt of my revolver.

"He then was quiet for a while, but soon started again to struggle, and when he threw the weight of his body against me while I was at the wheel, I crushed in his skull with my *manganello* [black-jack].

"Then when we saw that he was dead we did not know what to do next, for I had not really at first intended to kill him. We drove about for many hours and it was getting dark. Then we decided to cut up the body and burn it, and this we did in a lonesome byway near the Grotta Rossa [about twelve miles out of Rome]. What remained of the body we buried in different spots and I don't remember now where that was done."

The day following this admission the humorist Dumini changed his mind.

"We were riding along peaceably," he testified, "when suddenly Matteotti developed tuberculosis and died of a hemorrhage."

But this was a little too much for even a Fascist judge.

"Then how do you account for the thirty-six stab wounds," asked the court.

"Who said stab wounds?" demanded Dumini.

"Doctors—experts," replied the judge.

"Oh!" replied Dumini. "I thought in these modern days that 'experts' were no longer allowed to testify."

Testimony was offered that Dumini, some months previous, had been smuggled out of prison by Fascist agents, given a bag filled with 1,000-lire notes, and packed off to France. He had been recognized at the station of Termini and rearrested. A letter was found on him which again implicated Mussolini. This letter from his sister Blanche read:

"Vaselli [Dumini's lawyer] says all will be well, but it will take time on account of the judges, who are Freemasons, who war on the government and the party. They are trying to get rid of them as they did of one before. It takes time, but all will be well.

"What have you arranged for communicating with Vaselli?

"Why have you told so much to Vaselli? Why have you come to this extreme with the Duce? Do you want Rosati for defense? If you do, communicate by letter. Vaselli told us he let Mussolini know he had been betrayed. De Bono is already out. Which papers were they which concerned De Bono? It is not true what Cesarino [pet name for Cesare Rossi] said. Vaselli told mother he will make arrangements for your future with Mussolini. Do you agree? Is it true that you are taking the whole responsibility? Do not speak too much and remain where you are. Mother says the arrangements will be made as quickly as possible and a large sum will be deposited for you when you come out. Be calm. We are all interceding for you, but it is a terrible moment; nevertheless we will succeed. Kisses. Blanche."

This letter, together with the testament of Finzi and the confessions of Rossi, were not allowed in evidence.

But it is interesting to note that Dumini, the humorist, shortly afterwards walked about the streets of Rome, and when occasions came or he could make them, smilingly introduced himself: "Dumini, *twelve* murders." In fact, he talked too much. Bragging in the cafés of the capital of how easily he got off at Chieti and how Mussolini had stood by him so nobly, he became the object of Fascist concern. One day his demands for hush money reached their limit, for he addressed to Mussolini a legal summons,[1] in which *inter alia* is declared:

1. that he, Dumini, received 60,000 lire from the Directorate of the Fascist Party and

2. that the expense of the trial, 32,754 lire, was to be paid by the Fascist Party, in addition.

Dumini was arrested, tried, sentenced to a year in jail one day in September, 1926, and from that time on he has stayed in jail, in silence.

Albino Volpi, a professional assassin like Dumini, and likewise a member of the Fascist Cheka, testified:

"While we were beating and stabbing Matteotti he appeared heroic. He continued to the end to cry, 'Assassins,' 'Savages,' 'Cowards.' But he never had a weak moment and he never asked for mercy. And while we were stabbing him he kept repeating, 'Kill me, but the idea which is in me you can never kill.'

"Probably if he had been humble for a moment, and if he had asked to be saved and if he had confessed the error of his ideas, we perhaps would not have accomplished our work. But no. Just to the end, so long as he had breath, he cried out, 'My idea will not

---

[1] Registered in the courts of Rome, Bureau of Private Orders, No. 5555, Vol. 356.

die' and 'My children will be proud of their father' and 'The work-ingmen will bless my corpse.'

"He died saying, 'Long live Socialism.' "

This is the chef-d'œuvre of Fascist crime which the Duce was afterwards to call "a practical joke on Matteotti—he should not have resisted his jesters."

Viola and Malacria were acquitted. Dumini, Volpi, and Poveromo were found guilty of *unintentional* homicide, sentenced to five years' imprisonment, and freed almost immediately afterwards by Mussolini's amnesty for *political* offenders which had been issued in 1925. Rossi and Mussolini had reached an agreement whereby the former was to keep quiet; he was accordingly allowed to escape from prison, and from his refuge in France he turned against his chief and issued another confession and accusation, this second memorandum concluding with the words:

"All the moral responsibilities of the circle from which came the Matteotti crime are on Mussolini."

But the vendetta of Mussolini followed Rossi unrelentingly year after year, to France and Germany and Switzerland. Agents came with guns and knives and plots and secrets whispered in his ears. Rossi withstood all these. Then, in 1930, a charming lady appeared in Paris and Rossi was smitten. The lady proposed a honeymoon in lovely Switzerland, and Rossi went. He went too far. One day the lovely lady proposed an excursion to the Italian frontier, and although Rossi became a little suspicious he took great care never to come within a hundred yards of the border. But the lady made a signal and several Fascist police ran across the frontier into Switzerland, seized Rossi, and carried him off to jail. The lovely lady laughed.

Just before his trial the representative of Mussolini came to Rossi and told him that the death penalty had been ordered; if Rossi wanted to save his life he must withdraw all his confessions, especially the document commonly known as "The Thirty-seven accusations against Mussolini," and must swear never to accuse the Duce of the Matteotti murder again. To save his life Rossi withdrew everything, promised everything, and began a sentence of thirty years in prison for "libeling" Mussolini.

Marinelli and Filippelli appeared before the Court of Appeals in Rome, where on the 1st of December, 1925, the charges were dismissed because it was found that the accused had ordered the kidnapping, not the assassination, of Matteotti. General De Bono was acquitted of complicity at a trial before the Senate in July, 1925. The reason given was "lack of sufficient evidence."

It was at this time that the campaign for the suppression of the liberal press and the intimidation of foreign correspondents reached its height in Italy. Detectives followed every American journalist. The concierge of the house where the *New York World* correspondent lived was forced to report daily, while around the office of Emmanuel, representative of the Hearst Service, numerous spies were stationed. All the Italian journalists who acted as assistants in the American offices were ordered to report to Grandi's bureau. But special favors were shown to all members of the Cortesi family, who, representing the Associated Press of America, the *London Daily Mail*, the *New York Times*, and several other important publications, have done Fascist propaganda a greater service than all the paid agents. Without a single exception, every journalist who was not a voluntary or subsidized propagandist denounced the trial of Chieti. Even friends of Fascism did so. But no one resident in Italy dared do so in the press. During the trial John Clayton, then representing the *Chicago Tribune*, wrote privately:

"We are bound by the worst censorship ever imposed. We must not write anything that might reflect on the Fascisti. *We are confined to an apology for political assassination.* It broke my heart not to be able to report the Matteotti case as it should be done, but *it would have meant arrest and expulsion from Italy.*"

The truth about the Matteotti trial was almost completely suppressed by the régime. But because he believed it a most unusual and cruel miscarriage of justice, Bolitho, unable to withstand the dictate of his conscience, fled from Italy when the hearings were half over and from the first free town, in France, wrote for the *Manchester Guardian* and the *New York World* a series of dispatches which startled public opinion.

A few liberals in America protested. In England Professor Gilbert Murray wrote that the tragedy at Chieti was "a mock trial in order to give absolution and public thanks to the murderers. No element of fraud was lacking; . . . the Matteotti trial will probably remain for some generations a classic model of the perfect perversion of justice."

As Bolitho, in order to escape arrest on his return to Italy, had used a pseudonym which the Fascist Cheka had been unable to identify, the head of the press bureau in the Foreign Office called in all the Anglo-American journalists for cross-examination. He even threatened those in whose papers Bolitho's syndicated articles had been used. But to the credit of those who knew the secret it must be said none betrayed him. With two exceptions, in fact, the Anglo-American press corps in Rome rejoiced over Bolitho's successful publication of the facts they themselves had been unable to send. The exceptions were the Italians who represent American and British journals and news agencies.

In defense of Mussolini, Luigi Villari, his chief apologist in London, has written that "the trial was conducted with absolute fairness and in an atmosphere free from pressure or outside influences . . . not a scrap of real evidence had emerged incriminating the government or the leaders of the Fascist Party, and all the fantastic structure erected by the Opposition has crumbled."

Professor Salvemini of course produced the documents incriminating the government, the leaders of the party, the Duce himself. The reply of Signor Villari is one of the supreme achievements of the Fascist mentality. The prosecution, he wrote, "committed Dumini and his companions for unpremeditated murder, which is *not* the same as manslaughter. By rejecting the charge of premeditation the alleged complicity in the murder of political personages is evidently knocked on the head."

This is typical of the apologia delivered in foreign countries a year after Mussolini, powerful, restored in confidence, accepted "the full responsibility" for the assassination.

The cynical (and not unwelcome to the Duce) viewpoint was that of Mr. Bernard Shaw. Comparing Mussolini with Napoleon, he said they differed in that the former had no military victories; they were alike in one respect; for the murder of Matteotti, Napoleon had the murder of the Duke of Enghien on his conscience.

Contrasted with the Shavian cynicism is the naïveté of the lady biographers. According to Mme. Bordeux: "To accuse Mussolini openly of the murder of a member of his own parliament was next to impossible. . . . No, Mussolini was never openly accused of other than instigating the murder of Matteotti. . . . Matteotti's murder was premeditated and carried out by his own personal enemies in his own party."

Stranger still are the references to Matteotti in the long biography by Mussolini's Egeria. Whereas the Duce himself devotes thousands of words to denouncing his opponent and defending himself, Sarfatti in 352 pages of joy bells and hosannas of Fascism, slides over the thin ice of the greatest crisis in its history with two sidesteps. Page 181: "And after the assassination of Matteotti, Mussolini's first utterances in an address to the Grand Council of the Fascists was one of vehement impatience with the storm which then broke out, because it prevented him from applying himself to the task of 'ordinary administration'—the only task which he regarded as vital and essential, that of giving the people what they really wanted and were asking for, bridges, water, roads." Page 275: "He was really very much taken up by his dramatic schemes. A short time after the sinister Matteotti affair, which caused him such terrible suffering that for a while his life seemed completely wrecked, I met him going out one day looking more cheerful. He showed me a packet of manuscript, which he told me was his new play, with which he had succeeded in distracting his mind when in need of relaxation from his worries and his troubles. It was a play based on the life of the campagna, and this man, tired, exhausted, worn out by his bitter experiences, had found refreshment in recalling the incidents of his childhood." There are no other references to the assassination, the trial, or the vast results from the crisis.

In the judgment of Louis Roya, a French writer who prefaces his opinion by praising Mussolini as a patriot and friend of Latin civilization, the responsibility of the assassination "can be inferred from imponderable facts, from an ensemble of troubling circumstances, such as the letter to Dumini from his family, and finally and above all (this is the thesis of Rossi *contre* the Duce) from the orders for violence given by Mussolini. Seen from that viewpoint, the culpability of Mussolini is irrefutable in the eyes of the universal moral conscience. And, a thing most impressive, all Italians who have fled from Italy to escape the Fascist tyranny, unite in recognizing that the first and the highest responsibility rests on Mussolini: that too is the opinion of the international proletariat.

"There can be no doubt about it that when the day comes when Fascism falls, the Matteotti trial, the real trial, will begin again; and the principal accused will be—Mussolini."

CHAPTER XVI

The Sons of Brutus

GIOVANNI AMENDOLA INHERITED THE LEADERSHIP OF THE FIVE Opposition parties commonly known as the Aventine.

If Matteotti had been the Brutus of the Fascist régime, Amendola was the son of Brutus. He was one of the leading intellectuals of Italy, a savant, one of the ideal university men who had given up a cloistered career for politics and journalism and yet had found time for serious and learned creative work. He was brilliant, and like Matteotti he frequently employed irony in his unanswerable attacks on Fascism and illegal violence.

Shortly after the assassination of Matteotti many men said that Amendola would be the next to die. In fact, the first threat against his life had been made by Mussolini a year earlier when he wrote:[1]

"The Deputy Amendola demands why we do not suppress the national militia at a time when Fascism has general approval.

"To this gentleman, who again promenades himself in the streets of Rome without annoyances, we reply that the militia is not prepared against the people, but, on the contrary, against a minority of scoundrels, very vicious, without credit, scoundrels who have always betrayed Italy.

"This Amendola who craves liberty, just as if all the pits of Italy were full of cadavers, and all the lamp-posts decorated with anti-nationalist carcasses, has, up to now, enjoyed too much liberty.

"Fascism has been too generous to him, as it has been to other delinquents whose names are Nitti, Albertini, Don Sturzo, Treves, Modigliani, Serrati, Turati, and others. [Every man mentioned, except Albertini, has either been beaten up, arrested, or forced into exile, since then.]

[1] *Popolo d'Italia,* August 24, 1923.

"Ah, if Fascism, instead of being so good and so naïve, had done away with all these scoundrels who infest the nation! Fascism today is paying for its faults for having made a revolution with the blood of its soldiers instead of the blood of its adversaries.

"But, for this reason, to repair this first omission, the militia must remain at its post; the militia would do well to give a lesson to the scoundrels who have not already been nailed to lamp-posts."

The militia and also the Fascist university students and the squadristi gave Amendola, "this Amendola who craves liberty," not one but several lessons. This is the records of the assaults:

> December 26, 1923, in a crowded street in Rome.
> March, 1924, in Naples during a political speech.
> May 30, 1924, on leaving the House of Parliament.
> April 6, 1925, in Rome, after a speech on liberty.
> July 20, 1925, at Montecatini, in Tuscany.

The first attack occurred in the Via Francesco Crispi while hundreds were passing. Many noticed that an automobile filled with militiamen was slowly following Amendola and they knew that an assault was planned. The militiamen finally stopped the car a few feet ahead of the Deputy, leaped out, drove the passers-by away, and beat Amendola with their clubs, leaving him with his head bloody, apparently dying on the sidewalk. Adjutant-major Vico Perroni of the 112th Legion of Fascist militia, later testified under oath that the order to attack Amendola came from General De Bono, who was head both of the militia and of the Rome police. He asked whether the order came direct from the Duce. "I was impressed with the mention of Amendola's name," reads his signed confession, "so I personally made sure that His Excellency Mussolini required this to be done. Discussions followed with His Excellency General De Bono, who was particular in directing that Signor Amendola was merely to be clubbed."

The high court of justice which tried De Bono for complicity in this and other cases, was the Fascist Senate; in its findings, it states that it is true that the two carabinieri posted to safeguard Amendola were mysteriously recalled the day of the attack, that many persons saw the miltiamen preparing the attack, that it is a fact that the attackers fled to the militia barracks at Magnanapoli, and that the chauffeur, Zaccagnini, spoke to Colonel Candelori about De Bono as the official who had sanctioned the crime. But the court found insufficient evidence; this ground, in Italy, however, is in itself an accusation, for the law states that persons so freed must never hold government office, but as this was a pre-Fascist law, merely a constitutional law, Mussolini defied public opinion by appointing De Bono governor of Tripoli the night of the verdict.

The young Fascist squadristi gathered outside the offices of Amendola's newspaper, *Il Mondo*, and sang:

> *"Amendola, Amendola devi morire*
> *E col pugnale che abbiamo affilato*
> *Amendola, Amendola devi morire."*

> [*"Amendola, Amendola you must die*
> *By the stiletto which we have sharpened*
> *Amendola, Amendola you must die."*]

When this Opposition leader planned to speak in the province of Caserta, the Fascist Deputy Greco obtained an advance copy of the speech and took the text to Rossi, who took it to Mussolini. The Duce then told Greco that the Amendola demonstration must be stopped at any price. It was.

Ten days later, on leaving the Chamber, Amendola and his friends were again attacked by Fascist militia. As Amendola carried an umbrella that day, he defended himself, while the militia, although outnumbering the liberal Deputies five to one, ran away. The next afternoon the Fascist Deputies offered a resolution asking that parliamentary immunity be suspended so that Amendola could be arrested for assaulting a Fascist militia chief.

One can well believe that Amendola with an umbrella was the equal of five. He was an enormous man, about six feet high, huge but not fat, muscular and vivacious. I never spoke to him. Although I interviewed all the leaders of the Fascist government in 1925, I particularly refrained from trafficking with the Opposition, knowing that the Foreign Office would look upon such action as treason. As it was, my telegrams regarding Amendola resulted in

Mussolini's protests to our ambassador, our Mr. Fletcher, who in Mexico had shaken his fist when Carranza imprisoned an American journalist, but who, in Italy, preferred to act "diplomatically."

What I reported were the circumstances of the attempted assassination of July 20, 1925, when Amendola, already a sick man, left secretly at midnight for Montecatini for a rest cure. When Amendola arrived at the Hotel Pace there were one thousand armed Fascists waiting to kill him. Some of them had traveled twenty miles. All of them, as I learned and cabled, had received an *alerte* from the Rome Cheka headquarters which was in the same building with the militia offices, and orders had been given to the squadristi of several towns.

At first the hotel proprietor refused to surrender his guest; the Fascists then stormed the building, invading the rooms of Italians and foreigners, smashing down resisting doors, threatening with death all who stood in their way. Amendola, however, had fled in his car. An official offered him protection, but when they had ridden several miles, betrayed the chief. Several automobiles filled with Fascisti arrived and twenty men clubbed Amendola, leaving him for dead in his car. This is what I had reported. Amendola suffered agony until April 7, 1926, when he died of his wounds in southern France.

To his deathbed he called his friend Campolonghi and said:

"The Fascisti have abolished parliament, and so I have lost my liberty of speech. They have abolished the liberty of the press and so I can no longer write. They have assassinated me and so I have lost the liberty to live. All this is nothing. The evil is that they will end by assassinating Italy."

The death certificate shows Amendola died of clotting of the blood in his lungs, the result of clubbing. As a racketeer's crime it was perfect: they do not want to kill outright like their Chicago brethren.

Mussolini's *Popolo d'Italia* congratulated the squadristi.

In the case of Gobetti, the complicity of the chief Fascist condottiere is more clearly proven.

Gobetti was only twenty-five. In Turin he published a periodical called *The Liberal Revolution*, satirizing Mussolini, irritating Mussolini again. But there was not a word in Gobetti's irony which, if read in court, would sound libelous or insulting and the Duce could find absolutely no ground for suppressing the paper. Gobetti was ambushed and severely beaten. But he recovered and continued his satire. In January, 1924, Mussolini sent the following telegram to the prefect of police of Turin:[2]

> Prefect Turin I am told that Gobetti went to Paris recently but actually is in Sicily. Please inform me precisely. See to it again that life is made difficult for this stupid opponent of the Fascist government.
>
> MUSSOLINI.

Gobetti's office was pillaged, his possessions requisitioned, his correspondence stolen, his paper suppressed, and finally the prefect issued an order denying him the right to exercise the profession of journalist, his one means of making a living. The Fascist again beat up their victim and he fled to France, where, like Amendola, he died of lung trouble.

Further evidence is given by Guido Narbone, former vice-secretary of the Turin Fascisti, who writes proudly that when he and other leaders of Torinese Fascism were received by Mussolini at the Palazzo Chigi, the Duce said:

"You must act fascistically and with the maximum energy. You know Professor Gobetti in Turin? He needs a severe Fascist lesson. You are charged to give it to him."

Criticism, humor, irony—Mussolini could not withstand these forces, especially when they were employed by men of intelligence and power. The politicians, the scholars, the writers, and the journalists who attacked Mussolini with words were in turn "eliminated from circulation" or, in American slang, "put on the spot" by the student of Machiavelli.

Among the few left who dared use their voices were one or two of the great heroes of the war, and most notable among them was that same Raffaele Rossetti who, to aid d'Annunzio, had brought to Mussolini's office the enormous fund with which the nation had rewarded him.

---

[2] The original, in Mussolini's handwriting, was saved by his secretary and afterwards published.

But Rossetti, Italy's greatest war hero, was made a pacifist by his experiences in the war. He was opposed to all bloodshed. And as he watched Fascism consolidate its power by that means he became an anti-Fascist. The story of Mussolini's wrath is told in Part XII of Rossi's memorandum:

"In the spring of 1923 a Fascist ceremony took place at which, I think at Rapallo, certainly in the eastern Riviera, General De Vecchi was present. Among the onlookers was Signor Rossetti, one of the men who were awarded the gold medal for bravery during the war. He was a bitter opponent of Fascism. Although not provoked, he thought it good to arouse the anger of the majority of the crowd by calling out, 'Long live free Italy' and 'Down with Fascism.' The next day Mussolini complained of the long suffering of the Fascists of the region and expressed his astonishment that Signor De Vecchi had allowed such provocation to pass without prompt punishment. He remarked: 'Signor Rossetti, gold medal or no gold medal, was there to give provocation. Therefore, without further ado he should have been struck down dead on the spot.'"

Inasmuch as the Fascisti had failed to strike Rossetti dead, Mussolini ordered them to arrest the hero, and this was done. Rossetti, however, managed to escape from Genoa in a rowboat; he was wrecked in the Mediterranean, but dragged, more dead than alive, on to the beach at Nice, and today he is setting type in a Paris publication devoted to attacking the Fascist régime.

The physical and moral incapability of the Fascisti to tolerate criticism is called by Rossi "the fundamental fault" of the party in power; "this mentality is the key to the political tragedy of the Italian nation." In the view of H. G. Wells "the deadliest thing about Fascism is its systematic and ingenious and complete destruction of all criticism and critical opposition. It is leaving no alternative government in the land. It is destroying all hopes of recovery. The King may some day be disinterred, the Vatican may become audible again, the Populist Party of Catholic Socialism hangs on; but it is hard to imagine any of these three vestiges of the earlier state of affairs recovering enough vitality to reconstruct anew the shattered and exhausted Italy. Fascism is holding up the whole apparatus of thought and education in Italy, killing or driving out of the country every capable thinker, clearing out the last nests of independent expression in the universities. Meanwhile, its militant gestures alarm and estrange every foreign power with which it is in contact."

Men of good will, like Mr. Wells, may deplore the course of the régime and counsel the Duce to other methods. But he remains under the influence of the cynic of Realpolitik, the philosopher of dictatorship, Machiavelli, who wrote: "He who creates a tyranny and does not kill Brutus and he who creates a Free State and does not kill the sons of Brutus, will endure but a short time."

This is the guide-book to power which Mussolini read and underlined in his youth. It explains his present success.

CHAPTER XVII

Purge of the Freemasons

AFTER PERSONAL VENDETTA HAD PASSED ITS CRISIS, AFTER BRUTUS and the sons of Brutus had been "eliminated from circulation" in the brilliant euphemism of the Duce, there still remained, in addition to the impotent Opposition parties whose slogan forever was "No violence is ever justifiable," one formidable element of danger to the consolidation of the Fascist régime. This was Freemasonry.

In 1925 all the journalists resident in Rome, and notably the American, British, Scandinavian, and others who came from Protestant nations, were collectively and individually lectured by the Fascist diplomats concerning a decree Mussolini had prepared which would abolish secret organizations. We realized it was an attack on Masonry and the Foreign Office admitted it. But in this instance, we were informed, the Duce was for once doing something consistent with his past. Had he not attacked Freemasonry in 1914, when he was a Socialist, declaring that membership in both organizations was incompatible? Today it was the same with Fascism. When we asked why this was so, the answer was, "Because Masonry is a common enemy." When we protested that so far as we knew Masonry did not interfere with a man's politics, the spokesman for Mussolini explained further.

"You Americans and British," said he to the group of which I was a member, "do not realize that your Masonry and ours are as different as the tropics and the poles. Your Freemasons are all of the Scottish Rite; ours are all of the Grand Orient. While it may be true that these two organizations have relations in common, fundamentally they are different. Your Masonry is decent; it keeps out of politics, out of dirty intrigue; ours is nothing but an intriguing organization, undermining the army and the State; yours does not fight the Catholic Church, ours exists mainly for that purpose. Our Masonry is the secret enemy of the government; it is a plot against the government. Mussolini shows his consistency in always attacking Masonry, that is, Grand Orient Freemasonry."

The world press swallowed this propaganda. Every journalist cabled the viewpoint of the Fascisti and believed it. Some of them were members of the Scottish Rite. Never having had any connection with Masonry myself and, at that time, naïve enough to accept the word of all government officials as authoritative, I did likewise. It was a great surprise to me, later, to find in the official expressions of leaders and the official publications of the Order in Britain and America views completely denying the tenets of the Fascist statesmen.

However, in 1925, I did learn from the Vatican that Mussolini's decree, which did not name the Masons specifically, but abolished all secret organizations, had troubled and chagrined the Pope. The Catholic Church, I was told, was opposed to the new law. First of all, the Church was not fighting Masonry in Italy and was not the secret instigator of the decree, as had been hinted by some Fascists; secondly, the Pope realized that the law as promulgated in its ambiguous manner, could just as easily be used for the destruction of the Order of Jesuits. These views I also cabled.

Of Mussolini's rare consistency in attitude towards the Masons, the explanation is now quite simple. The Order, since its foundation, has always been a refuge for men who believed in individual and political liberty; it has always opposed dictatorship in any form, Socialist or Bolshevist or Fascist; it has always favored a constitutional government, and since the day Garibaldi impressed it with his great personal seal, it has remained the standard-bearer of freedom. That is why the most rabid of radicals, Benito Mussolini of 1914, sought to destroy it and why the most reactionary of dictators, Benito Mussolini of 1925, finally did so.

The Duke of Middlesex established the first lodge in Italy in 1773. Under warrant of the Grand Lodge of England he came to Florence and soon after the foundation, there was considerable papal opposition. In 1862 the Grand Orient of Italy was organized, and upon reorganization some eleven years later, it began to be a power. That there was antagonism between Italian Masonry and the Vatican is only too true. A writer in the *Masonic News*, an American publication, states that "owing to religious and political conditions in Italy it was almost impossible for the Grand Orient to remain outside of politics." The reason was simple: "On the one side was the Roman Catholic Church, always seeking to destroy it; on the other side was a government, suspicious of secret societies, which in Europe nearly always have a revolutionary purpose and liable at any time to fall under the control of the Vatican."

Garibaldi and Mazzini, founders of the New Italy, were both grand masters. The former addressed a letter to a general assembly in Naples, June 17, 1867, saying:

"Masonry being the oldest bulwark of liberty and justice and therefore the true antagonist of the papacy, which is the antithesis of progress and civilization, I implore all my brothers of all the Italian lodges to assist the poor Romans, oppressed by the immoral domination of the harsh enemy of Italy and Humanity." And of course it was Garibaldi who uttered the exclamation "The Vatican is a dagger in the heart of Italy."

The Freemasons, however, never did ally themselves with the radical movement in Italy, despite the anti-Vatican attitude of the latter; Masonry was religious and Christian, while the extreme radicals, of whom Mussolini, then the apostle of atheism, was the leader, were not only anti-papal but Antichrist.

When Fascism, under the atheist Duce, later began its punitive expeditions against its radical enemies, it found unexpected support in Freemasonry, and for many years, despite the suppression of the facts by the Fascisti, there was a brotherly understanding between the two organizations. From the time the first Fasci were formed until after the march on Rome Masonic lodges coöperated, went so far as to organize Fascist locals and to join the employers in subsidizing Mussolini. Professor Salvemini states that the amount of money they gave the Duce and his generals to assist in the capture of Rome was 3,500,000 lire, or $175,000. Signor Domizio Torrigiani, then grand master, published in November, 1922, a few days after Mussolini became Prime Minister, a declaration of confidence in the new government and in Fascist principles. It was not until the new party had been in power for almost a year, and when the necessity of a rapprochment with the Vatican began to impose itself, for purely opportunistic reasons, that the estrangement occurred.

Then events moved quickly—from the passage of laws to actual massacre.

First of all the decree which abolished the freedom of the press, the *sine qua non* of all Fascist repression, was of particular importance because many great and liberal papers were owned, edited, and supported by Freemasons. The journalist Mussolini realized that so long as he could not muzzle them he could not destroy them, and the decree which followed the Matteotti assassination silencing all opposition, silenced the Masons also. In 1925 the branch of the Grand Orient in Florence, the spiritual headquarters of the Order, realizing that Mussolini had begun his plans for a treaty with the Vatican and that the press muzzle was directed against it as well as the five political parties, began a violent campaign in the press. The Fascisti replied by seizing the Florence press club. Newspapers were suppressed, some were bought, editors were beaten up and all precautions taken to hold the massacre with as little publicity and opposition as possible. Freemason judges, magistrates, officials, were forced to resign, and in some instances bankers were replaced with enemies of Masonry.

Then the whispering began. In the cafés of Florence the Fascisti sat around and whispered about coming trouble, while in other cafés the Masons gathered to discuss the sinister whispers. At first they would not believe that any real danger to their lives was imminent; there would be the usual Fascist excesses, the burning of newspapers, the destruction of clubs, the clubbing of leaders, perhaps a few knife wounds and some revolver-shots were probable, but a massacre, never.

Then the atmosphere changed. "We must do all the good we can to our friends and must inflict all the harm possible on our enemies," said Mussolini. "Now as Masonry has fought us, as it has given us trouble, as it has attempted to split and divide us and as it has in certain cities succeeded in creating dissensions more than usually idiotic because of their underground origins, for all these reasons, even if there were no others, we are within our plain and sacrosanct right to defend ourselves and to proceed to the attack, because, as you are teaching me, the best defense consists in an attack."

These veiled words were followed with a notice to the press from the Fascist Directory. It is generally understood to have been written by Mussolini himself, but this has never been affirmed or denied. As it appeared in the *Battaglia Fascisti* it read:

"The Fascist Council assumes complete responsibility for the holy actions of retaliation and violence, performed by the Fascisti, even the slightest, and commands that every Fascist should endeavor to identify those unworthy Italians affiliated with Masonry so as to be able to know better what are the most useful means in order to accomplish a radical, a decisive punitive action.

"The fight against Masonry continues with a great intensity. The enemy is more ready, more prepared than before. The fight against Masonry is a fight to a finish and there is only one possible program:

"Masonry must be destroyed and Masons should have no right to citizenship in Italy. To reach this end all means are good, from the club to the gun, from the breaking of windows to the purifying fire. In one word, no avenue of escape should be left open to Masonry. . . . The Masons must be ostracized. Each and every one of their acts or movements must be stopped. Their very life must be made impossible."

The phrases "to render life difficult," to "make life impossible" for an enemy and "to remove from circulation," were well understood. The followers needed no explanation.

The massacre of the Freemasons of Florence began on the 26th of September and lasted until the 4th of October, 1925. There were at least 300 casualties and the number of dead has been estimated between 50 and 137. The order came from Rome. The massacre was not the usual wild debauch of bloodshed which characterized other Fascist "reprisals," but a highly organized, carefully planned military attack, with its objective in lives and property. "I have the names of every man in Italy inscribed on the rolls of Masonry," Mussolini had said, and the chief of the Florence Black Shirts had a list of the persons marked for death. Eighteen men were systematically murdered.

The Fascist squads, dressed in their uniforms, carrying banners and singing the "Song of Youth," went rioting in the streets (it is so strange that the thousands of our tourists who sing the praises of law and order and the trains running on time, these thousands who fled from Florence that week, have never said a word about the affair); the Fascisti looted shops, cracked safes, stopped innocent persons and felled them with their blackjacks.

Thirteen lawyers and notaries had their offices destroyed. All were Masons. One clinic was destroyed. The apartments of the Socialist Deputies Targetti and Baldesi were looted and burned. The Fascisti entered the home of one Becciolini, and during the riot he killed one of them. They returned in force, lynched him, dragged his body into the public square, and exposed it there as a warning. Cafés were looted, wine and spirits flowed in the streets, eager Fascist youth drank itself drunk and staggered. Houses were set on fire. In the week of rioting were heard the cries:

"Viva Mussolini! Viva Dumini! (My name is Dumini, twelve assassinations!)"

One of the most savage incidents was the assassination of the Socialist Deputy Gaetano Pilati, war hero and cripple. Pilati's widow tells the tragic story:[1]

"The assassination of my husband had been decided a long time in advance. I learned later from the café-keeper Pietro Serpieri, who lives opposite us, that during the month of September, 1925, my husband had been followed constantly by a young man. This man was able to inform himself on the location of our bedroom.

"The night of October 3rd a Fascist named Lupporini was killed when he entered, with a gun in his hand and followed by another militiaman, into the home of an old Freemason for the purpose of killing him. The Fascists, after having killed Benciolini, the presumed murderer of their fallen companion, organized more reprisals. Anti-Fascists were tracked down, their studies and their shops were sacked, their homes burned.

"It was almost midnight when several inhabitants of my quarter saw a black automobile, lights out, stop about 500 meters from our house. A dozen persons descended. One, drawing his revolver, stayed to guard the chauffeur. The others went along the Africo, obliging

[1] In *Liberta*, Paris, July 24, 1927.

all whom they met to run. In the street Fratelli Dandolo, where our house was, many were at their windows, watching the burning of the furniture of the Honorable Baldesi which had been thrown into the street. The Fascists fired several shots in the air, summoning all to withdraw. This did not stop anyone, the lights being out, to follow events in the street and in our house, by looking through the shutters.

"That evening my husband returned late after paying his workmen, and after dining, retired, being very weary. We slept so soundly neither heard nor perceived what happened in the street.

"Suddenly we were awakened by a great noise. I lighted the room. Before us was a man, small, sinister, with a hat over his eyes. He brandished two revolvers. A second person, who had also entered our room, approached my husband and in a menacing voice said, 'Dress and follow me to Fascist headquarters.'

" 'I will follow you,' replied my husband, and seated on the bed began to put on his trousers on the one leg he had left after the war.

" 'Come quickly,' said the Fascist. 'Are you really Pilati?'

" 'Yes.'

"Hardly had he said that word when the two bandits discharged their revolvers at him.

"After receiving the first shot in his left shoulder, my husband rolled from the bed to the door, either because he wanted to leave the bed so as not to expose me to more shots, or to block the door to our son's room.

"Maddened by terror, I screamed.

"At the open window suddenly appeared the sinister figure of a third bandit.

"I heard another shot, and the man who had already spoken cried, 'Quick, quick, let us depart.'

"He had hardly gone when my husband, groaning painfully, said to me: 'Look, look, how many wounds. Give me a bandage.'

"Another tenant saw the bandits flee. One of them, while the chauffeur was blowing his horn for all to return, proposed to them: 'Let's go have a drink on me. I was the one who killed him, you know.'

"My husband was taken on a stretcher to the hospital of Santa Maria Nuova. To the porter who asked what had happened to him he replied:

"'The Austrians have mutilated me; the Italians have murdered me.'

"After three days of agony he breathed his last . . . the funeral, by order of the police, was held secretly.

"In March, 1926, during the hearing, I was confronted with Ermini, who was defended by the attorney Meschiari. I, however, was unable to find an attorney to take the case. I recognized without hesitation, one of the assassins.

"When the day came for the trial I was the victim of all sorts of pressure and threats for the purpose of making me deny the identity of Ermini. I was offered much money, which I refused with indignation.

"I asked for passports for myself and my son. I was told I would get them if I would give up going to the trial. Everyone was organized to conquer my resistance, the Attorney Pacchi, the Colonel Lanari, the Deputy Delcroix, the prefect.

"Finally the attorney who had charge of my interests was summoned by the prefecture and by the Fascio to abandon me.

"I had to resign myself to do without assistance.

"The trial began in Chieti at the end of April. I was exhausted, sick, I was in bed. But the fear of betraying my dead husband by my absence gave me a new strength.

"At the trial I was veritably attacked by the lawyers. But I remained firm and confirmed my identification of Ermini.

"The assassins were acquitted. At Florence they posted police at my house. The assassins returned to my quarter, amusing themselves by coming under the windows and insulting me."

The listing of Masonic leaders and their destruction was partly the work of the head of the Florentine Fascio, Luporini, who, as fate would have it, was accidentally shot in a scuffle. It was the death of Luporini which supplied the immediate reason for holding the massacre in September.

On Sunday, October 4th, so many British, American, and other foreign citizens had been clubbed and robbed that the terrified tourists fled to the consulates for refuge. The American, British, and Swiss consuls raised their flags, as if for a holiday or for a war, the frightened nationals poured into the diplomatic buildings, and the consuls telegraphed their protests directly to Mussolini. It was the next day that Farinacci sent word to Florence, "Cease hostilities."

More than a week of rioting and murder and hardly a word in the foreign press about a state of revolution in one of the most beautiful and popular tourist centers of Europe. For Fascist censorship it was a great success. The cables were stopped in the post-offices, telegrams to Paris held up, letters opened, the foreign journalists held almost incommunicado. Then the Fascist press bureau began issuing statements which the venal Stefani agency, the Italian journalists representing the American papers, and some leading but betrayed American and British reporters, accepted as true and sent out. In these Fascist reports it was stated that the Masons and the Socialists had attacked a Fascist without warning and killed him, that the mob demanded vengeance and acted without authority. The government then pacified the city.

It was more than a week after the massacre before the honest journalists saw that the official reports were not true, but then it was too late to send out sensational news; the matter was now historical —and therefore dead. The *Ligue des Droits de l'Homme* later sent its protest:

"The savage onslaught on Masonry now organized at Mussolini's instigation is nothing more than a move to use these artificially provoked sanguinary upheavals as a plea for indefinitely putting off the date of the Matteotti trial: because Mussolini knows that the public hearing of the evidence in court it will not be possible for him to prevent the disclosure of his own direct personal participation in the atrocious crime, as having given the order to the murderers."

But that was not news, either.

A correspondent was invited to ask Mussolini questions about the massacre of the Freemasons. "Could your Excellency explain the reason for the Fascist war on Masonry?" His Excellency could:

"I am very glad you asked that question because there is a lot of misunderstanding in Anglo-Saxon countries over this question. We must once and for all make clear the great difference between Eng-

lish and American Masonry and the political Masonry of Italy. . . .
Italian Masons have nothing in common with English Masons except the name. . . . The work of Masonry on behalf of our independence has been much exaggerated.

"The sect must be absolutely abolished because its influence is
deleterious to discipline in the army, to the impartiality of the courts,
and a subversion of order that should obtain in all public offices.
Masonry has overturned all regulations. . . .

"Fortunately, Fascism has struck Italian Masonry such a blow
that it will be difficult for it to regain its legs again for some time.
. . . The grave attempt on my life on the anniversary of our glorious
victory, and the plot to throw the whole nation into disorder, show
what a sinister influence the Masonic sect—which undoubtedly inspired the criminal attempt on my life—has on the minds even of
Italians who, because of their social position and past military experience, ought to be better able to understand the folly and shame of
this latest exploit."

This "latest exploit" to which Mussolini refers is the Zaniboni plot
which will be told in due time. William Bird, the noted journalist
from Paris where he was free of censorship quoted one of Mussolini's admirers as informing him that "either Mussolini is rapidly
going mad or else the worst elements among his entourage have so
completely dominated him that he is longer free to act according to
his own judgment. This so-called plot is too obviously trumped up
to deceive anybody. It was intended simply as a pretext for dissolv-
ing the United Socialist Party and for closing the Masonic lodges."

The other point emphasized by Mussolini in his interview, the
difference between the Scottish Rite and the Grand Orient types of
Masonry is further shot to pieces by John Bond of the Fellowship
Forum, who tells what happened to the Scottish lodge at the time
the Fascists were killing the Masons of Florence. He states:

"In Rome the Masons of the Scottish Rite had their offices in the
great palace right opposite the church of the Jesuits. . . . While a
meeting of the lodge was in progress, Mussolinian thugs armed with
cudgels broke down the doors, beat the members of the lodge, and
then set fire to the premises. . . . No mention was made in the
Roman newspapers.

"Commendatore Raoul Palermi, the Grand Master of the Scottish Rite, well-known to leading Masons all over the world, a scholar and a gentleman in the truest sense of the word, had to give up his home in Rome, as several attempts had been made to break in and set it on fire. He had been spared in the general massacre because he enjoyed the esteem of men who were close to the King. . . . He was 'advised' by the prefect of the Roman police to leave Rome . . . and went to a little town near Palermo. . . . One morning he was found unconscious in his writing-room, stabbed. The police gave out a statement to his friends (no news of the fact was permitted to appear in the press) that the wounds seemed to have been self-inflicted. Happily they were not fatal."

It is an obvious fact that the Scottish Rite was suppressed in Italy, and it is another obvious fact that Fascist propaganda has not only ignored this, but perverted the news for the press. Mussolini frequently has come to his own defense with vast vague attacks. Thus on one occasion he links Masonry with Bolshevism when he speaks of "Italy's imps, the red dabblers, our organization of so-called Freemasons." Again he resorts to his habitual characteristic methods of using foul language; thus he cautions us not to forget that "this shady institution with its secret nature has always had in Italy a character typical of the briber and the blackmailer . . . the Masons of Italy have always represented a distortion, not only in political life, but in spiritual concepts. . . . Its secret character throughout the twentieth century, its mysterious meetings, abhorrent to our beautiful communities with their sunlight and their love of truth, gave to the sect the character of corruption, a crooked concept of life, without program, without soul, without moral value. . . . For my direct, methodical, consistent course of policy the hate of the Masonic sect persecutes me even now. . . . This is a war without quarter, a war of which I am a veteran. . . . I have always had against me our Masonry. But that organization, which in other times was very powerful, has been beaten by me. Against me it did not and cannot win. Italians won this battle for me. They found the cure for this leprosy. . . . I obeyed the positive command of my conscience, and not any opportunism. My attitude had nothing in common with the anti-Masonic spirit of the Jesuits."

And finally he speaks of the "corrupting, sinister, tortuous power as that of international Masonry of a political type, as distinguished from the Masonry known in the Anglo-Saxon countries." But here again a question of veracity arises. For despite all the Duce's efforts to distinguish between the two Masonries, an effort which for a while deceived the foreign press and aided in the apology for the massacre of Florence, we find that the Scottish Rite has everywhere stood by the Grand Orient. Thus, in the official organ of the Supreme Council 33° A. & A. Scottish Rite of Freemasonry S. J., U. S. A. the blood bath of Florence was denounced in this editorial opinion:

"The millions of Masons throughout the world at the present can only look on, impotent for the time being, to help their oppressed brethren in Italy, but their distress awakens the deepest sympathy. Masons of the world, especially the three millions of the Craft in this country, are well aware of the issues involved and their hearts vibrate with compassion for their suffering brethren overseas.

"There can be no doubt of the ultimate result. For the time the tyrant prospers. . . . The despot must fall, the wrong be dethroned and righteousness come to victory. In that day Freemasonry in Italy will be vindicated. It will be seen that the Craft has been the victim of malicious slander and that the people of Italy have no better friends than the men who wear the apron of the Masonic Order."

According to an American masonic investigation, the Fascisti destroyed 1,000 lodges and clubs, pillaging most of them, throwing the emblems into the street or auctioning them off with a ribald ceremony, and burning what they could not dispose of otherwise.

Grand master of the Grand Orient Domizio Torrigiani was deported to the isle of Ponza; General Luigi Capello, once commander of the Italian Second Army, was sentenced to thirty years imprisonment and became convict No. 3246; General Roberto Bencivenga, former chief of the general staff of General Cadorna, was also deported to Ponza.

Whether Masonry was guilty of anti-Fascist activities cannot be answered definitely. One fact is certain: from the time the Masons of Italy ceased to give money and moral support to Fascism, from the time they saw Fascism assume all authority and realized that

Mussolini was waging war against the lodges and their leaders, they began to draw to themselves all those who hoped for another risorgimento. Garibaldi had once called Masonry his bulwark of liberty; perhaps some new leader, some new Matteotti or Amendola, would join with Masonry and under the banner of the Aventine Opposition rally all elements for another battle of restoration of personal and public rights. So Masons thought in 1925. In destroying Masonry, therefore, Mussolini destroyed the one great secret habitat of a possible future enemy, an enemy which might prove dangerous to his soaring will to maintain himself throughout his lifetime in full and absolute power.

★ ★

CHAPTER XVIII

Mussolini Conquers the Mafia

AMONG THE MINOR FORCES DANGEROUS TO THE PROGRESS OF
Fascism was the Mafia, the secret terroristic organization which
was particularly active in Sicily and the southern provinces. This
menace Mussolini met and in his typical way conquered. It is one
of the achievements most loudly and universally acclaimed in the
press.

Especially vociferous are the pæan singers in America, where,
during the great and golden era of Prohibition, a system closely allied
to the Mafia flourished in the big cities and took its toll of millions
if not billions of dollars. Racketeering is not yet dead in America.
But few realize how closely allied it is to the Italian system.

In the early 1920's the present writer employed as his assistant in
Rome an Italian journalist named Camillo Cianfarra, who had for
many years served in the Italian diplomatic service and who had
made a survey of Italian emigrant activities in the United States.
Part of his work was to investigate crime in the United States, to
watch, study, and report on the number of Italians engaged in
criminal activities, so that the records in their home towns to which
they frequently returned could be kept efficiently.

When Colonel McCormick of the *Chicago Tribune* asked the Rome
bureau to investigate the question of Italian predominance in Chicago
racketeering, Cianfarra naturally undertook this work. His explanation of Italian criminality in America was simple and frank. In
Sicily, in the old days, he had found that the judges made it a point
to encourage habitual criminals, cut-throats, murderers, and bandits
to emigrate to America. As this was before Mussolini restored capital
punishment, it was found cheaper to deport murderers and gunmen
than sentence them to life imprisonment and feed them in Italy.

When a murderer appeared before a Sicilian judge the latter would say, well, it's life imprisonment for you, and the sentence will be pronounced Thursday morning. That is, if you are here. But there is a boat for New York on Wednesday.

And that is how many of Italy's worst citizens came to America. But when American laws were passed aimed most directly at that country, and a few American consuls took seriously the State Department's orders for selective emigration, the result was that bandits had a hard time getting to the United States.

Under these circumstances Mussolini had a brilliant idea. He found that in reality there were two big secret terror organizations called indiscriminately the Mafia. The one protected the countryside, the other the city, the one levied tribute on farmers, the other on urban merchants, and among themselves they fought. Everyone was a victim. If a peasant wanted to take a bullock-load of vegetables into Naples or Palermo he had to pay a small percentage to some gangster who would assure him "safety" on the trip both ways and his money. Likewise city merchants were mulcted. Sicily saw the origin of all the beer and movie and pants-pressing rackets of Chicago and it happened generations ago.

Mussolini soon realized that the urban Mafia was far superior to the rural Mafia. S. S. McClure, one of Mussolini's best apologists in America, believed that Sicily was "under a tyranny of the worst and most powerful criminal oligarchy that ever existed," making the American urban system of murder, robbery, blackmail, kidnapping, and other forms of violence "mild" in comparison. In the province of Palermo there were 1,750 murders in one year: Chicago would have to have 7,000 murders a year in place of 300 to equal it.

These thousands of Mafiosi, who for half a century had become a great power in the American underworld, who had established the Black Hand system in the Italian colonies in New York, Chicago, and other large centers, and who were later to take the leadership in bootlegging and racketeering, were now doomed to remain in Italy.

To meet the situation Mussolini appointed the Honorable Carnazza governor of Sicily and sent Cesare Mori to Palermo as prefect.

Some forty years ago Mori, an artillery officer, entered the police department as a delegato, the lowest rank, and began his new career in Trapani, which, with Palermo, shared the reputation of being the centers of Mafia activities. His chief work was rounding up the cattle-maimers whose specialty was hamstringing the livestock of landowners who refused to pay their "contributions." It was racketeering in its purest Chicago form.

So successful was Mori that he gained advancement and medals for courage, military, and civil valor. When Nitti was made Prime Minister he gave Mori the highest rank, quaestor in Rome.

In 1923, when Mussolini had been in power almost a year, the leading urban business men of Sicily came to Rome with the request that Mori be sent back to command the forces against the Mafia. Naturally enough, these prominent gentlemen who had contributed liberally to the Fascist cause wanted their business protected by the new government, instead of the bandits who were preaching "the pernicious doctrine that the police and the law were the enemies of the common people," and who were extremely active in levying a tax on the wealthy city merchants.

Mori, who did not play politics, went to work as a soldier; but Carnazza, who was a Fascist politician, carried out orders from Rome.

Mussolini, adding a new twist to the axiom, *divesa et impera,* ordered that a distinction be made between the city and the rural bandits; the former, which was the larger section, was armed and given moral encouragement, while the latter division was proscribed. Under these circumstances country banditry soon disappeared.

Mussolini then incorporated the urban branch of the Mafia into the Black Shirt militia. According to Don Sturzo it was the Honorable Carnazza who in addition to all their other weapons added the Fascist manganello to the Mafia equipment, and Bolitho, after an investigation two years later, found that "Carnazza took into his service the celebrated Mafia and the hardly less redoubtable 'squadra del baltico' for whom he found much employment in the elections."

The addition of this criminal element to the armed forces of the new state made itself felt. According to Gilbert Murray, "many parts of Italy have long been accustomed to the rule of private extra-legal societies like the Camora, the Mafia, and the Black Hand. The Fascist Society is only a Camorra on a grand scale."

Today there is no longer a vegetable-racket Sicily. The peasants come in peace, the merchants haggle in peace, and quiet reigns. Because the Mafiosi, the Black-handers, have been transferred throughout the kingdom, doing their work on a national scale, levying taxation upon men and industries, administering castor oil to small offenders, shooting workingmen who attempt to flee into Switzerland or France, clubbing critics of the government and generally engaging in the old racket.

Their work is to get the money from the little men and to keep the little men in the Fascist line. For big-time work there are more important persons, the podestas, the minor dictators of cities and provinces. Thus the street-repaving job in Rome in Holy Year 1925 was found recently to have entailed a graft of $350,000 for the Black Camorra, while other municipal improvements so highly praised by Holy Year pilgrims netted another big sum. In Milan racketeering reached unprecedented heights. In many cities and rural districts Fascist Party racketeers levy tribute on their original backers, the big banks and industries. Following is a sample instance, a communiqué sent by the ras of the province of Pesaro Urbino to the wealthy:

"I have audited recently the amount of subventions given the Fascio by the proprietors in this province.

"It is useless for me to declare that I do not know how to employ so much money flowing into our treasury.

"Certain gentlemen, proprietors of many millions, have offered us sums which, in proportion to the capital which Fascism has saved them, amounts to almost nothing. On this account, considering that by the system we have employed up to now we have taken in practically nothing, I warn the proprietors of the province of Pesaro Urbino that I will impose upon them taxes in proportion to their capital and in such a fashion that I soon will be able to systematize definitely the financial situation of our province."

So it is that today when a black shirt is buttoned over a leading Fascist bosom, the fingers frequently are those of an old Black Hand. When an automobile sideswiped another, somewhere in New York or Chicago in the old bad days, when a stream of sub-machine gun bullets "rubbed out" a gangster, the finger on the trigger very likely was that of an old Mafiosi of Sicily who had been able to get away in time. And when a man is put on the spot, whether in Italy or America, it is frequently by the same common methods because the same type of men from the same native towns are employed. Fascism instead of deracinating the Black Hand, Camorra, and Mafia system, found a new use for its clever members.

Instead of terrorizing, extorting money,[1] or killing for the purpose of private gain, the "totalitarian" Mafiosi are trained to employ their talents "for national and patriotic purposes." They are dispersed throughout the country and some have important positions in the new secret-service organization which the new régime found necessary for its existence.

[1] During the general strike in August, 1922, the following note was employed in several provinces:

National Fascist Party
Fascist Secret Provincial Committee of Action

We Fascisti are sacrificing our lives to smash this strike by every means. It is your duty to aid our movement financially in order to save the nation.

We therefore ask you to turn over to the bearer of this message — lire.

(signed) Secret Committee of Action.

CHAPTER XIX

The Cheka—spelled Ceca or Ovra

POWER RESTS ON FEAR AS WELL AS THE CONSENT OF THE GOV-
erned. The corner policeman still plays a part in our lives. We,
the fortunate who are governed by a President, a Congress or a
parliament whom we elect and who are not dictated to by a man
in absolute power, frequently may protest actions by the forces of
law and order as terroristic, but we cannot, even when we go touring
in foreign lands, completely realize the state of fear that exists under
a political system which employs terror as an instrument.

Even in time of war, when an enemy occupies a country, the very
necessary mass terrorism which frees the rulers from the alternative
of appointing one policeman for every inhabitant is mild in comparison to the dictatorial system.

Terrorism is the finest and cheapest weapon of the modern tyrant.
But if he wishes to avoid the ignominious fate of a weakling, a
Primo de Rivera for example, the tyrant of our day must be ruthless,
unsentimental, unswerving; he must have little regard for human
life; he must be implacable and he must remain fixed on the idea of
survival.

To meet that problem Mussolini found that the methods of his
predecessors were useless. After he had dispersed all the organized
elements of opposition, from the political parties to the comparatively
unimportant Mafia in the south, he realized that he had to employ
the same terroristic organizations which the rulers of Russia forced
upon Lenin in 1918 when leniency with enemies of the régime resulted in many plots and the attempted assassination of the head of
the government.

Mussolini already had his bodyguard, his little group of men who
carried out the secret orders. He now began to build a powerful

organization. At the same time he made public and press statements denying its existence and one day had the courage to repeat them to the Chamber of Deputies.

"Gentlemen," he said, "I am the one who brings forth in this hall the accusations against myself.

"It has been said that I would have founded a 'Cheka.'

"Where? When? In what way? Nobody is able to say. Russia has executed without trial from 150,000 to 160,000 people, as shown by statistics almost official. There has been a Cheka in Russia which has exercised terror systematically over all the middle classes and over the individual members of those classes, a Cheka which said it was the red sword of revolution. *But an Italian Cheka never had a shadow of existence.*

"Nobody has ever denied that I am possessed of these three qualities: a discreet intelligence, a lot of courage, and an utter contempt for the lure of money.

"If I had founded a Cheka I would have done it following the lines of reasoning that I have always used in defending one kind of violence that can never be eliminated from history.

"I have always said—and those who have always followed me in these five years of hard struggle can now remember it—that violence, to be useful in settling anything, must be surgical, intelligent, and chivalrous. Now, all the exploits of any so-called Cheka have always been unintelligent, passionate, and stupid.

"Can you really think that I could order—on that day following the anniversary of Christ's birth when all saintly spirits are hovering near—can you think that I could order an assault at ten o'clock in the morning? . . . Please do not think me such an idiot."

Yet despite his calling on all saintly spirits that Christmas day, 'despite his disavowal of violence, a Cheka which, it is true, still had no name or definite organization, was already flourishing in Italy in the Year One, Era Fascista. The Saint-Just of the Italian terror system was that same Rossi who was so prominent in the Matteotti case. He himself was a great admirer of Djerdzinsky of Russia, and commonly among themselves, Mussolini, Rossi, Dumini, and the others referred to their little group as the "Ceca" which in Italian is pronounced Cheka.

Following the threatened uprising in 1924 it was nationalized. According to its chief, "Several days before the Matteotti tragedy, facing the acts, gestures of indiscipline, and nonchalance of Fascist Deputies, such as Rocca and Ravazzola, Mussolini before me and others of the National Directorate, expressed his astonishment that the party police, the famous 'Ceca,' had given no sign of life. On that occasion he said in absolute tranquillity, 'Action against these parliamentary gentlemen cannot be taken by any legal arm; we deplore, we expel, we demand the resignations, but they do not give a darn. . . . There is nothing to do but beat them without mercy. This Ceca, does it function or not?'

"The mother-idea of this Ceca was Mussolini's alone. . . . The necessity of an organ for defense and for vengeance was explained by Mussolini as follows: 'The régime does not yet dispose of legal means for beating its enemies. Laws which exist represent the liberal spirit against which Fascism has arisen. To fill in this gap all governments in a state of transition have need of illegal powers to put their adversaries in place.'

"If as a result, in the activity of the Cheka there were committed acts which were arbitrary and inopportune, this does not diminish the responsibility of its author, Mussolini. To attribute them solely to Rossi and Marinelli is the height of audacity and puerility."

Several years ago, when the Cheka was still a mystery, Paolo Valera made the declaration that this organization was a part of the Ministry of the Interior and "appears to be a society of criminals and assassins. Its chief . . . is said to be Cesare Rossi, head of the press bureau of the Ministry. . . . Its agents are famous for their crimes." Prezzolini, one of the rare intellectuals who have spoken in favor of the régime, admits that "the Matteotti and preceding crimes force the admission that there existed a veritable criminal association preparing and executing the attacks and destruction inspired by Cesare Rossi."

So long as the censorship flourished and foreign correspondents were afraid to write anything which might offend Mussolini or were covetous of his good will, the Cheka was never mentioned. But on July 13, 1925, came the supreme test for honest journalists. It was on that day that of the 140 members of parliament who had seceded more than 100 signed an indictment against the Cheka. The signatories were not only Socialists who were mourning their secretary-general and leader, but also the representatives of the Catholic, Republican, Democratic, and Liberal Parties. Said this document:

"The conclusion is that the inquiry conducted by the High Court has brought out evidence more than sufficient to show that under the auspices of the Head of the Government (Mussolini), men in confidence sharing the functions if not the real and proper responsibilities of government, organized crimes to punish Deputies for their opposition to the régime; and that for the preparation of these crimes there was a special collective organization (Cheka) of which several members are known."

Journalists who cabled the above became *persona non grata* with the Fascist government and were expelled.

On the 29th of May, 1923, Misuri, member of parliament, who had quit the Fascist Party and therefore earned the undying hatred of its leader, made a speech of criticism to which the Duce replied by a public threat of punishment. Almost immediately Misuri was attacked by Cheka men and beaten up. In a statement to the press[1] Misuri charged Mussolini with giving orders for the assault to several gangsters, but there was no contradiction to this statement, no libel suit.

"The Misuri incident," reported James Murphy, "is a definite landmark and probably marks the first official operation of the Cheka in its official functioning as a normal organ of the government."

The complete exposure of the Cheka as a murder organization and also as a racket was made before the Senate of Rome by Dr. Donati, editor of the Catholic newspaper *Il Popolo*, during the trial of General De Bono. The evidence states in part:

"The criminal association—or the Cheka, as it is more commonly called—bound together under a pact of mutual common action in crime the highest leaders of Fascism (Rossi, Marinelli, and so forth), the professional assassins (Dumini, Volpi, and so forth), and the non-official coadjutors (*Corriere Italiano,* Filippelli, and so forth). It had its headquarters in a government building, the Viminal, where

[1] *Il Popolo,* Rome, December 21, 1924.

Senator De Bono also had his dual headquarters, as Director-General of Police and Chief of the Militia.

"The Cheka, which had already existed in embryonic form, was endowed with a regular constitution of its own at a meeting held in the private residence of the Premier, in the Via Rasella. Among those present was General De Bono, who had already been appointed Director-General of Police and First Commander-General of the Militia. There is explicit mention of this meeting in the affidavit drawn up by Finzi, which was submitted to three gentlemen who can give evidence as to its contents. These are Signor Schiff Giorgini, Commendatore Guglielmo Emmanuel head of the Roman office of the *Corriere della Sera*, and the journalist Carlo Silvestri. This is also borne out by the evidence which these gentlemen have already given before the Crown Prosecutor and confirmed by Finzi himself in a recent conversation which he had with Silvestri. Therefore the Cheka represented a constitutional organ of the Fascist Party and the Fascist Government.

"As we shall see, the Cheka was entrusted with a two-fold task: (1) to spy attentively on all movements of political parties and persons opposed to Fascism, also on lukewarm friends and open dissenters; (2) to suppress the more dangerous adversaries by violence in style,[2] under an astute system of protection which ensured the immunity of the assassins and their paymasters.

"The executive of the Cheka is identical with the General Command of the militia. The General Command recruited the hired assassins, furnished the material and financial means, arranged the plans, gathered information, provided—through the office of the Premier's press agency (Cesare Rossi)—for the 'working up' of public opinion, and made arrangements with the police authorities to guarantee the immunity of the direct culprits.

---

[2] "Bastonatura in stile" (bastinadoing in style) is the technical phrase used in the orders sent out from the headquarters of the National militia. It stands for a distinct type of cudgeling, and those who are entrusted with the task have been specially trained in the barracks, where they have a dummy figure on which they practise. The weapon used is a specially made bludgeon which is rather heavy towards the end and is somewhat flexible. Most of the blows are inflicted on the lower part of the face, for the purpose of breaking the jawbone and thus laying up the victim for months. Care is taken not to fracture the skull, lest death may ensue.

"The Cheka was considered as an instrument necessary for the government of the country, according to the literal expression used by Finzi in his affidavit. To this Cheka organization we are to attribute the well-known acts of violence committed against the Deputies Mazzolani, Misuri, Buffoni, Amendola, Forni, Bergamini, Nitti, and the journalist Giannini; also the murder of Father Giovanni Minzoni at Argenta, the murder of the laborer Antonio Piccinini, Socialist candidate in Reggio Emilia, and the murder of Matteotti."

While the Fascist Senate failed to indict General De Bono for complicity in the murder of Matteotti "for lack of sufficient evidence," it did not deny Donati's charges that there was a Cheka functioning in Italy and even referred to it as "the committee which has been organized against the enemies of Fascism." In corroboration of Donati's charges there were General Balbo's letter about the Minzoni murder, the confessions of Rossi and Filippelli, and other sworn statements, most of which the Senate refused to read. Threatened with immediate death, the Catholic editor fled to France the day the Senate report was issued.

In January, 1926, the French government discovered how vast and international the Fascist Cheka had become when Ricciotti Garibaldi, one of the grandsons of the founder of Italian liberty, who seemingly was active in France in the struggle for restoration of freedom in his native land, was arrested by the police of Nice.

At the trial, in November, testimony was given that there was a conspiracy in southern France to organize two armies, one of Spaniards, the other of Italians, and march against the dictators. Garibaldi had involved Colonel Francesco Macia, the ardent Catalonian patriot (and after the Spanish revolution, governor of Catalonia) in gun-running to Spain, and had furnished the information to Mussolini directly, so that the Italian dictator could retail it to his Spanish colleague De Rivera and thus further their secret treaty of coöperation and good-will. Moreover, Garibaldi had conspired with gunmen in Paris, with leading Freemasons and republicans, and with labor leaders and patriots who saw in him the possible liberator of Italy. So cleverly did he do his work that even Fascist agents were fooled. Thus Luigi Villari at the time wrote that the "neo-Garibaldian movement was being prepared under the leadership of,

Ricciotti Garibaldi, Junior . . . with the support of Italian and French Freemasonry. The aim was actually to attempt an armed invasion of Italy. . . ."

Villari indignantly reports meetings between the Paris Freemasons, Garibaldi and Torrigiani, head of the Grand Orient of Italy, and connects them all with the conspiracy of Tito Zaniboni to assassinate Mussolini. The fact is that Garibaldi was sent by Mussolini to do several jobs as an agent provocateur, but his main purpose in going to France was twofold: to earn 2,000,000 lire for stealing the documents signed by Mussolini[3] from Signor Fasciolo, one-time secretary to the Duce, and to earn another 2,000,000 if he succeeded in putting Fasciolo "out of circulation." He succeeded in neither of these things, but he did earn 645,000 lire for what he did accomplish.

On November 6th it was reported that "Garibaldi confessed to being an agent provocateur, a stool pigeon in the pay of Mussolini. Mussolini's government is exposed as deliberately fomenting plots; as sending its secret agents to France to play the spy and traitor; as paying 100,000 francs in a single sum for a mean piece of work done on French territory in violation of the French laws."[4]

The official criminal-court record at the Paris trial shows Garibaldi confessing that he had intrigued with a man named Scevoli to go on a mission to Rome; having obtained Scevoli's passport, Garibaldi sent it to Lapolla, chief of the Fascist police, who used it for secret trips between Garibaldi and Mussolini.

Of the 645,000 lire received, Garibaldi confessed, 400,000 came from Federzoni. Papers and letters from Federzoni and from Gino Lucetti, one of the would-be assassins of Mussolini, were introduced and read. At the close of the first day's hearings there was more than a suspicion that Garibaldi might have been involved in a plot to assassinate the Duce for the benefit of dissenting Fascist leaders, of whom the most notable in 1926 was Federzoni, the nationalist and royalist.

The second day's hearings, which coincided with reports from Rome of 100 dead and 1,000 wounded in the three-day riots which

---

[3] Gobetti telegram, etc., and letters relative to the American oil deal of 1924.
[4] *New York World*, November 6, 1926.

the Fascists carried out as reprisals for the Zaniboni shooting, Ricciotti was confronted by Sante Garibaldi.

"There is not one among us who would not have gone blindly to death at the bidding of this man, because of the name he bears," said Sante Garibaldi, pointing at Ricciotti; and then addressing the latter: "If you have the lightest sense of honor left, there is but one thing remaining for you to do. What are you waiting for? Why don't you beat out your brains against a wall?"

"I am a victim of fatality," muttered Garibaldi. He had come to court wearing his monocle and his Legion of Honor ribbon; he had tried for a few minutes to deny and to brave it out, but now he was almost in tears. "It was Mussolini who led me into a trap," he concluded.

"Traitor," shouted Sante Garibaldi; "you have dragged the name of our family, glory, and honor into the mire."

"I am a victim of an awful fatality," mumbled Ricciotti, "I have taken money, it is true, but I have not betrayed the cause of liberty." He fell on his knees, clasped the hand of his young brother to his lips, and asked forgiveness.

Macia and Garibaldi were found guilty. Mussolini apologized to France.

Altogether there were nineteen conspirators on trial. Maître Torres defended Colonel Macia.

"It is true. I admit," said the Catalonian patriot to the court. "It was my duty as a patriot. When I am free I will begin again." He confessed that the Catalonian arms were shipped as "brooms" to sweep out Catalonia; bayonets were marked "toothpicks," and rifles "flutes."

Garibaldi, Macia, and sixteen others were given short terms in prison for possessing firearms; as the seventeen men came up for sentence, each in turn dramatically walked past Garibaldi, pointed at the chest full of hero medals, and uttered the word "Traitor."

The trial also brought out the following facts:

That there existed in Europe and America a large organization of spies and agents provocateurs in the pay of Fascism.

That acts of violence committed in Paris, New York, Buenos Aires, and other big Italian centers against Fascists are frequently instigated by Fascist agents themselves for the purpose of furnishing pretexts for prosecutions and protests from the Italian government.

That Italian state functionaries did not hesitate to "sequester" persons, steal documents in foreign countries, and instigate attempts at assassination.

That all such actions were developed with the assistance of the Italian embassies. Ricciotti, for example, received his money and instructions in the diplomatic mail-bag to France.

All the foregoing is legal testimony; the French government has acted upon it, the Italian government has made amends, yet in Mussolini's autobiography there is only this reference: "The maneuver of the former Premiers definitely failed and became ridiculous, just as did other artificial structures attempted about that time. One was a movement inspired by Benelli, under the name of the Italian League, to create secession from Fascism, and another an underhand maneuver by some short-weight grandchildren of Garibaldi." Apparently the employee was not worthy of his hire.

It is of course possible for the head of a government, the founder of a secret police, to remain ignorant of its ramifications, its plottings, and its assassinations. Perhaps Mussolini never knew that the "short-weight grandchildren of Garibaldi" were employees of his own Cheka.

That the consulates abroad have been filled with Fascist squadrist leaders or former racketeers is generally admitted. Some of these young men now occupying diplomatic positions have never been anything but leaders of the "reprisal" gangs which terrorized small towns, administered castor oil, burned, looted, beat up those adversaries pointed out to them by Fascist political leaders. Street fights, political assassinations, and espionage trials have proven that everywhere the Italian embassies and consulates are centers of Fascist intrigue.

Several high Fascist officials were some time ago recalled from Brazil to explain numerous "incidents." There have been demonstrations against the embassy and consulates in which not only anti-Fascisti, but native Brazilians, have taken part as retaliation for Fascist racketeering. In San Paulo the police had to rescue the

Fascist consul from an infuriated mob. In Buenos Aires a Fascist consul tried by force to shanghai an anti-Fascist engineer who was visiting an Italian warship; the result was a fist fight and a public scandal; another consul to Brazil was accused of plotting the murder of a rich man in order to marry the widow; in Argentine a Fascist consul was arrested for dealing in obscene post cards. Almost all the consuls were members of the former squadristi.

In a more recent international scandal, in Brussels, it was testified in court that the Fascist agent Menapace, who planted the dynamite, revolver, and incriminating papers in the home and pockets of the anti-Fascist journalist, Cianca, was an employee of the Italian embassy. Menapace was exposed by the liberal paper *Le Soir*, but the embassy succeeded in helping him to escape the country. Some time later the pro-Fascist newspaper of Switzerland, *Suisse*, demanded the withdrawal of the Italian consul at St. Gall and eight other Fascist spies, so flagrant had become the racketeering in that canton. The Swiss government easily expelled the eight gangsters, but had to negotiate with the Italian ambassador because the Fascist gangster-consul claimed diplomatic immunity.

After four years of officially denying the existence of a Ceca, or Cheka, Mussolini, by virtue of Article 8 of the law of November 25, 1926, "legalized" the organization by establishing exceptional tribunals "for the defense of the State," a euphemism which the French used during the Commune, and the Soviets in 1918. The law provided that it was to remain active until December 6, 1931, Mussolini expressing the hope that within five years he would extirpate all opposition. Meanwhile a new penal code was written, which went into effect July 1, 1931. But the Fascist Party, realizing that its strength of a little more than 1,500,000 was not enough to intimidate the majority, held a special session of the Grand Council on March 6, 1931, which decided that "political crimes, as comprehended by the new penal code, must be submitted to the special tribunal for the defense of the State, whose functions are prolonged until 1936." The special tribunal is the O. V. R. A., Organizzazione Vigilanza Repressione Antifascismo;[5] it is the terroristic arm of Fascism and Mussolini's personal vengeance; it is

[5] Also called Opera Volontaria Repressione Antifascista.

the old bastard child of Fascism, the Ceca, grown up and legitimatized by its brilliant father.

Today the work of the O. V. R. A. is international; it employs thousands if not several hundred thousand agents; in fact, Bolitho believed that every tenth man in Italy is at least a part-time worker of the organization.

Ever since its emergence from secrecy, the activities of the Cheka have received notice in the official press, usually a few lines like the following:

"The special section O. V. R. A. of the department of public safety, a part of the Ministry of the Interior, has discovered a clandestine organization. . . ."

"The O. V. R. A. has likewise identified a Communist organization in Emilia and has made arrests, denouncing the chiefs to the special tribunal."

"The O. V. R. A. has discovered in Rome an anti-Fascist group developing criminal activity by the clandestine distribution of defamatory literature. The chiefs have been arrested: Mario Vinciguerra, Renzo Rendi, and Madame Widow De Bosis."

Thus, many years after Mussolini had officially denied that in the Ministry of Interior, the Viminale, he had under him a branch of government commonly called Cheka, it is officially announced that the O. V. R. A. of the Viminale Palace, where Mussolini still presides, is functioning excellently.

It was the third of these announcements which interested America because Signora De Bosis was born Lillian Vernon, of Springfield, Missouri. Her father was dean of a college in upper New York State, and her son, Dr. Lauro De Bosis, of Columbia University, was head of the National Alliance which the O. V. R. A., through an agent provocateur, succeeded in crushing. This Alliance had three objectives: to tell the news which the press suppressed, to form a union of the constitutional parties, and to prepare the "men of order" to take over the government when Fascism collapsed and a Bolshevik reaction followed. The Alliance sent out circulars written by Lauro De Bosis; Vinciguerra and Rendi were sentenced to fifteen years' imprisonment on the charge that they mailed the circulars. Both are journalists, the former once on the liberal *Mondo*, the latter occasional and literary correspondent of the *New York Evening Post* and *New York Times*.

Another plot netted twenty-four intellectuals. The O. V. R. A. always had an able instrument. From the time of Rossi and Dumini, Mussolini has always had some important, usually quite intelligent, man in his Cheka who carried out personal orders and pursued personal enemies.

This agent was sent by the O. V. R. A. to visit prominent leaders abroad who were Mussolini's enemies. In October, 1929, for example, he came to Brussels to interest Count Sforza in a little dynamiting. He began by asking the former Minister of Foreign Affairs if ideas were enough and whether violence were not better; he had some nice chemical plans for bombs and believed it would be a fine gesture to throw one at the Pope, or at least blow up Saint Peter's, as a sign to the world that there was anti-Fascist activity. Count Sforza asked the agent to leave the house, so the agent went after smaller game.

Returning to Milan, he trafficked with numerous professional men; one of them, the chemist Umberto Ceva, member of the old Republican party, liberal and democrat, he tried to interest in his bomb schemes. Ceva answered he would not care to play the game of violence. However, on leaving the house, he placed a piece of paper with the design for a bomb, on Ceva's table, and it was found in the place indicated to them, by the O. V. R. A. agents and militia who made the arrest the next morning.

Given the third degree in the prison, Ceva, believing the agent an honest if too violent anti-Fascist, refused to admit the origin of the paper with the bomb design. He committed suicide rather than betray the betrayer. A few days later the press officially announced the agent of the O. V. R. A. Ceva's suicide was kept secret by the Fascist government until a protest from groups of British intellectuals asking for a fair trial was sent to Mussolini.

Another of the agent's victims was Mussolini's personal enemy, Ferruccio Parri, who with Carlo Rosselli aided Filippo Turati, for many years head of the anti-Fascist movement in France, to escape from Italy. Parri, major of the general staff during the war, liberal-democrat-republican, was sentenced to a year in prison, then "forced domicile," then to the island of Ponza, then Lipari, and finally, having expiated not only his original crime, but every charge the O. V. R. A. could bring, he returned to Milan. Here the agent attempted to get his consent for a dynamite plot, and despite Parri's being declared not guilty by the Special Tribunal, he was in 1931 sent to an African colony for five years.

Another personal enemy of Mussolini's, Camillo Berneri, professor of philosophy, was the victim of the O. V. R. A. agent Menapace, who placed a false passport and a quantity of an explosive called cheddite in Berneri's pockets, then informed the Brussels police. As this occurred at the time the Italian Crown Prince was shot at in Belgium, Berneri was arrested, deported, then arrested in France and in Luxembourg and in France again. The professor to this day doesn't know what all the political intrigue is about.

An American journalist of many year's residence in Rome, one who is forced by circumstances to send glowing reports via the daily cables, and one of many who has smuggled true reports to the present writer, thus sums up the situation:

"The Fascist system has given modern Italy the atmosphere in which the Medici and the Borgias would find themselves perfectly at home. After years of Fascist rule and consolidation, the Italian people are still deprived of all liberties. They accept this as a measure of force majeure, silently, but they suffer from a sense of slavery to an oligarchy which does not represent the best elements in Italian life. The right to keep silent is practically the only one left.

"The opposition is watched, tracked down like wild beasts. No one can find out how many unfortunates are imprisoned in the unhealthy isles or in the prisons of the mainland. The special tribunals have condemned wholesale, large groups. One tribunal in one year condemned 400 persons to 2,000 years' imprisonment. . . . All these events are carefully concealed so that no indignation may be aroused abroad. . . . The Duce admits 100,000 professional policemen. There are even more in plain clothes. . . . Amateur spies are daily denouncing persons they suspect according to the best traditions of a reign of terror. Petty and private tyranny takes the most exasperating and minor forms. . . . All this is never felt nor suspected by the visiting tourists. . . .

"All this is accepted supinely and in silence by the Italian people, who are waiting for something to happen which will deliver them from a domination and a fate which they do not think they deserve and from a system which is entirely alien to their civilization and beliefs. . . . It would require too much space to recall the incidents revealing the miasma of oppression and repression under which Italians live. . . . The special revolutionary tribunal functions with harshness and ferocity. . . . Families of persons sent to *confino* (island exile) and of those who are *fuorusciti* or exiles, are subject to reprisals and held almost as hostages. . . . The secret police and system of national espionage penetrate every corner of Italian life. Persons are careful in talking to anyone. Everyone, accordingly, lives in an atmosphere of submission, without open expression.

"General Capello, hero of Gorizia and friend of the King, is in confino. No one except Mussolini knows how many Italians are there. The estimate is as high as 200,000, but Mussolini put it at 1,500 and the truth is somewhere between these two extremes. With hundreds of persons being sentenced monthly to the islands, the figure is certainly not Mussolini's. Hundreds are in the Mediterranean Siberia without trial.

"The régime has gained little hold on the majority of the upper and educated classes. . . . The surveillance of Benedetto Croce and Professor Ferrero is no longer kept secret. Fascism's hold today is sustained by military dominance of the Black Shirts and the secret police."

No one knows how many persons have been killed by the Fascisti. Labriola, former Minister of Labor, announced that from the time Mussolini went into the employ of the employers' associations in 1920, until he entered Rome in 1922, his squadristi murdered 4,100 non-Fascists of which full case records exist. There are also lists of thousands of victims in the ensuing years of Fascist rule. Mussolini's one reply has been that the Bolsheviki in Russia killed more.

Mussolini defends not only violence as his means to power and means of maintenance in power, but terrorism as well. "In the creation of a new State," he says, "which is authoritarian but not absolutist, hierarchial, and organic—namely, open to the people in all its classes, categories, and interests—lies the revolutionary originality of Fascism, and a teaching, perhaps, for the whole modern world, oscillating between the authority of the State and that of the individual, between the State and the anti-State. Like all other revolutions, the Fascist revolution has had a dramatic development, but this in itself would not suffice to distinguish it. The reign of terror is not a revolution: it is only a necessary instrument in a determined phase of the revolution."

This phase of the Fascist revolution has now officially been extended for almost ten years.

★ ★

CHAPTER XX

The Fate of Heroes

IN THE MARCH OF THE FASCIST PARTY FROM A WEAK, OPPORTU-
nistic compromising minority to absolute dictatorship it was
necessary to employ methods tested in medieval times, proven in-
valuable by the Germans when they held enemy Belgium, and more
recently used with abundant success by Hitler. Sentimentalists and
idealists alone raised horrified hands against the taking of hostages
and the shooting of high officials, but realists and militarists knew
only too well that it was impossible for Ludendorff in 1914 to withstand the plotters and the snipers unless he used terrorism.

In Italy Mussolini was ably assisted by his generals. Of the original Quadrumvirate, the Generals De Bono, De Vecchi, Italo Balbo
and Michele Bianchi, who more or less led the march on Rome, all
but one shared in the work of establishing the necessary Black
Terror, and Bianchi died too soon to enjoy its fruits.

Many of the original minor heroes of Fascism have already been
mentioned: Dumini, Rossi, Marinelli, Filippelli, Finzi, Volpi. Of
the major heroes, the most impressive is Italo Balbo. At the age
of twenty-five he was repaid for his devotion to the Duce by being
put in command of the Black Shirt militia and given the title of
ras, or sub-dictator, of the province of Ferrara. Here in the town
of Argenta he found the leading anti-Fascist to be the veteran
priest, Minzoni, who remained a follower of Don Sturzo and who
preached the old Catholic Party ideas of social-reform. On August
23, 1923, Balbo's militia organized a "punitive expedition" to Argenta, where they burned and destroyed Catholic institutions and
murdered the priest. More than a year later public opinion forced
the government to stage a public trial of the murderers. It was then
testified that all violence in Ferrara was under the direct leadership

of Balbo. The charges were so grave that Mussolini asked him to resign. But lieutenants of the Balbo type cannot be replaced easily. A year later he was given a higher position.

During the hearing, in November, the following document was published in the Opposition press. It relates to a trial of several men accused of anti-Fascist activities, but as no evidence, real or falsified, was produced, the Fascist judges were forced to free them. Whereupon Balbo wrote:

"To the commanding general:

"As far as the men acquitted December 2 are concerned, it will be necessary to explain to them that a change of air and establishment in another province is necessary. If they insist on remaining and consequently causing moral discomfort, it will be necessary to beat them—not too much, but as is customary—until they decide to leave.

"Show only this part of my letter to the prefect and say to him in my name that I have sufficient evidence to justify my demand that the ruffians should leave the city and province. The *questura* will do well to persecute them at least weekly and let the prefect notify the King's *procuratore* that for a possible beating, which must be *in style*, a trial is not desired. Read this part of the letter to the *consiglio federale*. If I write this from Rome it is certain that I know of what I speak. Basta.

"ITALO BALBO."

Despite the publication of documents which he could not refute and which accused him of fomenting violence and being implicated in bloodshed, Italo Balbo continued to gain in power. He became the commander of the Italian air forces, and led one squadron to South America and another to the United States.

On the occasion of a luncheon given the hero by the Lord Mayor of London in December, 1930, the latter read a long series of telegrams of congratulations. Among them this one:

"Unable to participate at your luncheon in the flesh, I am present in spirit. DOM MINZONI."

There was a fine burst of British applause, but Balbo went as white as Macbeth on first seeing Banquo's ghost. After his flight to America Balbo was honored with an invitation to the White House and thousands of columns of praise, with no mention of his racketeering past, were published, nor did the press explain the riot in New York or the effigies inscribed "assassino" which greeted the hero on arrival.

But almost immediately upon returning to Rome to receive the congratulations of a proud nation, Balbo was surprised to find every newspaper publishing an official history of his conquest of the Atlantic, a history which gave credit to Mussolini for organizing and directing the entire adventure. This surprise was turned into chagrin a little later when Balbo was sent to Africa as governor of Libya. Again the world understood that there was room for only one Caesar in Rome.

Quadrumvir De Vecchi alone has escaped the Duce's jealous wrath. Shortly after the "capture" of Rome, at a time the Opposition ridiculed the event which the victors called a "revolution," the Fascisti realized that a "blood bath"—to use the exact phrase and proposal which Mussolini once made—was necessary to consolidate the victory. On December 17, 1922, occurred the Massacre of Turin. On that day and the next several hundred anti-Fascists were beaten and at least a score murdered. Several more succumbed later. When, on the first day of the massacre, the Fascist dictator of Turin, Brandimarte, was informed by journalists that only fourteen of the men listed for execution had been found dead, he replied, "The Po will deliver up the remaining bodies." But the glory of this "purge" was not given to Brandimarte. On the 1st of January, 1923, Undersecretary of State De Vecchi said in a public speech:

"Yes, the reaction of a few days ago was necessary; and though I was not there, I accept the responsibility for all that happened."

In Part XXV of his confession Rossi states that "I must in good faith declare that in this case no orders were sent from Rome. The responsibility lay entirely with the group of Turin Fascists gathered by Deputy De Vecchi. . . . [His] assumption of responsibility was easy enough for him, since he enjoyed parliamentary immunity, and justice and the police were in acquiescence."

The extent of the massacre having surpassed all in Fascist history, it caused a tremendous reaction throughout Italy. In Mussolini's cabinet, at the time, there were still several liberals who opposed violence and demanded that the guilty be punished. A commission of inquiry was sent. Gasti, its chief, took testimony which, while convicting Brandimarte of the murders, proved the inspiration of the action was De Vecchi.

Mussolini immediately recalled Gasti and dissolved the commission. The Grand Fascist Council met; instead of expelling De Vecchi as the nation expected, it sent him out of the country—as governor of Somaliland. Later he was named ambassador to the Vatican, and today he is a member of the cabinet.

General De Bono, who actually planned the march on Rome, is now Colonial Minister. On one diplomatic visit to London and Paris he heard the word "assassin" frequently. In Paris thousands of leaflets were distributed and their contents republished in some papers:

"The French government today receives officially the Italian Minister of Colonies, General De Bono. On this occasion we have the duty to bring the following to the knowledge of the French public:

"1. General De Bono is one of the principle accomplices of the assassins of the Deputy Giacomo Matteotti. He aided and favored the assassins and Mussolini, saving them from justice. He was then chief of police and his responsibility is officially shown in the sentence of the Italian Senate, which judged him as a high court.

"2. General De Bono had in his hands the bloody clothing of Matteotti; he hid them and let disappear the traces of the crime which led directly up to the Duce.

"3. On Christmas day, 1923, General De Bono, chief of police, organized the bloody attack against the former liberal minister, Giovanni Amendola, chief of the Opposition parties. . . ."

Farinacci of Cremona, a railroad worker who became the chief exponent of terrorism, surprising Mussolini himself, devoted his home-town newspaper to advocating reprisals, punitive expeditions, "making life unbearable" for his opponents. One day his racketeers rounded up the small Socialist delegation and chased them; the latter found refuge in a barn of a peasant. Petroneschi was felled with one blow and left for dead. In this way he escaped death, but his colleague, Bolderi, president of the workers coöperative of Cremona, was clubbed to death. The chief murderer was Giorgio Passani, aged sixteen. Although Mussolini later deplored the crime, Farinacci declared in an interview with the press of all factions that he accepted "on behalf of Fascism the responsibility of the murder of Bolderi."

Farinacci brilliantly and sadistically conducted the trial of the corpse of Matteotti at Chieti, but immediately afterwards, instead of being rewarded by Mussolini, was permitted to resign his high offices. He accepted a provincial secretaryship. The cause of the downfall was a mystery for many years, but now it is known that Farinacci the sadist was also Farinacci the bank manipulator. He had been pardoned several doubtful banking transactions, but the list had grown too long and important to save him from political disgrace. He did save himself from jail.

Volpi, one of the confessed murderers of Matteotti, had been sentenced previously to fifteen years for killing a man during the Fascist attack on the Socialist club Foro Bonaparte. As Volpi had fled, he did not serve a day. On returning, he was absolved and went to work for the Cheka.

The chief assassin of the Fascist Cheka, Dumini, known everywhere as "The American," according to the régime's press agent, Villari, was "a discredited and disreputable Fascist from Florence, born in the United States, who had been mixed up in various acts of violence and shady transactions. . . ." For all his crimes Dumini had never served time. There are eyewitnesses to a double murder in Carrara on June 2, 1922, when Dumini struck a girl for wearing a red carnation, the symbol of the Socialist Party. The girl's mother and brother protested, in fact struck Dumini with their hands, whereupon he shot and killed them both.

Many of the "punitive expeditions" which Mussolini boasts of in his autobiography, were led by Dumini.

He also had a personal reason for assassinating Matteotti. The Opposition leader had promised that when he had finished exposing the 1924 election frauds in which he claimed 1,500,000 false ballots had been counted by the Fascisti (enough to lose them their ma-

jority in parliament if there was a true recount) he would take up
the subject of commercial corruption of Fascist officials, predicting
he would tell who was to get the graft if the (American) Sinclair
Oil Company concession was made, and how a "household friend"
of the Duce's was getting rich betraying Italy by smuggling arms
to her arch-enemy, Yugoslavia. The smuggler was Dumini.

Various testimony has been given regarding this record-breaking
racketeer. Colonel Sacco, ordnance officer and director of the secret
police—he was forced to resign later for telling this—said that
just an hour before the kidnapping of Matteotti, Dumini said boastfully "We are about to make a fat expedition; it will be *punitive*
and *it is I who will lead it.*" Signor Giurin, vice-president of the
provincial deputation of Milan, pictures Dumini as fatalistically sad-
dened when he declared "I now have twelve murders on my conscience, but they were done under orders and I am chained and in
the power of those for whom I am working. Now there is nothing
I can do but continue in this work. If I refuse there is nothing left
for me but to be crushed, denounced, taken as a galley slave."

Prezzolini, defender of Mussolini, says it is difficult to understand
how the Duce could not only tolerate but actually accept with pleasure
the friendship of such men as Finzi, Rossi, De Bono and even
Dumini, "who have dealt a serious blow to both his own prestige
and to that of Fascism. . . . He allowed the most intellectually and
morally worthless people to group themselves against him. . . . From
the day when he formed an exclusive Fascist Ministry began his
conflict with Fascism. His most serious troubles, his most insuper-
able obstacles, his severest threats, have always come from Fascism."

But here again there is a counter-picture. The Fascist press not
only at one time lionized Dumini, but one paper wanted to erect
a monument to him. Said the *Popolo Valtellinese* of Sondrio: "It
appears to us that Dumini and his co-accused are deserving of a
monument because if they themselves are really the murderers of
Matteotti they have delivered the nation from a furious calumniator
of the fatherland, a sabotageur of the World War, in other words,
a traitor."

Another hero, "a Fascist from the first hour" in the Duce's
roll of honor, is Dino Grandi, who for many years was called in

the popular press the probable inheritor of Mussolini's toga. Grandi began his political career as head of the Bologna squadristi; later he headed the local Cheka branch, and in 1926, when there was a plot in the Fascist ranks to upset Mussolini, it was he who saved the career of his chief.

In the early days of Fascism the Bolognese ras, Baroncini, exposed graft amounting to 300,000,000 lire in the building of the 700,000,000 lire Florence-Bologna railroad tunnel. He accused "the Grandi Gang" of taking the money. Grandi was Baroncini's greatest personal enemy. The so-called Grandi Gang hired a physician to administer disease germs to the ras, but at the critical moment the doctor probably remembered the Hippocratic oath, since he repented, confessed, and published his confession in the local newspaper. Grandi did not sue for libel; instead, he challenged Baroncini to a duel, the latter refusing to cross swords with a man he called a common gangster.

The biggest swindle in Fascist history involved the $30,000,000 loan to the city of Milan which was floated in America by Dillon, Read & Co. Belloni, podestá, or vice-dictator, of Milan, was one of the leaders of Fascism and at one time Italy's representative in the League of Nations. Yet under his rule almost every cent of the thirty millions was stolen. Again the Duce sent a commission of inquiry and again it was disbanded. It obtained evidence not only against Belloni, but against Arnaldo Mussolini, with whom the clever Belloni had made a business alliance. Belloni was sent to the penal islands.

Filippelli, one of the Matteotti assassins who escaped punishment for that crime, met a similar fate. He was caught in a municipal swindle. As long as the gangsters, the former members of the Mafia, the high officials of the party, and the members of Mussolini's household cabinet limited their activities to enemies of the régime they usually escaped all penalties. When, however, they became financial embarrassments instead of political assets, the Duce never hesitated to treat them as common criminals or anti-Fascists.

The fate of heroes pursues the new men as well as Fascists of the first hour. In 1932 the Stefani agency issued a simple announcement: "It is reported from Turin that Signor Augusto Turati, former secretary-general of the Fascist Party and former director of the *Stampa*, has been interned in a sanitarium." That was all. It was the epitaph on the political grave of the most powerful man in Italy next to the Duce. Three years earlier Turati had renamed Mont Blanc "Monte Mussolini," despite French protests that the peak lies within the French frontiers. The only plausible explanation of the break between Mussolini and Turati is the enmity of Farinacci for the latter, which translated itself in published charges of immorality. The "sanitarium" officially announced as Turati's present residence is generally understood to be an insane asylum.

In August, 1934, Leandro Arpinati, who since the downfall of Turati was known as "Mussolini's right hand," was removed as Undersecretary of the Interior and sentenced to five years in the penal islands. Twenty of Arpinati's Bolognese friends were also dismissed from the party on the charge of "connivance." No explanation has been given.

There is the famous fable of the ruler who sent a messenger to a colleague asking him how to deal with ambitious men within the kingdom. The second ruler, unwilling to commit himself to writing, took the messenger walking in the garden, and during the conversation knocked off the heads of all the taller flowers. So it has been in Fascist Italy. Whatever head has risen above the crowd has invariably fallen. Federzoni, Farinacci, Grandi, Balbo, Turati and Arpinati each in turn became a power second only to the Duce, and each in turn was struck down.

Arpinati is the only leader within Fascism to whom a suspicion of plotting against Mussolini is attached. However, there have been many plots inside and without the party against the existence of the régime and the life of the Duce.

★ ★

CHAPTER XXI

"'Live Dangerously' Is My Motto"

AT THE LAUSANNE CONFERENCE THE JOURNALISTS FOUGHT FOR THE first interview with the new dictator. Lincoln Steffens found him with his large eyes sharply scrutinizing everybody and a revolver ready. He asked a pertinent question.

"I was looking for the fellow that is out to shoot me," replied Mussolini.

"Why that, what for?"

"To shoot him first."

"What makes you think you'll be shot?"

"History," replied Mussolini.

"History?—Yes, that's right. History says dictators are apt to be shot. . . ."

"Ah," continued Mussolini, "if a dictator knows history, the dictator can look out and—shoot first."

In the early days of 1923 a report circulated in Rome that one of the guards of the Chigi Palace, then dictatorial headquarters, fired on the Premier. There is the record of the arrest of a guard, no record of a trial, and the fact that the censorship suppressed all cablegrams on the subject.

That same year Mussolini, returning from an excursion in the country, chose to drive his car, placing his chauffeur in his accustomed seat. As the automobile passed the Colosseum and was slowed in traffic an unidentified assassin fired from a window of a neighboring house. The chauffeur was killed.

In September, 1924, Mussolini returned to Rome alone from the Badia San Salvador, but the entire entourage, which he was supposed to lead, followed in the evening. It was fired upon.

No mention of these three attempts on the life of the Duce appears in the world press, but on the 4th of November, 1925, occurred an incident which had tremendous repercussions. It was Armistice Day in Italy, the national celebration of victory and honor for the Unknown Soldier. In the afternoon the foreign journalists were informed by the press department that a certain Signor Zaniboni had been caught with a rifle in his hand standing at a window facing the palace, ready to assassinate the Duce. For once foreign correspondents were told they could go as far as they liked without fear of censorship.

Mussolini himself, after referring to Zaniboni as "a vulgar Socialist," the recipient of "two checks for 150,000 francs each from Czechoslovakian Socialists to lead an anti-Fascist struggle," and "a drug addict," complains that Zaniboni "chose the sacred day of the commemoration of victory. He ambushed himself in the Hotel Dragoni, just in front of the Palazzo Chigi, from the balcony of which I usually review the processions which pass on the way to the altar of the Unknown Soldier to offer their flowers, their vows, and their homage. Having an Austrian rifle with fine sights, the fellow could not miss his aim. . . . He was discovered. He had been followed for a long time. A few days before, General Capello had generously given him money and advice. Masonry had made of him its ensign. But by simultaneous action, Zaniboni, General Capello, and various less important personages in the plot were arrested one hour before they planned the attempt."

The journalists,[1] however, did not cable the sensational news as Mussolini himself wrote it. They were too well aware that the underlined sentences belied the truth of the information officially given them. They could not afford to repeat the statement of the supreme journalist of Italy.

Months later an investigation showed that Zaniboni was a Freemason, one who had suffered injury and desired revenge. But he had had no violent intentions until one day he met a man named Quaglia who expressed sympathy and suggested a plan for assassination. For months Quaglia urged Zaniboni on, alternately postponed the date,

[1] In November, Bolitho wrote, "Zaniboni would have been unable to see him, much less shoot him. . . ."

and finally hired the room in the Hotel Dragoni and supplied the gun.

The reason for the postponement was simply this: Quaglia was a Fascist agent, and the greatest showman in the world wanted the attempted assassination staged on the most patriotic of national holidays so that the sympathy of the world would be stirred more easily, and the political actions he had planned more easily put into practice.

However, to make sure that no accident would occur, the Fascist secret service arrested Zaniboni in his room an hour before Mussolini was scheduled to appear on his balcony for the great oration of the day.

And still another precaution was taken. The would-be assassin's room, which faced Mussolini's office, was just across the street from the Palazzo Colonna, in which, incidentally, was situated the office of the present writer. These three buildings and the open square of the Piazza Colonna complete the scene. Mussolini, as seen frequently by the present writer, had to appear on his balcony facing the square in order to speak to the multitude, whereas the Dragoni faced the other wall of the Chigi. It would therefore have been impossible for an assassin to see Mussolini unless he had, in addition to his Austrian rifle and its fine sights, a new invention which made it possible to fire around a corner.

These stone-wall facts explain why the American reporters of the Zaniboni affair usually referred to it as an "alleged" attempt at assassination.

At his trial Zaniboni testified that Carlo Quaglia had for eight months talked to him about the matter, had lived in his house, had reported almost daily to the police, had arranged everything, and had in fact offered to do the shooting himself. "I swear by my child, the dearest thing I possess," he said, "that you, Quaglia, told me you would like to have the honor of shooting Mussolini."

The Honorable Violet Gibson, sister of Baron Ashbourne, shot Mussolini in the nose just as he emerged from the Congress of Surgeons on the 6th of April, 1926. Mussolini went back to the congress and a piece of sticking-plaster was put across his nostrils. He then stood for the photographers.

The would-be assassin in this case was a recent convert to Catholicism. It was testified by the sister superior at the convent where Miss Gibson lived that the Englishwoman was subject to hysteria. There was also evidence that she was incensed over Mussolini's professed atheism and the treatment given several priests and Catholic institutions by the Fascist squadristi. "A supernatural force entrusted me with a lofty mission," she said.

The Roman mob smashed the windows of the Soviet Embassy in reprisal. The Milan mob smashed and burned the offices of the *Avanti* and the *Unita*.

Mussolini ordered an end of violence. "I do not want reprisals," he shouted. "It is my Will."

To the jubilant crowd the dictator said:

"The episode which provoked your magnificent demonstration, whose sincerity I appreciated, has now faded from my memory. If I do think of it, it is with a feeling of annoyance, of boredom, as for foolish things.

"I do not want exaggerations. Mussolini has that in his composition which loves to participate in risk, and although I understand a certain anxiety, I declare I have not the least intention to hide or lose touch with the Fascist masses and the Italian people. . . . In no case, under no circumstances, will Fascism soften its program. At this moment everything is prepared. Let it be known at home and abroad, because Fascism will continue to rule the destinies of the Italian people with an iron hand."

To an American journalist the Duce said: "The bullets pass, Mussolini remains."

It was the first time he used the third-person-royal.

Almost immediately afterwards he sailed for Africa at the head of the Italian war fleet. "We are of the Mediterranean and our destiny has been and always will be on the sea," he said to accompanying journalists. The words "Our destiny lies on the sea" appeared in thousands of red, white, and green sheets on all the kiosks and walls of the country. Landing in Tripoli, the conqueror exclaimed, "Rome carried the beacon lamp of strength to the shores of the African sea. No one can stop our inexorable Will."

In Rome, on the 11th of September, as Mussolini was motoring to the Chigi Palace, a youth named Gino Lucetti threw a bomb which hit the car, bounced back, and exploded, injuring eight persons. It so happened that this, the third violent attempt of the year, came at a time relations with France were strained and the annual charge that France harbored anti-Fascist emigrés was made in the daily press. To the 50,000 Fascisti frantically gathered in the Colonna square Mussolini thundered: "This must end. It would be well for responsible governments to take note of this because otherwise their friendship for the Italian people may be fatally compromised.

"Tell the Americans and the Italians of America that neither pistols, bombs, nor other instruments of death can make me desist from my course. This is the third attempt against me in the brief space of several months, but like the others this one has not disturbed me in the slightest.

"I consider myself a soldier who has specific orders and is ready to confront any risk."

To Percy Winner of the Rome bureau of the Associated Press, who brought him a fifty-pound bundle of American clippings on the Lucetti affair, the Duce said:

"My star protects me as Italy is protected. I shall die a natural death. As I live now there is adventure."

At the same time he asked the death penalty for assassins and would-be assassins. The King of Italy reminded the Premier that his father, King Humbert, had been assassinated and that there had been a popular clamor for the death penalty for regicide to which he, the present King, had refused to listen.

While press and politicians debated the question, still another attempt at assassination occurred.

On October 13, 1926, a triumphant procession of automobiles headed by the Duce was thrown into disorder by a revolver shot. The bullet hit Mussolini's chest but glanced off. Bolitho's report that the Premier was wearing a bullet-proof vest was thereby confirmed.[2]

In the next car were high officials of the Fascist Party. Signor Arconovaldo Buonaccorsi slit the throat of the boy accused of the shooting. Signor Italo Balbo fired his revolver twice into the writhing body on the ground. The other notables, amidst terrifying shouts

---

[2] In September, 1935, the *New York Times* published an interview with the Vienna manufacturer who had sold Mussolini the steel garment.

and common frenzy, shot, stabbed, kicked, and rushed at the body in such a fury that two of them were so badly injured they were taken to the hospital. This fact even the Fascist press recorded. And, by a mistake of the censor, the report was also passed that the would-be assassin wore a black shirt. The Associated Press sent to America a completely false report that a Communist plot had been discovered. To this great American news agency the Duce said a little later: "To discredit Fascism certain journalists give proof of an inventive power which would well be used to write a movie scenario. They have not as yet invented—it would be the height of absurdity and ridiculousness—that I purposely invent the attacks on my life, one after another."

To the United Press the Duce said: "I don't know what it is that protects me from assassins. Certainly it is a mystic something."

To his townsfolk he declared, "Nothing will happen to me before my task is done."

But in a public address to the inhabitants of Milan, the reinstated administrative secretary of the Fascist party, Signor Marinelli, who had been sent to jail for the murder of Matteotti and amnestied almost immediately, said that "the first words of the Duce yesterday after the attempted assassination were these: 'Italy and the whole world must know that the criminal has been lynched.'"

The body was identified as that of Anteo Zamboni, fifteen years old, a Fascist belonging to the Balilla. Inasmuch as Mussolini himself had said to his companions that the man who had fired at him "was a man of medium height, in a light suit, who had stepped a pace in front of the protective cordon," and the policeman who had spoiled a second shot by tearing the revolver from the man's hand confirmed Mussolini as to the gray suit, it was quite obvious that the wrong man had been lynched. The Cheka thereupon proceeded to make a case of it by arresting the entire Zamboni family.

As it was impossible to contradict Mussolini, the public prosecutor then declared that apparently two men had fired simultaneously, but the Duce, his four companions, and the policeman had noted only one of them—the one who got away. As for Zamboni, the prosecutor admitted he was a mere boy, "never interested in politics, and his association with the young members of the Balilla would certainly not lead him to think of our Duce as a tyrant." Therefore, it was argued, he had accomplices, and the man in gray must have been Anteo's brother, Ludovico. "The proved innocence of Ludovico would destroy the very basis of the charge," continued the prosecutor, and in the following day Ludovico proved so satisfactorily that he was innocent that the court acquitted him. There was now nothing left for the Fascist prosecutor but to accuse the father and aunt of the two boys—the mother went insane before they could arrest her. It was therefore testified that in 1907 [*sic*] the aunt had carried a red flag in a funeral procession, and that the father had never been legally married in a church nor had he had his children baptised. The august court thereupon sentenced the father and aunt of the two loyal enthusiastic Fascist boys to thirty years' imprisonment for inciting to assassination and the press was instructed to drop the matter.

On the 9th the Fascist Assembly passed the Duce's law making it a capital crime to attempt to kill Mussolini. The King, opposed to this act, could not do anything about it. In that exciting week the Fascisti invaded the home of the philosopher Croce in Naples and that of Roberto Bracco, the dramatist, in Caligari. They also smashed into the French consulate in Vingtmille and the offices of *Nuovo Mondo* in New York.

In the two years which followed the passage of the law reinstating capital punishment there were no publicly announced plots against the Duce, although bombs were exploded in various parts of Rome now and then. In June, 1928, the Fascist press made the claim that a bomb which went off in Milan was timed to kill the visiting King. According to Bolitho many enemies of Fascism were arrested, but the authors of the crime were never caught nor were any names ever published. Arnaldo Mussolini used his newspaper to accuse the "intellectuals" generally. Bolitho expressed the opinion the whole affair was a little Fascist scheme to make it appear that the Fascisti had saved the life of the King; to bind the King closer to the party; and at the same time to arrest and imprison the intellectual enemies of the régime.

In November, 1930, there were mass arrests of the former liberal and conservative leaders for an alleged conspiracy with certain military chiefs, royalists, to overthrow the régime. In Trieste, numerous

Yugoslavs were imprisoned. The authorities of this former Austrian city announced that one Yugoslav prisoner, on trial for "terrorism," had given the court a written confession of a plot to kill the Premier. Accordingly, four Yugoslav boys were sentenced by General Cristini, head of the military Cheka, to be shot. Throughout Yugoslavia there were mass demonstrations against Mussolini, based on a report that the King of Italy's desire to pardon the youths was negatived by Mussolini.

In 1931 Michele Schirru, a naturalized American citizen who had been a banana-dealer in the Bronx, New York, was found guilty of planning Mussolini's death. There was no evidence that the bombs which Schirru was accused of owning were intended for that purpose, but Schirru promptly was shot. In 1932 Angelo Shardellotto, who, according to the Fascist press, confessed he had come to Rome to avenge Schirru, was killed by a firing-squad. At the same time one Domenico Bovone, accused of being the director of the plot, was also put to death, although the co-accused, his mistress, Margharita Blaha, was sentenced to prison and later reprieved. Bovone, according to the Italian newspapers, was not an anti-Fascist, but merely an employee of Mussolini's enemies in Paris who had offered $50,000 for the death of the Duce and $5,000 for the death of the Crown Prince. The obvious contradiction—the Crown Prince being notorious for his enmity to Fascism—was not noted in the general press. A Swiss newspaper, answering its Italian colleagues who accused France of harboring and encouraging would-be assassins, said that "what is important is the confirmation that the life of the Duce of the Black Shirts is continually in danger. That is the fate of all tyrants. Zaniboni, Lucetti, Zamboni, Schirru, Shardellotto . . . the series of unfortunate terrorists grows longer. But it is oppression which creates the atmosphere of attempted assassinations; it is injustice, atrocities, cruelties of the Fascist régime which they seek to avenge. . . . Perhaps Shardellotto wanted to avenge Schirru. And tomorrow Shardellotto may in turn find an avenger. The executioner shall find justice; it is the destiny of régimes based on violence."

In March, 1934, Leonardo Bucciglioni, Renato Cianca, Claudio Cianca, and Pasquale Capasso were accused of firing a bomb in St.

Peter's and, as a Fascist corollary, plotting the life of the Duce. They were not executed. The press was told this was the best proof of the stability of the Fascist régime.

In Italy today it is said, generally, that Mussolini has escaped sixteen attempts on his life. Although the more important were probably more theatrical than real, it cannot be denied that he has lived dangerously. Ever since he had read Nietzsche in Switzerland he had proclaimed the phrase "Live Dangerously" as his motto. And in another way his own words have come home to him—with a vengeance. It was he who said that assassination was the employment hazard of rulers.

But in the time between his Swiss exile and his supreme rule he had learned his Machiavelli well. He had become not only the philosopher of violence, but the brilliant exponent of the political uses to which press-made national hysteria may be put when violence in turn was directed against him.

★ ★

CHAPTER XXII

The Silent Revolution

PLANNED OR FORTUITOUS, EACH OF THE MANY ATTEMPTS ON THE life of the Duce were with Machiavellian opportunism exploited by him in enforcing a Fascist program on a people whose majority was still frankly anti-Fascist.

If one takes the dates of the passage of the most drastic laws, the so-called "Mussolinian reforms" which completely repealed every individual and collective liberty which Italy had enjoyed since the days of Garibaldi, he will find that they coincide with the days of excitement following an attempted assassination, when the emotions of the masses were deeply stirred, when the calm, calculating leaders could more easily enforce stern decrees. That several of these moments were artificially planned is a conviction shared by most of the foreign correspondents in Rome and not a few diplomats.

"All my adversaries," said Mussolini on one of these exciting occasions, "from the most hateful ones to the most intelligent, from the slyest one to the most fanatical, thought that the only way of destroying Fascism was to destroy its duce. . . .

"A policy of force was absolutely necessary. . . .

"I launched the laws for the defense of the régime. . . .

"I abolished the subversive press whose only function was to inflame the minds of men."

The Fascist "revolution" does not date from the bloodless march on Rome of 1922; it stems from the murder of Matteotti in 1924 and really dates from the time Mussolini, no longer trembling with fear, could make the "sequestration" one of the victories of Fascism. It dates from the era when he could say, truthfully or otherwise:

"In all that time I credit myself with the fact that I never lost my calm nor my sense of balance and justice. Because of the serene judgment that I endeavor to summon to guide my every act, I ordered the guilty arrested. I wanted justice to follow its unwavering course. Now I have fulfilled my task and my duty as a just man. . . ."

At the very moment when that change in the mentality of the trembling leader came about, the real Fascist revolution began. It was to lead to hierarchy, an attempt at a "corporate" state, the "totalitarian" idea, and finally "Italianity" as an international cause, newer, therefore superior to Pan-Slavism, Pan-Islamism and Pan-Germanism.

To achieve "totalitarian" Fascism, it was necessary to destroy the entire edifice of liberty begun by Garibaldi and built by many liberal leaders in half a century. Press, parliament, the Freemasons, and the Liberals all represented the Garibaldian State; to achieve the Fascist State, Mussolini determined to crush them all. Only by this means could he assure himself he would never have to face another Matteotti crisis.

The Fascist revolution's first act was the abolition of the free press.

Of the score of decrees by which the dictatorship established itself, this is the only one issued in 1924, the year of Matteotti's assassination. The others followed, most of them in 1925. But it is important to note how powerful Mussolini, "an old newspaper man himself," considered the power of the press, because the edict of July, 1924, had been prepared by him and signed by the King in 1923 for just such an occasion: a national mutiny against the ruling party. The decree provides for "warnings"—i.e., suppression—"if any newspaper or periodical by false or misleading news causes any interference in the diplomatic action of the government in its foreign relations or hurts the credit of the nation at home or abroad, causing undue alarm among the people, or in any way disturbs the public peace. . . . If the newspaper or periodical, by editorial articles, notes, titles, illustrations, or inserts incites to crime or to class hatred or to disobedience of the laws of the established order or upsets the discipline of those engaged in public service or favors the interests of foreign states, groups, or persons as opposed to Italian interests, or insults the nation, the King, the royal family, the Summo Pontifex, the religion, the institutions, or the authority of the State or of other friendly powers.

"Newspapers or other periodicals published in violation of the preceding provisions shall be suppressed. . . ."

(This decree was supplemented on December 31, 1925, with a new censorship law which suppressed all independent publications and forced all journalists into a police docket register. It contained ten points of which the last was:

("Prefects of police are empowered to seize editions of newspapers which attack the government press, or which injure the national cause at home or abroad, or which alarm the people without justification." Any reference to Mussolini and Matteotti was under this decree termed an injury to the nation and resulted in the suppression of the paper.)

Under the press law, the first dictate of absolutism, Mussolini acted slowly but inexorably. Any criticism of himself or Fascism was announced an act of treason, the newspaper confiscated, and frequently, on orders from the Cheka, the editors beaten and the printing-plant destroyed. No other violent decrees were issued until the press had been so completely subjugated that all danger of it causing a serious reaction had passed. Then came laws in quick succession.

At the end of November, 1925, (the Zaniboni affair), decree 2029 abolished the right of public association. Freemasonry in Italy was destroyed.

Actually the law requires all associations, organisms, or institutes functioning in the kingdom or the colonies "to communicate to the authorities of public surety their constitutions, their interior regulations, the complete lists of their membership, their social functions, and all other information relative to their organization, their activity, everything that may be required by the aforementioned authorities, for reasons of public order or surety."

The police and government are given the fullest power of intervention so that they can dispose of the life and functions of all associations. In addition, Article 3 of the municipal and provincial code was interpreted giving the prefects the right to limit and almost to suppress the right of individual citizens to join associations.

The abolition of parliament came next. Again there was no clean direct action, but the first of a series of decrees, each a little stronger, until the present state of parliamentary zero was reached. The first decree, Christmas Eve, 1925, made the Chamber of Deputies merely consultative; it could discuss and ratify, but nothing more. The head of the government (Mussolini) was given the right to initiate laws, the parliament could initiate nothing but could suggest and present only those ideas approved by the Duce; the Premier was responsible only to the King and could no longer be criticized or checked or overruled by the Chamber.

The liberty of teaching and the liberty of the magistracy were abolished the same evening. The decree, No. 2300, declares that "all functionaries, employees, agents of all orders and grades, civil and military, those who are in the administration of the state upon which they depend, who by any manifestation, in and out of service, do not give complete guaranty for the accomplishment of their duties faithfully, or who place themselves *in a situation incompatible with the political directives of the government*," may be removed.

This law was used almost exclusively to force university teachers to be friendly to Fascism and to force the magistrates of Italy to free Fascists accused of violence and punish anti-Fascists, guilty or not guilty.

Naturally, free speech was next suppressed. The rights of the individual having already been circumscribed in every way, it was hardly necessary to pass a new decree, so one day in conferring more power on the Duce it was announced that anyone criticizing the head of the government was punishable with six to thirty months in prison and a fine of three hundred to three thousand lire. Nor is anyone under this law allowed to criticize the *policies* or the *purposes* of Mussolini or his government. It is under this law that from two thousand to six thousand men, mostly intellectuals, were sent to the terror islands in certain years.

Two decrees stripped King Victor Emmanuel III of all his powers. One took the command of the army and navy away from him; this was a mere formality, as the King could not use them in the old days without the approval of parliament and premier, but now the soldiers and sailors of the nation were placed at the disposal of the dictator. The King was denied the right to change Prime

Ministers. The second law placed, above parliament and the crown, the Grand Fascist Council as the highest ruling body, a veritable "Comité de Salut Public" of the old French Terror.

Universal suffrage was abolished. It is one of the ironies of history that shortly before this decree was passed Mussolini, after listening for hours to a debate on the question of enfranchising women, banged the table, said, "Basta," enough talk, and ordered parliament to vote as he directed, in favor of the law. The Marquesa Piccolomini, one of the Duce's first women converts, and an ardent suffragist, was in the balcony, beaming upon her hero, who turned his limpid, passionate eyes upon her and passed her law for her. Shortly afterwards, suffrage for men and women was suppressed. Later, by order of the Grand Council, on February 20, 1928, it was decreed that in the future the Fascisti would announce a list of candidates, and everyone, men and women, would have the right to vote "Yes" or "No," but only for these candidates, and woe to the man who dared vote "No."

In turn the law courts were Fascistized. Article 71 of the Statutes, guaranteeing freedom in the courts, was abolished and the clause "there must never be created either special tribunals or extraordinary commissions" was erased, when Decree 2008 of November 25, 1926 (following the Lucetti and Zamboni affairs) was put into force. A special tribunal "for the defense of the state," a tribunal composed with a majority of the Fascist militia, came into being. It denied the last of the human liberties (including habeas corpus), and functioned arbitrarily, sending thousands of persons to the islands, to prison on the mainland, and to confino, or enforced domicile, under police surveillance. The militia tribunal is commonly known as the Fascist Inquisition.

The inviolability of private homes was abolished. Local police authorities, as well as the national militia, were empowered to invade anyone's domicile at will, search and seize, while all the janitors of Italy were registered and made espionage agents of the régime.

The inviolability of private correspondence was abolished. It is very interesting to note that whereas other dictatorships mark letters "censored," the more modern Fascisti employ numerous agents in the main post offices to steam letters open and to seal them as carefully as possible in an effort to hide the fact there is a censorship and to fool as many customers as possible. The present writer not only has many such envelopes, but has proof from three journalistic colleagues still in Rome that letters to all persons on the "list of suspects," which includes several American and British newspaper men, are steamed open and secretly resealed. The government reserves the right to confiscate outgoing and incoming letters, and frequently does so.

The right freely to choose and exercise a business or a profession was abolished. This was done by a series of legislative and ministerial measures dating from the law of April 3, 1926, to the publication of the Labor Charter on April 21, 1927. The order of the *questore* (chief of police) of Alexandria illustrates this law. When the time came for the new lawyers and students to be registered at the bar, those suspected of not being Fascisti received a legal document to sign. This document reads:

"I, the undersigned, Lawyer . . . . , who until now have remained outside the Fascist Party and régime on account of my sectarianism or my views, believe it my duty today to declare:

"1. I disown my past, in as far as it concerns open or secret dissension with the action or régime of the Fascist Party.

"2. That on my own volition I have deemed it necessary to renounce this apostasy as reparation for conduct politically damnable.

"3. That from now, with sincerity and conviction, I will give my adhesion to everything which the party and régime do in carrying out their powers.

"4. That I recognize that Fascism has saved the country and is deserving of that recognition by all Italians.

"5. That from now on I will exercise my profession and develop all my activity, not only without any factious spirit, but with the purpose of collaborating to make of Fascism the sacred religion of every Italian.

"In confirming the authenticity of this declaration I sign it and authorize the Fascist Party to make what use of it it desires."

Free movement was abolished. Two classes were caught by this law, the peasants who frequently moved from province to province, seeking better working conditions, and the victims of the régime who sought freedom in Switzerland and France. The workers, by this law, came under a sort of serfdom, being required to stay in certain localities and work for wages imposed upon them, and under unbearable conditions. As for those seeking liberty, they were chased, fired upon, and in many instances killed by the frontier guards.

Liberty of conscience and religion were curtailed by the laws which favored the Catholic Church as a State Church.

The right of an Italian-born subject to choose another nationality was denied. Before the war only two semi-civilized countries, Russia and Rumania, had such laws; at present Italy is the only country which cannot admit that a man may change his nationality. The Italian law, moreover, provides for the confiscation of property of those abroad who criticize Fascism or change their nationality, and although the law does not provide for this, the families of emigrants are frequently held as hostages, subjected to terrorism or blackmail.

Article 30 of the Statutes, containing the consecration and traditional guarantee that no unjust taxation shall be levied unless passed by the Chambers and sanctioned by the King, was abolished.

Finally, on February 4, 1926, all municipal liberty was suppressed.

On more than one occasion one of these decrees was passed a day or two after one of the attempts on Mussolini's life; on more than one occasion the publication of a decree led to violent reaction by the public and a massacre. Accused of violence, Mussolini in his speech on May 26, 1926, assumed all responsibility.

"It is I," he said, "who have dictated the measures taken: repeal and revision of all passports for foreign countries; the order to shoot without warning anyone trying to cross the frontier secretly; suppression of all anti-Fascist publications, daily and periodical; dissolution of all groups, associations, and organizations which are anti-Fascist or suspected of anti-Fascism; deportation (to the islands) of those who are anti-Fascists or conduct an anti-revolutionary activity; creation of a special police force; creation of secret bureaus of investigation and a special tribunal.

"All the opposition newspapers have been suppressed, all the anti-Fascist parties have been dissolved. The special police already gives signal service. The political bureaus of secret investigation have been created. The Special Tribunal has been created, it functions in a remarkable fashion."

The democratic state was destroyed. The monarchial constitution was broken. The individual was robbed of all liberty.

Violence, which from the day of Fascism's coming into power, in 1922 and throughout 1923 and 1924, had remained actual but illegal, was made legal in 1925.

In 1925 Fascism and the nation became one.

The revolution, which failed to occur in 1922, came about through the passage of decrees in 1925 and 1926. Quietly.

Fascist absolutism was built over the body of Matteotti.

Mussolini's revenge for the Matteotti uprising was complete.

Part III

MUSSOLINI VICTORIOUS

★ ★

CHAPTER XXIII

Mussolini versus the Pope

THE HISTORY OF THE CATHOLIC CHURCH IS DIVIDED INTO THREE parts: the Church Persecuted, the Church Militant, and the Church Triumphant. The first refers to the early days, the second includes the centuries of successful establishment and our own times; the third refers to heaven. But with Fascism, as with Communism, the three eras are more condensed and the third stage, Triumphant, refers to the present.

Mussolini Victorious asked the people of Italy to endorse his régime in the plebescite of March, 1929; for this event the Fascist Party published its list of achievements, which may be summarized as follows:

Bolshevism and social disorder have been abolished.

Industry and commerce have been revived.

The trains run on time; magnificent automobile roads have been built; the marshes have been drained.

Employment has increased.

Wages and the cost of living have been balanced.

Order, Discipline, Hierarchy (the Fascist slogan) have been made actual.

The budget has been balanced; the nation's finances have been placed in a state of prosperity despite the abolition of many taxes.

Agriculture is flourishing.

The army, navy and air force have been enlarged and restored to high efficiency.

The prestige of the nation has been restored. Italy is now respected and feared abroad.

It is the purpose of the concluding portion of this book to discuss these and later claims of Fascist achievements. At various times

243

Mussolini has called the creation of the Corporate State, the stabilization of the lire, the increased grain or child production, the victory he prized most, but future historians, who are able to take the long view, will most probably place the settlement of the Roman Question first under the name of the Duce.

And if this truly happens they will have a magnificently ironic caption for their chapter; they could call it "The Atheist who liberated the Pope."

We have already witnessed the struggle between Mussolini and his chief political opponent of 1922, Don Sturzo, the Catholic leader; we have seen the youthful Benito defying God to send a thunderbolt against him, and we have heard him saying bitter things about the popes, the priests, Christianity, and all religions. We know he was born an atheist. In fact, in the province where he was born the majority of the poor and oppressed were Socialists and the majority of Socialists were atheists; all the rebels against the social system were enemies of the Church; Socialism was a sufficient religion for them and they hated equally the rich, the employers, the monarchist politicians, also the priests and the established Church, whom they considered the protectors of all the economic forces against which they fought.

The early struggle between the deeply religious mother and the agnostic father for little Benito's soul ended in easy victory for Papa Alessandro. It was not necessary for him to use his belt or the whip, as he did for other corrective purposes. Had he done so it is likely that the child would have fled to the consoling dogmas of the Church which his mother represented. Atheism, however, was in the air, Benito was nourished on it, it became part of his being, and it has remained there. In vain did the mother drag the child to church where the smell of incense in the vitiated air sickened him; in vain did she send him to the Salesian friars, because their moral and physical beatings served only to increase the boy's disdain for religion and make him swear a revenge against the priests, their Church, and their God.

The Swiss episodes are not the only proof of this vendetta. At the time of the execution of Francisco Ferrer in Spain there was an outbreak of anti-clericalism in Italy also, and in Forli it was

Mussolini who led the mob which stormed the central square of the town and destroyed the column surmounted by the Virgin Mary. In the trenches one day the corporal read one of the King's exhortations to the troops which concluded with a call for divine providence to aid the noble Allied war. Mussolini sneered. "We shall conquer without God," he said.

After the war, addressing a convention of veterans one day, he said, "I love a pagan and warlike people, a people which refuses its allegiance to revealed dogma and which is not fooled by miracles." At about the same time he wrote, "There is only one possible revision for the Law of Guarantees [the act that made the Pope the "Prisoner of the Vatican"] and that is, its abolition, followed by a stern invitation to His Holiness to leave Rome, to reënter Avignon, or, in conformity with the taste shown by the Vatican during the war, go to the Boches."[1]

Mussolini seemed to have a grudge against the popes. He never forgave Benedict XV for calling the war a "useless massacre"; as late as 1928, in his autobiography, he attacks the memory of Europe's first pacifist, calling his effort to make peace in 1917 "ambiguous conduct," adding that the "Catholic Church had ever been a stranger to wars when she did not provoke them herself." He insulted Pius XI on more than one occasion. In April, 1924, there was a savage attack by the Fascisti upon the Catholic institutions of the district of Brianza which had voted the Catholic ticket. The Pope sent 500,000 lire to restore the buildings and addressed a bitter message against Fascist violence. Mussolini replied by dubbing Pius XI "Papa Brianzolo."

But now we must look at the seeming contradictions in the behavior of the Duce towards the Pope. The sending of emissaries to the Vatican in preparation for the march on Rome was not a sudden impulse; it was penultimate action in a well-thought-out plan. Even before that was done, in June, Mussolini had written that "Fascism has nothing to gain by exiling God from the sky and religion from the earth," and immediately upon taking office the Duce, in the convention of all statesmen and politicians, called upon God to direct his endeavors. Such expressions shocked those atheist Fascist

[1] *Popolo d'Italia.* November 18, 1919.

followers who had understood from the original program that among
the first actions on gaining power would be a concerted and continual attack on the Catholic Church and the Vatican. But they soon
learned of Mussolini's change of program, if not change of heart.

The first climax in the relationship between Mussolini and the
Vatican followed the Matteotti affair, when the populace turned
against Fascism and the Fascisti took off their black shirts and
removed the lictor's emblem from their buttonholes and pretended
they had never trafficked with the party which stood accused before
the world as one of bloodshed and assassination. Mussolini turned
toward the King, whom he had more than once intimidated with the
plan to replace him, and toward the Church, which he had spared
on entering Rome. The Duce's agents called upon Monsignor Pizzardo, the confident of the Pope, and immediately afterwards there
was a campaign against the Socialists and the Popolari launched in
certain newspapers. This was the only moral support Mussolini had
at the time. But it was important. It helped him emerge from his
pose of remorse, his cringing attitude, and assume his old rôle of
superman. It was then that he announced that he was certain the
Matteotti affair had something to do with Freemasonry, which was
seeking to ruin his authority, and that he would soon settle that
matter, too.

The whole history of the negotiations with the Vatican is a record
of threats, provocations, and promises. One morning Mussolini would
write in his *Popolo* that the Fascisti would tear down the cross from
St. Peter's and replace it with the lictor's ax if the Pope interfered
with his régime, and the next day there would be an emissary waiting on a papal representative. In the spring of 1925 Mussolini applauded the production of Pirandello's "Sagra della Nava" in the subsidized art theater, while the Catholic press denounced the Duce,
Pirandello, and the theater for producing one of the most subtle
and dramatic attacks on the Catholic faith. Then in turn Mussolini
would forbid the American Methodists to build the church they had
planned on a hill overlooking the Vatican or he would propose a bill
for outlawing Masonry.

In July, 1925, and again in August and December, Fascist violence against Catholics was especially intense in Florence and Pisa.

Cardinal Maffi, the leading intellectual of the Church, who had received the second largest number of votes on several ballots at the conclave which elected Pius XI Pope, assumed the leadership of Catholics versus Fascists. And because there was a censorship of the press, Cardinal Maffi issued his anathema of Fascism in the form of a pastoral letter, which called the Duce and his followers the "Race of Cain" and concluded with these words:

"It is said of murderers that they boast of the number of their victories. But the word is merely on the lips, presented rather than pronounced, in a moment of confusion and excitement. Other words come in the night and ring with a different sound, causing fears to arise that are uncontrollable and sometimes even insane. O, Cain! O, Judas! O, all ye who shed the blood of your brothers, you lie when you speak of security; for we know you have it not. Nor could you have it. Do we not see you turn pale and look furtively around, as if seeking some way of escape, at a chance sound that may strike the ear, at a chance light that may strike the eye, even at the murmur of the wind, at the chirping of the birds? . . .

"War had and has its poison-gas, its liquids of destruction; but bear this well in mind: No acid, sulphuric or nitric or prussic and no sublimate is so corrosive as one drop of blood criminally shed. There is no chemical basis that will resist or neutralize it. There are no forces to control it. Armies will not hold it in check. It flows on. It corrodes. It destroys. Woe to the hand that sheds blood. Woe to the feet that trample on the corpse. O, Dynasty of Cain, carry on. But listen to this: where men fail, God is to the rescue—God, who gives no quarter to the culprits but incessantly pursues them, crying out judgment over them: Accursed. Accursed. Accursed in time. Accursed in eternity!"

Following the publication of this pastoral letter, Cardinal Maffi called upon other Catholic leaders to join with him in united and continuous action against Fascism. Mussolini then apologized to the Pope, and Federzoni, strong nationalist and devout Catholic, again made overtures of friendship to the Vatican.

The objective of the Fascisti was the destruction of the power of the Azione Cattolica, the association of elders, and the Catholic Boy Scouts, which enrolled children. Fascism, claiming to be the true leader of youth, in 1926 established the Opera Nationale Balilla for the political and military education of the young of Italy. "The organization," explained the Hon. R. Ricci "requires that its pupils at the time that they will have come of age, will be capable of suitably entering in the higher schools of the army, the navy, and aviation. It will try, above all, to develop the sentiment of absolute devotion to the country in peace time as in time of war. This preparation of young people for military life has properly scandalized faint spirits in certain so-called democratic countries.

"Peace and war are two phases in the life of the people, equally necessary to their development, to their greatness and their growth. Fascism wants only to realize in Italy what the modern states have realized among themselves since the beginning of time, the ability to defend with arms, at all times and against whoever threatened their existence and their prestige."

Militarism and nationalism, the ideals of the Balilla, were the exact opposites of the ideals of the Catholic organizations. On January 9, 1927, Mussolini rushed through a royal decree abolishing all existing Catholic Boy Scout organizations in localities of less than 20,000 population. The Pope, in a letter to Cardinal Gasparri, replied by abolishing the entire organization, explaining he did so because he had to yield to force and that the Scouts still remained "the apple of my eye."

The world at that time, however, had only a suspicion that serious negotiations were under way for the settlement of the Roman question. Behind the acts of violence and reprisals there were diplomatic advances. Actually on the 8th of August, 1926—as the Marquis Francesco Pacelli, brother of Eugenio Cardinal Pacelli and later general counselor of the Vatican State, revealed—Domenico Barone began the definitive negotiations with representatives of the Pope. By autumn of that year there had been considerable progress. Mussolini had asked and received a complete statement of the Vatican's terms for peace. Signor Pacelli, in transmitting them, informed the Duce that there were two questions on which he could cede nothing: the sovereignty of the Pope in a recreated papal state, and the recognition of religious marriage on a par with the civil rite.

In 1927 Mussolini, who had already known that the Pope disapproved of the plan for the Corporate State, announced the Labor Charter. The Pope again showed his displeasure. The official *Osservatore Romano* said it was "contrary to the Christian conception of the State and individual liberty." This and similar declarations by the Pope and the official organ, by order of the Duce's press department, were not reprinted in Italy.

Early in 1929 the rumor of a treaty was confirmed. And then arose the question, why is Mussolini making peace with the Pope, why is the atheist so anxious to please the head of the Catholic Church, why is he making concessions which were not even demanded of previous Prime Ministers, from Cavour to Nitti?

The reasons were many. First, and most important, Mussolini, who had studied his Machiavelli and followed many of the precepts, had been convinced, in the course of years, that the dictum which he had questioned was, after all, the most logical in Italy: one must rule with the aid of the church. Seven years of conflict had convinced him. But perhaps more important still was the politico-economic situation in which Mussolini found himself in the two years of negotiations. In 1926 it was already apparent that a crisis was imminent: unemployment was increasing, exports were down, emigrant remittances had taken an alarming drop, the officially announced balanced budget was in fact not near an equilibrium and dissatisfaction was spreading.

By 1928, despite the flotation of billions of lire in loans in the United States, the crisis was on. Wage cuts and increased taxation were not the cure. And now the bankers and the large industrialists, the subsidizers and owners of the Fascist party, as well as the general public were aroused against Fascism. While the front of the edifice still glittered with decorations and looked imposing, the foundations were sinking into economic mud.

Mussolini was hard pressed. There was even a possibility that at this point he would actually revert to his original program, the plan for a socialized coöperative State written nine years earlier out of Karl Marx, and give the world the semi-Communist régime which was obviously his original intention. He did, in fact, begin taking over certain industries—those which were in unsolvable financial difficulties—and making the State participate in production and distribution. But again he changed his mind.

Something was needed to restore his prestige, at home and abroad, some newer, greater gesture which would unify the masses again, rally them in his vanguard against the threatening desertion of the business leaders. Politics and economics and Machiavellian opportunism dictated the move; it is a practical masculine world and only feminine naïveté, as exhibited by female biographers, has Mussolini, like Saul of Tarsus, seeing the great light on the road to Damascus and becoming a repentant Paul. His was not a gesture of a repentant. It was a politico-economic move.

On February 7, 1929, Cardinal Gasparri, Secretary of State of the Holy See, announced to the diplomats accredited to the Vatican that the temporal power of the Pope had been restored, the Pontiff released from his prison,[2] a new state created.

Behind the present accord stands the figure of Father Tacchi-Venturi, who for years has guided Mussolini in his relations to the Holy See. It was this powerful Jesuit who had planned to have Mussolini make a public confession of faith during the anniversary celebration of St. Francis of Assisi, but there was too much ribald hilarity over the atheist-politician's proposed action to make it profitable. However, the Duce's children—those he so gallantly calls his "first series"—having grown up and noble marriages being proposed, Mussolini permitted himself to be married in the Catholic Church,[3] thereby legalizing their birth, had his "second series" baptized, thereby saving their souls, and allowed himself to be photographed in dark-eyed prayer before the statue of St. Peter in the Cathedral, thereby reaping another harvest of publicity.

Explaining this treaty to the Senate on the 13th of May, Mussolini began with Cavour's formula "a free Church within a free State," adding that the new situation created "a sovereign State within the Kingdom of Italy; the Catholic Church with a certain preëminence loyally and voluntarily recognized; free admission of other religions."

[2] On November 1, 1870, the Vatican had announced that "His Holiness declares that he is in a state of imprisonment and that he will not partake with Belial."

[3] This is the now generally accepted report, but no official document of marriage to Rachele Guidi has ever been found by investigators.

To a Senator who proposed "free and sovereign Church, free and sovereign State," Mussolini said:

"This formula might create the belief that there are two sovereignties coexistant, but they do not coexist. One counts as the Vatican City, and one counts as the Kingdom of Italy, which is the Italian State. It must be understood that between the Italian State and the Vatican City there is a distance which can be measured in thousands of miles, even if it requires only five minutes to go and see this State and ten minutes to walk around its confines.

"There are, then, two sovereignties perfectly distinct and well differentiated: perfectly and reciprocally recognized. But within the State the Church is not sovereign and is not even free. It is not sovereign and is not free because in its institutions and its men it is subject to the general laws of the State, and is even subject to the special clauses of the Concordat."

Of Christianity the Duce said, sarcastically, "This religion was born in Palestine but became Catholic in Rome. If it had been confined to Palestine it would in all probability never have been more than one of the numerous sects which flourished in that overheated environment, like that of the Essenes or the Therapeutæ. The chances are that it would have perished and left no trace."

After giving flat denials to several of the Pope's statements, Mussolini exclaimed:

"We have buried the temporal power of the popes, not resuscitated it."

"Any other régime than ours," he continued, "may believe it useful to renounce the education of the young generations. In this field I am intractable. Education must be ours. Our children must be educated in our religious faith, but we must round out this education and we need to give our youths a sense of virility and the power of conquest."

The Pope read Mussolini's speech May 14th at eleven in the morning, an hour and a half before the first pilgrimage was to visit him. To the professors and pupils of the College of Mondragone he made the famous reply in which he referred to Mussolini as the devil.

The Pope began by attacking the Fascist Spartan educational

principle that children belong to the State. "The State should interest itself in education," said the Pope, "but the State is not made to absorb and annihilate the family, which would be absurd and against nature, for the family comes before society and before the State. The State should perfect the activities of the family in full correspondence with the desires of the father and mother, and it should respect especially the divine right of the Church in education.

"We cannot admit that in its educational activities the State shall try to raise up conquerors or encourage conquests. What one State does in this line all the other States can do. What would happen if all the States educated their people for conquests? Does such education contribute to general world pacification?

"We can never agree with anything which restricts or denies the right which nature and God gave the Church and the family in the field of education. On this point we are not merely intractable, but we are uncompromising. We are uncompromising just as we would be forced to be uncompromising if asked 'How much does two plus two make?' Two plus two makes four and it is not our fault if it does not make five or six or fifty. When it is a question of saving a few souls and impeding the accomplishment of greater damage to souls we feel courage to treat with the devil in person. And it was exactly with the purpose of preventing greater evil that we negotiated with the devil some time ago when the fate of our dear Catholic Scouts was decided."

Although the Pope's reply was suppressed in the Fascist press, some weeks later Mussolini published his speech, retaining all its violent language, misquotations, and insults to the Pontiff. The Pope addressed a letter to Cardinal Gasparri, published June 5th, calling the Duce's words "heretical, and worse than heretical."

Two years after the signing of the peace treaty the Fascisti were again breaking into Catholic clubs and using violence against members; the Pope was reported making plans for leaving Italy, and Mussolini's newspapers were again using language such as this: "If the Duce orders us to shoot all the priests, we shall not hesitate an instant. . . ."[4] In 1931 Mussolini regretted his surrender to the Vatican.

[4] *Gazzetta Fascista,* quoted by the French writer, Emmanuel Bourcier.

The two years of peace had not been two years of harmony. The Church continued to insist on its right to rule the family and raise the children of Italy; the régime continued to enforce the decrees making the State the supreme power over the individual and especially over youth. A brilliant paragrapher has summed up a situation which whole books might expound. "As we understand the controversy between Church and State in Italy," said Howard Brubaker, "the whole question is who gets the custody of the child." As both the Pope and Mussolini rest the future of their régimes on the education of the coming generations, the conflict was bound to occur, and is bound to occur again and again.

The Concordat was based on ambiguity. The two parties had agreed to collaborate on the following points: nomination of priests, status of the religious Orders, recognition of religious marriage, dogmatic religious instruction in the primary and secondary schools, etc. But the grave problems were not definitely settled; the question of the education of youth, the question of the attributes of the Church and the question of the State control of the individual, remained unanswered.

On these questions Fascism has its own moral thesis completely independent of the Church: the State is absolute, it absorbs the family, the individual, the new-born babe, the future citizen. The thesis of the Church: the family is the original unit, independent and fundamental, where the child is to be raised; the individual is an atom in the mass, but sacred for society, possessing inviolable rights which the State cannot curtail or restrain.

The theses are opposed; the treaty, however, could perhaps be maintained had there been unbounded good will and no political intentions on the Fascist side, because compromises are always possible when politics are concerned, much more difficult when religious and moral issues are disputed. Here the incompatibility was profound and fundamental, ancient Christian doctrine clashed with new Fascist doctrine, and a retreat by one force became inevitable.

Meanwhile Catholic institutions had been making unparalleled progress. Not only were the youth organizations strengthened, but the Azione Cattolica showed from twenty-five to fifty per cent membership increases in a short time. According to the Fascisti the old leaders of the Popolari and their followers were swamping the Catholic organizations for the purpose of using them as political centers.

The Fascist organ, *Lavoro Fascista,* accused the Catholic League of debating "explicit proposals for supplanting Fascism"; on May 26, 1931, it accused Monsignor Pizzardo, diplomat and chaplain-general, of declaring that "Catholic Action must be strong enough to seize power." "It is time to resort to extreme measures," concluded the official organ.

A fortnight of violence throughout Italy, and especially in Rome, followed. Fascists attacked priests, plundered the Catholic clubs, the Jesuit house of the Civiltá Cattolica, and invaded the palace of the chancellory, which is protected by extraterritoriality. In the Piazza Colonna, near the Foreign Office, they burned copies of a book *The Pope.* One group found an oil-painting of the Pontiff in a Catholic club and marched with it through the streets, finally trampling it with cries of "Traitor." A bomb was thrown into the Catholic headquarters at Imola.

The Pope replied, on June 29, 1931, with his encyclical *Non abbiamo bisogno.* Because of the strict Fascist censorship the Pope himself was forced to smuggle his encyclical. He called in two notable dignitaries, Monsignor F. J. Spellman, who is now assistant to Cardinal O'Connell, archbishop of Boston, and Monsignor Vanneuf-ville, canon of the Lateran and member of the higher council of the Propaganda Fide, also correspondent of the Catholic organ, *La Croix,* in Paris, and published the encyclical in France.

"They have tried to strike to death all that was and will be always dearest to the heart of Our Father and Pastor of Souls," wrote the Pope in his encyclical, recounting numerous "brutalities and beatings, blows and bloodshed—and all this lamentable accompaniment of disrespect and violence accomplished with such intervention of members of the [Fascist] party in uniform, with such condescension from the authorities and from the forces of public safety, that it is necessary to believe that these decisions came from above." The Pope then denies the official versions sent from Rome, "genuine slander spread by the party press," and the Radio d'Italia;

finally the Pope denounces as ridiculous the statement that the Azione
had become a "nest" for the Popolari. Of the directors of 250
diocesan organizations, 4,000 sections of Catholic men's clubs, and
5,000 groups of Catholic male youth, only four men were connected
with the old Popolari, "and, we must add, that in the four cases
in question there are those who are sympathizers with the régime
and the party which they look upon favorably."

"And here We find Ourselves," continues Pius XI, "confronted
by a mass of authentic affirmations and no less authentic facts which
reveal beyond the slightest possibility of doubt the resolve (already
in great measure actually put into effect) to monopolize completely
the young, from their tenderest years up to manhood and woman-
hood, for the exclusive advantage of a party and of a régime based
on an ideology which clearly resolves itself into a true, a real pagan
worship of the State—the Statolatry—which is no less in contrast
with the natural rights of the family than it is in contradiction with
the supernatural rights of the Church.

"We have seen, in fact, in action a species of religion which rebels
against the directions of higher religious authorities, and imposes or
encourages the nonobservance of these directions . . . a religious
sentiment that goes to extremes, and permits others to indulge in
insulting words and actions against the person of the Father and of
all the faithful, even to cry out 'Down with the Pope and death to
him!' This is real teaching of parricide. It is a semblance of religion
which cannot in any way be reconciled with Catholic doctrine and
practice. . . .

"A conception of the State which makes the young generations
belong entirely to it, without any exception from the tenderest years
up to adult life, cannot be reconciled by a Catholic with the Catholic
doctrine and cannot either be reconciled with the natural right of
the family. . . .

"You ask Us, Venerable Brethren, in view of what has taken
place, what is to be thought about the formula of an oath[5] which
even little boys and girls are obliged to take about executing without

[5] "I swear to obey the orders of the Duce without questioning them and to serve the
cause of the Fascist Revolution with all my force and if necessary with my blood."

discussion orders from an authority which, as we have seen and experienced, can give orders against all truth and justice and in disregard of the rights of the Church and its souls, which are already by their very nature sacred and inviolable, and to have them swear to serve with all their strength, even to the shedding of blood. The cause of a revolution that snatches the youth from the Church and from Jesus Christ and which educates its own young forces to hate, to deeds of violence, and to irreverence, not excluding the person of the Pope himself, as the latest facts have very evidently demonstrated. . . . Such an oath as it stands is unlawful."

This encyclical, suppressed for several days by the Italian press, made a great sensation and won worldwide sympathy for the Pope from Protestants as well as Catholics.

On July 9th Mussolini ordered Fascisti to abandon the Azione Cattolica. The Pope declared Catholicism and Fascism incompatible; Mussolini declared Fascism and Catholicism incompatible. Both are right. After two years of trying to render unto the Duce the things which are the Duce's and unto God the things that are God's, the real crisis had come and both sides realized that there can be no friendship between two opposing ideologies.

On September 3rd the Vatican and the Chigi Palace announced a compromise agreement which made the Azione Cattolica strictly diocesan, dependent on the bishops, aloof from politics, foreign to trade unions. It was considered as a codicil to the Lateran Pacts. The Fascist government restored compatibility between party and Catholic institutions. On the third anniversary of the Vatican treaty Mussolini, accompanied by his ambassador, Count Cesar-Marie de Vecchi di Val Cismon, the same gentleman who voluntarily assumed responsibility for the massacre of Turin and who during the Matteotti uprising proposed "three minutes of shooting to destroy the Opposition," paid a grand ceremonial visit to the Vatican. The Borghi and neighboring quarters were put in a state of seige and several thousand persons were obliged to spend their time in jail until the 13th of February. Mussolini was closeted with the Pope from 10:45 to 11:15, one of the longest interviews ever given a visitor.

Did Mussolini kiss the Pope's slipper? European diplomatic circles and the whole Catholic world were greatly intrigued by this visit. *Le Peuple* of Bruxelles, which claims editorially it obtained the description from one "in close touch with 'the eye of the Vatican,'" thus describes the historic occasion:

"A painful silence reigned. . . . Finally Mussolini precipitated himself at the feet of the Pope and kissed the slipper humbly, at the same time giving himself great blows on the chest. With infinite bountifulness the Successor to Saint Peter raised his visitor and said to him:

"'Repent, repent, my son. All is not yet lost for you.'

"A few minutes later the Pope asked Mussolini what time it was. Mussolini went pale. He quickly caught the significance. He said:

"'I have only a Swiss watch, but it is not the one I placed on the table at the time the police of His Majesty the King of Italy, Victor Emmanuel, did me the honor of tracking me down as my men now track down those who now think as I then did. The cheap nickel watch which I placed on the table in addressing an ultimatum to God was pawned by me when I was outlawed. In this connection I have to confess that I have failed to reimburse those comrades who aided me out of their pocketbooks in those regrettable times.

"'But today I no longer deny God by according him five minutes in which to strike me dead as proof that he exists. I now know why I was not struck by lightning: the Church needed me.'"

Interviewing the Duce some time later, Emil Ludwig asked him whether or not he kissed the Pope's slipper. Mussolini replied:

"In general I do as the Romans do. That is to say, I accept the custom of the country where I am being entertained. At the Vatican I was left to follow my own bent."

Has Mussolini been converted? In the Fascist Catechism he had written "Fascism is not atheistic, but any army of believers. Religion alone makes possible the realization of great human ideals. Science . . . cannot explain all the phenomena of life; there remains always a closed wall on which one word alone should be written: 'God.'" To an American woman admirer he was even more outspoken. "I feel God deeply," he said, lifting his eyes. "While God protects me no

human force can stop me. I live dangerously and God protects me."
But to the astute Ludwig, whose interviews Mussolini himself cor-
rected and officially stamped, he admitted frankly that he is still a
free-thinker. This paragraph, it is not strange to say, was deleted
from the second Italian edition.

With considerable irony a Catholic newspaper headlined Mussolini's visit to the Vatican "Caesar and Peter have shaken hands."
It had in mind Mussolini's favorite poet, Carducci, who wrote:

> *Quando porge la mano Cesare a Piero*
> *da quella stretta sangue umano stilla;*
> *quando il bacio si dan Chiesa ed Impero,*
> *un astro di martirio in ciel sfavilla.*

[When Caesar shakes hands with Peter, human blood flows;
when the Church and the empire embrace, the star of a martyr
is lit in the heavens.]

The press of Italy considered the new accord a Fascist victory.
It declared that although the encyclical was extremely violent, although the Pope denounced the "Totalitarian" idea of Fascism, the
Vatican has come around to the thesis of the régime. Although it need
not be admitted that the Catholic Action has been engaged in politics,
it is certain that in the future it is pledged never to do so. By the
new arrangement, not only must members restrain themselves to
religious and spiritual works, but they cannot engage in social action,
cannot in any way rival Fascist action, and the youth movement loses
all its character which was antagonistic to the Fascist or militarist
youth movement.

It marks the end of the plan of a vast Catholic party with a
Christian as opposed to a Fascist program.

If the Vatican, through Father Tacchi-Venturi, has obtained as-
surances that the Totalitarian plan will be changed, that religious
teachings of youth will be liberalized, that the incompatibility of
Christianity and Fascism will be compromised, these facts are secret.
That a tacit understanding of this nature exists has been admitted by
La Croix, the official French Catholic publication.

Officially, it must be said, the settlement of the Roman question has been a magnificent example of political opportunism. The old axiom, *Religio instrumentum regni,* has taken on new life in Italy. "Fascism," in the opinion of the editorial writer of the London *Times,* "respects pietism, bigotry, and superstition so far as they serve to keep the peasants, particularly in the south, in ignorance and submission, but it does not allow, for instance, the Church to take any part in the education of youth (hence the abolition of the Catholic Boy Scouts), or to take care of the moral and social welfare of the faithful (hence the persecution of the Demo-Christians). The crucifix is in the schools, but several priests are in the prisons."

In the first large engagement, 1929, Mussolini had won a Pyrrhic victory; in the pitched battle of 1931 Mussolini triumphed. According to non-Fascists it was a triumph of desperation made necessary by the growth of the movement within Catholicism against the political régime. It is quite true, as Fascists contend, that all the liberal, democratic, and intelligent minority in Italy, driven under cover, had taken refuge in the Azione Cattolica, the only institution in the country where there was a trace of freedom left. And now the Catholic Action has been emasculated as a political body.

On Mussolini's proud chest today appears, surrounded by the decorations of a military character, the Order of the Holy Sepulchre. Good Catholics ask, can this cross over his heart cover the years of Fascist violence, the assassination of Matteotti, the bombs sent to Cardinal Ferrari with Fascist compliments, the murder of the heroic priest of Argenta, the attacks on the Catholic Scouts, the destruction of Catholic clubs and coöperatives, the dissolution of the Catholic Party, and finally the emasculation of the Azione Cattolica? Good Catholics shake their heads doubtfully.

The Pope, like the King—it is no secret in Rome—remains anti-Fascist. He knows that his adversary is acting a part. He knows also that a dictatorship can disappear as suddenly as it is born and that the Church goes marching on. He watches all the reverences, the kneelings, and the professions of faith of the neophyte as that of an atheist of yesterday and probably of tomorrow. The Pope's own verdict on Fascism is very simple. "Nothing built on violence ever endures," he said. The Totalitarian or Corporative State in the opinion of Pius XI remains "unchristian." The Pope has not changed his mind.

For the time being the victory is Caesar's. But the Kingdom of the Pale Galilean and the Hierarchy of the heretic of Predappio cannot exist forever, morally function, side by side, and one within the other. The eventual triumph lies in the future.

CHAPTER XXIV

Diplomacy: Corfu to Ethiopia

IN DIPLOMACY, THE WAGING OF WARS AND THE DIRECTING OF THEIR occasional interruptions, peace, Mussolini's course has been rather helter-skelter: in fact, in this field more than any other he has proven himself a zigzag Caesar.

The record can be divided into three important sections. First there was the flamboyant period with the attack on Greece, defiance for the League of Nations, loud fulminations in praise of violence, demagoguery in international affairs on a par almost with internal affairs, imperialistic gestures without corollary actions, all in all the manifestations of the same youthful spirit which was first in evidence on the Socialist soap-boxes of three countries. The Duce became an international figure at the age of thirty-nine.

But the years of contact, as journalist and colleague, with Lloyd George, Curzon, Chamberlain, Simon, Poincaré, Barthou, Stresemann and other professional diplomats of the conventional school, and the fatality of compromises, softened Mussolini in his second phase. He learned quickly and adapted himself to circumstances with the unequaled ability which he had demonstrated throughout his career. This, then, became the period of the great Anglo-Saxon flirtation when the Duce dropped his threats against Britain, whom he never forgave for being the possessor of Gibraltar, Malta, and Cyprus, and became in turn the chastened follower of Downing Street diplomacy, at the same time espousing the cause of the German people and Germany's allies, the Revisionist nations.

The third, or present, stage of Mussolinism contains many elements of the first: instead of Greece the enemy is Ethiopia, and the army and navy are again on the road to conquest, and again the League of Nations, which Mussolini at one time dominated through

the brilliance of his representative, Dino Grandi, is the object of
scorn; imperialism again rules his mind, although his utterances lack
the reckless defiance of a decade ago, and there is more evidence
today that growing desperation of a broken home economy demands
foreign recompenses.

The first test of Mussolini's diplomacy followed an incident on
the Greek-Albanian border. An Italian general named Tellini and
his staff of four were ambushed on August 24, 1923, and assassinated
by Albanian bandits in the forest near Janina. Without a moment's
hesitation, in which he might have learned on whose soil the murders
occurred and the nationality of the murderers, Mussolini, who had
yet to wage his first war, sent an ultimatum to Greece. He demanded
(1) an official apology; (2) a formal memorial service for the dead;
(3) honors for the Italian flag; (4) an inquiry into the affair within
five days; (5) capital punishment for the murderers; (6) an indemnity of 50,000,000 lire within five days; (7) military honors for
the Italian victims, and (8) a reply within twenty-four hours.

Greece accepted five of these points immediately and asked for a
compromise on the others, notably the size of the indemnity, which
Greece could not deliver at once. On the advice of the council of
ambassadors which was held in Paris on the 30th Greece agreed to
meet Italy in a conference.

That same day, however, Mussolini mobilized his fleet with remarkable speed and efficiency. The battleships sailed proudly out of
the harbors of Italy and the nation recaptured the hot transcendental
feeling of patriotism. At three in the afternoon of the 31st an Italian
officer visited the prefect of Corfu to inform him of the imminent
capture of the island. The prefect replied that the old fort was not
occupied militarily, but was used by refugees. (A later Italian statement claims the officer did not understand this statement.) The prefect said he had no troops, that he had no means of fighting, and
that his only course could be passive resistance.

The ultimatum having been delivered, the Italian navy began its
bombardment at five o'clock. Shell after shell crashed down on the
police barracks and the fort. There was no reply. For an hour the
bombardment continued, and at six the victorious Fascisti landed
and stormed the silent fort. From its wreckage came the screams of

wounded and the groans of the dying. Of the hundred victims, according to Colonel Bowe of the American Near East Relief, there were twenty dead, of whom sixteen were infants, the wards of American charity.[1] Greece appealed to the League of Nations; the American Red Cross buried the dead; in Rome Fascism celebrated its first military victory.

An astonished and indignant world accused Mussolini of a "brutal assault" upon a peaceful and innocent nation. Outside of Italy press and public united in sympathy for Greece. Mussolini sent special cables to many newspapers. In one of them he explained his actions in this way:

"I ordered the Italian navy to occupy Corfu because I know the Greeks and was aware that if I did not take a pledge for their payment of reparation I would get nothing out of them. I have now taken a pledge and I will retain it until there has been a complete and literal fulfillment of the conditions of my ultimatum to them. If the Greeks fulfill these and pay up I will withdraw from Corfu, but they had better pay soon, for next week the price will be higher. These naval operations are expensive. Battleships won't steam on songs. If for any reason Greece does not pay I will remain in Corfu indefinitely. It was Venetian territory for four centuries, anyway. I have no intention of occupying more Greek territory or inflicting other penalties, unless, of course, the Greeks are foolish enough to attack Italian subjects or property. In that case I shall be forced to take immediate military action.

"Italian public opinion does not like the League of Nations, for a very good reason. We respect its aims, but I completely deny its authority to intervene in a matter affecting Italian honor. The present affair does not come under the League Covenant, as there is no danger of war."[2]

But the League thought otherwise. Lord Robert Cecil on the 1st of September informed it there was no doubt whatever of its competency to deal with the conflict nor its duty to do so, and Branting of Sweden demanded action against Italy. The Marquis della Tor-

[1] U. S. Ambassador R. W. Child, later a Fascist agent, hinted that the Greeks purposely placed the refugees in the fort.

[2] *New York Herald.*

retta stated to Lord Curzon that the League had no business in the Corfu affair; Lord Curzon replied that the whole weight of British prestige was behind the League, and the press began speaking of an international boycott and joint naval action against Italy.

But bravely Mussolini stuck to his guns. "In case the Council of the League of Nations declares itself competent," he said in an official statement dated the 4th, three days after the Council had already done so, "the question whether to remain or resign from the League of Nations arises in Italy. I have already voted for the second solution."

That week, not for the first and not for the last time, the tension at Geneva reached a breaking-point and the collapse of Woodrow Wilson's foundation seemed imminent. But, as was to be repeated when Japan withdrew, and when Germany withdrew, and when Italy again threatened in the summer of 1935 over the Ethiopian crisis, the directors of the society of peace capitulated before the man of war. As in all diplomacy, a "formula" to save faces had to be found, and in this instance it was decided that, although the League was not to insist on its competency, the council of ambassadors in Paris, consisting of the same set of diplomats, should make the decision. This decision, naturally enough, was on the side of force and possession: the evacuation of Corfu was traded for Greek fulfillment of the ultimatum, the 50,000,000 lire in cash having been provided, according to report, by Sir Basil Zaharoff.

From all points of view, military, political, patriotic, the victory was Mussolini's. His and Italy's prestige rose. Europe sat up and took notice of a new man who would probably have a lot to say in its international affairs in the future. The official report of the mission headed by a British, a French, and a Japanese colonel, which after a month's investigation found that Greece was entirely innocent in the Janina affair, made no impression outside of Athens.

There was, however, one important diplomatic aftermath. "The first anniversary of the occupation of Corfu," writes V. Demetrio in *La Politica estera di Mussolini*,[3] and neither the Italian nor the British Foreign Office has denied it, "was celebrated by Great Britain, not by Fascist Italy.

[3] Milan, 1925 (before the suppression of the free press), p. 27.

"It was exactly twelve months after the ephemeral occupation by the Italians that the British admiralty organized large maneuvers in the Ionian Sea, and it was on this occasion that the British government obtained from the Greek government the permission to debark heavy artillery in Corfu for the purpose of participating in the mock war.

"A similar permission had never before been asked for nor granted.

"This was the reply to Mussolini.

"Unfortunately, on this account, Italy was obliged to watch impotently the making of a wicked precedent on whose account the Mediterranean equilibrium has been, without motive, troubled."

But the Greek adventure, with its sixteen dead children and its indemnity of 50,000,000 lire (the expedition cost 288,000,000, a fact almost successfully hidden in the budget), and its salute for the Italian flag, while not the great military success anticipated, still did lead to something for Mussolini. In Livorno, on the 30th of September, 1926, Mussolini and Sir Austen Chamberlain held a Machiavellian conference, from which came reports that the Italian Premier had promised support for an expedition against Turkish Anatolia, where territory could be seized for both nations, or, should the adventure be canceled, Mussolini would be given a free hand in seizing Albania, provided, however, that he support the British in intimidating the Turks, who were claiming Mosul and preparing a descent upon Bagdad.

Whatever arrangements were made between the two great statesmen is their own affair, and the records, if they exist, remain archive secrets. Historically, however, what happened was that after this famous meeting of Livorno, Chamberlain without a blow drove the Turks from the Iraq frontier and Mussolini without a blow began the complete economic, military, and political penetration of Albania.

The first important nation to adopt Mussolini's brand of Fascism was Spain, and the latest is Germany. The universal Fascism of which Mussolini speaks also embraces Austria, Hungary, Poland, Bulgaria, Yugoslavia, and Esthonia, while in the Far East the government of Chiang Kai-Chek may be termed completely Fascist, while that of Japan the nearest to Fascism of all reactionary governments.

In addition Fascist parties have grown extremely powerful in Ireland, Finland, Rumania, and Spain, and Fascist elements of considerable varying strength have appeared in Portugal, Holland, France, and Greece, and there have been initiations in England, Switzerland, Czechoslovakia, Sweden, Cuba, and—although leaders and membership deny and express abhorrence of the name—in the United States.

In Spain, Germany, Austria, Bulgaria, Greece, Hungary, and Rumania Mussolini has played a not unimportant part. In September, 1923, General Miguel Primo de Rivera established a Fascist dictatorship with the approval of the king and the aid of the artillery officers, and in November he came to Rome for a consultation. Mussolini laid down the principle of Discipline, Order, and Hierarchy; Primo agreed; together they made a secret military pact against France[4] and a commercial pact against the United States—they agreed to exploit South America together and undermine the influence of Yankee traders—and like two commercial travelers they divided the market for spaghetti, oranges, wine, artificial silk, olive oil, and other products. Commenting on the success of his visit, Dictator Primo uttered these exalted words:

"On Mussolinism has been formed a creed, a doctrine of redemption, which is drawing to it an army of recruits throughout the world."

In 1926, following Mussolini's example of 1924, Primo held a plebiscite to endorse dictatorship, and like his preceptor, he ordered that no opposition votes should be cast. Announcing the resultant great popular victory, the Spanish dictator declared, "I believe with Mussolini that the principle of liberty is pretty as a principle, but is no longer effective as a rule of conduct for a nation and must be replaced by the principle of authority.

"Public opinion must be strictly controlled.

"The masses must not direct the government, but the government the masses.

"The parliamentary system has had its day . . . it is no longer indispensable; it is harmful.

---

[4] The contents of which were published by the Spanish diplomat, Santiago Alba, after his exile to France.

"My system will last, not for my personal convenience, but for the good of the country.

"Mussolini's actions showed me what I had to do to save my country. Mussolini is a torch which affords light to nations."

Two years later de Rivera supplemented his views. "There are few who can deny," he said, "that from a material point of view dictatorships in Europe have, on the whole, proved profitable.

"I condemn noisy and sterile assemblies. It is true that when nations and their parliaments reach a high degree of culture they escape the peril. Sr. Mussolini has declared that a democratic parliamentary régime is a luxury for rich nations. He is perfectly correct. In rich countries and highly civilized ones, parliament has its uses.

"As for Italy, everyone is aware that chronic strikes have ceased, that the lira has been stabilized, that the provinces of the south are making progress, and that regions formerly unhealthful are now being developed.

"As for my own country, dare anyone deny that the dictatorship has made considerable material progress, manifest in every branch of our economic life?"

The answer to this question was given by the republican government which followed the resignation of de Rivera on January 28, 1930, and the collapse of his successor, General Berenguer, on April 12, 1931: in 1928, it was announced, the economic system of dictatorial Spain had broken down, but was saved by a loan of 25,000,000 pesetas from Wall Street; in 1931 the complete collapse was so imminent that the dictatorship was negotiating with the banking houses of Morgan, Chase, National City, Kuhn Loeb, Guaranty Trust, Dillon Read, and Lee Higginson for $38,000,000 and the Banque de Paris et des Pays Bas for an additional $22,000,000.

Tremendous financial scandals were brought to light, proving that the business men and militarists behind Primo had made millions of dollars' profit, while the dictatorship had falsified the budget for years; instead of the officially announced balances there had been expenditures of 4,000,000,000 pesetas and a deficit of a quarter of a billion; the treasury had only 68,000,000 pesetas on hand instead of the officially announced 320,000,000; the Duke of Tetuan blamed the dictatorship for the flight of capital, loss of confidence, financial crisis, dishonest elections, suppression of liberty, unparalleled waste, and the general distrust of the people of Spain.

Niceto Alcala Zamora, emerging from the prison where the dictatorship had placed him, assumed the Presidency, and one of his first actions was to send a cablegram to Italian anti-Fascists to make Spain their home and look upon the republic as their friend. Francesco Macia, once imprisoned in France as a result of a plot by the Fascist agent Ricciotti Garibaldi, was proclaimed President of the Catalonian Republic. The military treaty between de Rivera and Mussolini was denounced.

Thus, if only temporarily, ended the first of the important Fascist dictatorships modeled upon that of Italy.

In February, 1925, the Grand Council of the Fascist Party under the presidency of its duce discussed "Preliminary examination of the possibility of a universal understanding between the Fascist and similar movements." There was little repercussion in the world press. But within the next decade, as Fascism made headway in many parts of Europe, journalists questioned the Duce.

"Fascism is purely Italian," the originator replied to one; "Fascism is not an article for export," he said to a German, and "America has no need for Fascism," he remarked to an American. Then in the spring of 1930 he wrote, signed and sold an article recounting seven years of the achievements of Fascismo, in which he said:

"Fascism is a typically Italian product, as Bolshevism is a typically Russian product. Neither one nor the other can be transplanted and live outside its country of origin."[5]

However, in his tour of northern Italy in May, Mussolini when not rattling the sword, defying France and Yugoslavia, extended an invitation to other nations to follow his successful methods. "Europe, tormented, uneasy and disheartened," he said in Milan, "will not find its salvation except through the coming of Fascism."

(On September 14, 1930, Reichstag elections were held in Germany, giving the Fascists—the still little known National Socialist Labor Party of Adolf Hitler—a considerable victory.)

Celebrating the eighth anniversary of the taking of Rome, il Duce made one of the most important explanations of Fascist diplomacy

[5] *New York World*, March 2, 1930, magazine section, p. 1.

of his career: he explained the Spring tour of oratory which had offended a large part of the peace-seeking world; announced Italy as the champion of the Revisionist bloc which sought to amend or destroy the peace treaties upon which the Status Quo nations led by France insisted, and announced the universality of Fascism. He said:

"By the year 1950 Italy will be the only country of young people in Europe, while the rest of Europe will be wrinkled and decrepit. People will come from over the frontier to see the phenomenon of this blooming spring of the Italian people. . . .

"Only toward the East can our pacific expansion occur. . . .

"Their phrase [referring to the German press] that 'Fascismo is not an article for export' is not mine. It is too banal. It was adopted for the readers of newspapers who in order to understand anything need to have it translated into terms of commercial jargon. In any case it must now be amended.

"Today I affirm that the idea, doctrine, and spirit of Fascismo are universal. It is Italian in its particular institutions, but it is universal in spirit; nor could it be otherwise, for spirit is universal by its very nature.

"It is therefore possible to foresee a Fascist Europe which will model its institutions on Fascist doctrine and practice, a Europe which will solve in the Fascist way the problems of the modern State of the twentieth century."

Then, in 1932, Mussolini and Ludwig engaged in the series of interviews already mentioned. Ludwig, mindful of the German press report that Mussolini had said, "Fascism is not an article for export," and then said it was not his phrase, since it was so banal, asked:

"Can Fascism be exported to Germany?"

"To no country," replied Mussolini. "It is an Italian growth. . . ."

Thus ended many years of preaching the gospel of Fascism as an indigenous miracle. Up to the end of 1930 Mussolini had had only one important follower, Primo de Rivera of Spain, but in 1933 one of the really great nations of the world was apparently ready to accept the dictatorial, militaristic, big-business State which he had created. The pragmatic politician, therefore, felt he was at liberty not only to deny his signed statement on the impossibility of Fascism to live transplanted in foreign soil, but to ridicule those who had published the manuscript he had sold them.

"Fascism," he announced after Hitler came into power, "is a religion; the twentieth century will be known in history as the century of Fascism"; and celebrating the anniversary of the founding of the party, he said to the Grand Council on March 18, 1934: "Since 1929 . . . Fascism has become universal. . . . One need only look about him to see that the principles of the past century are dead. We admit unreservedly that they had their period of fecundity and grandeur! But it is over.

"Those who would check the course of history, those who would arrest its movement or stem its tide, have been overwhelmed. The political forces of the last century—Democracy, Socialism, Liberalism, Freemasonry—are spent. . . . The trend is toward new forms of civilization, both in politics and in economics. The State is resuming its right and its prestige as the sole and supreme interpreter of the needs of society."

Pending the years of mere protestations of friendship and declarations of the indigenousness or universality of Fascism, Mussolini had more than platonic relations with Fascist minorities in many countries of Europe. He went the Bolsheviki one better. Whereas the Third Internationale had been accused by almost every nation in the world of spending sums which would total many times more billions than the world possesses on propaganda work abroad, the Fascisti engaged in the more practical and paying business of smuggling arms to Fascist parties in Europe.

Thanks to the social consciousness of several Austrian railroad workingmen, Italy was caught black-handed in January, 1928, in a plot to send twenty-two freight-cars loaded with munitions to Rumania and five car-loads of machine-guns, marked for delivery in Poland but intended for sidetracking into Hungary. This became known as the St. Gothard affair.

The League of Nations intervened and reported. The Italian diplomats attempted to have the report suppressed and it might have been but for the astuteness of American journalists. Not only was the 1928 case reported in full, but evidence was obtained from the archives of the League that Italy had been engaged in smuggling arms to Fascist parties from 1922 on. In 1925 the main shipments were to Hungary, Bulgaria, and Adolf Hitler in Bavaria. The sender of the arms was revealed as the Commercio Universale di Ferramenta Ordigni, which Geneva reported a blind under which were hidden the factories under control of the Fascist government and whose stock was held by Fascist generals.

It was found that in December, 1925, eleven freight-cars passed Bozen, Austrian-Italy, for Rosenheim, the military headquarters of the Hitler-Ludendorff movement. The addressee was Marx & Co., a commercial house in Rosenheim, the sender Frumenti, a well-known Fascist vice-duce in Bozen; the contents were small arms, machine-guns and ammunition. Upon seizure by Austrian border authorities, the Fascist Frumenti came to the customs-house, paid a fine of 27,000 lire for false customs declaration, and the next day sent Fascist militiamen to Rosenheim to investigate the report that Italian railroad workers had given away the secret.

The League of Nations in the St. Gothard affair warned Hungary to preserve the evidence intact, but the Hungarians sold the 2,000 machine-guns—a number enough to equip fifty regiments—for junk. Mussolini, although failing to deny Fascist complicity, issued an order to the press to attack the League for interfering with business and to accuse "certain nations" who were afraid of the arming of "defenseless Hungary," as "cowards."

Smuggling continued. Occasionally there was a scandal. Then in January, 1933, came the Hirtenberg affair. Italy, Hungary, and Austrian Fascists were caught in a conspiracy to violate the Trianon and St. Germain treaties in the smuggling of 50,000 rifles and 200 machine-guns to Fascist elements, notably Prince Stahremberg, who with M. Mandl operated the arms factories at Steyr and Hirtenberg. Prince Stahremberg, friend of Hitler, commanded the Austrian Fascists in 1933 with the blessings of Monsignor Seipel, the ex-chancellor who planned to make himself dictator.

Again Socialist workmen exposed the plot, and the Allies, more concerned with Austria than with the shipments to Bulgarians, Hungarians, and Hitlerites, sent an "ultimatum" to Dollfuss which, despite a request for secrecy, was published by the Fascist press bureau. Dollfuss, having to choose between a $40,000,000 loan from the

Allies and the support of Stahremberg, was forced to return the shipment. The guns, accordingly, were started for Italy. At this moment Berthold Koenig, head of the Socialist Railway Workers Union of Austria, according to information given by him in the Austrian parliament, was offered 150,000 shillings for the association if the workmen would permit the shipment to take a wrong switch at a point indicated, so that the guns would be delivered at Sopron, in Hungary, where, the arms having been removed, the cases would be sealed officially and sent on to Italy.

Upon exposure of the plot by Julius Deutsch, Socialist leader in parliament, Dollfuss was forced to dismiss Dr. Egon Seefahlner, director of the state railroads, but he did not prosecute the case farther. Koenig testified that Seefahlner, although the author of the bribe offer, had conspired with the Hungarian government for the delivery of the guns and with the Fascist government in furthering this scheme and arranging to accept the empty cases in silence. At this moment Sir John Simon acted. Britain brought such pressure upon Austria that Stahremberg could by no means retain the guns, and in July the British Foreign Minister announced the safe return to Italy.

In France this scandal was followed by another involving the delivery of Italian war planes to Hungary in contravention of the peace treaty: Eighteen Fiat pursuit and thirty two-seaters and twelve Caproni bombers, also twenty tons of gas and twelve tons of aerial bombs.[6] In Prague Mr. Benes informed parliament that "only one or two out of a hundred contraband lots are caught"; he demanded in the name of the Little Entente that the League take action to prevent Fascist smuggling operations in the future.

At this point Mussolini broke his unusual silence. On his instructions to the press there followed a series of articles showing that France, Czechoslovakia, and Britain were shipping about a hundred times as much arms as Italy. There was one point, however, the Fascist press was instructed to overlook: the Allied arms were being shipped to Allies, which was legal, whereas the Fascist arms were being shipped either to ex-enemy countries in violation of the peace treaties, or to extra-legal organizations, in defiance to law and ethics.

[6] *Journal Officiel*, March 10, 1933.

In all Mussolini's intrigue in Germany, Austria, the Balkans, and Africa, his proposed union of dictatorships, his alternate defiance and attempted leadership of the League of Nations, the penetration of Albania and the various enterprises in Tangiers, Tunis, and Ethiopia, the visits to Cyrenaca and Tripolitania, and the final declaration of the universality of Fascism, there runs the thread of a dream: the old Roman dream. Charlemagne was the first of the long series of imitation Caesars who attempted to conquer and rule the old empire, and the refugee Wilhelm in Doorn is not the last to have that dream. The son of the Forli blacksmith sitting under the bust of Julius cannot escape it.

World empire through Pan-Fascismo seemed a possibility for a little while in 1930, but that dream was torn by shell-fire in the battle of Vienna when the impossibility of coöperating with Hitler was made evident. But before that event and even now there has persisted an idea for a Holy Roman Empire to be divided equally with the Pope, which would embrace the Catholic countries from Italy to the Danube and including the Rhineland, Hungary, Croatia, a part of Yugoslavia, and Bavaria. And a third idea of similar nature was presented to the world in Mussolini's 1932 "Cry of Alarm," published universally, in which he suggested himself as a leader of a coalition of all the European nations in a holy crusade against that Russia which in the face of universal depression was announcing the successful completion of the first Five-Year-Plan in four years.

In one form or another, therefore, the Caesarian idea remains. Either as the commander-in-chief of the Revisionist nations against the Status Quo nations, or as the leader of Europe against the common enemy, the Red Menace, or as the founder of a new African empire, or as the directing head of a Danube confederation or a Catholic bloc, Mussolini's mind can find the right place for himself. When Briand proposed his United States of Europe the loudest advocates of nationalism were not opposed; on the contrary, the Fascist viewpoint as shown by one of the semi-official publications was an approving one—under conditions. If Europe united as one super-nation, "it would be necessary," declared the Roman voice, "to present a new and formidable political idea, a code of life, which could assure the collaboration not only of languages, of nationalities, but also of classes, and provoke a rapid development of equilibrium and economics, and envisage at the same time a wise valorization of all creative possibilities. It will therefore be a Fascist idea because only Fascist Italy has been able to realize that which might serve as a model. In organizing the United States of Europe it will be necessary to name a president, a chief, and a man must be chosen, the most genial, the most celebrated, the strongest and the most respected on the continent. Evidently it will be Benito Mussolini because he combines all these qualities."

The future may bring Mussolini some realization of the hope of world empire; the past can be summed up as follows: Corfu was a failure, but the penetration of Albania a good success; the intrigue with the Bavarian Nazis was at first a success, and now, at least temporarily, a failure; the secret coöperation with the dictator of Spain was a complete failure; the rôle of patron saint of discontent is no longer applicable, because Germany, chief of the Revisionist nations, has, without Mussolini's aid, destroyed rather than revised the Versailles Treaty, and yet vicariously that success, whether pleasant or not for the Allies and for the world, must go to Mussolini.

He has made Italy an imperialist nation. Whereas that other Caesar of our time said that "Germany, like the spirit of Imperial Rome, must expand and impose itself," the Duce exposed his principal objective in a declaration to a German editor when he said: "We are obliged to fight on our soil, too small for our overpopulation, for the smallest grain of nutritive substance. Despite scientific effort, Italy cannot nourish its people. *We must expand or explode.*[7] I do not feel myself authorized to believe in the humanitarian idealism of the pacifists."

For the explosion itself Mussolini then named the year 1935. In 1935 Italy was at war in Africa. The admitted overpopulation is a danger to the peace of the world, intensified by both the encouragement of the birth rate and the refusal of the colonial nations to cede rich land to Italy. And more important than all else is the necessity of imperialism to explode because its economic structure makes that, instead of peaceful methods, the one way out of its own dilemmas.

[7] To Theodore Wolff, editor of the *Berliner Tageblatt*, January 30, 1930. The Associated Press, whose Rome correspondent was then an Italian, cabled a similar interview with the italicized phrase as "We must expand or suffocate."

CHAPTER XXV

The Corporate State: People under Fascism

ALTHOUGH IN TURN THE BATTLE OF THE LIRA, THE BATTLE OF THE Grain, the Battle of the Babies, and many other triumphs have been announced by Mussolini as the outstanding event of his reign, the Duce is also the author of the statement that his greatest gift to civilization and the harassed modern world, the accomplishment for which he will be remembered forever, is the Corporate State.

"There is one battle which I intend to win—the battle for the economic restoration of Italy," he declared in July, 1926; "I am now giving my earnest attention to the restoration of the balance of trade and the stabilization of the lira." That same day the following decrees were also issued:

Abolition of the eight-hour day.

Abolition of the right to strike.

Limitation of newspapers to six pages; crime news must be diminished.

Luxury hotels, cabarets, and the building of luxurious homes prohibited. Abolition of luxury imports.

Potato-raising must replace spaghetti-making.

A ten-o'clock curfew for tea, coffee, and alcohol.

This was part of a program of "prosperity by edict"; in the press of the United States and the free nations of Europe labor-leaders declared that "Labor's greatest gains in a century of struggle have been wiped out." Almost immediately afterwards Mussolini announced the completed Corporate State.

"For the first time in the history of the world a constructive revolution like ours realizes peacefully, in the field of production and

275

work, incorporation of all the economic and intellectual forces of the nation to direct them today in a common purpose. . . ."

Simultaneously with the establishment of the Corporate State came a series of loans in America and intensification of the propaganda, begun the year before, when the $100,000,000 Morgan loan was floated, that Fascism was the antithesis of Bolshevism, that Mussolini had saved not only Italy, but perhaps all of Europe, from the Red Menace, that the Corporate State was the answer to the universal Utopian urge which elsewhere, notably in Russia, was making itself known in a manner quite unacceptable to the organized profit-making system.

This new phenomenon, therefore, must be judged from three important points: whether it is actually the "salvation" from Communism; whether it actually functions; whether the people under the Corporate State have gone forward or backward.

To begin with, it must be said that despite the best American public-relations counsel employed by the international bankers, despite the newspapers and magazines which voluntarily surrendered to the Fascist propaganda machine, it is a historic fact that the whole Mussolini-Bolshevik story was a pure myth which dates from the time of the foreign loans, and the most important historian who first admitted that the Bolshevism of 1920 (the worst year, the time of the occupation of factories) had disappeared long before the victory of Fascism, wrote in 1921:

"The Italy of 1921 is fundamentally different from that of 1919. It has been said and demonstrated several times. Fascism must not have the air of monopolizing for itself the right of such a profound national change. It is enough to count Fascism among the forces, the most powerful and the most disciplined, which have operated in that direction. After having thus limited our merit, there is no man or party which can attack us.

"To say that the Bolshevik danger still exists in Italy is equivalent to trying to exchange, for reasons of self-interest, fear against the truth. Bolshevism is conquered.

"More than that, it has been disowned by the leaders and by the people."

This editorial is signed by Benito Mussolini.[1]

This same statesman who in 1925 and 1926 informed American journalists that Fascism rose to destroy Bolshevism is the same Mussolini who advocated not only confiscation of wealth, but the lynching of the patriotic body of war profiteers, the confiscation of land and industries, and in short played the part of the devil's or Lenin's advocate in Italy. But in December, 1920, three months after the factory seizures, he had also written in his *Popolo*:

"It is honest to admit that for the past three months, or precisely after the referendum on the occupation of the factories, and after the return of the mission to Russia [Serratti and others had brought back unfavorable reports on Bolshevism] the psychology of the working-masses has profoundly moderated. The famous wave of disgust and weakness seems conquered. . . . It is indisputable that the Italian working-class continues to offer the spectacle of laborious activity and discipline; one cannot refuse them participation more or less vast in the government of the nation."

If Mussolini's statement that Bolshevism had ceased to menace Italy after 1920 needs corroboration, he has had it from modern historians like H. G. Wells and Professor Salvemini. If liberal and anti-Fascist historians are not enough, we have the testimony of Professor Aulard of the Sorbonne, who states that long before the march on Rome "Bolshevism had been conquered, annihilated in Italy by the efforts of the sane democratic elements." Sanford Griffith reported in the conservative *Wall Street Journal* that "it is a distortion of fact to picture Italian business conditions as in a state of chaos, and the country on the brink of Red terror, when Mussolini and his Fascisti came into power." And Fascism's defender, Prezzolini, wrote that "Fascismo can hardly be called the destroyer of Italian Bolshevism, because when Mussolini's movement assumed the violent forms which gave it such a spectacular history, Bolshevism was already on the decline as a result of discouraging reports brought back by the emissaries from Russia. . . . In more than one sense it [Fascismo] is the heir to Italian Bolshevism."

But popular opinion—and the bankers—needed a Saint George and therefore refused to accept Saint George's own admission there

[1] Vide *Popolo d'Italia*, July 2, 1921.

was no Bolshevik dragon for him to kill in 1922. Popular opinion, therefore, finds consolation in those American economists, literateurs, and philosophers of the daily press and weeklies which boast readers by the millions. One of these writers[2] states that "Ruin impended. Mussolini took the short and unconstitutional cut which is the dictatorial way. He smashed precedents, turned red terror into white fear, and brought order and—what was even more important— economic revival out of the dust and din of class war and political bicker. In the last analysis, Fascism is not only a political force of historic moment, but it has been the impetus of an impressive commercial renaissance as well." This same political economist precedes this statement with an unqualified declaration that "the traditional parliamentary systems of Europe are failures," and a suggestion that France should join the dictatorships. It is true that the same writer in 1930 ate all his praise of dictatorships, but he remained the agent of the Italian Bolshevik myth. He wrote:

"Sovietization, with its attendant social and fiscal dislocation impended. The workers had seized the factories in all the important productive centers. Chaos loomed. In the darkest hour a strong man rose up and saved the day. The stern will of Mussolini, reinforced by the cohort of Black Shirts, imposed a régime that made for historic rehabilitation. Dictatorship achieved its best."

Another writer, a more flowery one,[3] believes that "everybody who has looked into the Fascist movement in Italy is agreed that it was a greatly needed movement and that it saved the nation from descending into a chaotic whirlpool of Communism and financial disaster that would have made Niagara's whirlpool look like a placid puddle of rain water in comparison." This is incidentally the same historian who glorifies Cesare Rossi as "the hero," who defends the castor-oil treatment, and who tells Americans that "in spite of his [Mussolini's] many changes, there has never been a word uttered against his absolute sincerity and honesty," and that "Mussolini's dictatorship is a good dictatorship."

This version of the Bolshevik myth accepted by such eminent gentlemen as Isaac Marcosson, Sir Percival Phillips, Kenneth L. Rob-

[2] Mr. Isaac Marcosson.
[3] Mr. Kenneth L. Roberts.

erts, Lord Rothermere, Luigi Villari, Lord Beaverbrook, Otto H. Kahn, Thomas Lamont, and Judge Gary of the United States Steel Corporation, eventually was noticed by the superman himself. The clever journalist realized that the world of big business was honoring him for something which he had denied, and he was opportunist enough to seize the tribute. From the time of the American loans onward he has been declaring himself the original Bolshevik-fighter of Europe.

"Adversaries of Fascism," he said in an oration in 1927, "have for a long time past been attempting to deny the revolutionary character of the events which took place towards the end of October, 1922, bringing the following argument in support of their allegations. First, that there was no real resistance, and therefore no conflicts, leading to bloodshed; secondly, that all the anti-Fascist parties withdrew, leaving the road open, because—these commentators of evil faith add—the Bolshevist danger had already disappeared since 1920, when the occupation of the factories ended in a bubble of soap. . . . In the face of these untrue assertions aimed at diminishing the generous and bloody effort of the Black Shirts we must never tire in our work of affirming and riveting the facts which led to the Fascist revolution." The Duce concluded by naming his facts: Bolshevik danger existed; the march on Rome was a bloody battle; etc. Forgotten were the signed editorials of another day, forgotten the statement to the King, forgotten everything which the opportunist mind *wills* to forget.

And so we find Mussolini in 1931 publishing his "Cry of Alarm" in which the world is warned that unless economic remedies are found for the economic collapse "Bolshevism will break through the Vistula"; again he made his bid as the leader of the united nations against Russia, and again he recommended in interviews that Europe adopt his Totalitarian idea in order to prevent the Communist idea from spreading.

What, then, is this new Corporate State, this substitute for Bolshevism which Mussolini has invented and recommends? It is, to begin with, philosophically based on Hegel; from this thinker who also influenced Karl Marx is drawn the first article of the Labor Charter which defines the new Italian nation as "an organism having aims, life, and means of action superior to those of the single or grouped individuals who compose it."

But after Hegel there came d'Annunzio, who in his *Carta della Regenza Italiana del Carnaro,* in his nineteenth article, created ten corporations which were to include all the people of Fiume and its dependencies, as follows: salaried workers of industry, agriculture, commerce, and transportation, etc.; members of technical and administrative bodies of industrial or rural firms; commercial workers who are not laborers; employers; public employees; intellectual flower of the people, studious youth, teachers, sculptors, painters, architects, musicians, etc.; free professions; coöperative societies of production, labor, and consumption; seamen. . . .

D'Annunzio put into noble strophes the ideas of his Prime Minister, De Ambris; Mussolini recooked d'Annunzio's poetry and combined it with the "philosophy" of nationalist-syndicalism of Alfredo Rocco; he was aided in this by Edmondo Rossoni, a former member of the American Industrial Workers of the World, whose habitat had been Brooklyn, New York, and who proposed the syndicalization of workers in vertical unions embracing all parts of an industry. All these gentlemen helped themselves from the writings of Georges Sorel, the French syndicalist.

The most important document of the new State is the Labor Charter, whose first eight articles were written by Mussolini. These provide that:

> Labor, intellectual, technical, manual, is a social duty.
>
> Syndicates are organized and controlled by the State.
>
> Collective labor contracts are established.
>
> Labor courts are established; the State intervenes and settles controversies.
>
> Each corporation constitutes the organization of one field of production, nationally.
>
> Private initiative is encouraged.
>
> Wages are paid "as best suited to the needs of employees and the undertaking."

The Labor Charter is a statement of aims, not a series of laws. It does emphasize the Totalitarian State idea, that the State is everything, the individual nothing. Although the workingman is called a "partner" in industry, he has no voice in it. Although lockouts are barred equally with strikes, and although the corporations which consist of employers and employees are entitled to elect the political directors of the Corporate State, it has surprised no one to find that in the hundreds of thousands of cases of labor unrest there are few instances in which the arbitration boards have to deal with lockouts, and politically the corporations are in the control of either the employers or of the Fascist Party.

The best summary of the corporate idea was made by Giuseppe Bottai, who represented it in the Fascist cabinet:

"The Corporate State idea, which Fascism has conceived and enforced, is an absolutely modern idea. The corporations of the Middle Ages were closed institutions; Italian corporativism, on the contrary, is founded essentially on the idea of syndicates, organizations to which access is on the principle freely open to all those who ply the same trade. Italian corporativism preserves the syndical structure likewise in the workers' syndicates as well as the employers' confederations, the two parallel organizations being united in a higher state which is the corporation.

"The directing idea is to integrate the syndical forces within the State, to utilize them. We do not deny the existence of the war of the classes; we do not suppress it; we simply enforce regulations by means of collective contracts of which 9,000 have been made, of which 300 to 400 apply to all of Italy, the other being of provincial character.

"The corporations penetrate all branches of public life. They are represented in the Chamber of Deputies by the Deputies, employers and employees, and equally in the Grand Council of the party. Furthermore, there exists a central committee of corporations.

"The influence of the corporations has produced in Italian industry a concentration whose happy results have been felt in its rationalization."[4]

When the Labor Charter was published, Rocco called it the Bill of Rights of Labor, but Rossoni, admitting it did guarantee minimum rights for the employee, said the employers would take advantage of

Prager Presse, January, 1933.

its vague terms. Rossoni was asked to resign. Labriola and Buozzi, the exiled labor-leaders, said simply it was a charter of slavery. But in February, 1929, Mussolini asked Buozzi, who had been head of the Italian Federation of Labor, to return from France to head the labor syndicates. In his refusal Buozzi said that the Duce's proposal showed that seven years of Fascism had not reconciled labor to the movement; that the workmen still trusted the old leaders; that he had once before refused to sell them out or to compromise his ideals and would not now.

The first practical step in the formation of the Corporate State was the prohibition of strikes under penalty of fines and imprisonment. In confirmation of Buozzi's views came the confession, at the Congress of Fascist Syndicates, June 30, 1929, that labor was not getting a new deal. Arnaldo Fioretti and the Hon. Begnotti, Fascist syndicate leaders, according to the official publication *Lavoro Fascista*, told the congress that workingmen were not fairly treated by employers, that the new labor contracts were not respected by the captains of industry, that the workingmen had lost faith in the Fascist syndicates, and that the Corporate State cannot be said to exist until the hostility and reprisals of employers against workmen had been removed and unjust dismissals stopped. No newspaper in Italy printed these official statements.

In May, 1930, Mussolini announced that the National Council of Corporations had been inaugurated, "to crown the Corporative State." He called it an economic revolution: not only was peace between capital and labor enforced, but prices would be regulated, and the quantity of production as well. The syndicates were announced as complete: six employers' federations in industry, agriculture, commerce, land transport, sea and air transport, and banking; and six corresponding employees' confederations. In addition there was a federation of all intellectual workers.

"We have thus created a united Italian State," said Mussolini. "Since the fall of the Roman Empire, Italy has never been a unified State. It is the State alone that makes the nation self-conscious."

In the national council there were fifty-two of Mussolini's picked men and thirteen representatives of the corporations.

In 1932 Fascist official figures showed that 4,181,848 Italians out

of some seven or eight million workingmen had become members of
the syndicates. What is remarkable about this figure is that it is
comparatively small because employment in Italy, as in Russia, is
extremely difficult, if not impossible, for those who do not join the
State organization. But more remarkable is the figure of 995,828
employers who have joined, out of a possible 3,707,893 who come
under that classification.

In 1933, despite the fact that the Rome correspondent of the *New
York Times* and the majority of correspondents of the other important newspapers resident in Rome had been announcing from
two to seven times, in the course of seven years, that the Corporate
State was functioning, Mr. John Strachey made the statement that
"No corporations exist except on paper." He was immediately attacked by unbelieving critics and reviewers. Mr. Strachey's declarations seemed stupid in the face of unanimous reports in the daily
press.

Shortly afterwards there appeared the first complete volume dealing with the problem. It was written by a Fascist with the coöperation of the officials of the Ministry of Corporations. On page 110
of this study[5] in a chapter entitled "The Corporations in their actual
working" [sic] the author states: "Only a single corporation, viz.,
that of the stage, has so far been established in Italy."

However, the only important thing for us to consider is whether,
functioning or not as a Corporative State, the Fascist system of
planned economy, the substitute for the planned economy of Bolshevism, has or has not achieved anything up to date. It is Mussolini
who said that the State's ultimate goal is "the well-being of the
Italian people"; it must be "judged and measured directly by the
masses as instruments through which these masses may improve
their standard of living. Some day the worker, the tiller of the soil,
will say to himself and to others: 'If today I am better off practically, I owe it to the institutions which the Fascist revolution has
created.'"

In just this manner let the following facts pass judgment.

In 1926, when the few untrammeled journalists reported that there
was already a crisis in Fascist economics and that the publicly an-

[5] *The Italian Corporate State,* by Fausto Pitigliani, London, P. S. King & Son.

nounced balanced budgets were mere jugglery, official figures showed that wages were below 1921 and that the cost of living had gone up 30 per cent. In 1927, with the stabilization of the lira, Mussolini found a much more serious economic crisis. He therefore announced a reduction in rentals, reduction in the price of manufactured goods, and a wage cut throughout the nation of between 5 and 20 per cent. He promised that the cuts ordered in the high cost of living would more than recompense the reductions in salary. At that time the general price index was 670; wages stood at 585; in real wages the workman was 13 per cent worse off than before the war.

That Fascism had proved a failure so far as the working population of Italy is concerned long before the world crisis of 1929-35 is openly admitted in the 1932 report of the Secretary of State for Corporations, who wrote:

"Between June, 1927, and December, 1928, the wages of industrial workers have gone down by about 20 per cent, and a further reduction of 10 per cent was made in 1929; during 1930 there has been a general reduction, varying for the different categories of workers from 18 to 25 per cent. Many other adjustments [*sic*] have been realized in 1931."

But that is not all. The decree effective December 1, 1930, cut the salaries of those earning more than $3,000 a year by 35 per cent and those below $2,000 by 12 per cent, and wages of 300 lire ($15.70) to 1,000 lire ($52.35) a month 8 per cent, and those above 1,000 lire 10 per cent. This cut affected 1,000,000 laborers in the industrial centers of the north—Milan, Turin, and Genoa. The government announced it "hoped" to reduce prices of commodities accordingly.

Then, on the 1st of April, 1931, Mussolini in another of his great public orations informed Italy that it need fear no more wage reductions. Frankly he admitted that "We have reached a limit in wage cutting; there is danger that the antidote may become a poison. . . . Italy was the first to apply what has now been adopted by almost the whole of Europe. . . . On the whole, certain symptoms of recovery may be seen, but . . . we are still waiting for the factors of recovery—in the first place *moral* factors—to enter into play simultaneously and collectively."

By 1932, however, an official of the Fascist syndicates[6] figured that the wages of glass-workers had declined between 30 and 40 per cent; signalmen's earnings down 40 per cent; silk-workers, 38 per cent; bricklayers, 30 per cent; miners, 30 per cent; while the cost of living had declined 20 per cent.

In 1933, moreover, despite the Duce's poison-warning, every Italian salary and wage was ordered reduced an average of 10 per cent and Mussolini announced a similar reduction in rents, food, manufactured goods, etc.

And again, on April 14, 1934, "the urgent necessity of lightening the national budget, which shows an annual deficit of between 3,000,-000,000 and 4,000,000,000 lire"—the admission is made by Mr. Cortesi of the *Times* himself—"caused the cabinet council . . . to apply a general reduction in the salaries of State employees, effective April 16th." Twenty per cent was removed from the income of high-salaried officials such as cabinet members; 6 per cent, the minimum, was the tax on those making more than 500 lire a month; others were exempt. When it is considered that one man in five works for the government, the size of this, the sixth reduction since 1927, will appear evident. The Fascist apologist, Cortesi, claims that the 1934 cut brings wages down to the pre-Fascist era and says "the general lowering of the cost of living which will ultimately result in the lowering of production costs in industry and agriculture, is deemed necessary by economists. . . ." The facts, however, are that real wages are far below the pre-Fascist era; that living costs have never paralleled the decline in wages; that the buying power of the Italian people has decreased rather than increased, and that while the philo-Fascist journalists continue to find explanations and publish excuses in the *New York Times*, the official figures of the League of Nations and the statements of Mussolini himself and other lesser enthusiasts for Fascism than the *Times* correspondent, have admitted the economic degeneration of the Italian people.

To complete the chronicle, it was announced by Mussolini on December 11, 1934, that a nation-wide and simultaneous reduction in salaries and the cost of living was being worked out which directly affected every person in the kingdom, directly and indirectly, the cut

[6] *Living Age,* May, 1934.

being similar to that of October, 1930, and similarly carrying with it a reduction in cost of rent, light, heat, food, and transport of between 10 and 12 per cent.

But instead of mentioning the obvious collapse of the Fascist economy, the American press heralded each of these seven events with an appropriate excuse furnished by the Fascist propaganda department. The headlines, for example, said that the 1927 cut was due to the success of the stabilization on a gold basis; in 1933 Mr. Cortesi of the *Times* supplied a story which was headed "Italy cuts wages to aid recovery"; the first 1934 reduction was linked with one in Russia and the joint headline read "Russia and Italy slash payrolls in Economy Wave"; the second 1934 cut was reported by the *Times* as "Italy to slash wages and cost of living to meet competition of non-gold nations."

Before presenting the documentary proofs of failure of Fascist economics, it may be interesting, perhaps, to give another sample of pro-Fascist journalism, typical of some magazines as contrasted with the newspapers. Whereas the daily press is supposed to deal with facts, the monthly journals devote themselves largely to opinion and interpretation. Here, then, are some extracts from the work of Howard R. Marraro[7] of the Italian department of Columbia University:

"In a world whose troubles are at bottom mainly economic, nations are rightly judged according to their success or failure in terms of genuine human welfare. What then has Fascism done to bring about a happier state of affairs in Italy? . . .

"The Italian today is much better fed than he was. . . .

". . . the standards of living of the Italian people have improved from 1913 to the present. This improvement is particularly marked during the twelve years of the Fascist régime, and it has not been interrupted by the world economic crisis. . . .

"Thanks to the labor legislation of the Fascist régime, there has been no important strike or lockout in Italy since 1926. . . . Of the 153 strikes which have come before the courts, a considerable number were due to the uncertainties prevailing in the early days as to the interpretation of the act. . . .

[7] *Current History*, May, 1935.

". . . the economic and social achievements of Fascism are truly impressive . . . a more prosperous and happy nation."

So much for opinion and interpretation. The facts are that under Fascism, from 1923 to 1932, the cost of living was reduced 5 per cent and wages reduced 40 to 50 per cent; if this is not a fact, then the League of Nations has been badly fooled. These statements are from the *Bulletin mensuel de statistique*, Geneva, February, 1933, page 74. Fascist official figures show a reduction in the cost of living of only 10 per cent as compared with 1914.[8] In other words, six wage cuts averaging 40 to 50 per cent and a cut in living costs of 5 or 10 per cent. The Fascist *Corriere della Sera* (July 27, 1932) admitted that in four years the wage cuts totaled 50 per cent. The official *Lavoro Fascista* (November 29, 1931) admitted that in some provinces wages had been reduced from 45 to 60 per cent in 1931.

The International Labor Office of the League of Nations made the following report on real wages, in July, 1930:

United States	190	Poland	61
Canada	155	Austria	48
Great Britain	100	Jugoslavia	45
Holland	82	Spain	40
Germany	73	Italy	39

The *International Labour Review*, March, 1932, gives the daily farm labor wage in 1923 as 12.88 lire; 1926, 14.24 lire; 1931, 10.49 lire. Real wages for agricultural workers stood at 107 in 1923, 89 in 1926, and 87 in 1931.

An examination of Fascist official figures shows that the average wage in 1928 was two lire an hour; that it fell to one and three-fourths lire in 1932, and one and a half, or eight cents an hour, in 1933. In other words, labor is worse paid in Italy than in any country in Europe.

Before Fascism arrived it is true that Italy was not among the first of the thirty or more nations which reported to the League, but neither was it the very last. It reached that position in a steady retrogression from 1926 on. Moreover, the Labor Office in its statistics on social welfare of workmen throughout the world also lists

[8] *Bolletino dei prezzi*, January 12, 1933, p. 44.

Italy last among the important nations of Europe because it spends less per man and because it has not yet (1932) organized a decent system of assurance against unemployment.

If the foregoing facts require an objective interpretation, here is one made by Constantine E. McGuire with the coöperation of the Institute of Economics :[9]

Rents are nearly four times higher than before the war.[10]

The low wages earned by employees and often by professional men frequently render it impossible for them to bring up their offspring according to the pre-war standard.

The deduction may fairly be made that the standard of living of students living in university dormitories has distinctly fallen.

The universities and higher institutions of learning are relatively deserted.

One may gather . . . that those who are students today are likely to have in the life of tomorrow an efficiency below that of those who were students before the war.

It is evident that a condition of this sort can hardly continue without progressive decay of the Italian national organism. At this very moment that organism is in a pathological condition. . . . By a pathological condition we mean precisely one which cannot continue without bringing about the breakdown of the organism itself.[11]

When the problem of the high cost of living continues on and on and for a greater or less fraction of the population without any other fraction thereof being able to realize exceptional profits—which is precisely the state of affairs existing in Italy for some time—the conviction that living is costly really signifies that at least for some categories of the population the national income is insufficient to maintain the standard of living which they have accustomed themselves to observe.[12]

So low is the standard of living of the Italian workman that it could not be lower without impairing his productive powers. The wage level . . . in Italy . . . is the same as in Austria, over whose

[9] *Italy's International Economic Position* (1927).
[10] *Id.*, p. 545.
[11] *Id.*, p. 547.
[12] *Id.*, p. 548.

population the world is in the habit of weeping; and Italy's wage level is actually lower than that of Spain or that of Poland.[13]

The facts are that the standard of living of Italy has fallen dangerously under Fascism; the question is whether or not it has fallen below the subsistence level.

In 1932 Professor Bottazzi, physiologist and member of the Fascist National Academy, published an academic study of this subject. It showed conclusively that the masses were not eating enough to satisfy hunger. In 1929 Mussolini had admitted that "there are communes in Sardinia and in South Italy where for months at a time the inhabitants have to live on wild plants,"[14] and the Deputy Zingali had reported to parliament that "I have been collaborating in the preparation of the material concerning the American debt. It was my duty to ascertain the standard of life in Italy, and I arrived at this disturbing conclusion: that the food ration per head and per day amounted to only 3,100 calories—i.e., to 200 calories less than the physiologists consider necessary for adults. Our ration is probably lower than that of any other European country."[15]

And finally, for the benefit of the Cortesis and Marraros, here is the original language of the *Discorso* of the Duce in the Fascist Chamber of Deputies December 12, 1930:

"Fortunamente il popolo italiano non è ancora ambituato a mangiare molte volte al giorno e, avendo un livello di vita modesto sente di meno la deficienza e la sofferenza." "Fortunately," said Mussolini, "the Italian people is not yet accustomed to eating several times per day and, having a modest standard of living, feels want and suffering less."

The "modest standard of living" is the lowest standard in Europe, one of the lowest standards in the civilized world; it was reached during the Fascist régime and it is one of the chief results of the Fascist economic program. In the United States, in 1935, there was a serious discussion among the physicians attending their annual national convention, whether or not the amounts paid the unem-

[13] *Id.,* p. 535.
[14] Discourse, Chamber of Deputies, June 22, 1929.
[15] *Parliamentary Reports, Chamber of Deputies,* December 5, 1929.

ployed and their food ration were sufficient to keep these millions
above the subsistence level. Yet under Fascism not the unemployed
on the dole, but the entire working nation, has been reduced to just
about or below that level.

And at the same time the burden of taxation has increased. In
proportion to income, the Italian people pay more taxes than those
of any other important country. In 1914 the taxation as percentage
of national income was 13; in 1925 it had already reached 20 per
cent, and in other Fascist years it has been higher. Concludes Mr.
McGuire: "Even with much more substantial allowances per capita
for the minimum of subsistence, it is probable that no other important country would show so great a percentage of income absorbed
in taxation. Thus, Italy's appearance of vigor and prosperity [in
1926] cannot cover the fact that from an economic point of view
her people are poorer, taken on an average, than they were before
the war."[16]

Compared with war time, rents increased from two to three times,
according to testimony given to officials by the Home Owners' Association[17] while the purchasing power of money had fallen to one-
fifth or one-sixth; taxes, on the other hand, had increased four-
fold and various expenses and dues increased an average of sixfold.
From these figures the home-owners concluded that the effective
income has been reduced to one-half.

In 1932 a study of official figures revealed that taxation had almost doubled under Fascism. The amount was 20,000,000,000 lire
a year, or 30 per cent of the national income, as compared with
12,000,000,000 lire or approximately 15 per cent in pre-dictatorial
days.

Bread is taxed 1½ cents a pound, sugar 13 cents, salt 3 cents,
and other necessities of life in proportion. Returning to his ancestral
land, Anthony M. Turano was surprised to have a friend say to
him, "You are fortunate you can smoke without counting the puffs.
Smoking has become the privilege of the upper classes." Mr. Turano
investigated. He found[18] that an assistant stone mason earned one

---

[16] McGuire, *Italy's International Economic Position*, p. 103.
[17] *Id.*, p. 535.
[18] *American Mercury*, September, 1934.

and a quarter lire an hour and the cheapest cigarettes were four lire for twenty; in other words, a man must work three hours to half a day for his cigarette money. Unemployed who for a time are allowed 3.70 lire a day cannot, therefore, buy a packet of cigarettes with their dole.

To Mussolini's declaration, "I am the first to declare that the pressure of taxation has attained the limit"—quoted by Mr. Marraro —Mr. Turano adds that despite this warning "not to tax the taxpayers to death," it continues. Bachelor taxes have been increased, but when the desperate bachelor marries he is told he must pay 25 lire a year as family tax; he is taxed for keeping a hog and he is taxed if he slaughters the hog; and so it goes.

The latest available figures on the subject show that the workingmen of Italy have to contribute 160,448,000 lire for the maintenance of the embryo corporations. The individual worker pays not only his regular dues, but contributes to the unemployment fund, sick benefit fund, summer resorts fund, winter insurance, federal secretariat, Fascist home fund, and to extraordinary levies, a total of somewhat over 216 lire. The American trades-unionist pays about $30 a year; the Italian pays less in dollars, but more in real wages, since the American gives up about one week's pay, whereas the Italian is legally forced to surrender almost one month's pay to the corporations.

It is true that there has not been one first-class strike since 1926. In every instance where workmen threatened or began a strike the Fascist militia has suppressed it with violence and bloodshed. And this is, of course, one of the great achievements of Fascism—from the point of view of the chambers of commerce and industrialist associations. The Labor Charter prohibits strikes. The militia see that the charter is enforced. That is about all there is to the struggle between capital and labor in Italy.

And yet in the reports of Fascist officials there is the proud claim that of the 142,000 labor disputes in 1932, 37,000 were settled in the courts, the balance by the syndicates. The claim to settlement is also an admission that disputes exist. But the Italian press has been ordered, and the foreign correspondents warned, not to emphasize or mention social unrest, labor troubles, tax revolts. Although the *Manchester Guardian* and London *Times* have frequently reported such episodes, there has been almost no mention of them in the American press.

In May, 1927, an armed rebellion against the Fascisti was led by Don Galbiati, the parish priest of Inveruno, and there were other uprisings and riots throughout Italy in protest to the wage cut and the increased cost of living. At that time the anti-Fascist press, secretly printed, still had a circulation of 500,000 copies daily. Early in 1931 the weavers of Parabiago and Legnago walked out. Wages had been reduced to 62 cents a day. In the American press this was reported as the first strike since the announcement of the Corporate State; it was, in fact, the first of thousands of strikes which was reported in the foreign press. The Fascist militia soon reduced both the Galbiati uprising and the weavers' strike to silence.

On the 8th of September, 1931, there was a revolt of the peasants of Montenero di Basaccia. The podestá, or vice-duce, of the province had imposed taxes the people could not pay. With cries of, "Death to the podestá," and, "Death to the famine-makers," the populace stormed and sacked the mayor's office, tearing up the pictures of Mussolini and destroying the archives. The officials fled. The Fascist militia deserted.

In the afternoon a commissioner of police arrived from Campobasso with regular police (carabineers). He informed the populace the Fascist officials had been sacked and a better régime would begin, but that night he began arresting the supposed ringleaders. The peasants sounded the alarm. In a battle with the police the latter fired 200 shots, killing three men, Antonio Lonzi, Antonio Suriani (aged over seventy) and Pasquale d'Aulero, and wounding thirteen others.

That same month there was a bloody demonstration of workingmen of Carrara in which the Fascisti killed two and wounded many. On the 27th at Roccacasale in the Abruzzi the angry populace stormed the mayor's palace. At Villa Santa the podestá and the municipal secretary were shot by peasants. At Vereno di Piave, near Treviso, during the Vatican-Fascist conflict over the school régime, the population shouted, "Our hour has come," barricaded the provincial route, and attempted to surround the Fascist barracks.

On January 8, 1933, the *Chicago Tribune* reported that the militia and carabinieri were sent to the villages to Monte San Giacomo and

Sassano to quell disturbances which followed attempts by the authorities to collect taxes. On April 19, 1934, the Associated Press carried a fifty-word report of "a violent outbreak in protest against provincial taxes in which one person was killed and fifteen wounded," at Pratola in central Italy. "Mountaineers chased the collector to the railroad station, cut the telephone and telegraph lines, and damaged public buildings before they were quelled by Fascist militia."

The plebiscite of 1934, according to Robert Briffault,[19] was an indispensable preliminary "to putting into force the drastic reductions of wages and other measures imposing misery and starvation, rendered necessary by the economic bankruptcy of the Fascist State, was attended by a terrorism not excelled at the time of the 'March on Rome.' The balloting was open, and the most violent intimidation was exercised by the State forces. Nevertheless, in Turin the negative votes have been estimated at between 12,000 and 15,000, and those who abstained from voting numbered 40,000. Similar reports were forthcoming from Milan. In Venice the 'plebescite' led to violent riots, which the militia were unable to control before several of the 'Dopolavoro' houses had been wrecked.

"Open opposition to Fascism, despite all measures of terrorism, is assuming ever larger proportions in recent months. Practically the whole of Sicily and Calabria is now manifesting openly its anti-Fascist spirit. At Bistari, Mussolini was burnt in effigy. At Catanzaro, a procession was stopped by masses of rioters shouting anti-Fascist slogans. At Udine, in February, large demonstrations, including women and children, paraded, crying 'Down with Fascism.' Anti-Fascist riots have taken place in Licorno. Everything indicates that the opposition to Fascism, which is in reality almost universal among the working-classes, is daily becoming bolder."

So it is apparent that there is unrest and occasional revolt.

It was said by the late William Bolitho that the Duce's agricultural program in 1928 was making serfs out of Italian farm labor. More recently Professor W. Y. Elliott, of Harvard, summed up the situation as follows: "Fascism has succeeded in depriving the laborer of the weapon of free association and the right to strike, and has reduced him, at least for the time being, to a condition of State-con-

[19] *Forum,* October, 1934.

trolled serfdom," and in October, 1934, the secretary of the British Trade Union Congress, Walter M. Citrine, urging the American Federation of Labor to declare war on Fascism, declared:

"The record of Fascism is one of repression, brutality, and terrorism. Personal liberty has been destroyed, trade-unionism has been crushed, and the status of the citizen has been reduced to that of a serf.

"Far from being saved by Fascism, Italy has been brought to the verge of economic bankruptcy. Since 1922 wages have been reduced 40 to 50 per cent and are now the lowest in western Europe. Even Mussolini admits that the living standards of Italian workers can be reduced no lower. American money is helping Mussolini to maintain his power.

"Fascism's record in the constructive sphere is one of failure and futility. It has contributed more than any other factor to the feeling of insecurity which has brought the possibility of widespread war to the forefront."

In 1934 the National Joint Council representing the Trades Union Congress, the Labor Party and the Parliamentary Labor Party of Britain issued "British Labor's Call to the People," an official declaration of war on Fascism, Italian as well as German. On October 13th of the same year the American Federation of Labor declared a boycott of goods made in dictatorial countries, including Italy. In February, 1935, following an investigation of Italian agents' activities against the trade unions, President Green of the A. F. of L. publicly condemned Italian Fascism.

Of course the fact that free labor throughout the world is anti-Fascist—seeing in Italian, German, and other forms of Fascism a return to medieval serfdom—can be interpreted conversely, that Fascism would be highly welcomed by the employers of labor. It was, in fact, by Judge Gary of the United States Steel Corporation. And that leading philosopher and economist of big-business, Mr. Marcosson, glorifying the Corporate State, wrote in 1930 that "under the Fascist trade-union law strikes have been outlawed and compulsory arbitration is enforced. No Mussolini measure was so fraught with constructive possibilities."

In Britain, America, France, and other free countries labor is becoming the chief antagonist to the Fascist movement. After all, it is labor which is hardest hit. One man's Corporate "constructive possibilities" is another man's Helot State.

The evidence is therefore overwhelming that Mussolini did not save Italy from Bolshevism; that the Corporate State, which may or may not be a substitute for Soviet-planned economy, does not function; that the standard of living of Italy has gone down with six or seven wage cuts; that under these circumstances "the well-being of the Italian people" has not materialized, but their misery increased; that, in short, Fascist economy is a failure.

CHAPTER XXVI

Fascist Finance

THE CONFESSION THAT FASCIST ECONOMY HAS FAILED IS MADE by Mussolini himself.

Addressing the Chamber on the 18th of December, 1930, the dictator who had stabilized the lira, announced balanced budgets for many years, proclaimed the economic viability of Fascism, and invited other nations to adopt the Corporative instead of the Communist idea of economic planning, informed Italy and the world that: "The situation in Italy was satisfactory until the fall of 1929, when the American market crash exploded suddenly like a bomb. For us poor European provincials it was a great surprise. We remained astonished, like the world at the announcement of the death of Napoleon, because we had been given to understand that America was the country of prosperity, of endless and absolute prosperity, without eclipses. Everyone was rich there.

"Everyone knows the data of American prosperity—there was one motor-car for every eight inhabitants, one radio set for every four, one telephone for every three. Everyone gambled on the stock exchange and since stocks rose incessantly, everyone bought at 20, sold at 100, and pocketed the difference, with which he purchased a motor-car, radio set, and telephone, or made a trip to Europe, paying for it by installments, and built a house in the country. All this was fantastic, and we on this side of the Atlantic had a sense of envy.

"Suddenly the beautiful scene collapsed and we had a series of black days. Stocks lost, 30, 40, and 50 per cent of their value. The crisis grew deeper.

"Black days followed black days, and prosperity was replaced by long lines of unemployed waiting for soup and bread in the great American cities.

"From that day we also were again pushed into the high seas, and from that day navigation has become extremely difficult for us."

The best American comment on this great explanation was made by Howard Brubaker. "Mussolini," he said, "has calmed growling Italians with the information that Wall Street is responsible for their lower salaries, their unemployment, their low returns on farm products. About the only crimes not attributed to Wall Street were the earthquakes of last July."

But shifting the blame on America does not shift the main issue, which is simply this: does Fascism offer the world a new and workable economic system; is it merely part of the universally (outside Russia) accepted system, and has it succeeded in meeting a crisis successfully? By blaming Italy's financial failure on Wall Street's failure Mussolini confesses that his is no new or different or independent system, or, if new and different, it is not a better one because it, too, has broken down.

In fact, the making of the Wall Street scapegoat is one of the master strokes of the modern Machiavelli, because Fascist economy broke down long before Wall Street collapsed. It is the purpose of this chapter to discuss the finances of the years 1922 to 1929 and to show, from official Fascist figures, that the crisis of Fascism began in 1925 and reached an alarming condition in 1927 and 1928. Paradoxically, Mussolini was saved the *political* consequences when the rest of the world—outside Russia—also joined in the collapse of 1929. The world was now in the same boat, and growing discontent in Italy was therefore stilled.

The first economic victory which Mussolini reported was the stabilization of the lira. It seems that the whole subject of economics first came to his attention in January, 1922, when he as a journalist, preparing to attend the annual peace conference (at Cannes, on the French Riviera), exchanged some money in Milan. For each one-hundred-lira note he was given a fifty-franc note.

"It was a grave symptom. It was a humiliation. It was a blow to the self-respect of a victorious nation, a vexing weather vane; it indicated our progress towards bankruptcy: up leaped the thought that this situation must be cured by the vital strength of Fascism."

This emotion engendered in the patriotic breast was not ephemeral.

It took root. It was later to flower in a gold stabilization which was higher than that of France. What is significant is the behavior of "the man of action," the ideas and the procedure of an economist like Mussolini, whose nationalistic egotism, whose Italian pride, is hurt by the financial situation, and who thereupon rules that "Fascism must change all that."

And so, commenting in 1928 on his actions of the past year, Mussolini with pride declares that "in December, 1927, at a meeting of the Council of Ministers, I was able to announce to the Italian people that the lira was back on a gold basis, on a ratio which technicians and profound experts in financial questions have judged sound."

He flatly makes the statement that "today we have a balanced budget. Self-ruling units, the provinces and the communes, have balanced their budgets, too. Exports and imports and their relationship are carried in a precise and definite rhythm—that of our stabilized lira."

He has the pleasant unbelievable surprise of a child which for the first time turns an electric light off and on, when he says that he had "solved a complex and difficult problem of national finance, such a problem as sometimes withdraws itself beyond the will and influence of any political man, and becomes subjected to the tyranny and mechanism of more material relations under the influences of various and infinite factors. Only a profound knowledge of the economic life and structure of a people can reach, in such an insidious field, conclusions which will be able to satisfy the majority."

"I felt the pride of a victor," exclaims Mussolini, and well might any man feel the pride of a victor who has not only marched into Rome, but who had smashed the tyranny of economics, laws which rule world finances, and which no other politician or nation has ever been able to conquer.

It was nothing short of a miracle: the sun of economic fatality stood still in the heavens at the command of the prophet, and the American international bond-floaters sang the epic of the great deed as they issued $600,000,000 in loans to Italy.

Six hundred million American dollars is a sum. It was surely worth the employment of public-relations counsel and the aid of the banking houses in protecting it. Time after time, between 1925 and 1929, the American public dumped the Italian bonds back on the market, and each time the dozen houses which floated them intensified their campaign which created the Mussolini-balanced-budget myth while they threatened the banking and brokerage firms which represented them with cutting them off from participation in future business if they failed to dispose of the Italian goods.

The Duce, of course, has always been party to the financial myth-making. He declared the stabilization at 19 was approved by "profound experts in financial questions," but it was later proven that Finance Minister Volpi and his good friend, Andrew W. Mellon, had advised against that figure.

It was always the head of the government who struck the note for the orchestra of the press to follow. When the bankers and the press agents and the Italians who wrote for the Associated Press and the American newspapers reported the stabilization at 19 to the dollar a victory, that Bolshevism threatened in 1922, that the budgets had balanced, that the municipalities were out of the "red" literally and figuratively, and that prosperity had crowned the planned economy of Fascism up to 1929, they are but playing variations on the tune which the master musician originated.

This tune, of course, is the only one heard in Italy and America. From his exile in England, however, Count Sforza, the former Minister of Foreign Affairs, has issued a statement calling it "an offense to Italy to give the impression abroad that she wants truth to be wrapped in gentle lies." "To pretend today that the present difficult financial situation in Italy is due to the American crisis," he continues, "simply means that the men now in office in Italy do not dare to face their responsibilities, that they slander the brave, thrifty Italian nation by showing her up as a sick person to whom only lies can be administered. . . . The truth is that the specific present Italian crisis has nothing to do with the general world crisis. Indeed, the general world crisis is a crisis of over-capitalization, while that in Italy is one of lack of capital. . . . But there are more direct proofs of my assertion. The Italian crisis began years before the American and general crisis—precisely, between 1924 and 1926."

Count Sforza is one of Mussolini's enemies. But so are the official statistics of the Fascist régime. In 1922 Italy's bankruptcies—commercial failures, personal bankruptcy, does not exist under that country's laws—were 3,858; in 1926, 8,580; in 1929, 11,106. In 1926 there were 181,000 unemployed in Italy, and in 1928, 439,000 or more. In fact, it is estimated, non-officially, that there were 800,-000 unemployed, including those kept inside the factories by Fascist orders and those working a day or two a week for their food. Imports in 1925 were 26,000,000,000 lire, and exports 18,000,000,000, while in 1928 imports were 22,000,000,000 and exports 14,000,-000,000.

The American commercial attaché, H. C. MacLean, reported from Rome on January 16, 1928, that "the outstanding characteristic of Italy's relations with the rest of the world is the large excess of the country's merchandise imports over its merchandise exports, a condition prevailing for many years. To compensate the large adverse trade balance invisible terms (notably remittances from Italians resident abroad and expenditures of foreign tourists in Italy) must be largely depended upon."

The attaché then points out an adverse trade balance of almost 5,000,000,000 lire for the first ten months of 1927, adding, "Having accepted 5,000,000,000 as Italy's adverse trade balance and 1,500,-000,000 as its net outgo on financial transactions, we have a total of 6,500,000,000 lire, for which compensation must be found on the credit side of the country's international accounts."

He then shows that "emigrants' remittances have sharply declined. Whereas in 1926 the withdrawals from postal saving banks were practically compensated by new deposits, during the first ten months of 1927 such withdrawals exceeded deposits by no less than 570,000,000 lire."

On July 9, 1928, Commercial Attaché Mowatt M. Mitchell cabled that "Italian industrial and business conditions continue unsatisfactory and are at present still further depressed by the growing seasonal slack."

The continuation of unsatisfactory conditions was confirmed by the January 14, 1929, report of Mr. Mitchell, who radioed: "Foreign trade suffered from the high stabilization point of the lira. Imports increased and exports decreased, resulting in an adverse trade balance of nearly 7,000,000,000 lire as compared with 5,000,000,000 in 1927."

The American attaché was of the opinion, however, that the government finances were in good shape, with large cash reserves, but the Italian treasury report[1] showed that the cash reserves had decreased continually until they were half of 1926: cash reserves, June 30, 1926, 2,841,000,000; June, 1928, 1,706,000,000; November 30, 1928, 1,389,000,000.

In fact it is Mussolini's first economic triumph, the boasted stabilization of the lira, which marks the intensification of the Fascist economic crisis. It must be remembered that the Italian, as well as the French, money had been guaranteed by the Allies during the war. When the guarantees were removed both fell; the lira was 8 to the dollar in the first half of 1919, and reached its just value somewhere above 20; its lowest was 23.91 in the second half of 1920, those fatal days of the so-called Bolshevik occupation of the factories, after which it improved generally so long as the democratic government existed. The lira was back to 20.15 just before Fascism in 1922. When, then, did the "humiliation," this "progress toward bankruptcy," occur? Under Fascism the lira dropped consistently, semester after semester, until it reached 30.53 under the miracle-working Duce in August, 1926. These are official figures. (Yet lady biographers of the Duce[2] can state without hesitation that "under the new government the lira ceased its downward trend.")

Mussolini stabilized at 19 plus, and the American commercial attachés immediately reported bad results, although "experts" writing for the million-circulation weeklies applauded. Mr. Marcosson of the *Saturday Evening Post* had to confess in 1930 that "much of the disruption is traceable to the stabilization of the lira at too high a price. Despite the advice of the best banking brains of the country, Mussolini, with a characteristic imperialistic gesture, decreed the figure at 19 to the dollar, which was out of proportion to the exigencies of the situation. All experts agreed that the lira should have been anchored to stability with the French franc . . . at 25 to the dollar. Instead, the will that has dominated every other activity had

[1] Conto del Tesoro, November 30, 1928.
[2] Mme. Jeanne Bordeux, *Mussolini the Man.*

its way here, and with the result that industry, because of high price of raw materials and inability to meet competition in the world markets, has been increasingly handicapped."

In 1925 the first reports were sent from Rome that jugglery, trickery, and distorted official figures and statements have marked Fascist finance. The Irish journalist and former diplomatic attaché in Rome, James Murphy, has published in the German, French, British, and American magazines numerous articles charging fraud which have never been challenged. He states, for instance, that the Fascisti, to maintain confidence and good will abroad, especially among banking interests, have organized a system of propaganda about their economic position, have given to the public "a state budget which has little or nor relation to the real financial condition. It is simply a piece of propaganda. I should not make such a statement without being in a position to bring forward proof. Take De Stefani's budget for 1923-24. For that year I find that under one heading alone there was an expenditure of fourteen billion of lire ($700,000,000) not a cent of which is debited in the State budget. The expenditure was officially announced in the official gazette.[3] It figures in the treasury accounts, *but it is carefully* kept out of the budget that has been published. That sum alone would practically consume the whole income from taxation for the same year. Therefore De Stefani's first budget had really a much heavier deficit than those of his predecessors, even if we confine the deficit to the above expenditure and say nothing of other treasury debts incurred. To keep all such questions dark, the press is muzzled and foreign journalists are watched and persecuted lest they begin to pry into the question of Italy's finances. By such means and by the expenditure of huge sums for propaganda abroad, the Fascists think that they will be able to stave off the day when their real economic and financial position may become known to foreign bankers and foreign industrialists."

Mr. Murphy likewise questions both Mussolini and American bankers on the subject of balanced budget by the municipalities. "One of the immediate purposes of the dictatorship obtaining control of the municipalities," he declares, "is the facilitation of Fascism's shady

[3] *Gazzetta Ufficiale*, June 27, 1924, p. 16.

finance. It is well known that a favorite trick practiced since Mussolini got control of things is to falsify the State budget by transfer-
ring State expenses to the municipal budgets. All the municipal
budgets show a deficit; but this does not appear in public. And there
will be no chance of its coming into the light now when there will
be no local supervisors appointed by the people. The system will be
understood if we imagine all the municipalities as subordinate corporations grouped under the one parent corporation, which is the
State. The balance sheets of the subordinate corporations are being
thrown more and more into a state of insolvency in order to make
the parent balance sheet look healthy. Yet the parent corporation is
solely dependent on the solvency of all the subordinated corporations
taken together.

"American financiers who have visited Italy have been too simple-
minded to spot this trick. They have also been too simple-minded
to ask for the treasury accounts and collate them with the budget.
And so the Fascist financial bluff has gone ahead triumphantly.
Mussolini wants to show the unwary Yankee how splendidly everything is going in Italy, so that he can raise loans in the United
States."

To such general statements must be added the official figures
from the Fascist government's publications. The debts of the provinces as of January 1, 1925, are 954,000,000 and January 1, 1928,
1,326,000,000, while the debts of the capital cities of the provinces
are as follows:

January 1, 1925...............................	3,066,000,000
January 1, 1928...............................	5,481,000,000
Increase in debt...........................	2,415,000,000

which somehow does not agree with Mussolini's statement that "the
provinces and the communes have balanced their budgets too."

Fascist Italy, say European economists, is the only country in the
world which announces balanced budgets while showing deficits in
the treasury.

Strange things have happened. For instance, Mussolini with his
annual pride announced a credit balance of 2,200,000,000 lire in

1925-26, but the announcement of the treasury-audits court added that "from this surplus 1,800,000,000 were deducted in order to provide for expenses in connection with the economic reconstruction of the country for the period of the same fiscal year 1925-26." Only Fascist finance has provided this minor miracle of eating one's surplus and having it too.

When Count Volpi and Mussolini quarreled about this ultra-modern way of dictating to the economic system, the former was dismissed and the latter declared that "from now on the data of the budget will be of crystalline clearness." Immediately afterwards 1,211,000,000 lire were canceled from the cash items of the treasury account published the following month, July 31, 1928. It was declared that it represented a sum "not liable to be spent." Apparently Mussolini was trying to show Volpi was making a slight error of a little more than a billion. But the next year the treasury account announced that the fiscal year had closed on June 30th with a surplus of 2,352,000,000 lire, while a supplement published a month afterwards showed a slight correction necessary, a reduction of 2,845,-000,000, with an explanation of "crystalline clearness": "reduction of the cash fund for operations to be credited to the preceding fiscal year." Next month there was another correction of 83,000,000, so that two months after Mussolini had informed the world and particularly the American bond holders he had more than two billion credit, there was a deficit of 574,000,000 lire.

In 1930 the budget showed a cash surplus of 2,261,000,000. The supplementary account, published a month later, brought a correction of 1,581,000,000, which reduced the surplus to 680,000,000, and there was no explanation, crystalline or otherwise.

One billion lire of national bonds, due the Vatican under the Lateran treaty, was taken from the "Cassa depositi e prestiti" under agreement to return it in ten years,[4] but the Cassa enters in its assets this billion which the treasury owes it, while the nonchalant treasury, which should enter a corresponding liability, enters only the annual installment of 85,000,000 and the interest on the rest of the principal.

Although the Bank of Italy lists assets of 1,801,000,000 gold it

[4] Decree 851, May 27, 1929.

claims is deposited abroad, due to it from the State, in the treasury account no mention is found among the liabilities of this State debt. The treasury explains that it means to return to the Bank of Italy the gold deposited with the Bank of England. Economists, however, declare that while the State debt is real, the gold in London is a security which will be returned "if and when" Italy pays the fifty-eight annuities still due of the sixty-two (or about 30,000,000,000 lire) under the Volpi settlement.

The Bank of Italy reserve just before stabilization was 12,516,-000,000 lire, but in April, 1929. only 10,004,000,000, at which figure it fluctuates only slightly, and this loss of about two and a half billion is claimed to be due to the stabilization at 19 instead of a reasonable, logical 25.

Although Count Volpi announced that the new silver currency which replaced a billion and a half of small paper notes "have their counter-value in pure metal," the value in silver is about one-sixth legal value.

A search through official Fascist figures reveals that in the year 1928-29 State receipts were 19,447,000,000 lire and payments 22,741,000,000, or a deficit of 3,294,000,000. More recently the régime issued several series of statistics, an explanation of the 1928-29 budget, the finance Minister Mosconi's revelations to the Chamber of Deputies[5] which neutral economists declare "render equally unintelligible the real financial situation in Italy." It is said that the actual state of the budget cannot be determined from all these figures, but the movement of cash reserves (page 33) shows that the treasury revenue for 1928-29 was 23,015,000,000 lire and expenditures 25,960,000,000, making a deficit of 2,945,000,000.

Minister Mosconi then attempted by various statements to reduce this deficit to 575,000,000 lire, claiming there were important credits abroad, but on page 51 mentions a credit of 6,358,000,000 and a debit of 11,829,000,000 in the budget.

On page 73 the Minister speaks of the extreme gravity in the local financial situation, but having admitted a rotten state of affairs, concludes with an oration: "The government of Benito Mussolini

[5] *Exposizione finanziaria fatta all Camera dei deputati nella seduta del 31 Maggio* 1930-VIII.

does not dissimulate the difficulties of the present time, but one must not doubt that he has unshakable confidence and profound force, which continues with a will of iron, with a lively energy, with an obstinate passion, to march towards the future."

The apparent fraud of the official announcements of balanced budgets, the apparent paradox of tremendous increase in national works expenditures without increased public debt and increased national income, which was first discovered and reported in 1925 to 1928 by Messrs. Motherwell, Murphy, and Bolitho, has now been completely substantiated and explained by Professor Gaetano Salvemini, former professor of history of Florence University and more recently of Harvard. The time for the exposé was extremely appropriate. The United States in 1935 was keenly interested in substitute systems of national economy; it was watching both the Fascist and Communist governmental planning; the American government was engaging in public works expenditures totaling many billions and the national debt was rising proportionally. How then was Mussolini able to produce balanced budgets while great land reclamation projects were going forward successfully, magnificent public buildings were being erected, express auto roads were being completed, new ships for commerce and war were built, a modern army equipped, the military budget doubled, and a vast list of minor Fascist achievements—all costing millions if not billions—were announced to a despondent and jealous world?

The Fascist mystery and miracle play was not easy to explain. Italy's budget is unlike Anglo-American budgets, which are integral and clear; the Italian consists of two, one showing revenues and expenditures legally assessed, the other as they actually resulted. Moreover, Professor Salvemini points out[6] "one set of official figures for the four years from July 1, 1928, to June 30, 1932, gives yearly deficits of, respectively, 2,576 millions, 507 millions, 288 millions, and 2,300 millions, a total deficit of 5,671 millions.[7] Another set of official figures for the same four years gives, respectively, surpluses of 555 millions and 170 millions and deficits of 504 mil-

[6] *Foreign Affairs*, published by the Council on Foreign Relations, April, 1935.
[7] Cf. Rendiconti Generali Consuntivi.

lions and 3,867 millions.[8] The difference between the figures amounts to 2,025 million lire."

Professor Salvemini examines the infallible index to the nation's financial status, the national debt, using the official Fascist statistics, the parliamentary reports, and the annual reports of the finance ministers. And here he discovers the magnificent modern contribution the Duce has made to national economy: the government instead of paying for its activities out of current revenue and borrowing from the public as other nations do, has issued promises to pay in installments, ranging from ten to fifty years. The list of annuities and dates contracted for are: March 29, 1924, 6,546,000,000 lire; end of 1928, 26,219,000,000 lire; December 31, 1930, 65,390,000,000 lire; March 31, 1932, 75,118,000,000 lire and February 28, 1933, 74,315,000,000 lire.[9]

This vast indebtedness incurred from 1924 to 1933, which has been hidden from the Italian people and the world, aggregates an increase of more than sixty-seven billion lire, as the parliamentary finance committee reports show. In plain words Fascism has taken up the installment idea somewhat like the American people who bought their furniture, cars, radios, and electric refrigerators in the boom days, mortgaging their futures at a time salaries were good and prospects grand. "One of the remarkable features of this situation," continues Professor Salvemini, "is the fact that out of the 74,315 million lire of annuities outstanding as of February 28, 1933, nearly two-thirds, or 51,243 millions, were for ordinary expenses, and only one third, or 23,072 millions, for extraordinary expenses."

Inasmuch as the 74,315,000,000 lire is to be paid out in installments up to 1986-87, Professor Salvemini has taken the present capital value of the debt, which is 35,000,000,000 lire and added that, instead of a sum more than double, to the national debt, which he has compared with the last pre-Fascist statistics. Here follows the result:

[8] Bolletino Mensile di Statistica, August, 1934, p. 746.
[9] These figures are from the Conto del Tesoro, *Gazzetta Ufficiale*, March 29, 1924, No. 76; the Parliamentary Report on the Budget of 1927-28, Camera dei Deputati, No. 30A, and the Reports of the Senate Finance Committee for the years 1931-32, 1932-33 and 1933-34.

	National Debt of Italy			Increase or
	June 30, 1922	June 30, 1932	June 30, 1934	decrease over 1922
Consuls	44,576	71,736	9,892	−34,684
Redeemables	12,010	18,907	83,055	+71,045
Floating debt	28,188	6,657	10,233	−17,955
Miscellaneous	5,901	7,554	9,282	+ 3,381
Autonomous authorities		1,184	1,184	+ 1,184
Current capital value of State annuities	2,700	35,000	35,000	+32,300
Total	93,375	141,038	148,646	+ 55,271

Fascist apologists bring up the fact that the liberal régime which preceded them raised the national debt by 37 billion lire from July, 1919, to June, 1922, and while these statistics are a fact, the national budgets also show that between 1919 and 1922 the liberal régime paid out a war debt of 55 billion lire; it paid out 20 billion in 1921-1922 and left the Fascists to pay only 6 billion in the next fiscal year, 5 billion in 1923-24 and about a billion and a third in future years. In other words, the pre-Fascist deficit and enormous budget increase was the result of the World War; the Fascist deficit is the result of Fascist economics. It is the equivalent of waging a war. Only in the latter instance it is a war against the Italian people.

Naturally enough, the Fascist innovation in hiding the bankruptcy of its finances has been termed a fraud by leading economists the world over. Fascist apologists, however, have tried explanations. The leading business magazine of the United States, *Fortune,* devoting an entire issue[10] to the glorification of the Duce and Fascism, had this to say of the social-economic-financial system:

"Fascist accounts are not faked: they are merely divided or delayed—on the general principle that solemn news is accepted more easily if delivered in parts, and that no news is commonly accepted as good news. Thus the Fascists delay payments on budgeted expenses up to the legal limit, and delay the charge-off of those expenses to the same limit. . . . But these annuities are not reflected in the regular public-debt statement. We have seen how 40 billions

[10] July, 1934.

of these annuities help to raise the *regular* debt statement of 98 billions to the *actual* debt figure of some 170 billions.

"And still 170 billions fails to tell the whole story. . . .

"A great question remains: does Fascist finance pay dividends to the Italian people? The long-established poverty of the Italian masses has been emphasized elsewhere. . . . Like the Japanese, the Italians have for centuries been used to living on next-to-nothing with a smile. In recent years that next-to-nothing has been reduced. The average wage of Italian agricultural and industrial workers has fallen perhaps 25 per cent in the last five years. The last published figure is 1.5 lire (eight cents) per hour. The masses are struck at every turn by the indirect tax policy of the State. Unemployment has been slowly increasing, with a January official estimate of 1,160,000. The standard of living of Italian labor has been estimated as the lowest of any country in Europe. An indication of the effects of Fascist economy of middle-class levels is provided by the gradual increase of bankruptcies from 1,800 in 1921 to 14,000 in 1933. The conclusion seems inescapable that if Fascism has paid dividends to the Italian people, they have been paid in the coinage of patriotic excitement. . . . Fascism has paid its people no cash dividends. . . ."

We can now arrive at objective conclusions: Mussolini announces that the budget for many years was balanced: *Fortune,* typical of the apologists for Fascism, states that the budgets are not "faked"; American bankers, on behalf of finance capital, declare that the budgets were balanced; official statistics show that annuities totaling 74 billion lire and having a present capital value of 35 billion have been kept out of the budget and from the knowledge of the people; the official Italian national debt has been announced annually as hovering in the neighborhood of 90 billion lire, only a fractional increase from the pre-Fascist figure. It is obvious, therefore, that the question revolves about a euphemism. If the budget has not been "faked" it has been "tricked" and "juggled," and these are the very words used by Messrs. Motherwell, Murphy, Bolitho, and the present writer in reporting on Italy from 1925 to date.

"Since 1925," concludes Salvemini, "the Italian budget has never been balanced. The Italian national debt in the last ten years has increased, on the average, by a yearly amount of over 5 billion lire, even though the war claims had been reduced to negligible proportions. . . . The government is concealing from the public at large the true composition and size of the national debt."

On the 8th of July, 1935, the ace of Fascist apologists[11] was permitted by the Fascist censorship to report that "The public debt, which has increased considerably, now stands at 105 billion lire, against 102 billion in May, 1934, and 97 billion in 1933." Apparently Mussolini at last has decided to show at least a part of the 148 billion lire burden which the Italian people, its children and grandchildren, must pay. It means increased taxation, a still lower standard of living, and resultant misery and degeneration.

[11] The Rome correspondent of the *New York Times*.

CHAPTER XXVII

A Journalist Suppresses the Free Press

IN THE CHRONOLOGY OF FASCIST PROGRESS THERE HAVE ALREADY been references to Mussolini's decrees and methods dealing with the free press of Italy. Here, for once, the dictator has been consistent and logical.

The foundation of all free, democratic, enlightened States is liberty, and the bulwark of liberty is the free press. Axioms, even platitudes, these statements are nevertheless true, and were as well known to the Duce as they are to us. But whereas we do little or nothing to safeguard the freedom of the press, permitting that phrase to be made into a slogan by certain publishers who want to keep wages down and their men from organizing for their economic and moral freedom, the Duce, who regarded liberty as a "rotten carcass" over which Fascism had to pass, devoted a large part of his time to destroying the first and last bulwark of the Italian people.

It must be admitted, of course, that the press of Italy, as that of practically all continental Europe, with a few notable exceptions in Scandinavia, Switzerland, and Holland, has never been nor is it today a news press. There are thousands of journals, almost no newspapers. The journals are expressions of opinion, the policies of special interests which range all the way from the Catholic Church to the munitions-makers. There are the publications of capitalist organizations and parties, Communist, Socialist and labor organizations and parties, personal organs of bankers, politicians, and other men seeking or holding political, social, and economic power.

In Italy, with the exception of the *Corriere della Sera* and two or three smaller liberal journals, there were no real newspapers, in the Anglo-American sense; the task for Mussolini was, therefore, the easier. He had simply to order the suppression of all the organs of the Opposition, of unfriendly bankers, industrialists, politicians, and parties, and encourage the journals of the banks, the industrial associations, and the rich individuals who supported Fascism.

In many respects Mussolini followed the methods of other dictators. Lenin had been editor of the *Iskra*; Trotsky practiced journalism in Siberia, Switzerland, and Second Avenue, New York, while Stalin undermined the Kerensky régime when he edited the Petrograd *Pravda*. Pilsudki was once a Socialist editor of the *Rabotnik, The Worker*, Kemal Pasha also published a paper to further his aims, and Hitler for years raged in his *Voelkischer Beobachter*. A large number of leading dictators gained by experience in journalism the knowledge of the power of the press, and all in turn knew enough to abolish opposition newspapers as the first and probably most important act to insure stability of a régime. Dictatorship and a free press can never co-exist.

The difference between the radical and reactionary dictatorships is this; the Bolsheviki have promised Russia a Utopian era of unlimited freedom once the various five-year-plans have been successful, the nation is economically independent, and the danger of invasion from Germany and Japan and perhaps a coalition of European nations, is over. They consider themselves in a state of war with the capitalistic world. In war time everyone agrees censorship and suppression of opposition opinion are necessary. In Moscow, therefore, there is a censor functioning publicly.

In Rome, however, Mussolini makes no such admission. Foreign correspondents who seek to send true news out of Italy are either bribed or intimidated, flattered or censored; if they are honest they make the best of things, trim their sails, smuggle out a little news when possible, indulge in almost daily compromises. Numerous correspondents have been arrested, imprisoned, or expelled. Meanwhile, with perhaps humorous cynicism Mussolini makes the statement that "The press of Italy is free, freer than the press of any other country, so long as it supports the régime." He denies publicly that he has instituted a censorship, but orders the telegraph office to hold up all doubtful cables, submit them to the foreign office, and frequently "lose them through bureaucratic carelessness." There is no censorship; the moment a journalist sends news which is factual but which offends the Duce or the régime, he is sent an official warning; the second time he is deported.

In the journalistic situation in Italy control of the Italian press is the most important feature for two reasons: because it has succeeded in a totalitarian way in making the newspapers the propaganda organ of the régime while completely destroying the possibility of getting true news to the Italian people, and because, after all, the newspapers and the government press bureaus which supply them are the main source of news for the rest of the world.

Mussolini himself, his official press bureau, the local governors, and the police departments of cities and provinces give instructions to the nation's editors. Here is a verbatim example as set down by an editor who has since escaped to Switzerland. The telephone in his sanctum rang and the following conversation followed:

"To whom am I speaking?"

"The director of the paper."

"*Bene.* This is the civil governor."

"I am Editor Fulano."

"Very well, Editor Fulano, take note that by order of the Chief of the Government (Mussolini) you are prohibited from mentioning the failure of Bank X. . . ."

"All right."

"Take note that you are prohibited from mentioning the fact that the family of Mussolini is visiting in Rome."

"Very well."

"Note that you are not to mention the aviation disaster of yesterday."

"Of course not."

"By order of the secretary of the party you are not to mention the violence which occurred yesterday in Savona."

"All right."

"And one more thing, refrain from republishing any article from yesterday's *Osservatore Romano.*"

And so it goes day by day.

Another editor kept a record of the important orders of suppression received during four months:

August 5: It is prohibited to publish any news of the interview Rabindranath Tagore gave the *Neue Frei Press* in Vienna in which he denies that he expressed himself as an admirer of Fascism as reported in the Italian press.

August 20: The President of the Council orders that the press refrain from discussion of the return of the gold standard, whether favorable or critical.

August 25: It is prohibited to reproduce the manifesto of a group of intellectuals in London against conscription.

It is prohibited to mention that between Rome and Sant'Ilario an automobile in Mussolini's suite upset a wagon.

August 30: It is prohibited to publish any information about war materials purchased in Italy by foreign countries.

September 3: It is prohibited to mention details of the swindle of 200,000 lire from the saving bank of Milan.

September 4: No allusion must be made to the incident in the Eden theater (Fascisti invaded the theater and prevented the showing of a French revue).

September 12: It is prohibited to mention incidents which followed the Lucetti attentat and especially the hostile demonstration against the French consulate.

September 15: The prefect recommends the greatest prudence in the publication of foreign articles, especially on the subject of differences between France and Italy.

September 16: The order is given by the President (Mussolini) that all polemics with the French press cease immediately.

September 21: It is prohibited to mention the visit to Rome of the Egyptian Minister of Foreign Affairs for the settlement of the Zarabub question.

September 23: By order of the President (Mussolini)

1. No mention must be made of the inquest on the death of the Fascist Luporini and the anti-Fascist Becciolini in Florence.

2. It is prohibited to speak of the economic, financial and political penetration of Albania.

September 24: No mention must be made of the voyages of Mussolini.

October 1: No mention must be made of the Greek book by Jewos on "The Dodecanese Question."

October 9: No mention must be made of the visit of the King to Trani last Sunday.

October 13: It is prohibited to publish anything about the thefts committed by Italian soldiers in the hotels of Merano.

November 6: All discussion of Franco-Italian rapports is prohibited. It is also prohibited to mention the difficulties of the Pordenone Bank.

November 9: It is prohibited to publish news of the destruction of political clubs following the Zaniboni attentat, or the arrest of deputies.

The range of these prohibitions is all the way from the ludicrous and trivial to the influence of international diplomatic relations. But even those which appear of no importance may have a bearing on world reaction to Fascism. Thus Tagore's visit to Rome was exploited by the Fascist press; naturally British, American, and other foreign correspondents, some of whom at times like to do the Duce a good turn, sent out columns of praise of Fascism and Mussolini, quoting from local papers. But Tagore was not the author of the statements attributed to him; guileless philosopher, he did not know what was happening, and when he found out it was too late to obtain satisfaction from the Fascist press. In Vienna, however, he explained his horror of Fascism and Mussolini, denounced the Italian press, denied the reports sent to foreign newspapers, and concluded with words which of course never found their way into Italy, perhaps not even to London or New York.

"It is absurd," said Tagore, "to imagine that I could ever support a movement which ruthlessly suppresses freedom of expression, enforces observances that are against individual consciences, and walks through a blood-stained path of violence and stealthy crime." This is Tagore's true opinion. Yet the Fascist reports of his praise linger in the public mind. Thus are explained the beauties of the censorship, the making of international opinion, and the astuteness of a dictator, himself a journalist, who knows how to rule the press.

As proof of the assertion that many Fascist editors are really anti-Fascists at heart is the frequent appearance of Mussolini's secret orders in the anti-Fascist press. In 1932 an Italian editor brought to Paris the following illuminating dossier of Mussolini's "Notes and recommendations":

"It is necessary directors and editors-in-chief of the newspapers attentively review the articles and all that is eventually to be published, in order to avoid the appearance in the dailies and the reviews, paragraphs or correspondences and articles that are in opposition to the interests of Italy and the action of the régime.

"During the course of the past few days, there appeared, for example: In the *Resto del Carlino* an article on the fight against flies. In the *Mattino* an article on the damage to the harvest of nearly one thousand million, caused by the rotting of the wheat. In the *Tribuna*, finally an article entitled: "Are the Summer Climatic Cures Really Useful?"

"But it will have been enough that the director, or at least the person in charge of the newspaper, had considered the things that we are going to enumerate from the political point of view, to be persuaded that they should not in any way allow these things to be printed which are in obvious and evident contradiction with the action of the régime in the same way as they are with the interests of our country. . . .

"The journals are also formally asked to abstain from all propaganda in favor of spas and thermal resorts of foreign tourism."

("Note—Recommendation" by Mussolini, July 25):

"(1) The papers are asked to support the summer cruise which will go into effect beginning the 28th of August on the steamer *Giulio Cesare*.

"(2) The papers are asked to recall the general strike in Italy the 30th and 31st of July, 1922, the principal references to be the transmission of the powers on the part of the central Committee of the Workers Alliance to a secret committee, the threats of Filippo Turati, the revolutionary manifesto: in order to prove one more time an evident historic truth, namely that the march on Rome has only been the counter blow to destructive forces."

In a "note" of July 27, 1932, the papers are asked "to write an article on the return to the land," calling attention to how the régime has since 1922 made an eminently rural policy; "to emphasize the words spoken by Gorguloff during the course of his questioning and in which he says: 'All my sympathies go to the socialists' which proves once more that those who attribute the quality of Fascism to Gorguloff lie with impudence."

(Service order of July 29, 1932):

"(1) One calls attention to the newspapers of the necessity of applying in the strongest possible fashion, the dispositions already given to avoid publication in papers and periodicals of pictures of thin women. The phenomenon of the slim woman has no other significance than the reduction of the birth rate.

"In Italy, also, one owes it to the decrease in the birth rate that our enemies have not failed to emphasize with apparent pleasure.

"Now it is absolutely necessary to avoid all that which gives pleasure to our enemies. To this end, the papers should with a great deal of tact deplore the phenomenon of the decrease in births, by remarking, for example, that it has already been the object of satisfaction to our enemies."

(Service order of August 1, 1932):

"(1) The newspapers are asked to make no mention of the automobile accident which unexpectedly happened to the Minister Di Crellalanza, near Montefiascone.

"(2) They are asked to prominently place the dispatch of the Duce for the aqueduct of Monferrate and to do the same for the message of Sidky Pacha.

"(3) They are asked to make outstanding the noticeable affluence of travelers in the popular trains in calling attention to the fact that a similar initiative has never been realized by past governments and that abroad like facilities for the benefit of the working classes do not exist to such an extent.

"(4) Concerning the German elections, they are asked to bring out the defeat of the Weimar coalition and the victory of the Hitlerites.

"August 4: (1) Play up on the first page that one hundred battleships will participate in the naval maneuvers, and the same holds true for thirty submarines.

"(2) Always, apropos of the next naval maneuver, take into consideration that, although aviation also participates at the maneuvers, the important rôle is held by the navy.

"That the papers take account of this fact and that they do not make the mistake of a Rome paper, which in a headline gave the most prominence to the airplane manifestations.

"It is further recalled to the papers that, being given the dispositions in power, it is absolutely forbidden to speak of eventual trips of the King. This prohibition holds equally for the next naval maneuver.

"August 6, 1932: The big naval maneuvers will be placed in the most prominent place possible and on the front page. Publish the most extensive reports and each day the photographs of ships and submarines. Furthermore, make note of the fact that the Italian war navy is equipped according to the most modern technique and that it has been entirely renovated and modernized by the Will of the Duce during the course of the ten years of his régime."

It must be noted that one of the first powerful groups to be thoroughly Fascisticized by Mussolini was composed of editors, reporters, and publishers; nevertheless these confidential instructions from the Duce, which are sent with the utmost secrecy to the responsible editors of Italian newspapers, all of which support the régime, are always being betrayed to the outside world. In December, 1933, *La Stampa Libera*, an Italian-language paper published in New York, was able to obtain still another of Mussolini's list of do's and don't's by which he rules journalism:

August 4, 1933. Anno XI (Era Fascista):

The greatest prominence should be given tomorrow to the inauguration of the township of Sabaudia. Meantime, on the first page a long article should be published today on the ceremonies to be performed tomorrow.

It is earnestly requested that no mistake shall be made in the spelling of the name of the Hungarian Secretary of Commerce.

By the use of large type, great prominence should be given on the first page to the orders issued by Il Duce for the celebration of the Mother and Child's Day.

Warning is hereby given to abstain from using the words "supreme hierarchies," as the party has only one: Il Duce.

In announcing the celebration to be performed on the arrival of the Atlantic fliers in Rome, the *Carlino* made use, in yesterday's number, the word "apotheosis." This adjective [*sic*] is too extravagant, because the arrival of the fliers is several days off and also because up to that date the event must be kept within reasonable bounds.

August 7, 1933.

Small space should be devoted to the preparation for the arrival of the fliers in the Azores; great prominence, instead, should be given to the reports of their take-off for America.

All correspondence appearing in foreign papers on the visit of Il Duce to the Pontine Reclaimed Land should be quoted at length.

With regard to the step taken by France and England in Berlin, too much stress should not be laid upon it.

Do not advertise the success of the loan in the United States and do not speak of America's inflation policy.

Feature the acclamations to Il Duce by the 2,800 teachers of the Opera Nazionale Balilla.

By an adequate use of italics, stress should be laid upon the importance of their teaching in the education of the youth.

Some papers have announced the creation of the new province of Littoria in 1936. The news should not be reproduced, for nothing has been resolved yet and all decision is reserved to Il Duce.

The following line appeared in the *Corriere della Sera*: "Instruction by H. E. Rossini on motherland and childhood." Bear in mind that all circulars by under-secretaries are issued not on their personal initiative, but by Il Duce's order, and that at any rate they are an emanation from the régime, not from individuals. This instruction should serve as a guide for the future as well.

August 8, 1933:

Of course, the take-off and the arrival at the Azores of the flying squad are the most important events of the day, and all news bearing on them should be given the most prominent place in the papers under headlines running across the page.

Reprint from this morning's *Popolo d'Italia* the Duce's Day and add a comment to it.

Feature: (a) the meeting of the wheat standing committee; (b) the reports of the Commanders of the Avanguardista Legions; (c) the statistical report on circulation.

Do not make up the paper in such a way as to have all the reports of accidents and crimes follow one another, for it is not desirable to fill half pages with catastrophic news.

Your attention is called once more to the fact that for no reason whatever mention should be made of region and regionalism, for the policy of the régime is solely unitarian and anti-regionalistic.

Some papers in their outside editions have extravagantly praised prefects and hierarchs on account of certain orders issued by them. Such a mistake should never be repeated, for they are but executors of orders issuing from the center.

August 9, 1933:

Feature, avoiding all exaggeration, under a two-column headline, the visit paid by Il Duce to camp Sandro Mussolini.

Reproduce extensively the comments of the foreign press calling attention to the rightness of the course followed by Italy.

In the out-of-town editions of the *Popolo di Roma* there appeared some accounts of the military maneuvers. You are reminded of the order forbidding the publication of news on the subject, unless an official communiqué is issued.

An article study on the depression has appeared in the *Régime*. It is not timely. The papers should rather concern themselves with the signs of recovery. The depression will be examined and studied when it has disappeared.

August 10, 1933:

Today, too, the news of Balbo's flight and the comments of the foreign press should be given the greatest prominence on the first page.

With regard to the news success of the foreign policy of Il Duce all news appearing in foreign papers on the subject should be reprinted without, however, undue exaggeration in the headlines and in commenting. No surprise is to be shown at this recognition by foreigners, as this is not the first time Il Duce has embarked on the right course.

The *Ambrosiano* had yesterday a headline on the increase of monetary circulation. In this regard it will be advisable to abstain from commenting on the constant increase of the gold reserve in order to avoid drawing to it the attention of foreign financiers. Emphasize the soundness of the lira as a political-social element, but avoid all technical discussion.

August 17, 1933:

The comments by foreign papers on the record set by the *Rex*, and also on those that eventually may be set by Balbo's squad, should be given prominent display.

Recall by an article the famous speech made by Il Duce at Pesaro, August 14, 1926, setting forth its great results in the way of stabilizing the lira, which is a mainstay of the social and economic policy of the régime, but do not enter into details on the gold reserve, the increase of gold, etc.

Reprint from *The Daily Mail* the article, "Will France Go Fascist?" by Huddleston.

Feature the telegrams sent by Il Duce to Balbo in the course of the flight, but do not reprint integrally the article published by the *Popolo d'Italia*.

September 4, 1933:

Give great prominence, by a suitable typographical display, to the text of the Italo-Sovietic pact and have it followed by a comment.

Have a large service ready for the Eastern Fair at Bari, which is to be opened September 6. It is better still to send a special correspondent.

In an interview with Acerbo published yesterday by the *Corriere della Sera* there appeared under a showy headline a statement to the effect that the wheat will always be sold at a profit; this statement is too bold; no paper can make such unqualified pledges. . . .

With great frequency the Duce, with his old-time insouciance, reverses himself in his dictates to the press. Thus, for instance, in July, 1928, he gave the example to the press for the glorification of Nobile, the unfortunate explorer who had been driven by the impatience of the Fascist press to fly over the North Pole on a day his experts warned him was meteorologically dangerous. Nobile flew, dropped a gigantic crucifix, the Italian flag, the Fascist insignia, and nevertheless was wrecked. When the Russians saved the Nobile expedition, two stories, one rumor and the other fact, appeared in the world press: Nobile, the captain, had been the first rescued— that was the fact; two of his associates had committed cannibalism, the victim being the Swedish scientist Malmgren—that was the rumor. But fact or rumor, it was obvious to every nation except that controlled by the Duce's press that the expedition had been a sad failure and that the only heroism was Bolshevik.

"The greatest polar explorer in the history of the world." Thus the Fascist press under Mussolini's orders. It was a Fascist achievement of the first rank. Mussolini struck the note; the whole Italian press responded as a helot orchestra. Meanwhile the press of the rest of the civilized world without instructions or censorship poured criticism, ridicule, and abuse upon this great Fascist triumph. The bitterness of the French press wrecked treaty negotiations and led to challenges from Roman journalists to duels. The French government made an official protest asking the Duce to stop the flow of billingsgate in the Roman papers. But from the Brenner Pass to Milan, from Milan to Rome, the people met Nobile with rejoicings ordered by Mussolini and with their hymns of praise were mingled the shouts, "Down with the jackal anti-Fascist press of the world."

Three months later Mussolini ordered the newspapers of Italy never to mention the name of Nobile again and threatened the arrest of those who went to interview him or those who printed his apology or explanation of the North Pole fiasco. (Nobile found refuge in Russia until 1935.)

Similarly with a matter of great political importance. We have already seen Mussolini order the press to play up Hitlerite victories; in 1933 the reward was close coöperation between the two Fascist régimes, and in July 1934, when Hitler again went Mussolini one better and instead of the Italian slow method of "purgation" resorted to two days and nights of murder and assassination of men and women, the Italian press chief again ordered support for his colleague. "The ability to put an end to such a situation is an excellent example of power," said the keynote article in Mussolini's *Popolo d'Italia.* . . . "The right to execute traitors and enemies is not a new discovery. It is the most legitimate revolutionary reality that exists." Courts and trial by jury were all right at times, but there are "exceptional occasions when the individual servant of revolution has the right to administer justice with his trigger finger." (Never had Bolshevism, at the time the Allies were invading from all sides and traitors in its own ranks were selling their country to the enemy, dared make such an open declaration for bloody violence.) The press of the world accused Hitler of murder; Mussolini alone supported him.

But a few weeks later Nazi terrorism broke loose in Austria. Dollfuss, who had approved the machine-gun killing of hundreds of workingmen, was in turn assassinated. He was the ally of Mussolini and his murderers were Hitlerites. Mussolini immediately gave the order to the Fascist press to join the universal chorus of disgust and repudiation of the Hitler régime. Expediency, opportunism, as usual dictated the dictates of the Duce. The Italian people were, as usual, merely the huge woodwork of the piano upon whose keys, the newspapers, the Hierarch was playing his own international tune.

The chief instrument for the control of public opinion in Italy is the official press bureau, Stefani. In the old liberal days this organization, which ranked with the American Associated Press, England's Reuters and Germany's Wolff, gave its subscribers the news with only a natural nationalist tinge; it did not resort to perversion, censorship, and falsehood, nor was it ever corrupted by the money of a foreign power, as was proven in the case of France's Havas when the Russian archives were opened.[1]

[1] L'Abominable Vénalité de la Presse.

Fascism has changed all that. That the Stefani issued nothing but Fascist propaganda and pro-Fascist news after 1922 is of course true, because it had orders from the régime which it could not disobey. But from 1925 on Stefani began to take liberties with the news. Here is an example of how news was changed in the Stefani office:

The Official Stefani Agency:

Lloyd George declared that after the war Socialism in Italy had a disastrous effect on industry. The nation in desperation accepted Fascist succor.

"I recall the joy with which the Liberal Party approved the Fascist revolution, its admiration for the Fascist movement, and its powerful chief, the honorable Mussolini . . ." said Lloyd George.

Official Record of Speech:

I recall how the Fascist revolution has caused and is still causing in the ranks of the Conservative Party, admiration and adulation for the Fascist movement and for its powerful chief. Italy, a terrestrial paradise where the snake of anarchy was chased out by cherubim clad in Black Shirts who guarded the garden against a return of the reptile! That was the picture of a year ago.

You can see for yourself what there is now: Liberty is entirely suppressed. Repression, menace, arson, confiscation, assassination have become the instrument of government . . . (Lloyd George).

And here is another example of how the Fascist press rewrites criticism of Mussolini to make it into flattery:

Statement by Bernard Shaw:

Mussolini has done for Italy what Napoleon did for France, except that for the Duc d'Enghien [who was murdered by order of Napoleon] you must read Matteotti.

The Same in the Italian Press:

Mussolini, without Napoleon's military prestige, has done for Italy just what Napoleon did for France. (From the *Gazzetta del Popolo*, October 12, 1927, page 1, col. 6.)

But while it must be admitted that Mussolini has had a complete success with the press at home, his efforts to influence international opinion have not rewarded him as fully. This is due largely to the fact that foreign correspondents from free nations, led by the Anglo-American group, are the real upholders of freedom of the press in Europe. Frequently these journalists, some of whom represent papers friendly to Fascism and other dictatorships, have had opportunities to show Mussolini just where they stand.

A notable example is the Locarno Conference of 1925. When that "peace" congress was drawing to an end Mussolini burst into the scene in his usual sensational manner—racing motor-car breaking all traffic laws and endangering himself and pedestrians, racing motor-boat from Stresa to Lake Maggiore to Locarno, shouting and bustling entourage, clearing the road for the victor.

The day after his arrival Mussolini summoned the world press for a conference in the Palace Hotel where all the delegations were staying. It was hinted by the Fascist attachés that a world-shattering pronunciamento was about to be delivered. It behooved every journalist, and there were between two and four hundred of them at each of the peace conferences, to be present.

But the time was just after the most flagrant suppressions of journalistic liberty in Italy and the expulsion of a British, a German, and an American newspaper man, all of whom wrote for liberal newspapers. In the lobby of the hotel these facts were discussed. A Frenchman, a German, and an Englishman, George Slocombe, representative of the *London Herald*, mouthpiece of the Labor Party and Ramsay MacDonald, determined not to assist at the Fascist conference. Within a few minutes the word went the round of the hotel and other press meeting-places and a spontaneous boycott of Mussolini occurred. Slocombe relates the incident:

"Mussolini descended the stairs of the hotel, swept like Caesar at the head of a Roman legion across the hall into the press room, followed by Fascist officials and Fascist journalists. In the conference-room there was consternation written large on the faces of the Fascists. Only a handful of correspondents, some of them servile, a few friendly, to hear Mussolini. The others were with me filling the lounge of the hotel. Even the great news agency men boycotted the conference.

"In the almost empty large conference room, I was told afterwards, Mussolini asked a Frenchman if all the journalists were there. The Frenchman, embarrassed, replied that he thought there must be some kind of demonstration elsewhere. But Mussolini sensed the boycott. He said with his usual jeer, snarl, or sneer, or whatever it is:

" 'If they have a protest to make I have a waste-paper basket ready.'

"But he was visibly annoyed. He read abruptly a short statement of his policy, refused to entertain any questions, stalked out. When he appeared at the entrance of the lobby of the hotel he saw me standing at the other end and walked haughtily towards me—afterwards he gave out that he had approached me in the most friendly manner since we were old friends from the Cannes conference before the Fascist coup d'état, when I met him for the first time. Anyhow, he stalked up to me, followed by his Roman cohort, and when he was within a few inches of me said:

" '*Eh bien est ce que le communisme marche toujours?*' ('Well, how is Communism getting along?') I do not know why he should have taken me for a Communist unless it was because we had discussed Communism, Socialism, and Sorel's philosophy of violence on the Cannes occasion.

"I stared at him coldly, keeping my hands in my pockets, although he had put out his hand, and said, '*Je ne saurais pas vous dire*' ('I am not able to tell you.')

" '*Eh bien pourquoi?*' he asked.

" '*Parce que je ne suis pas communiste*' ('Because I am not a Communist.')

" '*Alors,*' he replied, '*je me trompe*' ('Well, I've made a mistake.')

" '*Oui,*' I replied, looking him in the eyes, '*vous vous trompez*' ('Yes, you make a mistake.')

"Then a Dutch journalist who was standing at my elbow made the really devastating remark.

" '*Ça vous arrive souvent,*' he said ('That happens often to you.')

"With that Mussolini almost broke a blood vessel. He looked at us speechlessly for a moment and then said '*Peut-être*' ('Perhaps,') in a theatrical voice, and stalked away, followed by his trembling satellites.

"The Fascist headquarters announced later in the day that I had misunderstood the attitude of the Duce and that he had meant to be friendly, but there was no mistaking the unfriendly nature of our boycott. I think really he had approached me in order to let me know he had remarked our abstention from attendance at his press conference, but did not intend a little thing like that to affect his superb disdain or to affect our own personal relations or ironic semi-affectionate understanding. However, we never met again and I have heard since that I am on the Fascist blacklist."

The second important episode occurred in Washington in 1928 when the board of governors of the National Press Club approved Mussolini's application for non-resident membership and the president committed "an impulsive mistake" by sending the Duce a cablegram congratulating him on his election and expressing "the pleasure of the members of the club in having him as a member."

A protest was organized. Those who signed a paper against Mussolini were Charles Ross of the *St. Louis Post-Dispatch*, Laurence Todd of the *Federated Press*, Leo Sack of the *Scripps-Howard Newspaper Alliance*, Mark Thistlethwaite of the *Indianapolis News*, Roy Roberts of the *Kansas City Star*, F. W. Wile, H. C. Bryant of the *New York World* and Robert Allen of the *Christian Science Monitor*.

The board held another meeting. President J. Fred Essary of the *Baltimore Sun*, and Edgar Markham of the *St. Paul Dispatch and Pioneer Press* moved and seconded the following resolution, which was unanimously adopted:

"Resolved, that a constitutional protest of more than ten active members, assigning reasonable cause, having been filed against the nomination of Benito Mussolini for non-resident membership, his name is hereby withdrawn from further consideration in accordance with the by-laws of the club."

It is unnecessary here to recount the stormy session of the club when the leading Washington correspondents denounced Mussolini as "the archenemy of a free press in our time, and perhaps all time." Naturally enough, the party press of Italy which printed columns of eulogy of the Washington club and congratulated everyone on the election of the Duce, emphasizing particularly the supposed fact that American journalists are not inimical to the Italian situation, but are, they said, really supporters and lovers of Fascism, printed not a word about the Duce's expulsion a few days later.

At this point the reader may ask how it has come to pass that Fascism has enjoyed a tremendous popularity in America and other countries when it is evident that the foreign journalists in Rome are almost unanimously opposed to the movement and its Fuehrer. There are many answers.

First and most important is the fact that the chief propaganda agency of Fascism, the aforementioned Stefani bureau, had and still has an exclusive contract with the Associated Press of America. And, although this may appear unbelievable to laymen, the Associated Press correspondent for the entire first decade of Fascism was an Italian journalist who loved Fascism, hated the Opposition, and (upon the authority of his American assistants) refused even to read the Opposition press, let alone send out Opposition views. If the Associated Press had employed Karl Radek, No. 1 Bolshevik propagandist in Moscow, the situation would have been paralleled.

The *New York Times*, the most powerful and influential newspaper in the United States, employed from the beginning of Fascism, and still employs today, an Italian journalist who has become a greater apologist for the Duce and his régime than any of the public-relations counsel hired in America. And there are other Italians who represent or have represented foreign newspapers, notably the *London Daily Mail* and Reuters. Thus, if one takes the correspondence of the Associated Press, Reuters, the *New York Times,* and the *London Daily Mail*, all friendly to Fascism, it is apparent that a body of public opinion in the two countries has been formed which the rest of the journalists working (and censored) in Rome cannot possibly change.

By the Fascist decree of February 20, 1928, Article 1, a roll of professional journalists was created and no Italian is permitted to practice journalism unless his name appears on the list. "Professional journalist, apprentices, and publicists are minutely controlled. Every applicant for admission to the roll must give ample proof of good moral and political standing, the latter being judged not only by the officials in charge of the roll, but also by the prefects of the provinces. Foreigners may practice the profession of journalist provided they fulfill the same requirements."[2] In other words every Italian journalist must be a Fascist; if a foreigner he must be pro-Fascist. "The Agenzia Stefani, a press agency similar to the Associated Press in America and Havas in France, is still intact and furnishes national and international news. . . . By means of this agency it is obviously easy to supply uniform, censored, and official approved political news to all Italian papers. Official announcements and news favorable to Fascism are continually issued by Stefani both at home and abroad."[3] The journalists' syndicate, according to an official of the press bureau, Amicucci, has been made into "an instrument uniquely political, at the orders of the Duce and the Fascist Party."

One distinction must be made: the foreign correspondent, who is forced into almost daily compromises, will suffer merely deportation if he offends the government, whereas the Italian who represents foreign newspapers faces five years imprisonment on the penal islands if he writes news unfavorable to Fascism.

And yet, under these circumstances, the Associated Press, which still claims it is the most honest and truthful organization in America, employed an Italian for ten years in Rome, and the *New York Times*, for all its declarations of "All the news that's fit to print," is still printing news out of Italy which gives only the Fascist viewpoint. For years the house organ of American publishers, *Editor & Publisher*, the liberal weeklies, *The Nation* and *The New Republic*, and also the weeklies *Time* and *News-Week* and the unique *New Yorker*, have remarked upon this amazing situation. It grew even more so when a special writer for the *New York Times*, an American, in July, 1935, published an uncensored article which made odious comparisons inevitable:

Extracts from cables from the "Times" regular correspondent, Signor Arnaldo Cortesi:	Extract from wireless from the "Times" special correspondent, Anne O'Hare M'Cormick:
The people have become accustomed to the idea that war is not	. . . Mr. Mussolini has not gone out of his way to make unnecessary

[2] Summary of Articles 5, 6, and 7. From *Making Fascists* by Herbert W. Schneider and Shepherd B. Clough.
[3] *Idem.*

only inevitable, but also necessary for a solution of some of Italy's most pressing problems.

Nobody who watched the troops leave the cities for embarkation points en route to East Africa could doubt that they were keen and happy to go.

The present Italian public opinion was shown during Mr. Mussolini's recent trip to Sardinia. The population of that proud, warlike island, which supplied the army's best divisions during the world conflict, gave overwhelming approval to the course he has followed. The Sardinians were roused to great patriotic fervor. . .

With public opinion in its present mood, Mr. Mussolini's truculent policy has the support of all Italians. . . .

enemies. Yet he faces the most difficult time since the killing of Giacomo Matteotti, Socialist deputy, by Fascisti.

In many years this correspondent has not heard such widespread open grumbling, particularly among the peasants. The war boom and active building operations keep money circulating in the cities, but privation pinches in the rural districts. The people everywhere are restive under the tightening of political, economic, and financial restrictions.

The Cortesi item is dated July 5th and the M'Cormick item July 2nd; on June 13th Mussolini had ordered the expulsion of the *Chicago Tribune* correspondent, David Darrah, who arrived in Italy to take the present writer's place almost ten years ago. For ten years Mr. Darrah had honestly tried to cable all the news about Italy, stopping short of facts which he knew would lead to his expulsion, and waiting, as most correspondents in Rome wait, for a story important enough to risk that eventuality. It came in the Ethiopian crisis.

In the Cortesi cable it will be noted that Sardinia is the happiest of all Italian provinces over the prospects of the bloodshed in Africa. In the Darrah correspondence, for which he was deported, a different story is told. On the Saturday before his expulsion from Italy Darrah had "a story commenting on the situation of a quasi 'revolt in Sardinia culminating in the sending of the cruiser *Zara* to Cagliari to impress the population with Il Duce's visit and his distribution of *largesse* to the suffering Sardinians. He also sent another story pointing out the catastrophic conditions to which thirteen years of Fascism had brought the Italian public finances, with an incredible increase in the national debt."[4] Darrah had also cabled that there were mass arrests in Italy, a fact which the *Manchester Guardian* had published weeks earlier, and a report that the King and several high officials were opposed to adventure in Ethiopia.

The foregoing episode is the latest in a thirteen-year series of deadly parallels which have been[5] or might be made between the cables from Signor Cortesi and his father, Salvatore Cortesi, who was recently retired by the Associated Press, and the cables of the majority of the journalists in Rome. For these two gentlemen point 8 of the Fascist catechism, "Mussolini is always right," has apparently been the complete code of the ethics of journalism.

There are three types of correspondents in Rome: the volunteer unpaid propagandists, the bribed, the mental lackeys, and the Italians; the majority, fundamentally honest, who are realistic enough to trim sails and make necessary compromises until a situation arises which makes a decision imperative; and the few who defy the censorship, smuggle news across the frontier, fight the dictatorship, and accept deportation as part of the game.

The commonest form of bribery is the gift of free use of the Italian cables or wireless up to 5,000 words a month. Practically all the pro-Fascist press in the United States and other countries apply for or accept this bribe. When the present writer took over the *Chicago Tribune* bureau in 1925 he was almost immediately threatened with the loss of this Fascist gift if he failed to support the Duce. Needless to say the owner of the *Tribune* knew nothing about this bribe, but the business manager of the Paris edition of the paper not only knew about it, but wrote to my successor suggesting that he try to get the free cable restored.

A handshake from Mussolini has been found to work wonders in emotional reaction from leading democrats and self-announced exponents of freedom of the press. The only explanation members of the *New York Times* staff have been able to give for the continued use of pro-Fascist correspondence is that the late and famous owner, Adolph S. Ochs, never got over a visit his representative

---

[4] Cable from Paris to *Chicago Daily News*, from Edgar Ansel Mowrer.

[5] Cf. "You Can't Print That" (1929) and "Freedom of the Press' (1935).

arranged to the Chigi Palace and the handshake which resulted. There are also many American editors and correspondents who take the commendatore ribbon as seriously as the ubiquitous French *Légion d'honneur*. And there is of course the annual 5,000,000-lire propaganda fund for press propaganda abroad.

All in all, as has been said, Fascism has been a great success in the world press, and credit is due almost entirely to the journalist who is dictator. Thanks to his efforts, the vast majority of newspaper readers throughout the world believe that he led the march on Rome, that he saved Italy from Bolshevism, that he balanced the budget, that Fascism economy was a success until Wall Street crashed in 1929, and that Fascism is a social philosophy worth serious consideration among desperate nations.

The world may also have been told that freedom of the press exists in Italy. In January, 1927, the Duce said to a congress of journalists: "You express an error if you suppose I have suppressed liberty of the press." On May 26, 1927, he admitted that "all the journals of the Opposition have been suppressed," but in 1930 he wrote and signed and sold an article in which he stated:

"Italian journalism is free because it serves only a Cause and a régime; it is free because it can, and does, exercise functions of control, criticism, and propulsion, within the compass of the laws of the régime. I deny absolutely in the most absolute manner that the Italian press lives in the realm of dullness and uniformity."[6]

When Marmontel, author of *Les Contes Moraux*, was a prisoner in the Bastille he complained about it to the governor. The governor replied: "It is true you are not allowed to go out of here, but inside the Bastille you are as free as any man in the world."

[6] *New York World*, March 2, 1930, first page, magazine section.

CHAPTER XXVIII

Let There Be Culture!

Without Art there is no civilization. I believe that Art marks the dawn of every Civilization. . . . (Mussolini, address, Accademia delle belle Arti, 1926.)

E VENTUALLY THE NECESSITY OF EXHIBITING TO THE WORLD AN advance in culture as well as in patriotism and the train schedule, impressed itself upon the fulminating mind of the dictator.

Himself a novelist, essayist, student of philosophy, violinist, and associate of the Futurist artist Marinetti, Mussolini in the years of relative peace which followed the silent revolution felt himself competent to direct the seven great arts and censor the seven lively arts.

In politics he had accepted as his hero Machiavelli's prince, who was Borgia; he had proclaimed himself a modern "enlightened tyrant," but in the arts he thought of other tyrants, one contemporary with his hero, Lorenzo the Magnificent, the great patron, and another who long before Italy gave birth to the Renaissance ruled an era of grandeur in Athens.

The age of Pericles and Plato, the golden age of Greece when creative mind reached unequalled fruition, when art and science flourished, when even everyday workers, stone masons who cut the steles for the tombs of the dead, were possessed of a feeling of beauty such as has never been felt by a race or a people before or after, followed, it is true, closely upon victories at sea and on land, Marathon and Salamis. But Athens then did not become, as Kaiser Wilhelm once hoped or Mussolini now desires his people to become, swollen with military glory, dominating other peoples and spreading kultur to all lands considered inferior. All that Athens had after her wars was a feeling of safety and freedom: the enemy no longer

333

threatened its gates and the wolf no longer skulked at the doors of men who felt the creative instinct.

Mussolini, writing of tyrants, compliments his predecessor, Pericles. The Greek was considerably a demagogue and somewhat a tyrant, the true enlightened tyrant whom Mussolini once called the best of governors and whom he wished to emulate. Pericles had the breadth of mind of a statesman, a prince, and an artist. Under him Athens rallied to rebuild the ravages of war and to make life a finer, nobler thing; under the modern tyrant all life becomes a struggle for survival, a battle for food and clothing and shelter, and while the tyrant rebuilds the army there is no rebuilding of the human spirit. Pericles emptied the war chests for remaking and ennobling his city-empire; Mussolini spent the national wealth upon maintaining himself in power, by creating a private militia, doubling the strength of the army, preparing the nation for war.

Pericles, innately an artist, gathered about him the leaders in sculpture, architecture, philosophy, science, art, and learning, while he who calls himself an enlightened tyrant today, followed the example by creating a national academy, subsidizing its members, and organizing art exhibitions where the painters are given Fascist propaganda themes before they are allowed to put brush to canvas.

In April, 1929, when the thirty members of the first Fascist Academy were announced, the great men of Italy were conspicuous by their absence. D'Annunzio, Croce, Ferrero, Papini, Ugo Ojetti, Sem Benelli and Grazia Deledda had either refused membership or had not been asked to join. Croce the philosopher and Ferrero the historian were not asked because they were living under police surveillance since they were admitted, although inactive, anti-Fascists, and Signora Deledda, who won the Nobel prize for literature in 1927, had two failings—she was not a Fascist and she was disqualified by her sex. The absence of d'Annunzio was the most remarked. In 1930 he had occasion to explain the mystery. He had replied to Mussolini's invitation with a short note.

"A thoroughbred horse," wrote d'Annunzio, "should not mix with jackasses. This is not an insult, but an eugenic-artistic fact."

Notable members of the Academy are Pirandello, Marinetti, and Guglielmo Marconi. On accepting the presidency, the inventor of the wireless said: "Italy's soul is growing as its body grows. Arts never were on a higher plane. Intellectual freedom never was so prevalent." (That same month seven professors in almost as many universities were arrested for insisting on academic freedom.)

For the new academicians Mussolini established a new uniform consisting of a three-cornered hat reminiscent of the war of 1812, a coat similar to that worn by officers of the colored branch of the Knights of Pythias, with frogs, epaulets, and gold braid, and trousers like those worn by the Louisiana Zouaves in the Civil War but in the color of the French spahis; polo boots, a sword, spurs, and sidearms. The Academy was instructed to combat every foreign influence in art, notably American motion-picture films, German architecture, and French literary style. No artistic work was to receive approval unless 100 per cent Italian in style and inspiration.

The education of youth was entrusted to the only philosopher who has accepted Fascism, Gentile, whose first occupation was the reformation of the entire public-school system. The now famous Gentile reform is "based on the principle that the State should aim at a formative rather than a practical education, seeking to educate in the original sense of the word rather than to instruct; a humanist education would achieve this end."[1]

In practice the system has not been carried out completely; it has come into conflict with the Catholic Church, and it has been thoroughly corrupted by the militarization of youth which Mussolini later insisted must be injected into it.

Gentile aimed at humanitarianism; Mussolini established rifle practice in the high schools and machine-gun shooting in the universities of Italy. The one aimed at the ennobling of the character of youth, the latter made class hatred an absolute part of the intellectual life of the nation's fountains of learning and enlightenment. Mussolini has had all the textbooks rewritten so that today there is an actual perversion of the facts of world history, and he has banned from the public schools and from the universities all those who are not adherents of his party or who refuse to remain at least silent and docile followers of the course of instruction set down for them by the political party of which he is the hierarch.

[1] Prezzolini.

It would indeed be difficult for the Anglo-American mind or even the Latin mind in those nations living in a tradition of freedom, to comprehend the situation in Italy. It would require an American citizen, for example, to imagine such a situation: The Democratic Party, let us say, having organized a secret militia and obtained arms through conspiracy with the Secretary of War, marches into Washington and establishes a party dictatorship. Having pacified the country, it proceeds, in due time, to appoint presidents of universities who are judged more by their enthusiasm for the party than on pedagogical merits, orders every public-school teacher to become a politician or quit, then rewrites the history of the nation and gives orders regarding painting and science and general culture, all of which, in the future, must have a political party bias.

Under this new régime, then, George Washington and Abraham Lincoln, having been classified as Republicans, are pronounced inferior to say James J. Whiffletree, the man who led the "march on Washington," and the Battle of Gettysburg is placed second to that event. Eventually the Whiffletree-Democratic Party announces that it is the element which won the World War. It is so written in the new school books. Militarism is exalted as the rule for success and the defeatist words "First in peace" are erased from the remaining statues of Washington while "First in war" are underlined. Jefferson, the Garibaldi of his time, is erased from history books because of having been a "radical, traitor, and Bolshevik." Under the new régime whatever Whiffletree decrees is art, is Art.

This is just what Fascist education has done or aims to do. Going from the ridiculous to the actual, here is an instance: The government has published a series of "unique" textbooks, one for each grade, which are obligatory in private as well as public schools. In the reader for the fourth form there is given the life of the greatest man who ever lived in Italy, Benito Mussolini, paraphrased like the life of Jesus Christ, from the time of birth in the house of his poor parents in Nazareth-Predappio, until that day when his spirit conquers Rome. In this book the martyrdom of Christian saints is replaced by the history of "Fascist Martyrs," the young men who, despite being armed with guns and clubs, sometimes met their death in battles with their usually unarmed and outnumbered opponents.

"One can hardly believe that human barbarity had reached such depths," comments the textbook. The Fascist militia is exalted in many pages and children are taught it is their duty "to love at the same time, the book and the gun, the two arms of knowledge."

In geography, astronomy, and history, Fascist teachers have to acknowledge that there is a universe and that a few but less important nations exist, but practically all the teachings relate to Rome and Italy, to the Caesars who built the past empire and their successor who just as capably rules the present.

The second greatest event in recent history is the World War and it was won almost single-handed, too, by the Fascisti. I myself am not a military genius nor a superpatriot but with some pride I have heard from the lips of two men, Hindenburg and Foch, calculated statements that the 10 or 20 per cent advantage in troops which America had at the front broke the stalemate which the French and British, outnumbered and outgunned, had succeeded in maintaining, and won the war—it is not only historically but militarily true—but in Italy some millions of children repeat in the Coué fashion, over and over, "At the battle of Vittorio Veneto the Italian nation won the World War;—at the battle of Vittorio Veneto the Italian nation won the World War." The Italian nation, as every well-brought-up child ought to know, was the Fascist nation. Mussolini, single-handed, had forced the country into the war. He had reorganized the nation after Caporetto. It is true there were other nations involved, but they were merely allies of Italy.

But in all history the greatest event is the conquest of Rome in 1922. Much more important to world civilization than the war. Because here it was that Mussolini capitalized the war victory and gave the victors, the Fascisti, their reward, the rule of the nation. Their heirs and assigns, the children-readers of this textbook must drink deep of the fountain of militarism. They must repeat:

"Italy, a hundred years ago divided and enslaved, is today one of the greatest powers of the world, presenting an admirable spectacle of discipline, work, and faith. The heroes and the martyrs of the Risorgimento, of the Great War, and the Fascist Revolution have made our country free, united, prosperous, and strong. It is now your turn to grow up healthy in mind and body, to continue the work, so that Italy may once more be a splendid lighthouse of civilization. You must be ready, as were your fathers and grandfathers, if the country calls you, to fly to arms and die serenely should the safety and greatness of your country exact from you this supreme sacrifice."

In intellectual centers, today, there is no longer any protest. It is the accepted order. A critical date in the history of Italian cultural degeneration is March 28, 1926, when the universities held their national congress of philosophy in Milan. The subject for discussion the opening day was "Culture and Liberty." Both items scared the mayor of the city. He ordered the dissolution of the congress the very afternoon of the opening day, and the congress closed after voting a protest "against an act of violence which pretends, but in vain, to limit the domain of philosophy and the thoughtful life."

But the university men guessed wrong. It is neither a pretension nor is it in vain; it is a very real fact that from 1926 to the present day the minor inquisition of the universities has brought about their complete Fascistization. Today no professor may teach in the higher schools unless approved by the Fascist Party and given a card of legitimation or tessera. He must declare himself an adherent of Mussolini's. As first assistant to the Duce, Augusto Turati, had declared that "In my capacity as secretary of the party I assume the direct organization of the professors, lecturers, and assistant instructors of Fascist universities, the most important category of studies efficaciously operating in the kingdom, with the definite intention of giving them a solid and harmonic organization according to the principles of the necessity of Fascism. . . . [Outside the universities] in the Fascist federation, the university professors will bring the precious contribution of their wisdom. . . ."

Every day the Fascist press brings news of how things go under this "totalitarian" system which is making Italy a Fascist Utopian cultural state. As for example:[2]

Revocation.

The Professor Livio Prati is dismissed from the chair of psy-

[2] Bulletin of the Italian Institute of Bio-Chemistry, Milan, September 15, 1930, p. 432.

chiatry and neuropathology on account of incompatibility with the general political directives of the Government. (D.M. 14 July 1930.)

Professor Joseph Rensi, who for many years had the chair of philosophy at the University of Genoa and who is considered one of the leading intellects of the kingdom, was arrested, imprisoned, dismissed, because the post-office censor found some remarks derogatory to Mussolini in a letter which Rensi's wife sent him.

In November, 1930, the new secretary-general of the Fascist Party addressed a circular to the university students of Italy, asking them to spy on their professors and instructors; it was not only their right, it was their duty to do so. They could show their fidelity to the party best by denouncing their teachers if the latter at any time said or did anything offensive to Fascism. "Your judgment," said Giuriati's circular, "towards your professors must be free and dictated by the surest Fascist intransigence; it must not depend on the kindness or the severity of the professor." Students are asked to be the instruments, "the most vigorous will of the battle of Fascism against the old world of democratico-liberals" with which there could be no relations in common.

And so it goes.

First to see that culture would die under a political party's control of the universities was—Matteotti. He declared there was an internal police system at work in the universities, watching both students and professors and reporting to the Fascist Cheka on all liberal thought and action. Matteotti said: "With the imposition . . . of a State philosophy in the secondary schools and with the political oath imposed on all teachers, even in the universities, the education system has completely lost its lay quality . . . the teachers' organizations have been rendered valueless . . . the decrees promulgated by the Fascist Minister of Education, profiting by the plenary powers of the government, have thrown the education system of the country into confusion."

Education, that is, pure education, has ceased to exist. In Italy as in Russia it is now class education, in Russia Communist education, in Italy Fascist education, which aims to give a political propaganda bias to everything, succeeds in history completely, somewhat in geography and philosophy and other branches, in almost everything, in fact, but mathematics. (It is only in Germany, the present great stronghold of anti-Semitism that the universities and their students have rejected Einstein, not because they understand or fail to understand the theory of relativity, but because they know that after all its exponent is nothing but a "sau Jude".)

In Italy, as in Germany, the chief purpose of the ultra-nationalist movement is military superiority. The schools are merely primary grades for the Fascist militia and the army of the future. Militarism, inculcated in youth, will make easy the militarization of the whole country. Moreover, the first education in army training is distinctly Fascist, as distinguished from royal, or belonging to the King, and the spirit of the warrior is a party spirit, which the school-teachers are ordered to prepare.

Every Sunday and every holiday at least 400,000 youths aged eighteen to twenty, all too young to be called for the obligatory eighteen months' army service—a shorter term, it may be mentioned, than the three-year period which the Duce himself escaped by going to Switzerland when he reached the age of conscription—are lined up on all the army parade-grounds of Italy, which for those days become an armed camp, when officers give the first instructions. Anyone failing to attend is severely punished. Fearing a protest from the Pope, the Fascisti announced that "field masses" would be held and the blessing of God called down upon those preparing for future bloodshed.

"The dawn of life," "The hope of the nation," "The army of to-morrow," Mussolini calls his Balillas, or militarized youth movement. Each boy is given a rifle to mark his entrance into full Fascist membership. He is promised it in the Balilla booklet: "Youthful conscripts of the Fascist revolution receive the rifle as the youth of ancient Rome received the toga of virility. It is one of the most beautiful celebrations of the party and most significant."

At the age of eight Italian boys are taken into the Balilla and militarized until the age of fourteen, when the Avanguardisti take them up to eighteen. It was to fill the gap 18 to 20 that the Fascist Grand Council made its 1930 law which begins army training on Sundays and holidays for that period. The official figures for Balilla vary from 800,000 to 950,000; Avanguardisti from 300,000 to 400,000; there are, in short, more than a million of them being militarized and a little less than a million girls and young women, in two similar organizations, Piccole Italiane and Giovani Italiane, who also receive some military training.

Having thus militarized the national culture of the future, the "enlightened tyrant-Prince" with one of those grandiose gestures for which he is now famous, one day devoted his thoughts to culture. Contributing to *L'Arte Fascista*, he wrote this manifesto: "Let us not waste the patrimony that has come down to us from the past, and let us further and create a new patrimony which shall be the peer of that past. Let us create a new art, an art of our own, a Fascist art."

He then placed the future of painting in the hands of his companion in early prisons and his colleague in the original fascio, that same rebel artist Marinetti who in writing the Futurist Manifesto, began with these revolutionary words:

> We intend to destroy the museums and burn the libraries!
> We hate unto death vulgarity, academic mediocrity, pedantry, and the cult of antique and worm-eaten art!
> We intend to raise love to the sphere of danger!
> We shall sing the songs of war!

In 1930 Fascism was ready to show the world what it had accomplished: it held its first exposition in Paris, where a hundred canvases, reeking with paint in cubes and circles, with words written across them, were shown an expectant art world: the show was a decided black eye for perspective, a swift kick to harmony in colors, and a "morte" for composition, a thumbed nose to significant form, altogether a dizzying spectacle, a cry for Fascist freedom.

It was also a complete return to the modern art—of the spring of 1914. It was Marinetti's Futurists back to the very day they dropped art for war. On the canvases the Futurist corpse of 1914 was stretched gaudily dead, with the signatures and dates of the living moment.

In 1933 modern Fascist art repeated its show in the Kronprinzenpalast in Berlin. The noted critic, Walter Mehring, saw nothing modern nor Fascist in it. "Severini, who once painted a turbulent chef-d'œuvre in his 'Bal Tabarin,'" he reported, "shows us today a still life in the pure French tradition of Braque. Carra, co-founder of the *Valori plastici* and Futurism, has returned to Impressionism, and the canvases of Montarini have nothing modern about them but the date 1932. Chirico, in the portrait of his brother, 'The Black Shirt,' alone recalls Fascism in its effect on color. This canvas was painted in . . . 1910! Chirico, Carra, Funi have become first in Italy in the tradition of classicism. I repeat: the first in Italy. Because modern Italian painting has done nothing but imitate Picasso, the pioneer in all new styles and also in neo-classicism. *'Ils pissent sur mes talons,'* he says of all his young imitators. And, in fact, it is he who has revolutionized classicism."

But in Italy laws, decrees, orders can be issued regulating art. Painters, sculptors, architects, in order to participate in exhibitions, work on government orders, and produce statues for the cemeteries, the important lucrative outlet for the sculptors, must belong to a Fascist syndicate and must therefore imbibe Fascist politics and culture, translate them into their work. At the Venice International and the Monza decorative arts salons Fascisti are given the prominent place and almost all the prizes, and the only pictures and statues taken by the government are those of syndicate members. The jury in all cases receives orders from Rome; the commission of the ministries likewise sees to it that only members of the Fascist Academy and the party organization are honored by prizes and purchase.

But the Duce's latest stroke of genius concerned the 1930 Venice exposition when he gave the order that all the painters must symbolize Fascism in some manner if only by the title to their canvas. Most of the pictures were illustrations; many were symbolic concoctions of the spirit of Fascism; there were numerous military scenes —the Black Shirts charging—could it have been unarmed civilians?— with the bayonet, or Mussolini on a white or black or red horse, riding into Rome. (Somehow no one thought of painting him entering the Eternal City in a Pullman sleeper.)

In defense, the authorities offer the fact that from primitives to present-day portrait painters, artists took orders from popes, princes, and patrons; Titian and Michelangelo and the greatest painter of all time, El Greco, not excepted. They also hint that the Soviets influence writers and painters, but it is nevertheless true that the enforcement of politics upon æsthetics in Italy is unique in the history of the world. Up to now the results, too, are unique. They are mostly propaganda and make nice railroad posters.

Of the making of books there is no end: Fascist books dealing with party politics and party philosophy, if such a term can be used; the fiction produced in the past thirteen years outside of the works of the old writers have not been worth while translating or reading. The leaders of the march on Rome, De Bono, De Vecchi, and Italo Balbo, two of whom have the upbringing and training of men of violence, have written prefaces to books on poetry, and one of the new authors, Virgilio Fiorentino of Florence, is called the equal of Virgil and Homer, the master of Milton.

His great Fascist epic is called *Le 27 Cantate della Rivoluzione*, the twenty-seven songs of the revolution, in twenty-seven volumes, each illustrated in modern art, each bound in sumptuous leather, the total costing some $600. Once a month the lucky subscriber receives this reminder of Fascist creative genius, richer and thicker than has yet come from the mind of mortal man.

This is the story in Fiorentino's masterpiece: At the beginning there is a divine intervention of the Trinity against Satan, who is seeking to destroy Holy Rome by means of Russian Bolshevism. The Unknown Soldier, Dante, and the Virgin Mary appear before Almighty God—this writer has no intention of being sacrilegious, he is merely reporting the facts—and ask for aid. God decides to invest Benito Mussolini with supernatural power and in consequence sends the Archangel Gabriel to visit the offices of the *Popolo d'Italia* in Milan, to present to the future Duce the lictor's emblem, the fascio, as a symbol of Divine Will.

Hell becomes alarmed and Satan sends one of his worst devils to the Versailles Peace Conference, the devil enters into the soul of President Woodrow Wilson, takes on the body of Wilson, and sends Wilson to the infernal regions. At Versailles, the devil, replacing Wilson, persuades the plenipotentiaries to steal the Roman goddess of victory and to deliver her enchained to Yugoslavia.

This action infuriates Mussolini, who immediately forms the Fascist Party and burns the Socialist newspapers of Milan; then begins a continual battle with the radical forces, which, however, at the general elections of 1919 are able to capture the goddess of victory and place her on a rock in Dalmatia, for delivery to Lenin!

In nick of time d'Annunzio, with the eagles of his aviation, flies to the aid of Mussolini and even Satan cannot stop him, although he has the aid of Premier Giolitti. Nevertheless, God believes that the goddess of victory is still in danger and sends the angels to save her and to place her, for permanent safety, in the offices of Benito Mussolini in Milan. Mussolini, in a noble strophe, then swears to protect her with his life and until his death and to transport her to Rome, where she will rest eternally as the defender of the grandeur of Latinity.

There follows a bloody battle, the angels of the Lord and the Black Shirts on one side, the devils and the Communists on the other, and as the former begin to scent victory, Mussolini, like Saint Paul, is carried to heaven by the angels, where God points out the beautiful future of Fascism.

In the last chant the doors of the *Popolo d'Italia* are burst open by the heavenly host and the goddess of victory, alive and in resplendent armor, is led by the Duce into the Eternal City. God descends from his throne to contemplate the spectacle, as the chief of the Black Shirts presents the goddess to the King. The gates of Saint Peter's open and the Sovereign Pontiff advances to bless the goddess, and the epic poem terminates with a touching scene in which the Pope, the King, and the Duce embrace each other fraternally.

The author, being poet and politician, does not miss an opportunity to say nasty things about America, Britain, Protestantism, and ex-Premier Nitti. The great work was chosen from several hundred submitted in response to an appeal addressed to "the poets of Fascist Italy." Fiorentino compares his style to that of the "Chanson de Roland"; he has written 20,000 verses and expressed his purpose as aiding in the love feast of the Roman Catholic Church and the Fascist Party. (But that was before the break with the Vatican of the summer of 1931.)

The censorship of books was established with the following order:

"From now on the publishing-houses are invited to submit the proofs of all works which have a political character or content, to the Fascist federations, in order to permit a close censorship. In case of doubt, uncertainty, or controversy, the federations must transmit the proofs to the press office of the National Fascist Party, whose decision shall be final."[3] In addition, an index expurgatorius is sent to all book-dealers. Italy alone among civilized nations banned *All Quiet on the Western Front*. This book was considered dangerous to the spirit of militarism.

Under the circumstances, therefore, of censorship and supernationalism which Mussolini thought would create an atmosphere similar to that in Athens in the time of Plato, culture, instead of prospering in Italy, has, in the opinion of most foreign critics, gone to its grave. Even Italians admit it is moribund. Similar to the Nazi leader's declaration, "When I hear talk about culture, I want to draw my revolver," is the explanation the noted theoretician of Fascism, Signor Ugo Ojetti, makes for the decrease in book publication in Italy. "Reader," he says in his newspaper, "let not the small number of books under review amaze you. Ours is an era of action, when not books but deeds matter. Instead of reading superfluous books, read rather—and reread—the speeches of the leaders."

Ernest Boyd, reviewing the London *Times* 1935 special Italian number literary supplement, calls it "a frank confession of intellectual sterility; no name of any original distinction is mentioned belonging to a newcomer. Many fine writers are ignored, others are mentioned and praised in the precise degree of their acceptance of Fascism. . . . Italian culture, under Fascism, has nothing to offer the world. This may, as everyone assures us, make the trains run on time, but it does not interest those of us who heard of Italy before Mussolini invented this expensive way of advertising that not altogether obscure country."

In the preparation of the new Italian Encyclopædia the two Senators in charge reported that there was not a single savant among the Fascisti, not a single man of letters, not a single intellectual

[3] January 29, 1929. Circular issued by the Fascist National Party, signed by Augusto Turati.

capable of carrying on the great work, so they employed non- or anti-Fascist talent.

When the party press discovered this act of treason it let loose its polemical tirades. Senators replied there would be no encyclopædia unless the right men were employed regardless of politics. The semiofficial *Il Tevere* answered that "if there is penury of competence in the Fascist camp, if Fascism has little in common with culture, it is of no great matter. The Fascisti have done and are doing more important things than making encyclopædias. The matter might just as well be dropped."

At the end of the first half-decade of Fascism the Under Secretary of State, Giuseppe Bottai, admitted that "the sympathies of all those who in the academic field still occupy the first places are neutral or opposed to us."

As the years went on and the leaders of Italian culture still refused to accept dictatorship, the régime tightened its laws and decrees and deported a larger number of intellectuals to the Liparian Islands. On May 15, 1935, mass arrests of intellectuals took place in Turin, Milan, and other cities. Among the victims are noted university professors, including Professors Martinetti, Solari, Cosmo, Salvatorelli, and Giua, the scientist, whose wife also is in prison. The crime of the Giuas, however, is not intellectual opposition to Fascism, but being the parents of a political enemy.[4]

Returning from a visit to Italy, Anthony M. Turano wrote that "The atmosphere itself is so depressing that no outstanding writer has arisen here since the advent of the Dark Age of Fascism. Even the novelist is inevitably cramped and self-conscious, for fear he picture contemporary life in a manner unsuitable to the Fascist idea. The consequence might be imprisonment or exile. . . . Furthermore, the psychological emphasis has been so completely switched to patriotic stupidities, that there is no longer a reading public in the older sense. There is only the State and its trembling subjects."[5]

Angel Flores found that the young Fascist intellectuals have at last got around to transcendental quarrels over Form versus Content,

[4] *Manchester Guardian*, June 7, 1935. Arrest of intellectuals was apparently not of enough importance for the American press.

[5] *American Mercury*.

furious hunts for the *mot juste,* and an attempt to surpass "the perfect beauty of their idol, the fairy-like Wilde," while the "revolutionary" writers in 1935 discovered James Joyce and immediately issued books with interior monologue as the feature. Critics ballyhooed Ettori Settani's *Who Killed Giovanni Bandone?* as a Fascist triumph. It is one of history's present ironies that the only important novel out of Italy under Fascism is an anti-Fascist novel. Of *Fontamara,* by Ignazio Silone, one of the large group of intellectuals either in prison or exile, Clifton Fadiman says it is Italy's most valuable export in some years and adds that Fascism has "destroyed the simple, deep-rooted, and organic culture of agricultural Italy."

The collapse or death of culture under Fascism is probably a great surprise to Mussolini. He has willed otherwise. Early in his dictatorial career he made the following prediction: "The Italian school will again take its deserved place in the world. From our university chairs true scientists and poets will again illuminate Italian thought. . . . *I have willed* that in collaboration with the universities, departments of Fascist economics, of corporative law, and a whole series of fruitful institutes of Fascist culture, should be created. Thus a purely scholastic and academic world is being permeated by Fascism, which is creating a new culture through the fervid and complex activity of real, of theoretical, and of spiritual experiences."

But there is an apparent discrepancy between the will and the deed. Mussolini wills art, he wills Fascist economics, he brilliantly recognizes that civilization perishes without art, and in practice his assistants militarize and stultify, to use redundancy, the national mind. To the Duce's glittering generalities must be added the more practical expression of the president of the National Fascist Confederation of Intellectuals, who announced a goal for the membership: "Of journalists and writers we have requested that they engage in what may be called 'spiritual imperialism,' in the theater, the book, the newspaper, and by means of lectures."

The figurative donning of the black shirt by Italian culture was literally exemplified in November, 1934, when the corps of teachers of the nation, by order of the Ministry of Education, put itself into Fascist Balilla or Fascist militia uniforms consisting of black top boots, riding-breeches, tunic, black shirt, black fez. At the same time (November 7th) army officers in uniform took the places of the professors of the country and began in high schools and colleges the compulsory military culture courses announced two months earlier by Mussolini. No high school or college student can now pass from grade to grade unless he has a qualifying mark in militarism.

Under these circumstances the "liberation of the spirit" has no future in Italy; the present is best summed up by Professor Horace M. Kallen, who made a study of cultural conditions in Italy and reported that "What I saw and heard and read there left me with the feeling that where art and thought are concerned, Fascist Italy is not alive, but drugged and dead. . . . In the world of art nothing is happening: only the Futurists whipping a dead horse and calling him Pegasus."

★ ★

CHAPTER XXIX

The Imperialist Road to War

WE HAVE NOW SEEN MUSSOLINI TRIUMPHANT, IF ONLY TEM-porarily, in his dealings with the Vatican, totally victorious in suppressing opposition parties and press, totally unsuccessful in attempting to create art and culture.

Economically, the evidence is incontrovertible, Fascism has been a failure, and the lowering of the standard of living has been an inevitable result. The Fascist hierarchy, the manufacturers, big-business men, the bureaucracy and army may be better off in Italy than before the war, but the masses of people, workmen and middle class, are decidedly worse off.

Certain Fascist claims have already been disposed of in preceding chapters, notably that "Bolshevism and social disorder have been abolished," that "Industry and commerce have revived," or that "employment has increased," a claim which was justified in 1925, but which was made in 1927 and 1928, when it was untrue, and which is ridiculous today. But there are still propagandists who claim that "wages and the cost of living have been balanced," and that the budget has been balanced, and many things which official Fascist statistics themselves deny.

The most important of the achievements which Mussolini and philo-Fascists have listed, in addition to those discussed previously, are the following:

The trains run on time.
The marshes have been drained.
Public works.
Restoration of the prestige of Italy.
Rebirth and intensification of Nationalism.

"Order, Discipline, Hierarchy" (The Fascist slogan).
The Authoritarian State.

Celebrating the first decade of Fascism, Mussolini in a public oration recounted all the material achievements. "And furthermore," he continued, "I say that we have accomplished even grander things. Because the Fascist idea has become part of the Italian nation, has become the Italian nation itself, and is destined to live in the generations which follow.

"Ten years of Fascism have created, as I have said, an epoch. The material gains constitute only a part of the work. . . . Fascism is destined to live. Fascism is a living spirit and that spirit will live even after the death of the pioneers who created it.

"The great movements which have survived are those which are animated with spirit. . . . Ten years of power have given to Fascism a spirit which, above the material things which it has constructed, is destined to live like the other great movements of the past. The material realizations are useful for the nation for years. . . . The spirit which created material things will live and will continue even after these things themselves have disappeared.

"Already other nations begin to study us. The people of the entire world demand of us: 'What have you accomplished?' The spirit of Fascism today is penetrating other nations outside our frontiers and will live under other suns.

"It is not a matter of the simple functioning of a system nor of mechanical organizations of a government. Fascism regards itself as a living organism, it believes in and develops itself in a measure which the years augment in vibrant vitality. . . . In ten years its virility has been infused into the very existence and the life of the Italian people. Fascism has fortified this virility and has given it plenitude of the kind which all nations have which survive, and it has given to all humanity its spirit and its benediction. . . . Ten years have created a living organism, full of ardent life, promising us eternity. Fascism will transmit to posterity its heritage of Power and Will."

Fascism's achievements, according to Mr. Marcosson, "ranged all the way from purging the streets of beggars and the elimination of the once-dreaded Mafia to the stimulation of production, the reorganization of governmental departments, the transfer of public utilities to private ownership, the conversion of the railway deficit to a profit, the checking of currency gambling and the restoration of Italian prestige abroad." According to Mr. Cortesi[1] "whatever opinions anyone may hold concerning spiritual and doctrinal content of Fascism, it is almost universally conceded that from a purely material standpoint Italy has made great strides under the present régime." He then proceeds to sum up the gains under Mussolini:

The technical equipment of the nation has been greatly improved.

"The reclamation work covers an area of about 10,000,000,000 [*sic*] acres, involving the construction of 830 miles of drainage canals, 700 miles of irrigation canals, 2,000 miles of new roads, 105 rural aqueducts, and 3,500 farmhouses."

Five thousand miles of road resurfaced in 1932; 3,500 miles of new roads built.

Great improvements in State railroads; 350 new miles opened to traffic in ten years; 300 miles under construction.

"Especially important is the new Florence-Bologna line which has cost more than $70,000,000 and will soon be opened to traffic."

The gospel of Fascism, according to Howard R. Marraro of the Italian Department of Columbia University:[2]

The Italian today is much better fed than he was.

The standards of living have improved from 1913 to the present. This improvement is particularly marked during the twelve years of the Fascist régime.

Thanks to the labor legislation of the Fascist régime, there has been no important strike or lockout in Italy since 1926.

[1] *New York Times,* August 12, 1933.

[2] Columbia University's president, Nicholas Murray Butler, is generally regarded as the ace of liberalism in America. With equal thunders President Butler wars against Communism and Fascism, while he upholds the best traditions of American democracy. At least so he claims. Despite the fact that convincing proof has been given that Fascism flourishes at Columbia, that the Casa Italiana is a Fascist agency, directed by Fascists or philo-Fascists, spreading propaganda for a policy opposed to the American liberal tradition and in violation of academic freedom, nothing has been done by President Butler to remedy this situation.

The *Opera Nazionale Dopolavoro* supplies entertainment, education, physical exercise, health, and welfare work.

Increased wheat production.

Hydroelectric power tells another story of progress under the Fascist régime.

Unemployment kept down by public works . . . costing 24,-708,509,497.12 lire, or about $2,148,572,000, to August 31, 1932 . . . ; road building; land reclamation.

Gold reserve rose from 5,626,300,000 lire on December 31, 1931, to 6,838,500,000 in April 1934.

"Fascism in Italy has thus made genuine progress toward solving a series of fundamental economic problems. . . . The economic and social achievements of Fascism are truly impressive. . . . A more prosperous and happy nation."

Least important and most quoted is the argument that the trains run on time. The vast American tourist class, which includes bankers, editors, senators and representatives, mayors and mayoresses, army officers and just plain "folks," returned to its native land, where railroading is an accepted institution but not necessarily a yardstick for patriotism, and roared in unison, "Great is the Duce; the trains now run on time." A poor, simple, naïve minority which protested that some abstract and old-fashioned American things such as liberty of the press, freedom of the individual, equal justice, and the spread of culture were being slaughtered by the Corporate State, where an institution known as the O. V. R. A. exercised dictatorial terrorism, was squelched with the complete answer, "But the trains run on time." When the unruly minority timidly suggested that the Authoritarian State was the complete antithesis of the Magna Charta, the Declaration of Independence, and the Rights of Man, millions of tourists would leap up to chant the litany, "The trains run on time." The official press agents and the official philosophers of the Fascist régime explained to the world that the running of trains was the symbol of the restoration of law and order—Order, Discipline, Hierarchy.

No one has bothered to explain that the short period of railroad disorganization occurred just after the war, when Italy, in order to keep the troop and supply trains running, tore up the rails in many parts of the kingdom and was forced to neglect roadbeds and repair work everywhere, and that immediately after the war engaged upon a railroad reconstruction program of five years which resulted in June, 1922, with enough success to make "the trains run on time," a claim of the Liberal régime. (The Liberal régime, thoughtlessly, hired no press agent and no international bankers to publicize itself.)

No one ever denied that there have been disruptions of the Italian railroads due to strikes; everyone seems to have forgotten that not only did Mussolini advocate the ownership and control of the railroad system by the railroad workingmen, but he editorially supported them when they struck.

Do the railroads always run on time under Fascist discipline? An investigation during a fortnight in July, 1930, made despite the fact the press was forbidden to mention railroad accidents and delays, disclosed five cases: the Milan-Chiasso express was derailed at Seregano, two of the crew being injured; two days later the train carrying the Hon. Minister of Justice Rocco was derailed and arrived many hours late; on July 22nd the Rome-Milan Pullman was derailed at Targuinie; on the 26th a locomotive and fourteen coaches fell into the Meduna River near Udine, and there was one other derailment of small importance. It is true that the majority of big expresses, those carrying eyewitnessing tourists, are usually put through on time, but on the smaller lines bad rail and road-bed conditions frequently cause delays.

Wrote M. Vandervelde, noted Belgian Foreign Minister, after a trip to Italy: "The time is no more when Italian trains run on time. We always were kept waiting for more than a quarter of an hour at the level crossings because the trains were never there at the times they should have been passing."[3]

A word must also be said about the great public works. Mussolini has announced the completion of the aqueduct of Pouilles, the Naples-Rome railroad, the Sila hydro-electric works, and many others. Mussolini himself made grand orations at the openings. He did not state, however, that such public works take ten or fifteen years to finish, that ex-Premier Nitti projected the Sila and other works,

[3] *Le Peuple,* Brussels, April 19, 1932.

that the aqueduct was begun in 1915, and that the Naples-Rome railroad was all ready but for the oratory

And take for another example the famous Florence-Bologna line which Mr. Cortesi lists among Fascist triumphs. I have already mentioned the work in Chapter XX, "graft amounting to 300,000,000 lire in the Florence-Bologna 700,000,000 lire tunnel project," when the ras Baroncini accused "the Grandi gang," and the gang retaliated by hiring a doctor to poison the ras. On April 22, 1934, the Associated Press reported the opening of the world's longest double-track railway tunnel, "a high spot in Premier Mussolini's public-works program," but after paying this homage, revealed the fact that "work was started on the tunnel approximately twenty years ago"—*i.e.*, in 1913, by a Liberal régime.

The case of land reclamation is a similar story. Mr. Cortesi has reported that it "covers an area of about 10,000,000,000 acres," which is just about two thousand times the area which Mr. Mussolini claims, but this may all be a typographical error or a wish-fulfillment betrayal of the Fascist mentality.

Before the war the government announced that the total of drained marshland was 700,000 hectares, the hectare being 2.47 plus acres; in 1928 the Fascist régime announced that from 1918 to 1927 an additional 527,000 hectares had been put into cultivation by the Nitti, Giolitti, and Mussolini governments, and that work was being done on 568,000 hectares by the Fascist government, leaving some 589,000 hectares for future operations.

In fact, the work on the Roman Campagna began in 1911, when 9,585 hectares around Rome were reclaimed by government subsidy; in 1921 the total was 53,000 hectares and the government passed an act for further increases. The company for the reclamation of the Pontine marshes was formed in 1919 and began operations on a twenty-year project on May 12, 1922. The Piscinara area operations also began in that part of 1922 which the Fascists call "chaos and anarchy"—*i.e.*, a few months before they arrived.

Official statistics for electrification also reveal that the period 1913-14 produced 2,3 thousand million kilowatts and that in 1918 it had been increased to 4 thousand million. From 1908 to 1915, according to *Fortune's* survey, Italy's hydroelectric capacity increased an average of 17 per cent per annum; under Fascism, from 1922 to 1929, it increased 18 per cent per annum, therefore "Fascist policy does not score a triumph." But the triumph—without statistics—is stressed in all emotional ballyhoo for the régime.

On the success side of the ledger must be written militarism. Here something new under the sun has been accomplished and Sparta has been left behind: the Duce has finally militarized the cradles of the country.

From the day of birth until the child is capable of beginning his military training the Italian male will be under government supervision merely of a hygienic nature. But at the age of six he begins his service by joining the pre-Balilla military order. From now on his life belongs to the state. Here is the program as finally completed in November, 1934:

Ages 6 to 8: Sons of the Wolf
Ages 9 to 14: Balilla
Ages 15 to 18: Avanguardisti
Ages 19 to 21: Fascist militia
Ages 22 to 34: Regular army (18 months) service and active reserve
Ages 35 to 55: Reserves.

Fifty years of a man's life under militarization; special training for women in the medical, chemical warfare, and allied fields; mobilization of all citizens from sixteen to seventy in time of war—from babes in arms to a nation in arms—this is the undisputed accomplishment of the statesman who never tires of granting official interviews in which he declares, "Our policy is peace," but who writes for the new encyclopædia:

"Fascism rejects pacifism which implies renunciation of struggle and cowardness in the face of sacrifice. . . . Only war carries all human energies to the height of tension and gives the seal of nobility to peoples who have the courage to confront it."

Weighing the fact that Italy cannot feed its present population and the axiom that a superior population imposes itself, the Duce on the 26th of May, 1927, inaugurated the "battle of natality," to bring the Italian people up 60,000,000. Birth control is a crime;

bachelors have been taxed and the taxes doubled; exemptions in taxes and special privileges are given large families. As a result there have been "victorious" years in the Duce's baby war. In 1929, however, there was a nation-wide birth strike. Laws were proposed "against deserters from the good battle, to make them so strict that they are unbearable, that they will compel people to marry and have children out of sheer desperation."[4] In 1930 the 1927 mark was reached again. In 1931, however, the rate was 22.4 compared with 1927's 26.9. In 1932 the Duce ordered the idealization of the fat woman, the best breeder of children. But the battle is still on.

To "free the Italian people from the slavery of foreign bread" Mussolini announced the *Battaglia del grano,* and shortly afterwards his victory. That Italy has increased its wheat production cannot be questioned. But every year, when nature smiles, the crops of the whole world increase and it is only the Fascist press (on instruction from the official bureau) which sings the praise of the divine Duce; in those years, however, when the crops throughout the world are bad, the Fascist press (on instruction) puts the blame on elements over which the Duce still has no control.

Thus in 1932, when Italy's wheat yield rose from 67 to 75 million quintals, Fascism rejoiced in its leader in the battle of the grain. It was an increase of 12 per cent. That same year, however, abundant nature gave neighboring and still republican France an increase of 17, and Spain, which had just shaken off dictatorial tyranny, an increase of 13 million quintals, respectively, 23 and 34 per cent. Of this, no mention in the Fascist press.

Patriotism, Prestige, Order, Discipline, Hierarchy, the Authoritarian State, remain to be considered.

Patriotism and Imperialism have been restored.

Italian prestige has been enhanced.

Order obtains. In the chapter on the Corporate State there have been noted various strikes and uprisings; in the chapter on journalism a revolt in Sardinia has been mentioned, but it must be admitted that nothing that has happened under Fascism has seriously affected the stability of the régime. Wherever men or women have tried to strike or even to speak against the régime, the Fascist

[4] The Fascist leader, Scorza, in *Lavoro Fascista,* December 31, 1929.

militia has made short work of them. The prison islands are full of political and intellectual opponents.

Before the war there was a joke known to all the diplomats of Europe. It was simply this: "Order reigns in Warsaw." It was a reference to the periodical reports made to the Tsar of Russia by his governor in Poland, who, after listing the riots, battles, dead, and wounded, always concluded his optimistic message with the phrase, "Order reigns in Warsaw."

Order, Discipline, Hierarchy seem secure in Italy. On the last-named subject Mr. Percy Winner, one-time Rome correspondent and later foreign editor of the *New York Evening Post*, wrote: "To be a potential candidate for the Mussolinian toga is as much a political suicide in modern Italy as being a candidate for the Caesarian toga was on occasions in ancient Rome."

Which leaves for consideration the Authoritarian State.

Just when this conception sprang from the brain of the Duce cannot be determined. It was certainly not part of the original Fascist program. In 1920, moreover, Mussolini took the occasion of Nitti's proposal of the *ora legale*, or daylight-saving time, to write a magnificent exposition of his philosophy of the State:

"The proletariat detests the *ora legale* because it is wartime hour. I too am against the *ora legale* because it represents in another form the intervention and the coercion by the State. I do not make it a question of politics, of nationalism or utilitarianism; I take the part of the individual and against the State. Numerous individuals are in potential revolt against the State, not this nor that State, but against the State itself.

"The State, burdened with its enormous bureaucratic machinery, to the point of asphyxiation. The State is supportable so long as it sticks to soldiery and policing; but today the State does everything, it is the banker, the usurer, the shipper, the insurance man, the post-office, the railroads, the impresario, the industrialist, the maestro, the professor, the tobacconist, and many other things, instead of making, as it once did, the policing, the judiciary, and the agency for taxation.

"The State, Moloch with its horrible face, today does everything, sees everything, controls everything, and carries everything towards its ruin; every function of the State is a disaster. Disaster, the art of the State, the school of the State, the post-office of the State, the navigation of the State, the food supply—alas, of the State this litany can be continued into infinity.

"If only mankind had a vague sense of the abyss which awaits them, the number of suicides would increase greatly because it goes towards the complete annihilation of all individuality.

"This, this, is the great malediction which drives the human race back to its uncertain beginnings of history.

"The revolt against the legal hour is the supreme attempt of the individual against the coercion of the State, a ray of hope filtering into the spirit of our desperate individualists.

"Down with the State in all its forms of incarnation. The State of yesterday, of today, of tomorrow, the Bourgeois State and the Socialist State.

"To us who are about to perish as individualists there remains, in the present darkness or in the tenebrous tomorrow but one religion, however absurd but always consoling, *Anarchism*."

Within a few months Mussolini's entire "philosophy" of the State underwent a change. The State became a "hierarchy which must end in a pin-point," himself; several years of functioning as hierarch led him to the following conclusion:

"The sense of Stateship grows in the conscience of the Italians, who feel that the State alone forms the indispensable guarantee of their unity and independence; that the State alone represents continuity in the future of their race and their history.

"The State is the central idea of our government; it is the political and juridical organization of national societies, and evolves in a series of institutions of various kinds. Our formula is this: Everything in the State, nothing outside the State, nothing against the State.

"The government is the highest expression of the régime. Therefore everything which depends on and descends from government is Fascist. Fascists must be doubly disciplined, as Fascists and as citizens. It is wrong to conceive the grotesque and absurd anachronism that the Fascist State is an authority which it is possible to dispense with, thus falling into the foolish and anarchistic demagogy which we have cauterized with fire and sword.

"The Fascist State is the Fascist government, and the head of the Fascist government is the head of the revolution."

(Or, *"l'État, c'est moi"* all over again.)

We do know that Mussolini, like Marx before him, studied Hegel, and just as he never hesitated to rewrite the one in the original Fascist manifesto, he helped himself to the older philosopher in his remarkable *volte face*. Not only the idea, but the wording, is Hegel's:

Mussolini:	*Hegel:*
The State is a spiritual and moral fact. . . .	The State is in and for itself a moral whole
incorporates the political, juristic and economic organization.	. . . and realizes itself consciously.
and such an organization is in its birth and development a manifestation of the spirit.	The State is a spirit which arises in the world.
The State reaches beyond the short span of life of the individual.	. . . it self-consciously realizes its independent power, in which single individuals are only passing moments.

The announcement of this Hegelian State—which the Pope was later to denounce as Statolatry—came many years after the Fascist régime had already established itself. Behind the announcement stands one fact: in August, 1920, the State was "Moloch with its horrible face . . . the great malediction which drives the human race back to its uncertain beginnings in history"; in September, 1920, Mussolini made his bid to lead a socialistic or communistic army into Rome and was rejected; in 1922 the march was made in the pay of the bankers and industrialists, and in 1921 Mussolini asked the philosophers of Italy to supply a philosophy for Fascism.[5] Hegel was the only man out of the past who fitted the present.

[5] Unbelievable as this statement may seem, it is a fact. On August 27, 1921, Mussolini wrote to Michele Bianchi on the occasion of the opening of the school for propaganda and fascist culture: *"Ora, il fascismo italiano, pena la morte o, peggio, il suicidio, deve darsi un 'corpo di dottrine'* . . .

"La parola è un po' grossa: ma io vorrei che nei due mesi . . . si creasse la filosofia del Fascismo italiano. . . ." (*Messaggi e proclami.* Benito Mussolini. Milan, 1929, pages 38 and 39.) Not only must the philosophy of Fascism be created, but Mussolini wants it in two months' time.

And so we have Mussolini's Authoritarian State, a totalitarian dictatorship, facing the historical truth that every autocracy such as his, from ancient times to that of Napoleon III, has ended in revolution or war, and we have a Duce who sits with a revolver on his desk, intent on outwitting history.

Sometime recently Lloyd George, released from the strictures of political office, said to an Argentine journalist that "it will be on account of the errors and absurdities of its economics that Fascism will reach its dissolution." Mussolini replied by calling Lloyd George "only a second-class little lawyer," but the balance sheet of Fascism shows one thing surely, and that is that Fascist economics have been a record of errors and absurdities. They seem typical of all authoritarian dictatorships. They are or have caused:

> Dangerous decline in the standard of living;
>
> Alarming increase in taxation;
>
> Financial excesses relatively beyond those of any modern state, hidden from the public by budget manipulation and secrecy.
>
> Disastrous financial-economic actions, such as stabilization, for purely prestige reasons.
>
> Waste; graft; loss of billions through the necessary multiplied police and espionage and militia systems.
>
> Suppression of parliament, press, public assembly, and other critical or controlling factors.
>
> War preparations which lead to war.

Autocratic dictatorships always begin in enthusiasm and end in corruption or bloodshed. Dictatorships which make use merely of the Hegelian phrases, refusing to consider the "idealistic philosophy" which accompanied them; dictatorships which are imposed from above, refusing to alter the economic system either by bringing the masses of the people into coöperative ownership of the means of production or providing economic security for the majority while guaranteeing the profit system of the ruling class, always face the revenge of social and economic and moral forces which attack the weaknesses of absolutism. Dictators in our own time have disappeared, or have been dismissed quietly, or have been driven out, or into

exile, or been assassinated; dictatorships have been dissolved, peacefully altered, or drowned in fraternal blood, and usually for the
same reasons:

> The financial ruin of the State;
> The economic anæmia of the nation;
> The strangulation of the people by taxation and the public
> debt burden;
> The armament race.

"You can do anything with bayonets except sit on them," said
one of Mussolini's great predecessors, Cavour, and the Fascisti
celebrating their first decade laughed at the phrase. But Cavour took
the long view.

Dictatorships have always proven the most expensive form of
government and their few achievements have been overbalanced by
their inefficiencies and errors. The democratic State can commit and
admit its mistakes. The dictatorship of a class—Russia, for example
—can and does admit its mistakes, as, for example, Lenin's announcement of the New Economic Policy which was a refutation of
a great part of the Communist program and which the Opposition
called a reversal to pure capitalism. But the Authoritarian State dare
not err.

To hide its errors the Authoritarian State has absolutely refused
to permit:

> The approval or disapproval of the people by free election;
> The control of finances by the public;
> The controlling criticism by the press;
> Sharing responsibility by a freely elected parliament.

All of which, coöperating with a dictator would, while weakening
the personal ego, the Will, the régime, at least prolong both the
man and the system in power and eventually lead to a normal free
government without a violent interregnum. An example of the latter
type of dictatorship was that of King Alexander of Yugoslavia and
his successor. But it is difficult to imagine the magnificent ego, the
transcendental will to power, of the Italian Duce bowing for a moment to criticism, control, or indeed any outside influence. This

born proletarian, this real man of the people, more than any person living today, represents the socially and economically deaf, dumb, and blind ruling class, programless, unphilosophical, unideological and anti-ideological, but determined at any price including the always logical and ultimate one, imperialistic war, to maintain its supremacy.

We have passed slowly through the centuries of village economy, serfdom, and the feudal overlords; very quickly through the era of industrial and commercial expansion, the era of colonization, the opening of world markets, the exploitation of "inferior" peoples, and we have arrived at the most magnificent smash-up in history in the decade and a half of the World War and the economic débâcle of 1929.

The rule of capital, big business, commercial penetration, and colonial expansion has been a time of democracy and social reform. But apparently, as Mussolini himself claims, liberalism is dead and the Goddess of Liberty is a rotten carcass: the ruling class can no longer make their profits and afford to grant democracy and social reforms. The various imperialisms which have divided the world have left no new markets to conquer, no inferior people to make into slaves and serfs to produce wealth and to absorb the production of the superior people.

In this world emergency Fascism arose to perpetuate the system of exploitation of its own people as well as those which it could conquer. The Authoritarian State is also the Helot State, the Serf State, for the vast majority outside the reigning hierarchy. Year by year Italy has been returning to the time of serfdom and the feudal overlords.

The balance sheet of Fascism indicates it plainly. But while it must be admitted that the Authoritarian State is a complete success, it is also becoming apparent that the return to serfdom is a complete solution of the economic problem of Italy or any other State which has or may copy this successful plan. Big business imperialism in Italy has not been able to continue its rate of profit despite the tremendous increase in taxation, the dangerous decrease in wages, the most complete denial of the rights of man in post-bellum history.

Those opponents of Fascism who have always maintained that it presented no new philosophy, no new ideology, but was merely a restatement of a medieval system and that every step taken by Mussolini was a step backwards into a dead civilization, had proof of their view in the official reasons Italy gave to the League of Nations for war in Ethiopia.

The massacre of Ual-Ual was the first excuse given. But it was dropped even before the League's commission absolved both countries of guilt. Then came two new reasons: imperialism, or the necessity of expansion by powerful nations, and *Kultur*, or the right of a civilized country to take over a barbaric country where slavery still flourished.

Both reasons date from the eighteenth and nineteenth centuries; it is true they were used by Britain in building her empire, and were advanced by Wilhelm in an attempt to rule the world, but no nation has been hypocritical enough to use them again in our own time. As for slavery in Ethiopia, the League has taken actions, the Emperor of Ethiopia has done his best, considering the fact the country is a loose confederation in which tribal chiefs frequently refuse to listen to Addis Ababa, but the hypocrisy of the whole matter is best shown in the fact that Fascist Italy has herself admitted that slavery in the form of economic servitude still flourishes in her African colony of Libya.

The road to war has been inevitable. Even before John Strachey wrote that "Fascism means war," an Italian writer, Mario Carli, predicted that "Fascism issued from the war and in war it must find its outlet." Fascism means war because imperialism means war, and no one has ever denied that Fascism is imperialistic.

"Imperialism is at the base of the life of every people which desires economic and spiritual expansion," Mussolini once wrote, and again, "We must have the courage to say that Italy cannot remain forever penned up in one sea, even if it is the Adriatic," while in the famous June 5, 1923, speech against Yugoslavia, he said that "all Italians of my generation understand the lack of territory. It is not surprising, therefore, that our spirit is frequently excited as it turns towards imperialistic aspirations. This is an expression of immanent historic reality, because people who are progressing have their rights against people who are declining. These rights are marked with letters of fire in the pages of our destiny."

In justifying his imperialism Mussolini said in a recent speech:

"Invasion of sovereign rights has been in progress for centuries. Where is the nation today which during its history has not invaded the sovereign rights of others? Take the United States! How did you push your frontiers back?"

To Mussolini's credit it must be said that he did not, as other imperialist nations have done, resort to euphemism in announcing his imperialism, although diplomatic hypocrisy cloaked the Ethiopian apologia. Sordid and cold-blooded as a post-bellum world may consider his scheme to take by violence the only remaining unexploited piece of Africa, it must be admitted that the intention to seize and conquer land has been frankly stated for a decade.

Many of the preceding chapters contain the reasons for the Fascist road to war. The glorious period of 1922-25 when the industrialists, manufacturers, large employers, subsidizers of the party, were being repaid, was followed by an economic reaction which proved boom times artificial. After 1925 it became impossible for the "new" system to enrich the few and continue to impoverish the many. One by one Mussolini's promises, which once brought thousands of liberals, radicals, and idealists into his party, were dropped, and instead a program of ruthless taxation which took half the national income was enforced. And no nation could continue to flourish under that condition, even though the standard of living of the masses was reduced dangerously year after year.

Since the depression Fascism has come to a dead stop. All that it has had in the past four or five years is a record of broken promises, an unbearable debt burden, and the dynamic oratory of the Duce. But one cannot live on oratory alone.

We have seen the collapse of every financial and economic factor in Fascist Italy, exports, imports, emigrants' remittances, tourist trade; we have seen the debts grow mountainous, the national debt increase 15,000,000,000 in four years; we know that the international bankers have refused to issue loans, and we know that the tremendous population pressure has increased during the ten years which now mark the Italian depression. Every economist and every intelligent student has been aware of the forces which for a decade have been driving the dictator into either war or collapse; only in the *New York Times* (September 1, 1935, magazine section, page 2) is the opinion expressed that "Mussolini is the first ruler since Napoleon by his own will, without external provocation or internal propulsion, to lead his people into a campaign of conquest."

The internal propulsion has been progressive for years and now it has become headlong.

Like many a bankrupt business man who takes his last resources and plays them on a number in Monte Carlo, Mussolini, rather than take the other way out of his dilemma, the fulfillment of the social-economic program which he wrote in 1919, must play the game of war.

The prediction of Mussolini's course was made twenty-three centuries before John Strachey. Aristotle, founder of political science, wrote: "The tyrant who, in order to hold his power, suppresses every superiority, does away with good men, forbids education and light, controls every movement of the citizens, and, keeping them under a perpetual servitude, wants them to grow accustomed to baseness and cowardice, has his spies everywhere to listen to what is said in the meetings, and spreads dissension and calumny among the citizens and impoverishes them, is obliged to make war in order to keep his subjects occupied and impose on them permanent need of a chief."

The word "chief" in Italian is "duce."

Many years ago Mussolini wrote that "the proletariat should train for that great historic conflict when it will be able to settle accounts with its adversaries; for the Italian proletariat needs a bath of blood for its force to be renewed." From 1922 on frequently he claimed that Fascism was a real revolution, a bloody revolution, that the blood bath was the sine qua non of a great revolutionary change. Today the paralysis which has invaded Fascism, its finances, economics, culture, and spirit also demand a blood bath, and to forestall it in civil war and at the same time satisfy imperialism, which historically has advanced from one blood bath to another, Italy must take the road to a foreign war. Although black, the Fascist shirts have become very dirty, and must be washed in blood.

CHAPTER XXX

Ave Caesar!

WHATEVER THE FINAL OUTCOME MAY BE FOR ITALY, FOR Mussolini the one thing he confesses has worried him most has now been won: he has made his mark in history.

There is, of course, nothing strange nor abnormal in the concern which a leader of men feels about posterity; it is merely part of the problem of immortality which has confused and inspired mankind from its first intelligent beginnings. "I am obsessed with this wild desire—it consumes my whole being," said Mussolini to his Egeria; "I want to make a mark on my era with my Will, like a lion with its claw." It has been made. The dictator may fall gloriously on an African battlefield or pass away peacefully in bed half a century from now, but Clio has already provided ample pages for the Duce's record.

For almost a quarter of a century he has wooed this muse, acting the Hero, posing before men and moviemen, and time and history, eagerly watching for the signs of his immortality. Even in his youthful soap-box speeches he was already conscious of what press and public would say, and as he grew to manhood he worked on his clipping-books with more enthusiasm than a Hollywood star, but always he kept looking ahead, to a place in the future where his name would shine on deathless bronze, when statues would be erected of his likeness side by side with the Napoleons, and better still, the Roman Caesars, and the gods and demi-gods of all recorded time.

At the Lausanne conference a group of diplomats on an upper floor, looking down an elevator shaft, beheld their newest colleague with his back to the operator, making faces and gestures before the rear mirror. The Napoleonic attitudes were unmistakable.

In the history of the world no man has been more photographed.

The paintings, sketches, and busts of the Duce surpass in number those of any being to whom deity has not been seriously attributed. A great part of the leader's day is spent reading the press of the whole world, where every item dealing with him and his activities has been marked by subordinates. He reads them with the air of a man seeking something.

Although he never tires of fatalistic remarks about his destiny in the stars, he has retained the peasant superstitions of his childhood. Twenty centuries earlier analogous rulers, dictators, leaders, tyrants, conquerors, strong kings and frightened kings, were sending to the Delphic oracle or looking at blood and entrails, watching the flights of birds and reading signs in thunder and lightning. Mussolini seeks sybilline warnings in the newspapers and the history-books of other revolutions. With the same eagerness with which Lenin, Trotsky, and Stalin watched the Bolshevik revolution take the course of the traditional French Revolution, each acting in his own way to defeat the Brumaires and Thermidores and circumvent the Little Corporals, so Mussolini, warned that history takes an inexorable course, strives to impress his superior will upon it.

Curious, but not surprising to psychologists, is this mingling of the belief in free will, predestination, fatalism, and the commonest Forli superstitions. The village "witch," old Giovanna, taught Mussolini her "magic lore"; he became "an adept in interpreting dreams and omens and telling fortune by cards."[1] He is quoted often saying, "My blood tells me" and "I must listen to my blood," and he once declared proudly, *"Que voulez-vous? Je ressemble aux animaux, je renifle le temps qui vient, je suis mon instinct, et je ne me trompe jamais"* ("What would you? I resemble the animals, I scent the times, I follow my instinct, and I never make a mistake").

The Duce and the age of dictators have already been explained by the scientists. Freud has expressed his belief that nations, like human beings, can suffer a neurosis; Adler believes that people like individuals suffer from inferiority, struggle hard to shake it off and to become superior, and in the case of Italy and Mussolini the world has its best example. More recently Stekel has presented his authority complex to explain the weakness of the masses and the power of

[1] Sarfatti.

the Mussolinis, the "father-substitutes." The millions of inferiorities of the people mass together to become a superiority; the people identify themselves with the leader, partaking of his authority, and the leaders are usually neurotic, suffering from a "compulsion complex." "Dictators in general," continues my colleague, John Gunther, in expounding the Stekel theory, "are a sort of regression to childhood. Love of a leader is a reversion to infantilism." Stekel concludes that "For many generations men fought for democracy, liberty, the right of free assembly and free speech. Thousands of good men have died for these causes. But now one country after another gives up its free institutions, people even vote away their freedom. New dictatorial revolutions . . . are welcomed with relief, not opposed by force. There is a world scramble for authority, for the security of leadership. People everywhere, because their parental sense of authority has disappeared, are looking for a father-substitute, for a strong and beloved parental hand."

Germany in 1933 and Italy in 1922 are the most excellent proofs of the contentions of all three psychologists. Although Italy was known as one of the victor nations in 1918, it was greatly humbled in the peace treaty of 1919 which divided the war spoils among the stronger powers and left little more than a dispute over Fiume in the lap of their colleague. The Italian people, who had for a while come through the shroud of inferiority when Garibaldi and his Red Shirts appeared, were therefore in the psychologically ripe stage to accept the man of promises, the man of violence, the demagogue who defied the oppressors, gratified the national yearning for superiority, and wore a black shirt.

One of the seeming paradoxes of the Italian situation which Italy has not yet discovered, although it could do so easily by reading the officially printed works of the Duce, is that the embodiment of their wish-fulfillment neither loves nor respects the masses who follow him. Time and again Mussolini has quoted Machiavelli's opinion of the common people as "mud" and sneered at public opinion. But the more the Duce shows that he despises his followers, the more they shout their love and loyalty. Unlike the bourgeois gentleman, Lenin, who really loved the world-filling proletariat, the oligarch of Italy, in origin plebeian, almost hates them. "I do not adore this new divinity—the masses," writes the Duce, thereby confirming Stalin's view that even revolutionary leaders at times despise their following and that "an aristocratic attitude of the leaders towards the masses" frequently arises, an attitude which Lenin escaped because his faith in the nobility of the workingman was never shaken.

The greatness of Mussolini can only be measured by the lowness of his worshipers.

He stalks through the world like the one man who wears the mantle of Zarathustra, possesses the mind of Machiavelli, is the inheritor of the power of Caesar, while all the little minds, all the hundreds of millions of unimportant, unthinking, weak, and ineffectual human beings (whom Sinclair Lewis has both immortalized and crucified with a new word) grovel at his feet, proclaiming him the conqueror. Emperor or Galilean? The same hundreds of millions go to their churches on Sundays and proclaim an unarmed Man who was weak and humble, who preached humility and kindness and love and non-resistance. The other six days they arm for war and praise violence. The mob mind can worship both.

In all seriousness Mussolini has been compared by his idolators with everyone from Jesus Christ to Theodore Roosevelt.

After Farinacci's solemn declaration that Mussolini's only logical successor as Duce could be Jesus, the official Fascist press proclaimed the infallibility of its leader, a political dogma meant also for the eyes of the Pope.

No less a person than an American ambassador[2] wrote that "the Duce is now the greatest figure of his sphere and time. One closes the door when one leaves feeling, as when Roosevelt was left, that one could squeeze something of him out of one's clothes."

Inasmuch as the Duce himself permits painters to draw a lock of hair over the forehead in the Napoleonic manner, busts made very Caesarian, and a large proportion of the millions of photographs show him à la Bonaparte on horseback or assuming other heroic poses, it is obvious he invites comparison with the world-conquerors.

Mussolini would like to uphold the tradition of the "strong, silent man," but his passion for oratory prevents him from complete achievement. But that he should assume, consciously or unconsciously, the

[2] The late Richard Washburn Child.

traditions of the world-conquerors, Caesar, Alexander, and Napoleon, is quite natural. All men arriving at similar heights, even the catchpenny Central American dictators, have been known to succumb to the rôle; Mussolini steps into it as an actor into his make-up.

The Caesar pose was most obvious to those who in April, 1926, accompanied the Duce to Tripoli—to that very same colony the annexation of which caused the same Mussolini to attempt an armed uprising two decades earlier. Now he had mobilized more warships for himself than Giolitti had used for the war on Turkey; on the prow of the *Cavour* he strutted and took attitudes which every motion-picture operator worth his pay recorded deathlessly, or he sat with folded arms looking dreamily across the Mediterranean.

He disembarked, he stepped into Africa like a conqueror. The Tripolitans—at least those who were not at the time in rebellion— the native troops, the Italian army, the civilians and officialdom, made a grand uproar.

An American journalist, overcome with the sense of historic emotion, raised his hand and cried, "Ave Caesar!" To the Duce he said, "It is like the old days when a Roman emperor landed."

Mussolini, delighted, said, "Yes."

Others took up the cry. The sun-baked streets of a small African port in an unimportant African colony echoed with the shout of "Caesar," and that very evening numerous red, white, and green posters with the words "Ave Caesar," followed by Mussolini's speech, published by the Fascist officials, were placarded throughout the colony as the expression of its greeting.

Julius, the divider of Gaul, shines over Mussolini; the Duce looks into those cold pupil-less eyes every day while his press reminds him that he is the pure Roman emperor type in face and will, the true successor to the thrice-crown-refusing political ancestor. Even the textbooks of Italy have been changed so that today all the Caesars are unblemished heroes and the tyranny, corruption, and weaknesses of that ruler "who fell an easy victim to the cheap devices of the lewd Cleopatra" have been eliminated by the censor. To make their own hero greater, the idol of comparison has been cleaned and polished.

In the year of the Tripoli voyage Mussolini ordered that "within

five years Rome must be restored to the grandeur of the Caesars";
and within a few months he told an interviewer that "we are in the
process of renewing the glory of the Caesars. I have a bust of
Julius Caesar always before me." And, although neither glory nor
grandeur was completely renewed by 1931, in September of the next
year Mussolini ordered the prefect of his native district to change
the name of the Fiumicino River to "Rubicon." "Foreign visitors
ask me where the Rubicon is, and we cannot show them," explained
Caesar's successor; "Let us find our river." But he had already
ordered the event. Thus it was shown to the world that a problem
which harried historians and geographers had disputed violently
from mediæval times could be settled only through an act of dictatorship.

A year later, at ancient Arminium, where Julius Caesar supposedly
harangued the legions for *his*—or, as it is now called, the *first*—
march on Rome, a statue donated by the successor was unveiled to
"the great patron of Fascism, the first Black Shirt," whose "mighty
conception which he gave to Rome and the world exists again in the
blood of the race," and in Mussolini "the heir to the legacy which
he bequeathed to Italy."

So the orators. To the podestá of Rimini Mussolini telegraphed:
"The statue of Julius Caesar which I have decided to give to your
city is similar to the statue in bronze which adorns the Route of
Empire [Via dell'Impero, in Rome]. If possible, you will place high
on the column the words which Julius Caesar spoke to the militia
men of the Thirteenth Legion when, the die having been cast and
the Rubicon having been crossed, he decided upon his march on
Rome. Every year, on the ides of March, you will take care to be-
flower the statue of the founder of the Roman Empire."

Four times in his talks with Ludwig the Duce mentioned the man
whose bust broods over him: once he confessed that "Jesus was
greater"; another time that Shakespeare's play about the hero was "a
great school for rulers"; again, "in thrilling tones," "Julius Caesar.
The greatest man that ever lived. . . . Yes, I have a tremendous
admiration for Caesar. Still . . . I myself belong rather to the class
of the Bismarcks," and finally, "The assassination of Caesar was a
misfortune for mankind. I love Caesar. He was unique in that he

combined the will of the warrior with the genius of the sage. At bottom he was a philosopher who saw everything *sub specie æternitatis*. It is true he had a passion for fame, but his ambition did not cut him off from humankind."

Finally, in the summer of 1935, addressing several thousand former grenadiers, at the time of the mobilization for the Italo-Ethiopian conflict, he reminded them that "Julius Caesar once dominated the world and that every stone surrounding them should recall the fact." (They were crowded into the ruins of the Temple of Venus.) "Nothing forbids us from believing that what was our destiny yesterday may again become our destiny tomorrow."

From Alexander the Great, who sighed for new lands to conquer, and from the time of every prophet and messiah, men have wanted to rule the whole world or to make the whole world bow to their one idea. The men of power and egotism want to be king of kings and many modern rulers use that title. The Ethiopian is not bashful. Caesar, Kaiser, and Tsar are variations on the theme. The idea of world conquest will probably remain forever, even if it is to be eventually democratized into a sort of figurehead, a man of straw and sawdust, a super-secretary of a future super League of Nations, and appear to this individual only in his serenest daydream of desire.

The last man to seize a large part of the world, Napoleon, called by Wells, an adventurer, a wrecker, a man of egotism and vanity, a personality archaic, hard, capable, unscrupulous, imitative, and neatly vulgar, is still the hero of the mob. Mussolini has at least this much in common with the Corsican: they were both well-whipped children, therefore destined to a rebellious manhood. Bonaparte was whipped by his mother, Mussolini by his father; the one used a birch rod, the other a leather belt.

The mediocrity of the two minds is amazing. The Code Napoleon, which he claimed was a greater monument than his forty victories, was written by other men. The plan of the Corporate State is not Mussolini's. The "totally uncreative imagination" of Napoleon was influenced by Plutarch towards a revival of the Roman Empire; Mussolini in all his words and deeds has shown the influence of the latest book he has been reading, the last strong-minded politician who has been advising him.

Napoleon was not above issuing contradictory and lying statements, as, for example, proclaiming to Italy that he was coming to free it from tyranny while he told his soldiers to loot the country and wrote to Paris he was going to make the newly conquered State pay an indemnity of twenty millions.

When Napoleon faced the Council of Five Hundred he was as frightened as Mussolini the day he stammered about Matteotti and promised to "return to legality." Yet both men prided themselves on physical courage.

The Napoleonic plan by which the First Consul had under him an *appointed* Council of State, which had under it a legislative body and Tribunate, a Senate, etc., is very much the Mussolinian idea of a "hierarchy ending in a pinhead."

When Napoleon became First Consul the whole world was at his feet, there was peace, and any ruler with a first-rate mind would have done something creative to astound the centuries. (When Mussolini took office, he had the support of all parties, there was peace, and a man whose mind was not warped by egotism and lust for personal power could have given Europe a lead in governing well.) Napoleon, says Wells, could do no more than "strut upon the crest of this great mountain of opportunity like a cockerel on a dunghill. The figure he makes in history is one of almost incredible self-conceit, of vanity, greed, and a grandiose aping of Caesar, Alexander, and Charlemagne which would be purely comic if it were not caked over with human blood." If Bonaparte's aping of Caesar was so ludicrous and so tragic, what can one say of Mussolini's aping of Bonaparte? Perhaps that while he had not a thousandth of Napoleon's success, he has shed but comparatively few drops of human blood.

Both men denounced religion as "opium for the people," Mussolini, actually quoting Marx's phrase, Napoleon in making the famous Concordat saying it was necessary to give the people religion to keep them quiet: "how can you have order in a State without religion?"

Whether either dictator ever felt remorse is debated by historians and chroniclers. It is said that Napoleon, during his fits in St. Helena, regretted his order to murder the Duc d'Enghien and sometimes wept for the dead. Only one person records a sign of regret in Mussolini. "The dead weigh heavily," he once said. On the occasion of the banquet which Italy tendered Ras Taffari, king of Ethiopia, the King and Mussolini found two beautiful envelopes in their napkins. Mussolini opened his and read:

"You are Matteotti's murderer; prepare for the handcuffs."

The King opened his and read:

"Majesty, Matteotti's murderer sits next to you. Give him up to justice."

The King turned pale, but it is reported that Mussolini hid whatever emotions this dramatic reminder provoked under a small laugh.

It is also said that Mussolini sometimes has fits of terror and plans to escape from Italy in an airplane or a yacht. But there is no actual evidence that the conqueror regrets anything.

Napoleon betrayed the French Revolution. Future historians may well say that Mussolini betrayed, or at least delayed, the Italian revolution.

Much more appropriate is a comparison between the Duce and Louis Napoleon, who, like his uncle, also betrayed his republic. For the *décret-loi* of Louis there are the royal decrees which Mussolini forces the King to sign and issues at leisure; there is the same perversion of justice, the liberal magistrates suffering the same fate as the French republicans, expulsion; university professors in the Third Napoleon's time were made to obey the political wind, too, and the press was censored and corrupted. Louis placed government largely in the hands of the omnipotent prefects, and Mussolini appoints sub-dictators called podestas. Hierarchy is similarly established. The pageants, exhibitions, and sports in France preceding Sedan are duplicated in Rome.

Louis Napoleon was vain, empty, trivial. His writings show small culture. He was, like Mussolini, mixed up in liberalism, socialism, and Napoleonism and likewise preached nationalist superpatriotism.

The similarity between the Italian Dux and the last German Rex especially in egotistic oratory, has already been noted.

Of the men who make history today, especially of dictators, one expects great, rich personalities. But Stalin is known for his metallic colorless voice, the absence of flourish, for the tendency to remain inconspicuous, and his inability to sweep an audience with enthusiasm.[3] Like Lenin, he has "a sense of compressed energy, of reserved will power. He is not magnetic." Lenin and Trotsky I saw at the height of their fame; both surprised me because they had nothing of the Communist-Socialist-Radical speaker so well known throughout the world. Lenin reasoned as Socrates once reasoned in the house of Cephalus. The only dictator who answers conventional anticipations is Mussolini, who is magnetic and dynamic, wild, histrionic, who raises and lowers his voice as taught by the best professors of drama, becomes cold, waxes hot, erupts like his own Vesuvius and uses his hands, eyes, shoulders, and breath for the purpose of hypnotizing the mob.

Lenin was the only revolutionary who had a deep sense of humor; his successor, Stalin, makes jokes and laughs over them; frequently they are coarse jokes, and in this Stalin and Mussolini are similar, except that at times Stalin has been able to show a trace of objective humor, while Mussolini has never betrayed it. Intolerance is one of the secrets of Mussolini's success.

In almost every sentence of his speeches, in almost every page of his writings, Mussolini curses his opponents. He is always shouting "scoundrel," "traitor," "egotist" at some one; his enemies are "soft-brained cowards," "swelled frogs," and "a base and pernicious crew"; he never hesitates to call the man who differs from his opinions a liar; with the utmost contempt he speaks of political enemies and those who have fought duels with him as weaklings, cowards; referring to foreign statesmen and journalists who have said he threatens the peace of the world he replies these are the "accusations of fools"; when he can find nothing evil to say of those whom the world honors he calls them "egocentric," he speaks of their "unbridled egotism"; he is always attacking those who "sell themselves for money, for power," whom he despises—and frequently the word "turncoat" comes up and the six four-letter words in Joyce's *"Ulysses."*[4]

The words of attack most frequently heard are "traitor" and "physical coward" and "egotist"; with them he disposes of all who

[3] Isaac Don Levine, *Stalin.*
[4] All these beautiful phrases are culled from Mussolini's autobiography.

have met him on the field of honor or who write works on philosophy which fail to include the newest and greatest of all theories, Fascism; everyone who has ideas not in conformity is an egotist and anyone who acts non-conformingly is a traitor, while those who oppose him are cowards.

Need one go to a psychologist for the explanation of such behavior, or is ordinary intelligence sufficient guide? Proust speaks of "that habit of denouncing in other people defects precisely analogous to one's own." "For," he says, "it is always of those defects that people speak, as though it were a way of speaking about oneself, indirectly, which added to the pleasure of absolution that of confession. Besides, it seems that our attention, always attracted by what is characteristic of ourself, notices that more than anything else in other people . . . an unwashed man speaks only of the baths that other people do not take . . . a cuckold sees cuckolds everywhere, a light woman light women, a snob snobs." There can be no better explanation.

Again, when Mussolini declares: "I have annihilated in myself all self-interest; I, like the most devoted of citizens, place upon myself and on every beat of my heart, service for the Italian people. I proclaim myself their servant. I feel that all Italians understand and love me; I know that only he is loved who leads without weakness, without deviation, and with disinterestedness and full faith," a student of his character can find it the great self-confession of what he lacks most.

One thing he has is a blazing hatred. "Not," as one of his compatriots says, "the hatred of a social rebel which is but another facet of love, like the hatred of Brutus for Caesar, of Bruno for the Papacy, of Mazzini for the tyrants," or the hatred which inspired Milton and Byron and Shelley sublimely and which has made heroes and martyrs. Mussolini's dominating hatred, which was important to his success, was the drop of poison on the swift arrow of his Will.

Of this man's amazing egotism much has been said. It is the most natural trait in human beings who are failures to shout down the successful man, no matter who he is or what he does. Napoleon and Pericles are equally condemned. No distinction is made between the ego which drives a man to lead the world by developing all that is great and powerful within him, and the ego which leads another man to rise high by destroying others. Mussolini's ego is a compound. Sometimes it exhibits itself in all its naïve crudity.

Three days after he had seized the government his old friend, Paolo Orano, a comrade who could call him by his first name, came into Benito's office, saying, jestingly, "I want to see how you are preparing to rule Italy."

"Preparing? I?" replied Mussolini, as Orano afterwards recounted. "Why, I'm already in the middle of it. I am ruling. I'll show you how I rule."

Mussolini pressed a button, summoned a secretary, asked that a telephone call be put through to one of the leaders of the march and of Fascism.

"Hello. I am talking. Mussolini. Be—ni—to Mus—so—li—ni. Listen. You are expecting to receive the field-marshal's bâton. Fine. But you are not going to get it just yet. You—are—not—going—to get—it—just—yet. Get yourself a small cane. Good-bye."

"There," he said to Orano. "I'm not here as a tourist, but to give Italy a government and to govern it. That never was before, but is now: a government. I am it. And all, mind you, all Italians shall and will obey. Italians have never obeyed. The Italians must be ruled and shall be ruled."

Mussolini threw his head high, as if to snap it from his neck and shoulders—a movement that Orano saw for the first time in this man, but which was to be immortalized later in a million photographs and many films.

When *Piemonte*, a newspaper of Turin, printed a questionnaire regarding Mussolini's greatness in history, the dictator telegraphed to the prefect of police: "Call the editor of *Piemonte* and ask him to stop the referendum. Tell him that Mussolini himself does not know exactly what he is and therefore it is difficult for others to judge him. The referendum can be resumed fifty years hence."

At another time he declared that "I am convinced that I am destined to rule Italy some ten to fifteen years more. My successor is not yet born."

The egotism of the ruler is transmitted to the youth of Italy. The Fascist publication for the universities thus informs the coming generation: "The Italian of tomorrow, and that means the Balilla and the Avanguardisti of today, will be the natural heir of the Fascist mentality, and will not need to discuss these four points:

"1. That Italy deserves to be the biggest and strongest nation in the world.

"2. That Italy will become the biggest and strongest nation in the world.

"3. That the Italian laws are the finest in the world.

"4. That the men who now rule are the best and that we owe them honor and obedience."

Of the noble traits in Mussolini's character none stand out more than his emancipation from the degenerate desire for money, exceedingly rare in persons who are born poor and who, on acquiring riches, frequently remain miserly through the fear of ever being poor again. Mussolini insists six separate times in his autobiography that "money has no lure for me." "I ask nothing for myself, nor for mine; no material goods, no honors, no testimonials." "I have annihilated in myself all self-interest." "In politics I never gained a penny. I detest those who live like parasites, sucking away at the edges of social struggles. I hate men who grow rich in politics." "To me money is detestable; what it may do is sometimes beautiful and sometimes noble."

His enemies say that if all this is true, why did the Fascist official press, boasting of the new income-tax law, congratulate the Duce on paying his the first day—the sum of 200,000 lire, which would indicate an income of 500,000 lire and a capital of 10,000,000. And why, ask enemies, does Mussolini insist so much on his contempt for the lure of money, why does he mention it at least six times in his autobiography?

The truth is that Mussolini does not care for money—for himself. But he does not hesitate to use it as a means to power. The 1914 episode of the French funds for founding a newspaper, and the 1919 episode of the "diversion" of Fiume funds, and the 1920 episode of subventions from the employers, while exposing the ruthlessness of the man, are not, even in the charges of enemies, instances of personal greed. Money means power; more so in Europe than in America. In Europe a man is born in a class, and imprisoned in that class as in a fortress. The peasant begets peasants, the proletarian proletarians, and rare is the case of the youth who breaks the caste lines. The workman's son does not go to college and graduate into the professions, and the rich man's daughter never marries the foreman—a fact that causes a wrong laugh over many an American movie. Brains and talent and even genius are wasted in continental Europe because of class distinction and lack of money. And Socialism flourishes for the same reasons. Mussolini, hating money philosophically, has never hesitated to get it and use it to break himself out of his class prison.

Strangely enough, there is a mental parallel. He suffers from claustrophobia. All his life he has felt himself tied down, hemmed in, suppressed by invisible forces. He hated the confines of the schoolroom. He fled. One of the reasons he escaped military service was the dreadful appearance of the prison-like military barracks of his province, and although he tried to forget the iron bars of frequent visits by reading philosophy and politics, prison cells have left their lines on his character.

He cannot stand locked rooms. In the Chigi Palace every interviewer has remarked the enormous chamber some fifty or sixty feet long, which served him as an office. His spirit requires vast spaces. He loves to fly in an airplane, enjoying the power, the superiority, and the freedom of an unpeopled infinity. He has refused to enter the Blue Grotto of Capri.

In exhibitionism he surpasses all the notable men of our age. Chicherin, the timid intellectual, once appeared in a uniform of the Red Army and did not cut a brave figure. The Kaiser was magnificent in shining breastplates, but Mussolini goes in for Central American splendor. The first time he addressed the Chamber he rigged himself in an operatic gold and spangles which gave the foreign ambassadors their first good laugh under Fascism. Short, stocky, bulgy, myopic, and fairly bald, he poses so well the world believes him heroically tall, with the most magnificent flashing eyes.

His literary judgments are sententious and weak. He is the author of such philosophical gems as "smoking is a distraction" and "the Will to Power is a cardinal point in the philosophy of Nietzsche" and "The hills and the sea give one the feeling of infinity." He has a college freshman's enthusiasm for Nietzsche's "blond beasts" and "the egotism which in men of power does not admit of restrictions"; he is impressed with Nietzsche's quotation from the Arabian sect of Assassins "To see men suffer is good, to make them suffer is better."

Few of Mussolini's admirers have anything to say about his twenty-year record of changing parties and ideals. Sarfatti, for instance, describes her hero as "impulsive and meditative, a realist and an idealist perfervid yet wise, a romantic in his aspirations, but a classic in his handling of public affairs, Mussolini has a groundwork of consistency in him underlying all these seeming incompatibilities." But a more worldly, less fascinated person, Mussolini's Cheka agent, Rossi, goes deeper into his employer's character. "How," asks Rossi, "can certain noble sentiments which Signor Mussolini expresses in his speeches, be reconciled with facts which put such grave moral, political, and penal responsibility upon his shoulders?

"His temperament, unstable by nature, as I am certainly not the only one to know full well, has, together with his mania for Machiavellianism, led him in the last few years into numberless acts of duplicity and changeableness.

"By turns he is cynical and sentimental, impulsive and cautious, irritable and calm, generous and cruel, quick to decide and slow to move, uncompromising and conciliatory.

"All the qualities of heart and mind have in him contradictory aspects, but in his activities as head of the government and of the Fascist Party, the tendencies which predominate are duplicity, superficiality, and improvization."

An explanation of the seeming incompatibilities in Mussolini's character is offered by Adolf Saager: "This is the deeper reason for Mussolini's betrayals: His Unconscious always decides in favor of his hunger for power and his ruler instinct serves the political reaction in the nation; against which his Conscious is always still striving to some union with the Radicals. From that moment when his Unconscious (which is the unfalsified natural power of the man), becomes dominant, his actions gain certainty and continuity, such as would delight an æsthetic observer in the actions of a preying animal.

"This explains Mussolini's periods of trembling and anxiety, because his Conscious and Unconscious are at war.

"Nothing is more ignorant than to understand Mussolini's coat-turnings and contradictions, his 'hypocrisy' and his 'betrayals' as signs of character weakness; these things compose his very character, they are his destiny. This is his organic development."

There remains the question of greatness.

He is, for instance, a great journalist but a tenth-rate littérateur. His eloquence is marvelous—emotionally, not logically. He is a great politician, a great leader of the mob, but he is a demagogue and not a statesman.

He is a genius at assimilating the ideas of other persons and making them his own.

He is totally unscrupulous.

He has never done anything original.

He has a tremendous will but an inferior mind.

If achievement is to be measured by such qualifications as strong, well-conceived ambition; difficult struggle to reach the goal; complete accomplishment of ambition; and importance, human value of the success gained by the man, Mussolini easily passes the first three tests. His ambition has been superhuman, his struggle one of the most noteworthy in our time, and he has accomplished everything his heart desired. But whether there is any great significance to his work, or any human value whatever, cannot so soon be judged.

Mussolini may found an African empire. He may in a small way emulate Julius Caesar. Or he himself may be destroyed by the monstrous State he has created, but he no longer need worry about his place in history. He has made his lion's mark. Even Mr. Wells, who somehow prefers Jesus and Buddha and King Asoka to the Caesars and Napoleons and Wilhelm Seconds, will some day have to give more space to the Fascist phenomenon.

History will say that Mussolini shows the triumph of the superiority complex, the triumph of Nietzschean catch-phrases, the triumph of the adapter of other people's ideas, the triumph of the book-made egotist.

Reactionary dictators are men of no element of greatness, men with no philosophy, no burning humanitarian ideal, nor even an economic program of any value to their nation or to the world. Grand and imposing as they look in their flaming uniforms and shirts in nationalist colors on marching days, they are almost forgotten the hour a change is made. Who now remembers Waldemiras? What country did he rule? What became of Pangalos? How many Bratianus were there and what happened to them? And how ignoble became that same Primo de Rivera who one day before had stood arm in arm with Mussolini, his treaty-friend, his proud disciple? But it is not too fantastic to imagine a time after Mussolini's disappearance, when the commentators will say that after all he was only a renegade Socialist who could never be trusted, a puny, sententious imitator of Lenin, a rather foolish repeater of Kaiser Wilhelm's foolish phrases, a man mentally[5] and physically ill, a megalomaniac who thought he could change the course of economic forces by the use of magnificent phrases taken from Karl Marx, Nietzsche, Hegel, Vilfredo Pareto, and his former colleagues in the Socialist movement—and nevertheless a person worthy of statues. After all, he is the original Duce of Fascismo, and all the others are merely imitators.

All of Mussolini's monuments will be monuments to the strength of a weakling, monuments to the weakness of his opposition, to the cowardice of the masses, but, above all, monuments to an Ego and a Will.

Mussolini has made his mark in history, but history records the marks of warriors, suppressors, and vandals as well as saviors and liberators.

History and monuments will recall Benito Mussolini as a Caesar— not a Julius but perhaps a Caesar Borgia or perhaps a Kaiser Wilhelm. If not a Napoleon Bonaparte, then at least a Louis Napoleon.

Everywhere new statues appear of Benito Mussolini today and more will be erected in his lifetime. The statues of Julius Caesar will probably remain forever in Eternal Rome—but the day will surely come when in all the noble cities of Italy there will arise the statue of Giacomo Matteotti. A free people will then decide if there will be room also for those of our Sawdust Caesar.

[5] In September 1935 the respectable *New Statesman and Nation* of London in an editorial suggested "official recognition of what is already common gossip in political circles in Rome—namely, that Il Duce's notorious paranoia is nearing the pitch of certifiable insanity."

APPENDICES

APPENDIX 1

The First and Second Fascist Programs
Original Fascist Program (March 1919)

Fasci italiani di Combattimento
Comitato Centrale
Milano, Via Paolo da Cannobio

Italians!

This is the national program of a movement sanely and integrally Italian: revolutionary because it is antidogmatic and antidemagogic; strongly innovating because it has passed through all prejudicial objections. . . .

For the political problem:

a) Universal suffrage
b) Lowering of electoral age to 18
c) Abolition of the Senate
d) Convocation of a national assembly which is to function three years, to which will be confided the power of establishing the new constitutional régime of the state
e) Formation of technical councils for industry, labor, communications, social hygiene. . . . , elected by Corporations of professions or trades. . . .

For the social problem:

a) The eight hour day legal and compulsory
b) Minimum wage law
c) Participation of the workingmen in the management of industry
d) Proletarian organizations to manage public industries and public services
e) Realization of the rights of the railroad workers
f) Reform of the law of social insurance

For the military problem:

a) Creation of a national militia for defensive purposes
b) Nationalization of war works
c) External policy to valorize the Italian nation in the work of peace.

For the financial problem:

a) Heavy extraordinary tax on capital, progressive, for the purpose of causing a partial expropriation of all wealth.

b) Seizure of all property of the religious associations and suppression of the religious taxes [menses episcopales].

c) Revision of all contracts for war supplies and the seizure of up to 85% of the war profits.

OFFICIAL FASCIST PROGRAM PUBLISHED OCTOBER 1919

(1) National Assembly, intended as Italian Section of the International Assembly of all Peoples, in order to proceed with the radical transformation of the political and economic basis of society.

(2) Proclamation of the Republic. Decentralization of the executive power. Administrative autonomy of regions and communes through their own legislative bodies. Popular sovereignty exercised by means of universal, equal, and direct popular vote of all citizens of both sexes, with right to the people of initiative, of referendum, and of veto. Reorganization, ex-novo, of the administrative bodies of the State. The function of the State to be limited to the civic and political direction of national life.

(3) Abolition of the Senate and of every artificial and arbitrary limitation of popular sovereignty. Abolition of political police. Establishment of a municipal and national civic guard. Elective magistrates independent of the executive power.

(4) Abolition of all caste-titles, of princes, dukes, marquis, "commendatori," "cavalieri," etc. Only titles of honor, those of talent and of honesty in work.

(5) Abolition of compulsory conscription. General disarmament and veto to all nations forbidding the manufacture of armaments.

(6) Freedom of thought and of conscience, of religion, of association, of press, of propaganda, of individual and collective agitation.

(7) System of education with both cultural and vocational schools open to all.

(8) Maximum care and perfection of the social hygiene system.

(9) Abolition of stock-companies. Suppression of every kind of speculation of Banks and of the Stock Exchange. Creation of a national financial institution with regional sections for the distribution of credit.

(10) Census and reduction of personal wealth. Confiscation of unproductive revenues. Payment of the debt of the old State by the wealthy classes. Suppression of church revenues.

(11) Eight hours' work on a legal basis.

(12) Reorganization of production based on insurance principles and on direct participation of profits by the workers. All landed estates to be given over to the peasants. The management of transportation industries and of public services to be entrusted to syndicates comprised of technical experts and workmen.

(13) Abolition of secret diplomacy.

(14) Open international policy dedicated by the solidarity and independence of peoples in the confederation of states.

APPENDIX 2

Dieu n'existe pas[1]

BY BENITO MUSSOLINI

When we claim that "God does not exist," we mean to deny by this declaration the personal God of theology, the God worshiped in various ways and divers modes by believers the world over, that God who from nothing created the universe, from chaos matter, that God of absurd attributes who is an affront to human reason.

With each new discovery of chemistry, physics, biology, the anthropological sciences, of the practical application of sound prin-

---

[1] "God Does Not Exist," from "L'Homme et la Divinité" par Mussolini, Benito; Bibliothèque Internationale de propagande rationaliste; Chêne-Bourg, Genève; Juillet, 1904. This is Mussolini's first published work; the translation, such as it is, is my own.

ciples, dogma collapses. It is a part of that old edifice of religion which crumbles and falls in ruins. The continuous progress of the natural sciences now extending from city to country, disperses the darkness of the Middle Ages, and the multitudes desert the churches where from generation to generation they betook themselves to pray to God—that monstrous product of human ignorance.

Let us examine the nature of God. We force ourselves, therefore, to reason in a vacuum, the God of religions being their own image of their mental vacuum, the proof of the complete absence of any activity in reasoning.

How can the idea of a creator be reconciled with the existence of dwarfed and atrophied organs, with anomalies and monstrosities, with the existence of pain, perpetual and universal, with the struggle and the inequalities among human beings?

Epicurus, the philosopher who lived in Rome in the time of the decadence of the Republic, posed the following questions:

"Either God wishes to do away with evil in this world and cannot succeed; or he can do away with it and does not wish to; or he cannot and does not wish to; or finally, he wishes to and can. If he wishes to but has not the power, he is not all-powerful. If he has the power to do away with evil and does not wish to, he is not infinitely good. If, as affirm the deists, he can and wants to, tell me, then, why does evil exist on earth, and why does not God make it impossible?"

That which affronts human reason most is the inconceivable fact of the creative power of a God who from nothingness created everything, from chaos the universe. . . .

One would have to be completely without knowledge of physiology, botany, and psychology to claim today the existence of a "soul" independent of the body; on the contrary, one which does not form one of the two distinct aspects of the unique human nature.

Dogma is absurd because it presupposes immobility and the absolute. Nothing in the world is absolute, everything is relative. Nothing is entirely changeless, but there is a continual transformation, a perpetual movement of forces.

Dogma presents to human reason an obstacle to progress because it imposes limitations to the painful but salutary impulses towards the search for truth, because it checks the free expansion of all intellectual energy.

Science is now in the process of destroying religious dogma. The dogma of the divine creation is recognized as absurd.

"Religion is the opium of the people."—KARL MARX.

It being demonstrated that religious dogma presents itself to the human spirit and to rational criticism as "the absolute consecration of the absurd," let us see why moral religion is "immoral."

The evangelists are ridiculous when, instead of studying the Bible as a document of a certain historic interest, they try to credit it with real life and bring to the masses the principles of Christ (who perhaps never existed) as the ethical principles of a morality everlastingly young, permanent, modern, in complete accord with the present age. The Bible and morals called Christian are two cadavers which the evangelists attempt to galvanize into life with, it must be agreed, small enough success.

It is, therefore, clear that religious morality is one of resignation and sacrifice, a morality which may be dear to the weak, to the degenerate, to slaves, but which results in the diminution of reason and human personality. It bends man toward the earth, making him a slave to divinity. It favors the conservation of those primitive sentiments which belong to that period of animal life long left behind, and transforms the "thinking being" into a "passive sheep" who lives in the fear of the universal judgment.

Religious morality shows the original stigmata of authoritarianism precisely because it pretends to be the revelation of divine authority. In order to translate this authoritarianism into action and impose it upon humanity, the priestly caste of revealers has sprung up and with it the most atrocious intolerance.

Certain it is that religion is a psychic disease of the brain, a contraction, a tightening up of the individual who, if he is profoundly religious, appears to us as abnormal.

The history of many saints, beatified by the church, is repugnant. It shows nothing more than a profound aberration of the human spirit in search of ultra-terrestrial chimeras; it is a delirium which can attain the state of spasms of passion and which ends in madness.

Therefore, many of those who today hover over the altars of the

Catholic Church are pathological cases, hysterics, *déomanes* and demonomaniacs.

Even today in the more remote parts of Italy and Spain we can witness similar phenomena, Saint January for the people of Naples, and the Madonna of Lourdes for French bigotry. Are they not analogous aberrations?

If we read the history of religions, we find that it deals with the pathology of the human brain. If today the Middle Ages are retiring into the thick shadows of convents, it is due to triumphant skepticism; and if the epidemic disease of religion no longer appears with the terrible intensity of former times, it is due to the diminution of the political power of the Church which formerly placed on the heads of people its cap of lead.

Religion presents itself to our eyes in another characteristic: the atrophy of reason. The faculty by which man is differentiated from the lower animals is his reasoning power. But the devout believer renounces reason, refuses to explain the things which surround him, the innumerable natural phenomena, because his religious faith is enough for him. The brain loses the habit of thinking; and this religious sottishness hurls mankind back into animalism.

In concluding we say that "religious man" is an abnormality, and that "religion" is the certain cause of epidemic diseases of the mind which require the care of alienists.

Religion has shown itself in the open as the institution whose aim is political power by which to externalize the exploitation and the ignorance of the people.

APPENDIX 3

(Supplement to Chapter V)

MUSSOLINI'S FRENCH MONEY

Mussolini's money, or the betrayal of 1914, is an apt illustration of the fact that an ethical or moral problem depends on time as well as geography and circumstances. The heroic deed of one day becomes the treason of the next.

Even now the millions of persons who believe that every means was justifiable in winning the war for the Allies will be unable to see anything but nobility in Mussolini's accepting French funds for establishing a pro-Ally newspaper.

The most interesting fact about the matter is that Mussolini himself was proud of his actions in 1914. Accused of becoming an interventionist for money he wrote in his *Popolo d'Italia*:

"I am proud of the beauty, of the holiness of my sin and will kneel before no Jesus Christ to beg forgiveness."

In the great year of disillusion, 1919, when Mussolini was attempting to return to the Socialist movement, the press took up the matter of the French funds. On May 3, 1919, the *Italia del Popolo* wrote:

"Mussolini accepted checks from the French government; we have the proofs; we defy him to sue for libel."

In 1919, it must be remembered, Italy was still a free country and men had equality before the law. The Opposition was accusing Mussolini of the lowest crime a man is capable of, betraying his cause and fellow men for money, and the *Italia del Popolo* had made a national scandal out of the matter. It offered to place its documents before the courts. Mussolini did not sue. In fact he offered no answer.

In November, 1926, Deputy Renaudal said in the French Chamber: "Mussolini established his paper, the *Popolo d'Italia*, with French money." Asked for details, he published them in the *Quotidien* of November 9th, mentioning Marcel Cachin as the agent who carried the checks.

In the Chamber of Deputies, M. Paul Faure in 1928 stated that "Jules Guesde, then [1914] member of the cabinet, confided to us that we had a man down below, Mussolini, whom he had sent 100,000 francs to start a paper." Deputy Faure also enlarged upon his charge in the *Popolaire*, January 9, 1928, adding: "I do not know more precisely who was the material carrier of the money, but Cachin, if it pleases him, could inform his readers in *Humanité*."

Jules Guesde was an ultra-radical leader in France, sometimes called the founder of the French Socialist movement. In 1914, however, he joined the Premier, Viviani, in upholding the war. Viviani was an ex-Socialist. Cachin was then a Socialist, one of the many who believed in the war and joined in the Sacred Union, the *Union Sacré*, and opposed the Juarès-Rolland group who opposed war, Guesde chose Cachin, therefore, to visit Mussolini, since both were Socialists who had gone over to militarism.

Cachin, however, repented. In fact he went to the extreme Left and became the leader of the Communist movement in France. He has left his past behind; he does not want to be reminded ever of the *Union Sacré*, and for this reason he never mentions the Mussolini mission.

Before the suppression of the press numerous political writers in Italy explained the "conversion" of Mussolini and were never sued for libel, nor were their books or newspapers suppressed. Massimo Rocca, in *Quaderni del Nuovo Paese*, wrote:

"Mussolini . . . preached with great violence the absolute neutrality of Italy. . . . Mussolini went to see the Bolognese editor, Filippo Naldi, and promised him to change his views if he could get his own newspaper. This promise obtained, he wrote in *Avanti* an article on relative neutrality while awaiting intervention. . . . Once his object obtained, Mussolini . . . rushed to Geneva to collect the first funds for the *Popolo*. . . .

"If the Kaiser had offered him a double sum he would have defended neutrality. . . ."

Throughout Europe scores of post-bellum investigators mention the French funds which Mussolini used. Paul Ronin (French) says: "The editor-in-chief of the *Avanti* . . . at Geneva met Marcel Cachin . . . who gave him an important sum in the name of the French government to aid a favorable campaign of intervention and to create a daily newspaper for that purpose.

"Completely overjoyed, several weeks later, Marcel Cachin took into his confidence the Chamber [of Deputies] in terms vibrant with patriotism, pure and authentic.

"'Voyez,' he said, 'that which has happened in the Italian section. *Voilà* Mussolini, who in the *Popolo d'Italia*, today in its fortieth number, has had a lively success, declaring that revolution is an idea which has found bayonets. We register with joy the happy and concordant symptoms. Everything presages the inevitable intervention of Italy. She will help us finish the war, assuring victory against the militarist reactionaries, the Hapsburgs and the Hohenzollerns.'"

William Elwin (British) says: "Mussolini attempted to explain his support of Italian intervention on the side of the Allies as the direct outcome of his conscience as a Socialist. He was less ready to mention the sums of money received from the agents of the French government in order to launch and maintain the *Popolo d'Italia*. . . . The amount of money sums received by Mussolini, as always in official bribery, cannot be ascertained exactly, for those concerned will not speak; the fact remains, however, that he cashed 'patriotic checques' from the French government. Incidentally he admits to this in his autobiography. . . ."

L. Kemechey (Hungarian) asks where had Mussolini obtained the money for the *Popolo*, and answers: "From the French, wrote the Socialists on the first day. Others pretended to know that Lord Northcliffe, the powerful press king, had backed him up. There was not a day on which the Socialist press did not publish constantly fresh details of the bribing of Mussolini and particulars of his treason. He did not bother about them . . . it did not matter what they were shouting about; he was done with them. . . ."

De Ambris (Italian), ex-Prime Minister of Fiume: "Certain persons find that Mussolini is guilty because he took the money of the French government to found the *Popolo d'Italia*. But that is not the crime of Mussolini. If Mussolini had been an interventionist from the beginning . . . he could not be blamed. When a man sees his course traced out by his conscience, he may even accept money offered to aid him. The profound immorality consists in changing one's views for a personal advantage."

It is also extremely interesting to note the skill of the lady biographers. Says Mme. Bordeux: "It was insinuated in a few French papers of that time that Marcel Cachin and Charles Dumas had been the intermediaries charged to buy Mussolini for France—but an honest Frenchman considers it rather broadly calumniating the probity of Cochin [*sic*] who had the reputation for respecting even his adversaries. On the other hand Mussolini is not a man to sell himself; in fact, if there is one man in the world who is not for sale, that man is, was, and always will be Mussolini. . . .

"Admit, then, that France had offered Mussolini help. What would the next move be? She might have offered, and he might have accepted, in order to be able to see the triumph of right and justice. . . ."

And the untiring Sarfatti: "Strange rumors were set afloat. . . . The ex-editor of the *Avanti* was declared to have accepted money from France. . . . We knew him, of course, to be incapable of taking a sou for himself; but men afire with a great project and with the sense of an imperative call to fulfill it!—who could say but that in a moment of excitement he might feel justified in availing himself of any means to his hand for the purpose? It was decided to acquaint him with what was being said, for the slanders were calculated to damage seriously both Mussolini himself and the cause dear to us all. What was my surprise when I saw the two tiny rooms furnished with only four tumble-down chairs and a rickety table. . . ."

Signora Sarfatti then completes her complete refutation of the most important charge against Mussolini's probity by a long description of the poverty of the apartment in which the hero lived, and concludes by mentioning an advertising contract for 4,000 lire. "Such," she says, "was the 'capital' available! Quite enough, Mussolini felt."

The irrefutable evidence in l'affaire Mussolini is that compiled by Maître Torres, the Clarence Darrow of the French bar, and produced in open court in the trial of Bonomini for the murder of the Fascist Buonservizi. Part of it is given in the text. Maître Torres has published his findings several times, and although the present Italian government has intervened into French journalistic affairs scores of times, it was silent in the most important of all incidents disturbing international relations.

After 1919 the French government withdrew its subsidy of foreign newspapers and Mussolini had to shift for himself. The *Popolo* now existed on the advertising of the members of the League of Manufacturers, chambers of commerce, members and others who were financing the Fascist movement. It was a legal matter but nevertheless a form of subsidy equaling exactly the purchase of the good will of thousands of newspapers in America by the National Electric Light Association, of which the first ten volumes of the Federal Trade Commission investigation reports contain the evidence.

In addition to the joyful announcement in the official Fascist press that Mussolini paid 200,000 lire income tax, indicating that he had amassed a fortune of ten millions, there is the press account that he was able to give his daughter Edda a dowry of 5,000,000 lire when she married Count Galeazzo Ciano, head of the press and propaganda department of the Fascist government.

APPENDIX 4

MUSSOLINI AND THE "BOLSHEVIK ERA"

Writings and public speeches by the head of the Fascisti during the labor troubles, strikes, and uprisings of 1919 and 1920. Most of these quotations are from the *Popolo d'Italia* of June and July 1920:

(Editorial on the strike at Genoa): "We need a firing-squad to execute the sharks who are starving the people" (June 16).

(Uprising in Spezia): "The demonstration is violent but spontaneous, and, moreover, anticipated, against that ignoble race, those who speculate in the blood of a suffering people" (June 16).

(Uprising in Livorno): "The revolt is an absolute necessity to extinguish the voracity of those who starve us."

(Looting of the stores in Bergamo): "At Bergamo they have attacked the men [who raised the price of food] and we cannot do otherwise than approve that which has been done" (June 20).

(Riots at Imola and other towns in the Romagna, five dead): "In the Romagna the people have revolted against the venality of the speculators. . . . I recognize, without reticences, the fundamental legitimacy of the popular protest. It is proportionate to the actions of the speculators" (July 4).

Under Mussolini's guidance the central committee of the newly formed Fascist Party passed the resolution, July 5, 1919, proclaiming "our absolute solidarity with the people who have revolted against the speculators, and we applaud the seizures" (i.e., food riots, looting, etc., later called "Bolshevism").

Demonstration by the metal workers of Genoa and railroad men approved by *Popolo d'Italia*, January 8, 1919.

Strike of Post-office employees, approved by Mussolini January 15.
Strike of street-car men of Genoa, approved January 25.
Uprising of the rural workers of the province of Novara, approved in the *Popolo* of March 30th.
Strike of the railroad workers on branch lines. Signed editorial by Mussolini: "Convinced that the strikers are in the right, we promise them our disinterested support . . ." May 4, 1919.

The Seizure of the Factories

(1) "I fear no social change, provided that it appears necessary to me. That is why I accept, not only the control of the factories, but also their social-coöperative operation"—Mussolini, speech, "Politeama Rossetti," Trieste, September 20, 1920.

(2) "It is a veritable revolution which we are having in Italy; moreover, it is a phase of the revolution which we began in May, 1915"—*Popolo d'Italia*, September 28, 1920.

APPENDIX 5

Text of Pacification Treaty between Fascisti and Labor

For the realization of the return of normal conditions in the relations between the Italian parties and economic organizations, are met today, under the presidency of the honorable attorney Signor Enrico de Nicola, president of the Chamber of Deputies, the representatives of the national council of the Fasci di Combattimento, the Fascist parliamentary group and the General Federation of Labor.

To this congress were also invited the directorate of the Communist parliamentary group, the representatives of the Catholic parliamentary group and the Republican deputies.

The directorate of the Communist parliamentary group declared verbally to the president that the group in conformity with the declarations already published by the Italian Communist Party could not participate in the pourparlers.

The representative of the Catholic parliamentary group, the Honorables De Gasperi and Cingolani replied with thanks for the invitation and the wishes that the conference have a successful termination.

They stated however that doubting if the intervention of parties which do not find themselves in the same line of fighting as the Socialists and Fascists might prejudice in some way the efficacity of the accords to be arrived at, the group preferred to renounce its official adherence. However it engaged itself to collaborate for the realization of the goal so nobly pursued by the president in guarding scrupulously be it in the Chamber or in the country, its attitude of strict legality from which it has never wavered.

In the name of the Republican deputies the Honorables Chiesa, Mazzolani, Conti and Macrelli replied likewise they judged their intervention inopportune; the Republican party desired to remain neutral in the sad battle between factions.

1. First under consideration is the official communiqué of July 28 last to solve a prejudicial question, a proposal of the Fascist party, which desires the determination of relationship between the Socialist party and the Communist party.

2. The parties engage themselves to do all in their power to prevent all menaces, all reprisals, all punishments, all vengeances, all personal violence.

3. The emblems and ensigns of all parties will be respected.

4. The parties engage themselves reciprocally to respect the economic organizations.

5. All attitudes or all deeds which countervene said engagements are from now on disavowed and deplored by both representatives.

6. All violations of the regulations mentioned in this present act will be submitted to the judgment of a college of arbitration which will determine the responsibility.

7. For this purpose the organizations, political and economic will collaborate in each province for the formation of a college of arbitration composed of two Socialist members and two Fascist members and presided over by a third who will be named by the contending parties, failing which, by the president of the tribunal.

8. All accords signed in the provinces outside of the aforementioned agreement, shall be considered as of no value.

9. The organizations pledge themselves not to oppose by violence the reintegration of those who have been previously shorn of their powers by force.

10. The parties engage themselves reciprocally to restore all objects having a patrimonial value which have been carried away without any justice by the organizations and by private persons.

11. The undersigned representatives address a warm invitation to the press of both parties to align themselves with the accords concluded by them.

Of the preceding compromise, communication is given the public through the agency of the press in the hope that each citizen will understand at last all the gravity of the present hour and comprehend also the value and the force of the words of peace which have been pronounced.

> Rome. Cabinet of the President of the Chamber. August 3, 1921.
> For the parliamentary Fascist group:
> Benito Mussolini, Cesare Maria De Vecchi, Giovanni Giuriati.
> For the national council of the Fasci di Combattimento:
> Cesare Rossi, Umberto Pasella, Gaetano Polverelli, Nicola Sansanelli.
> For the directorate of the Socialist Party:
> Giovanni Bacci, Emilio Zannerini.
> For the Socialist Parliamentary group:
> Elia Musatti, Oddino Morgari.
> For the General Federation of Labor:
> Gino Baldesi, Alessandro Galli, Ernesto Caporali.
> Enrico De Nicola, President of the Chamber of Deputies.

APPENDIX 6

FASCISM: "REACTIONARY," "ANTI-LIBERAL"
BY BENITO MUSSOLINI

(The famous pronunciamento against liberty by the Duce in the March, 1923, issue of his magazine, *Hierarchy*)

FORCE AND CONSENT

Certain Italian Liberalism, which holds itself to be the one and only depository of true and immortal principles, is uncommonly like that moribund socialism, because it, too, as the latter, thinks it has "scientifically," an indisputable truth, good for all times, places and situations. Here is absurdity. Liberalism is not the last word, nor does it represent the definite formula in the theme of the art of Government. In this difficult and delicate art, which has to work with the most refractory materials and in a state of movement, since it works on living and not on dead things; in this art, there is not the aristotelian unity of time, of place and of action. Mankind has been more or less well governed in a thousand different ways.

Liberalism is the sun and the method of the nineteenth century, which is not stupid, as Daudet thinks, because there are not stupid centuries nor clever centuries, but there are alternate times of cleverness and stupidity in larger or smaller proportions, in every century. It is not said that the liberal method of government, good for the nineteenth century, for a century that is dominated by two essential phenomena like the development of capitalism, and the affirmation of the sentiment of nationality, must necessarily be fitted for the twentieth century, which already promises to have very different characteristics from those which marked the preceding century. Facts are worth more than books; experience more than doctrines.

Now, the greatest experience which has come to us after the World War in a state of motion under our very eyes—is the defeat of liberalism. In Russia and in Italy it has been shown that it is possible to govern outside, above and against the whole of liberalism's idealogy. Both Communism and Fascism are outside the bounds of liberalism.

But after all is said and done, what does this liberalism, for which all the foes of Fascism today more or less obliquely get excited, consist? Does liberalism mean universal suffrage and such like things? Does it mean to have the Chamber always open, in order that it may present that indecent spectacle which made everybody feel sick? Does it mean to leave, in the name of liberty, to a few the liberty to crush the liberty of all? Does it mean to give a free hand to those who proclaim their hostility against the State and work actively for its destruction? Is this liberalism? Well, if this is liberalism it is a theory and a practice of aberration and of ruin. Liberty is not an end; it is a means. As a means it ought to be controlled and dominated. Here fails this talk of "force."

The liberal gentlemen are asked to tell me if there ever was in history a Government based exclusively on the consent of the people and renouncing the employment of any kind of force. Such a Government has never existed and it never will exist. Consent is as changeable as the sands on the seashore. It cannot always exist. Nor can it ever be entire. No Government has ever existed which has managed to make everybody it governed happy. Whatever solution you happen to give to any problem whatever, you—even were you participants of divine wisdom—must inevitably create a class of malcontents. If so far geometry has not succeeded in squaring the circle, still less have politics managed to do it. Allowing as an axiom that any governmental decision creates discontented people, how are you to prevent this discontent from growing and becoming a danger for the safety of the State? You prevent it by means of force; by surrounding the mass with force; by employing this force without pity when it is necessary to do so. Take away force from any Government whatever—and physical armed force is meant here —and leave only its immortal principles—and that Government will be at the mercy of the first organized group which has made up its mind to beat it.

Now Fascism throws all these anti-vital theories to the scrap heap. When a group or a party is in power it is obliged to fortify itself and to defend itself against all comers. The truth, plain to the eyes of all who are not blinded by dogmatism, is that men are tired, perhaps, of liberty. They have had an orgy of it. Today liberty is no longer the severe and chaste virgin for which generations of the first part of the last century fought and died. For the intrepid youth who, uneasy and alert, face the dawn of new history there are other words which have greater fascination; these are, order, hierarchy, discipline.

This poor Italian liberalism, which goes in search of a greater liberty, groaning and struggling, is very much behind. It is quite outside all understanding and possibility. They talk of seeds which spring will find. Nonsense! Some seeds die under the coat of winter. Fascism, which did not fear to call itself reactionary when many liberals of today were prone before the triumphant beast, has not today any impediment against declaring itself illiberal and anti-liberal. Fascism does not fall a victim to certain commonplace tricks.

Let it be known then, once and for all, that Fascism knows no idol, worships no faith; it has once passed, and, if needful, will turn to pass again, over the more or less decomposed body of the Goddess of Liberty.

BENITO MUSSOLINI

APPENDIX 7

RESOLUTIONS ADOPTED BY THE REPUBLICAN, SOCIALIST, DEMOCRATIC, AND CATHOLIC PARTIES, FOLLOWING THE ASSASSINATION OF MATTEOTTI:

"To send greetings to the memory of Giacomo Matteotti, who, above party divergences, has become by his tragic destiny the symbol of the aspiration of liberty and civil order, in the service of which he was killed in a cowardly manner.

"The horrible character of this crime, so different from other political crimes because it was the result of a plot born in the protection of the high powers of the State, has shocked the public conscience, revealing the existence of a political mentality which cannot be compatible with the state of civilization of the present century. . . .

"Now, in the light of testimony made by the judicial authorities, forced by the pressure of public opinion despite the opposition of the police authorities, we know of the organization, outside the law, called upon to execute the condemnations against political opponents. This organization (Cheka) is grafted on the very organization of the government and directed by the confidants of the Chief of Government (Mussolini).

"In face with these troubling affairs, the assembly . . . serves the supreme interests of the State, unable to distinguish logically and morally the close or distant responsibility of the government. This responsibility is irremediably proven by the solidarity, paid and maintained, between the collaborators, who today have been demasked as the veritable mandatories of the ignoble crime and the constitutional regulation which makes the President of the Council (Mussolini) responsible before Parliament and before the country for the work of his coadjutators. . . .

"The government promises for the future, the work of normalization. . . . The Opposition cannot believe in the efficacy or the sincerity of this promise. They are contradictory, carried out by a party which maintains the intolerable privilege of defending with arms its place in politics.

"The circumstances of the assassination . . . oblige the Opposition to abstain, for the moment, from all parliamentary participation."

APPENDIX 8

EXTRACTS FROM LAW OF DECEMBER 31, 1925, ON THE PRESS

1. Every newspaper or periodical publication shall have a responsible director who . . . must be approved by the Procurator-General attached to the Court of Appeal of the district.

3. The printer and editor must furnish a list of the titles and addresses of all the proprietors.

7. In every town where there is a Court of Appeal there shall be an order of journalists. . . . Those journalists only who are inscribed on the registers of the order may exercise their profession.

ROYAL DECREE OF JULY 15, 1923

2. The Prefect of a province is empowered . . . to address a warning to the manager of a newspaper or periodical publication:

(1) if by means of false or tendentious news it impedes the diplomatic action of the Government in its foreign relations, or injures the national credit at home or abroad, or creates unjustifiable alarm in the population, or disturbs public order;

(2) if by means of articles, comments, notes, headlines, or illustrations it incites to crime or excites class hatred or disobedience to the laws and orders of the public authorities, or compromises the discipline of public servants, or favours the interests of foreign states, societies, or individuals to the prejudice of Italian interests, or holds up to opprobrium the

King, the Royal Family, the Sovereign Pontiff [the Pope], the religion of the state, or the institutions and organs of the state or friendly Powers. . . .

3. On the advice of the Commission referred to in the preceding Article the Prefect may cancel the recognition of a responsible manager to whom two warnings have been addressed in one year.

4. Newspapers or other periodical literature published in contravention of the preceding dispositions may be sequestrated.

SUBSIDIZATION OF VIOLENCE IN FOREIGN COUNTRIES

Under a Fascist law "for the compensation of protagonists in internal civil strife" party members injured in disputes with anti-Fascists were indemnified by the State. To insure the same benefits the Fascisti abroad, notably in France, the United States and South America, the following law, No. 1519, was passed on August 10, 1927, and published in the *Gazzetta ufficiale*, August 30, 1927:

"That the benefits of the law of 1925 are extended, without limit of time, to citizens who beginning on the 23rd of July, 1919, have, in foreign lands, in time of conflicts or aggressions, received bodily harm, etc. . . . provided that they have acted, calculatedly or spontaneously, in a nationalistic manner."

On the initiative of Minister of Justice Rocco the following decree was published October 27, 1927:

"Condemnations for crimes committed for a nationalistic purpose must not be inscribed on the judicial docket."

APPENDIX 9

THE LABOR CHARTER

Art. 1. The Italian nation is an organism, having aims, life, and means of action superior to those of the single or grouped individuals who compose it. It is a moral, political and economic unity which is completely realized in the Fascist State.

Art. 2. Labor in all forms, intellectual, technical and manual, is a social duty. In this sense, and in this sense only, is it protected by the State. From the national point of view all production is a unit; its objects are unitary and can be defined as the wellbeing of the producers and the development of national strength.

Art. 3. Trade or syndicate organization is free. But only the syndicate regularly recognized and placed under the control of the State has the legal right to represent the entire group of employers or of workers for which it is constituted, to guard their interests before the state or other organized economic groups, to draw up collective labor contracts, obligatory on all those belonging to the same group, to impose contributions (taxes) on them and exercise delegated functions of public interest relating to them.

Art. 4. In collective labor contracts, the solidarity of the various factors of production finds its concrete expression in the reconciliation of the opposing interests of employers and workers, and in their subordination to the superior interests of production.

Art. 5. The labor court is the organ through which the State intervenes to solve labor controversies, whether they deal with the observance of contracts or other existing standards, or with the determination of new labor conditions.

Art. 6. Legally organized trade organizations assure legal equality between employers and workers, maintain the discipline of production and labor, and promote its perfection. A corporation constitutes the organization of one field of production and represents its interests as a whole. Since the interests of production are national interests, the corporations are recognized by law as state organizations by virtue of this representation.

Art. 7. The Corporate State considers private initiative in the field of production the most efficacious and most useful instrument in the interest of the nation. Private organization of production being a function of national interest, the organization of the enterprise is responsible to the State for the direction of its production. Reciprocity of the rights and duties is derived from the collaboration of the productive forces. The technician, office employee and worker is an active collaborator in the economic undertaking, the direction of which is the right of the employer, who has the responsibility for it.

Art. 8. Trade associations of employers are obliged to promote in every way the increase and perfection of products and a reduction in costs. The representatives of those who exercise a liberal profession or an art, and the associations of public employees, join in the guardianship of the interests of art, science and letters, in the perfection of production and in the attainment of temporal aims of the corporate system.

Art. 9. The intervention of the State in economic production takes place only when private initiative is lacking or is insufficient, or when the political interests of the State are involved. Such intervention may assume the form of outside control, encouragement or direct management.

Art. 10. Labor disputes which involve groups can have no resort to the Labor Court until the corporation has exhausted its efforts for reconciliation. When individuals are involved in relation to the interpretation of collective contracts, the workers associations are empowered to attempt settlement. . . .

Art. 11. The trade associations are obliged to regulate by means of collective contracts the labor relations between the employers and employees. . . . Every collective labor contract, under penalty of nullification, must contain precise statements . . . of the amount and manner of payment of wages, and the hours of labor.

Art. 12. The syndicate operation, the corporations' mediation and the labor court decisions shall guarantee the relation between wages and normal living costs. . . .

Art. 13. Losses due to crises in business and the fluctuations in exchange must be equally divided between the two elements (capital and labor). . . .

Art. 14. Wages should be paid as best suited to the needs of employee and the undertaking. When payment is by piece-work . . . suitable weekly or fortnightly accountings must be furnished. Night work . . . must be paid at higher rates than day work. . . .

Art. 15. Employees have the right of a weekly rest day, Sunday. . . . Collective contracts . . . shall ensure respect for civil and religious holidays. Employees must scrupulously and earnestly observe working hours.

Art. 16. After a year's uninterrupted service in a concern doing continuous work, the employee has the right to an annual holiday with pay.

Art. 17. In companies functioning the year round the employee has the right in case of discharge through no fault of his own to compensation based on the years of service. Likewise, in case of death.

Art. 18. The transfer of a firm into new hands shall not affect the labor contracts. . . . Illness of an employee does not cancel his contract. Call to service in the army or navy or Fascist militia shall not cause the dismissal of an employee.

Art. 19. Infractions of discipline, and acts disturbing the normal functioning of a concern shall be punished by fine, suspension, or immediate discharge without compensation. . . .

Art. 20. Newly hired employees shall have a period of trial in which the right to cancel the contract is reciprocal and payment only for actual time of work.

Art. 21. Collective labor contracts extends its benefits to workers at home. . . .

Art. 22. The State shall ascertain and control employment and unemployment since these are the indices of production and labor.

Art. 23. Labor exchanges (employment bureaus) shall be controlled by the Corporations. Employers shall be required to engage workers through these exchanges, with freedom of choice among names inscribed except that other things being equal, preference must be given to members of the Fascist Party and of Fascist syndicates in order of seniority of registration.

Art. 24. Professional trades associations must practice selective action among members for the purpose of increasing technical skill and moral value.

Art. 25. The corporations must see that the laws are observed governing safety, preventing accidents, sanitation.

Art. 26. Insurance is an excellent example of the spirit of collaboration between classes. Employers and employees contribute to the cost proportionately. . . .

Art. 27. The Fascist State proposes to bring about

1. Improvement in accident insurance.
2. Improvement in extension of maternity assurance.
3. Compulsory insurance against occupational diseases and tuberculosis, first step towards compulsory insurance against all disease.
4. Improvement in unemployment insurance.
5. Adoption of special marriage endowment for young workers.

Art. 28. It is the duty of the employees associations to protect members administratively and legally in problems arising in connection with accidents or other form of social insurance. . . .

Art. 29. The associations must provide relief for workers they represent whether they be members or non-members. . . .

Art. 30. Education and training, especially technical training, shall be one of the chief duties of the professional trade associations towards members and non-members. They shall support the Dopolavoro (recreational institution) and other national educational enterprises.

APPENDIX 10

THE FASCIST DECALOGUE

I. Know thou that the Fascist, and especially the militiaman, should not believe in perpetual peace.

II. Days spent in prison are always merited.

III. One serves his fatherland even by standing guard at a gasoline tank.

IV. A companion must be a brother, first because he lives with you, and second because he thinks like you.

V. A rifle, the munitions belt, etc., are not intrusted you to be worn at your ease, but to be preserved for war.

VI. Never say "the government will pay," because it is you who pays and the government is that for which you wished and for which you put on the uniform.

VII. Discipline is the sun of the armies; without it there are no soldiers, only confusion and defeat.

VIII. Mussolini is always right.

IX. The volunteer profits by no extenuating circumstances if he disobeys.

X. One thing must be dear to you above all—the life of the Duce.

The Fascist Ten Commandments[2]

1. God and country first: all other affections come after love for these.

2. He who is not ready to sacrifice body and soul to Italy and to serve Mussolini without question is unworthy to wear the black shirt, symbol of Fascism.

3. Use all your intelligence to understand the orders you receive and all your enthusiasm to obey them and carry them out.

4. Discipline is not only a virtue for a soldier in the ranks. It should be a daily and hourly habit.

5. A bad son and a lazy scholar cannot be good Fascists.

6. Employ your time and talents so that work becomes a pleasure and pleasure becomes work.

7. Learn to suffer without grumbling, to be generous without expecting a reward.

8. Carry out good actions to their end; do not leave them only half accomplished.

9. Be daring and courageous in moments of difficulty and desperation.

10. Thank God every day that he has made you an Italian Fascist.

The Apocryphal Fascist Catechism

Five years in the penal islands is the usual punishment for political activity against Fascism. For smaller offenses, one to three years. Thus, one year in prison is the penalty for everyone found possessing the following satire which is being secretly circulated by the many thousands in Italy. It is called the "Catechismo fascista," the ten questions and answers being:

1. Who has created you?
   Mussolini created me.
2. Who is Mussolini?
   He is the eternal father.

[2] Issued by Giovanni Giuriati, Secretary of the Fascist Party, October, 1931.

3. Where is Mussolini?
   Mussolini is in heaven, on the earth, in every part, and he resides in the Viminale.
4. Does Mussolini know everything?
   Mussolini knows everything. He is omniscient.
5. Can Mussolini do everything?
   He can do everything. He is omnipotent.
6. For what purpose did Mussolini create you?
   Mussolini has created me to fight the Bolsheviki.
7. What are the verities revealed by Mussolini?
   They are comprised in the Credo.
8. Do you know the Fascist Credo?
   May I be damned if I don't.
9. Recite it.
   "I believe in Mussolini, the almighty father, creator of Fascism and the Black Shirts, conceived post-bellum, born of Karl Marx and Gabriele d'Annunzio, came into this world under the Red Flag, was crucified, died and was buried, descended into hell, but on the third day was resurrected with a blackjack (manganello) in his right hand and a bottle of castor oil in his left. He conquered Rome and now sits on the Viminale to judge the quick and the dead. I believe in the holy ghost Michele Bianchi, in the holy church of the seat of Fascism, and in the remission of the blackjack on the heads of the Bolsheviki, in the resurrection of the ax in the heads of the Socialists. I believe in the eternal life of Fascism. Amen."
10. Recite the Fascist paternoster.
    "Our Mussolini who is on the Viminale, thy Will be done in the Montecitorio as in the Quirinal. Give us this day our daily squadristi and remit us our blackjacks as we remit them on the heads of our enemies. So be it.
    "Blessed be the squadristi because theirs is the kingdom of Montecitorio. Blessed be the Fascisti, because theirs is the kingdom of the manganello. Blessed be those who accept Fascism because theirs is the kingdom of castor oil. Blessed be those who do not mingle in politics because they will never see the hospitals."

THE BALILLA CREDO[3]

Question: What does it mean to be a Fascist?
Answer: It means that the commandments, precepts, and sacraments of Italy must be observed.
Q. What is its creed?

[3] Denounced in 1926 as sacrilegious by the Bishop of Brescia, with the approval of the Vatican.

A. It is the creed given by the Apostles of Italy and of Fascism.

Q. Of how many articles does it consist?

A. Of twelve articles, as follows:

1. I believe in Rome Eternal, mother of my fatherland
2. And in Italy, her firstborn,
3. Who was born of her virgin womb by the grace of God;
4. Who suffered under the barbarian invader, was crucified, slain and buried;
5. Who descended into the sepulcher, and rose again from the dead in the nineteenth century;
6. Who ascended to Heaven in her glory in 1918 and in 1922 (by the March on Rome);
7. Who is seated at the right hand of Mother Rome;
8. Who will come thence to judge the quick and the dead.
9. I believe in the genius of Mussolini;
10. In our Holy Father Fascism and in the communion of martyrs;
11. In the conversion of the Italians; and
12. In the resurrection of the Empire. Amen!

APPENDIX 11

FASCIST FINANCES

THE PUBLIC DEBT

(in millions of lire)

June 30, 1926	1927	1928	1929	April 30, 1930
82,537	86,666	89,271	91,015	92,242

DEBTS: MUNICIPAL AND LOCAL BODIES

The 93 principal communes Dec. 31, 1925.............. 3,066,000,000
The 93 principal communes Dec. 31, 1927.............. 5,481,000,000

BANKRUPTCIES

(From *Annuario Statistico Italiano 1930*, p. 572, and the *Bollettino Mensile di Statistica*, May, 1930, p. 499)

1923	1924	1925	1926	1927	1928	1929	1931*	1933*
5,352	6,951	7,095	7,631	10,366	10,946	11,478	12,500	14,000

* press report

The Pre-War Decade and the Fascist Decade

In percentages of increase or decrease

	1904-13	1922-32
Foreign commerce	86%	—12%
Steel production	477%	46%
Exports of fabricated goods	194%	34%
Exports of cotton fabrics	118%	36%
Mercantile steamship tonnage	89%	36%
Railroad tonnage	54%	23%
Gold reserve	95%	—40%

(Note: 1913 was a year of crisis comparable to 1929)

THE FASCIST CRISIS

On October 9, 1927, two years before the collapse in Wall Street, Mussolini, addressing parliament, said: "Let us speak frankly, without pious euphemism. There is a crisis. The crisis is grave." Objective economists date the Fascist crisis from 1926; it became intense following the stabilization of the lira. The following official statistics prove these statements:

	1926	1927	1931
Failures	7,631	10,366	12,500
Foreign commerce (billions)	44	36	21
Unemployment (maximums)	181,493	414,283	982,321
Wholesale price index	708	495	328
Gold Reserve, 1927	12,100,000,000	(after stabilization)	
Gold Reserve, Sept., 1932	7,100,000,000		

	1925-6	1931-2
National Income (billions)	100[4]	68[5]
Total taxes	20	22,5
Percentage	20	30

[4] Official.
[5] Mortara, *Prospective economiche.*

APPENDIX 12

Fascism: Its Theory and Philosophy

BY MUSSOLINI

(Written for the Treccani Italian Encyclopædia)

LIKE all sound political concepts, Fascism is both practice and thought, action in which one doctrine is inherent, and a doctrine which, rising from a given system of historical forces, remains bound with it, and works from the inside of this system. There is no concept of the State that is not fundamentally a concept of life: philosophy or intuition, a system of ideas that moves within a logical construction, or is gathered in a vision or in a faith, whatever it is, it is always, at least virtually always, an organic conception of the world.

Thus Fascism would not be understood in many of its practical attitudes, as a party organization, as a system of education, as discipline, if it were not looked at in the light of its general way of conceiving life. It is a spiritual way. The world, for Fascism, is not this material world that appears superficially, in which man is an individual separated from all others, and is governed by a natural law which instinctively leads him to live a life of egoistic and momentary pleasure. The man of Fascism is an individual who is the nation and the motherland, a moral law which brings together individuals and generations in a tradition and a mission, which suppresses the instinct for the closed life in a short round of pleasure, so as to initiate as a duty a superior life free from the limits of time and space: a life in which the individual, through self-abnegation, the sacrifice of his own interests, death itself, realizes that totally spiritual existence in which is the worth of man.

Fascism demands the man active, and engaged in action with all his energies: it demands him vigorously conscious of difficulties, and ready to face them. It conceives of life as a struggle, and that it is up to man to conquer for himself that which is really worthy of him, creating first of all within himself the instrument (physical, moral, intellectual) with which to build himself up. Thus with the individual, thus with the nation, thus with humanity. Hence the high value of culture in all its forms (art, religion, science) and the tremendous importance of education. Hence also the essential value of work, with which man overcomes nature and creates the human world (economic, political, moral and intellectual).

This positive conception of life is evidently an ethical conception. Life, then, as conceived by the Fascist, is serious, austere, religious: poised in a world supported by the moral and responsible forces of the spirit. The Fascist disdains the comfortable life. Fascism is a religious conception, in which the man is viewed in his inherent relationship with a superior law, with an objective will that transcends the particular individual and elevates him to the position of a conscious member of a spiritual society. Those who, in the religious policy of the Fascist régime, have stopped at considerations of mere opportunism, have not understood that Fascism, in addition to being a system of government, is also and first of all a system of thought.

Fascism is an historical conception, in which man is not what he is if he is not functioning fully in the spiritual faith to which he adheres, in the family and social group, in the nation and in that history in which all nations participate. Hence the great value of tradition in the memories, the language, the customs, and the standards of social life. Outside of history, man is nothing. For this reason Fascism is opposed to all individualistic abstractions on materialistic bases of the 18th Century type; and it is opposed to all Jacobin utopias and innovations. It does not believe real happiness to be possible on earth, as it was in the desire of the economic literature of the Settecento, and therefore rejects all conceptions by which, at a certain period in history, there will be a definitive apotheosis of the human race. This means putting oneself outside of history and life, which is a continuous flux and reflux.

Politically, Fascism is a realistic doctrine; practically, it aspires to solve only the problems which are posed historically by themselves and which by themselves find or suggest their own solutions. To act among men, as in nature, one must enter into the process of reality and avail oneself of the forces at the moment.

Anti-individualistic, the Fascist conception is for the State; and it is for the individual (insofar as he coincides with the State) the universal conscience and will of man in his historic existence.

Fascism is against classic liberalism, which rose from the need to react against absolutism, and which has exhausted its historical function since the State was transformed in its own popular conscience and will.

Liberalism denied the State in the interest of the particular individual; Fascism re-affirms the State as the true reality of the individual. And if liberty must be the attribute of the real man, and not of that abstract puppet about which individualistic liberalism thought, Fascism is for liberty. It stands for the liberty which can be a serious matter, the liberty of the State, and of the individual in the State.

For the Fascist, everything is within the State, and nothing human or spiritual exists, and much less has worth, outside of the State. It is in this sense that Fascism is totalitarian, and the Fascist State, synthesized and united by every value and worth, interprets, develops and strengthens the whole life of the people.

Neither individuals outside of the State, nor groups (political parties, associations, syndicates, classes). For this reason Fascism is against socialism, which hardens the historic class struggle and ignores the unity of State which casts the classes in a single economic and moral reality; and, analogously, it is against class syndicalism. But within the orbit of the regulating State, the real needs from which originate socialist and syndicalist movements, are recognized by Fascism and made to count in the corporative system of interests, conciliated within the unity of the State.

Individuals are classed according to the categories of their interests; they are syndicates according to their differentiated but co-interested economic activities; but they are first of all and above all the State. The latter is not a number, like a sum of individuals forming the majority of a people. For that reason Fascism is against the democracy that equalizes a people to its greater number, lowering it to the level of the majority; yet Fascism itself is the purest form of democracy. The people is conceived as it should be, qualitatively, as the most potent idea because it is more moral, more coherent, truer, an idea which in the people is realized as the conscience and will of the few, even of One, and, as an ideal, tends to be realized in the conscience and will of all: of all those who from nature and history, ethnically, find reason to form a nation, bound in the same direction of development and spiritual formation, like a single conscience and will. Not race nor region geographically individualized, but progeny historically perpetuating themselves, multitudes unified by one idea: a will to existence and power, knowledge of self, personality.

This superior personality is, however, a nation only insofar as it is a State. It is not the nation that engenders the State, according to the obsolete naturalistic concept which served as the basis for the publicists of the national States in the 19th Century. On the other hand, the nation is created by the State, which gives the people, conscious of their own moral unity, a will, and therefore an effective existence. The right of a nation to independence derives not from a situation of fact more or less unconscious and inert, but from an active consciousness, from a political will of the moment tending to lay down its own law. The State, in fact, like universal ethical will, is the creator of law.

The nation as State is an ethical reality that exists and lives insofar only as it develops itself. Its halting is its death. Therefore the State not only is the authority that governs and gives form to laws and values to the spiritual life of the individual will but it is also the power that makes its will mean something abroad, making it recognized and respected, or rather, demonstrating with fact its universality in all the necessary determinations of its development. It is thus organization and expansion, at least virtually so. Thus it can be compared with the nature of the human will, which in its development does not recognize barriers, and which realizes itself by testing its own infinity.

The Fascist State, the most potent and highest form of the personality, is a force, but a spiritual one, which sums up all the forms of man's moral and intellectual life. It cannot therefore be limited to simple governmental functions of order and protection, as liberalism used to desire. Fascism is not a simple mechanism which limits the sphere of supposed individual liberty. It is an interior form and norm and a discipline of the whole person; it permeates the will like the intelligence. Its principle, a central inspiration of the human personality living in the civic community, descends deeply and lodges in the heart of the man of action as well as the thinker, of the artist as well as the scientist: it is the soul of the soul.

Fascism, then, is not only a giver of laws and a founder of institutions, but an educator and promoter of spiritual life. It demands to remake not the forms of human life, but the contents: man, character, faith. And to this end it demands a discipline and authority which descends within the spirit and there dominates unchallenged. Hence its sign is the Lictor "fascio," the symbol of unity, strength, and justice.

APPENDIX 13

IL DUCE TELLS FASCIST JOURNALISTS DUTY IS TO SERVE REGIME;
CALLS ITALIAN PRESS FREEST IN THE WORLD AND TELLS EDITORS TO
AVOID PUBLICATION OF CRIMES AND DEAL WITH NATIONAL
PROBLEMS

BY BENITO MUSSOLINI

Premier Mussolini expressed his conception of the Fascist journalist's duty in the following speech delivered before the editors of seventy Italian newspapers who met in Rome on Oct. 10, 1928, for the first time in six years.

COMRADES and Gentlemen: This important meeting of the journalists of the regime takes place only at the end of the sixth year thereof. You understand it could not have taken place before because it is only since January, 1925, and more particularly during the past two years that the problem of the Fascist press has been faced and almost entirely settled. In a regime which embraces everything, as any regime arising from a triumphant revolution should, *the press is an element of that regime, a force at the service of that regime.*

In a unitarian regime the press cannot be extraneous from the whole. This is why the whole Italian press is Fascist and should feel proud to militate compactly under the emblem of the lictor's rods. Starting with this undeniable fact, we immediately have a compass to guide the practical activity of Fascist journalism. We avoid that which is harmful to the regime and do that which helps it. Above all, and we may say it of Italy exclusively and apart from other countries, *journalism, rather than a profession, or trade, becomes a mission of great delicacy and importance, because nowadays it is journalism which circulates among the masses.* After the school has instructed the rising generations, it is journalism which carries on the task of information and formation.

Therefore, it is not absurd that, since we must continue the formative education of the multitude, journalists should be morally and technically trained. It is evident that journalists are not made in schools any more than poets. Nevertheless, nobody can deny the usefulness of schools.

This first meeting of the journalists of the regime is meant to be an honor and recognition. *Those old accusations that Fascist tyranny suffocates the freedom of the press are now entirely discredited. The Fascist press is the freest in the whole world.* Elsewhere newspapers are under orders from plutocratic groups, from parties, from individuals; elsewhere they have been reduced to the melancholy state of exchanging exciting news, the perpetual reading whereof saturates the public mind with a kind of stupefaction, with signs of atony and imbecility; elsewhere journals are grouped in the hands of a very few individuals who consider newspapers as true and personal industry like that of iron or leather.

Italian journalism is free because it serves but one cause and regime; it is free because within the laws of the regime it can and does exercise functions of control, criticism, propulsion. I most absolutely deny that the Italian press is the realm of boredom and uniformity. All who read foreign journals of all countries in the world know how gray, uniform, stereotyped, even to details, is their press. I affirm that Italian Fascist journalism must always and in greater measure differ clearly from that of other countries so as not only to build for the flag which it defends but also be a resolute, visible, very radical antithesis to the press of other lands.

This difference does not exclude another one equally important. *Let me use a musical simile. I consider Italian Fascist journalism as an orchestra. The—la—is common to all instruments. This—la—is not given out by the Government through its press bureaus under some sort of inspiration and suggestion made according to daily contingencies; this—la—is given by Fascist journalism itself. It knows how to serve the regime. It does not wait the word of command every day. It has it in its conscience.*

Once given the—la—there remains diversity of instruments and it is precisely their diversity which prevents cacophony and brings instead full, divine harmony. There is, besides, the diversity of the musicians' temperament, a necessary diversity because this imponderable but vital element makes execution ever more perfect. Each journal should become a well defined, that is, individualized instrument recognizable in the great orchestra. In a modern orchestra stringed instruments do not exclude wind instruments of unusual shape. There can be Fascist journals of serious aspect with perhaps an official tinge, and journals for assault, warlike, headstrong. There can be journals partial to certain problems; those which are big enough to be national, others which must be content as excellent regional or provincial journals.

For instance, it is absurd for a provincial newspaper to soak its readers with whole pages on world foreign policy. Their difference must be bound up with true and proper division of labor based upon Fascist journalism's common sense rather than upon instructions from above.

The national, regional, provincial press serves the regime by reporting its daily task, creating, maintaining an atmosphere and approval of its work.

It is a great adventure to live in this first extraordinary quarter century, a great adventure for you to be able to follow Fascist revolution in its progressive stages. Destiny has been particularly kind to you, permitting you to be journalists during a war and revolution, both rare, memorable events in the history of nations.

Now, do all those who think they serve the regime, serve it effectively, usefully? Not always. Those do not serve it who abandon themselves to laudatory adjectives, singing some obligatory rhyme for conventional purposes about every act and fact, even of small import, or every man even of modest stature. You must deflate and keep your distance. Six years of Fascist revolution are greater than

any words, especially than many words. Nouns make adjectives superfluous.

Nor do those who give excessive space to crimes, featuring them
for copy, serve the regime, nor those who neglect their journal's
make-up, who should take great pains over headlines and text, especially headlines. I read, for instance, of rewards given to the re-
porter who spends his time between prison and hospital for the
headline "Genius and Madness," as though genius inevitably dwelt
in madhouses. Accidents during work become terrifying catastrophes.
You feel bound to report that some young professor shoots his wife,
as if it interested anybody but the janitor and their nearest relations.
For the thousandth time you rehash the mystery of Rudolph at
Mayerling and reprint to boredom the story of Baker, the self-
styled Black Venus. All this is uneducative journalism of old regimes.

The new regime that is Fascist journalism must get off the rocks
of this mentality and set out in search of and write about all other
varied grand aspects, problems of individual and national life. Copy
about crime must be left to police reports, except in those exceptional
cases where great social, human or political interest prevails.

Those do not serve the regime who fail to keep their dignity before
foreigners who are enjoying Italian hospitality, even when they express their opinion about the regime or Mussolini. I repeat that the
highest marks assigned to me, with or without praise by any of these
illustrious personages, leave me entirely indifferent.

Exalt big men, all those who render service to their motherland
and humanity, not those vain ones who like to see themselves pictured
in the act of saluting the unknown warrior. Nor do those serve the
regime who lack discretion, especially in matters of foreign policy
or finance; who are inexact; who go in for Barzinism late in the day;
who cover themselves with incense or, in the heat of argument, stoop
to defamatory remarks and cannibalism. Nor do those who indulge
in the luxury of generic censoriousness and irresponsible moralizing,
who look at all and nobody when precise facts and names are needed
to correct evils betimes; nor those who fail to check facts and judgment passed upon people in their articles, thereby serving their adversaries with evidence against them.

This list of how to serve, or not to serve, the regime could be prolonged, but you already understand me and how to serve the regime.

I wish to stress that, apart from strictly political questions or those fundamentally embedded in the revolution, criticism can, with limitations, be exercised for all other questions. Before monetary reform was introduced I allowed polemics between those favoring and those against revaluation, not only in academic chairs but in reviews and dailies. In part, science, philosophy, a man's Fascist membership ticket must not give him privileges or immunity. *Just as it should be permissible to say that Mussolini as a violin player is a very modest amateur, so it should be permissible to criticise objectively art, prose, poetry or the theatre without any veto. Here party discipline is not at stake nor does revolution come into play.* When a man asks to be judged as poet, playwright, painter, novelist, he has no right to fall back on his party membership when judgment is unfavorable.

Jones or Smith may be a brave Fascist but a deficient poet. You must never give the public the alternative of being anti-Fascist because it hisses, or cowardly because it applauds all literary abortions, all bad poetry, all pictures which are daubs. The membership card gives no talent to those who lack it. I have not said all I could, but I think I have said the essentials. Above all this, your task will grow ever more important, nationally and internationally. Nationally because among other things the Italian people will within a few months' time be summoned to a plebiscite whereby it will record its effective consent to the regime in the eyes of the whole world. You must prepare this great manifestation and you have in your journals a means of doing so worthily.

In international spheres we are not marching toward easy times. The more Italy grows in political, economic, moral stature the more durable Fascist Italy becomes and the greater will be those inevitable reactions in anti-Fascist spheres which seem offended at having a new word of command in political and social camps. For this our press was vigilant, ready, equipped modernly with men who know how to argue with adversaries beyond our frontiers, who above all, are moved not by material but by ideal aims.

I hope that when I again convoke you I shall be able to see that you have always more decidedly, proudly served the cause of revolution. With this hope, accept my cordial greeting, in which there is a little reminiscence and homesickness.

APPENDIX 14

THE FOREIGN POLICIES OF FASCISM

Speech by Premier Mussolini

"Do you remember my speeches last May at Leghorn, Florence, and Milan? I will comment on them long after the event now that the tumult of others' comment appears to have abated. With these speeches I intended to *tear the mask from the face of hypocritical Europe, which stammers of peace at Geneva but prepares for war everywhere.*

"Naturally, those whose mask was torn off tried to invert the situation by representing Italy as the only wolf amid a bleating flock of peaceful lambs. But that trick is puerile. *Italy arms relatively because others arm. She will disarm when all disarm.*

"I repeat that as long as there are cannon they will always be more beautiful than beautiful, but often false, words. When words will be sufficient to regulate relations between peoples then I will say that words are divine.

"Let it be clear, however, that we are arming ourselves spiritually and materially in order to defend ourselves, not in order to attack. Fascist Italy will never take the initiative of war.

"As for Italy's policy on the Danube and in the East, it is dictated by reasons of life. We are trying to utilize the last square inch of our territory. What we are doing is gigantic. But soon our territory will be saturated by our growing population. We wish this and we are proud of this, because life produces life.

"By the year 1950 Italy will be the only *country of young people in Europe*, while the rest of Europe will be wrinkled and decrepit. People will come from over the frontier to see the phenomenon of this blooming Spring of the Italian people.

"Only toward the East can our pacific expansion occur. This explains our friendships and our alliances. The dilemma propounded at Florence still holds good. It goes hard with our enemies already, but we are marching side by side with our friends.

"Our foreign policy is sincere, without evasion or mental reservations. A written agreement is sacred for us whatever may happen. Nor do we know of any other means whereby a people can increase its prestige and the confidence others have in it.

"The longer our régime lasts the more the anti-Fascist coalition has recourse to expedients dictated by desperation. The struggle between the two worlds can permit no compromises. The new cycle which begins with the ninth year of the Fascist régime places the alternative in even greater relief—either we or they, either their ideas or ours, either our State or theirs!

"The new cycle must be of greater harshness, not of greater indulgence. Whoever has interpreted it differently has fallen into a grave error of interpretation. This explains why the struggle has now become world-wide and why Fascismo has become the subject of debate in all countries, here feared, there hated, elsewhere ardently desired.

"The phrase that Fascismo is not an article for exportation is not mine. It is too banal. It was adopted for the readers of newspapers who in order to understand anything need to have it translated into terms of commercial jargon. In any case it must now be amended.

"*Today I affirm that the idea, doctrine and spirit of Fascismo are universal.* It is Italian in its particular institutions, but it is universal in spirit; nor could it be otherwise, for spirit is universal by its very nature. It is therefore possible to foresee a Fascist Europe which will model its institutions on Fascist doctrine and practice, a Europe which will solve in the Fascist way the problems of the modern State of the twentieth century, a State very different from the States which existed before 1789, or which were formed afterward.

"Today even as yesterday the prestige of nations is determined absolutely by their military glories and armed power.

"*Fascism is an army on the march.* Its well-being, therefore, must be guaranteed by methods of safety. The Masons, who are sleeping, may reawaken. By eliminating them we can be sure that they will sleep forever."

"Italy is an immense legion which marches under the Fascist symbols toward a greater future. Nobody can stop her. Nobody will stop her."

(Rome, Oct. 27, 1930, Palazzo Venezia, 8th anniversary eve celebration.)

APPENDIX 15

CAPITALISM AND THE CORPORATE STATE

BY BENITO MUSSOLINI

(November, 1933)

Is this crisis which has afflicted us for four years a crisis in the system or of the system? This is a serious question. I answer: The crisis has so deeply penetrated the system that it has become a crisis of the system. It is no longer an ailment; it is a constitutional disease.

Today we are able to say that the method of capitalistic production is vanquished, and with it the theory of economic liberalism which has illustrated and excused it. I want to outline in a general way the history of capitalism in the last century, which may be called the capitalistic century. But first of all, what is capitalism?

Capitalism is . . . a method of industrial production. To employ the most comprehensive definition: Capitalism is a method of mass production for mass consumption, financed en masse by the emission of private, national and international capital. Capitalism is therefore industrial and has not had in the field of agriculture any manifestation of great bearing.

I would mark in the history of capitalism three periods: the dynamic period, the static period and the period of decline.

The dynamic period was that from 1830 to 1870. It coincided with the introduction of weaving by machinery and with the appearance of the locomotive. Manufacturing, the typical manifestation of industrial capitalism, expanded. This was the epoch of great expansion and hence of the law of free competition; the struggle of all against all had full play.

In this period there were crises, but they were cyclical crises, neither long nor universal. Capitalism still had such vitality and such power of recovery that it could brilliantly prevail.

There were also wars. They cannot be compared with the World War. They were brief. Even the War of 1870, with its tragic days at Sedan, took no more than a couple of seasons.

During the forty years of the dynamic period the State was watching; it was remote, and the theorists of liberalism could say: "You, the State, have a single duty. It is to see to it that your administration does not in the least turn toward the economic sector. The better you govern the less you will occupy yourself with the problems of the economic realm." We find, therefore, that economy in all its forms was limited only by the penal and commercial codes.

But after 1870, this epoch underwent a change. There was no longer the struggle for life, free competition, the selection of the strongest. There became manifest the first symptoms of the fatigue and the devolution of the capitalistic method. There began to be agreements, syndicates, corporations, trusts. One may say that there was not a sector of economic life in the countries of Europe and America where these forces which characterize capitalism did not appear.

What was the result? The end of free competition. Restricted as to its borders, capitalistic enterprise found that, rather than fight, it was better to concede, to ally, to unite by dividing the markets and sharing the profits. The very law of demand and supply was now no longer a dogma, because through the combines and the trusts it was possible to control demand and supply.

Finally, this capitalistic economy, unified, "trustified," turned toward the State. What inspired it to do so? Tariff protection.

Liberalism, which is nothing but a wider form of the doctrine of economic liberalism, received a death blow. The nation which, from the first, raised almost insurmountable trade barriers was the United States, but today even England has renounced all that seemed traditional in her political, economic and moral life, and has surrendered herself to a constantly increasing protectionism.

After the World War, and because of it, capitalistic enterprise became inflated. Enterprises grew in size from millions to billions. Seen from a distance, this vertical sweep of things appeared as something monstrous, babel-like. Once, the spirit had dominated the material;

now it was the material which bent and joined the spirit. Whatever had been physiological was now pathological; all became abnormal.

At this stage, super-capitalism draws its inspiration and its justification from this utopian theory: the theory of unlimited consumers. The ideal of super-capitalism would be the standardization of the human race from the cradle to the coffin. Super-capitalism would have all men born of the same length, so that all cradles could be standardized; it would have babies divert themselves with the same playthings, men clothed according to the same pattern, all reading the same book and having the same taste for the movies—in other words, it would have everybody desiring a single utilitarian machine. This is in the logic of things, because only in this way can super-capitalism do what it wishes.

When does capitalistic enterprise cease to be an economic factor? When its size compels it to be a social factor. And that, precisely, is the moment when capitalistic enterprise, finding itself in difficulty, throws itself into the very arms of the State; it is the moment when the intervention of the State begins, rendering itself ever more necessary.

We are at this point: that, if in all the nations of Europe the State were to go to sleep for twenty-four hours, such an interval would be sufficient to cause a disaster. Now, there is no economic field in which the State is not called upon to intervene. Were we to surrender —just as a matter of hypothesis—to this capitalism of the eleventh hour, we should arrive at State capitalism, which is nothing but State socialism inverted.

This is the crisis of the capitalist system, taken in its universal significance. . . .

Last evening I presented an order in which I defined the new corporation system as we understand it and wish to make it.

I should like to fix your attention on what was called the object: the well-being of the Italian people. It is necessary that, at a certain time, these institutions, which we have created, be judged and measured directly by the masses as instruments through which these masses may improve their standard of living. Some day the worker, the tiller of the soil, will say to himself and to others: "If today I am better off practically, I owe it to the institutions which the Fascist revolution has created."

We want the Italian workers, those who are interested in their status as Italians, as workers, as Fascists, to feel that we have not created institutions solely to give form to our doctrinal schemes, but in order, at a certain moment, to give positive, concrete, practical and tangible results.

Our State is not an absolute State. Still less is it an absolutory State, remote from men and armed only with inflexible laws, as laws ought to be. Our State is one organic, human State which wishes to adhere to the realities of life. . . .

Today we bury economic liberalism. The corporation plays on the economic terrain just as the Grand Council and the militia play on the political terrain. Corporationism is disciplined economy, and from that comes control, because one cannot imagine a discipline without a director.

Corporationism is above socialism and above liberalism. A new synthesis is created. It is a symptomatic fact that the decadence of capitalism coincides with the decadence of socialism. All the Socialist parties of Europe are in fragments.

Evidently the two phenomena—I will not say conditions—present a point of view which is strictly logical: there is between them a historical parallel. Corporative economy arises at the historic moment when both the militant phenomena, capitalism and socialism, have already given all that they could give. From one and from the other we inherit what they have of vitality.

We have rejected the theory of the economic man, the Liberal theory, and we are, at the same time, emancipated from what we have heard said about work being a business. The economic man does not exist; the integral man, who is political, who is economic, who is religious, who is holy, who is combative, does exist.

Today we take again a decisive step on the road of the revolution.

Let us ask a final question: Can corporationism be applied to other countries? We are obliged to ask this question because it will be asked in all countries where people are studying and trying to understand us. There is no doubt that, given the general crisis of capitalism, corporative solutions can be applied anywhere. But in order to make corporationism full and complete, integral, revolutionary, certain conditions are required.

There must be a single party through which, aside from economic discipline, enters into action also political discipline, which shall serve as a chain to bind the opposing factions together, and a common faith.

But this is not enough. There must be the supremacy of the State, so that the State may absorb, transform and embody all the energy, all the interests, all the hopes of a people.

Still, not enough. The third and last and the most important condition is that there must be lived a period of the highest ideal tension.

We are now living in this period of high, ideal tension. It is because step by step we give force and consistency to all our acts; we translate in part all our doctrine. How can we deny that this, our Fascista, is a period of exalted, ideal tension?

No one can deny it. This is the time in which arms are crowned with victory. Institutions are remade, the land is redeemed, cities are founded.

APPENDIX 16

Volte-face Caesar

If consistency in these pragmatic realistic days can still be regarded as a jewel, then our present Caesar should well crown himself with the largest and finest diadems of India and the Rand. For, *mirabile dictu,* the man who has belonged to every party and to many creeds, who has changed his coat and his face, his religion and his policies more often than any statesman of our time if not in history, is by this very virtue, the consistency of living a lifetime of almost annual inconsistencies, entitled to the jeweled honors.

It was Talleyrand who changed his parties often but never his opinions—at least we have his word for that—but it is our present Duce who has changed his opinions and never his party. For his party has never been the Socialist or Communist or Anarchist or Clerical or Republican or Fascist; it has been his own. He was true to one party—and that was himself, said Mr. Lowell of another older politician, and in our case the party has no officially registered name, but is the driving ego and the oft-announced inscrutable will of the demigod. Fascism is Mussolini; Mussolini is Fascism, cry the followers and worshipers, and that explains everything.

It is also Lowell who claims that the foolish and the dead alone never change their opinions; and herewith follow many opinions and also certain unchangeable facts. (The letter A or a number refers to the Duce's Autobiography. Documentation for all the other quotations is on hand.)

WAR AND PEACE

"Fascism believes neither in the possibility nor the utility of permanent peace. . . . War alone brings up to its highest tension all human energy and puts the stamp of nobility upon the peoples who have the courage to face it."—Written for the new Italian Encyclopedia.

"Three cheers for war! May I be permitted to raise this cry? Three cheers for Italy's war, noble and beautiful above all, with its 500,000 dead who are our surest wealth. And three cheers for war in general."

"I repeat that so long as there are cannon they will always be more beautiful than beautiful and often false words."

"Italy will never take the initiative of starting a war. Italy needs peace."—Christmas 1931 broadcast to the United States.

"We are arming ourselves spiritually and materially in order to defend ourselves, not in order to attack. Fascist Italy will never take the initiative of war."

"I should like to contradict the many rumors spread abroad about Fascism and the danger it is supposed to represent for the peace of the world. Such accusations are groundless. Neither I nor my government nor the Italian people desire to bring about a war."—Christmas broadcast.

"Mine is a policy of peace." (A)

THE LEAGUE OF NATIONS

"A congress of laymen, fantastics, impotents, and by these very facts dangerous."

Mussolini in 1919 spoke in favor of Wilson and the League. Cf. first edition of *Discorsi*, pp. 53 and 147.

"Fascism does not believe in the principles which inspire the pretended League of Nations. In that League the nations are not on an equal footing; it is a sort of Holy Alliance of the plutocratic nations, made to give the French-Anglo-Saxon group, despite their diverse interests, the exploitation of the largest part of the world."—October 1919, at Fascist Congress, Florence.

"We must stay in the League of Nations for the reason that others are in it, others who might be glad if we were to withdraw and who would arrange their affairs and protect their interests without us and possibly at our expense."

"We shall remain in the League of Nations especially as today the League is very sick and we must not abandon it."— Fascist anniversary discourse, October 1932.

"The League of Nations—a sort of monstrous idealistic-plutocratic abortion. . . ."

"The League of Nations declared itself incompetent to solve the [bombardment of Corfu] incident."—Autobiography, p. 25.

The League immediately declared its competence; Mussolini threatened to withdraw.

FINANCE AND ECONOMICS

(The budget deficit of six billions) "had come down to me as a legacy from the errors and

Preceding premiers had cut the deficit of 25 billions to six and prepared a balanced budget for weaknesses of those who had preceded me." (261)

"I would never approve of subjecting inheritance to a taxation which had almost assumed a Socialistic character of expropriation." (263)

"In December, 1927, at a meeting of the council of ministers, I was able to announce . . . the lire on a gold basis, on a ratio which technicians and profound experts in financial questions have judged sound." (271)

"I had not only led the Black Shirts and political forces, but I had solved a complex and difficult problem of national finance." (271)

"Today (1928) we have a balanced budget." (271)

"The provinces and communes have balanced their budgets." (272)

"We needed a strong capitalist tradition." (147)

1922-23, according to the official report of the first Fascist Finance Minister.

"Confiscation of the super-profits of war; heavy taxation on inheritance; partial expropriation of capital."—Original Fascist program and editorial, *Popolo,* April 20, 1921.

Secretary of the Treasury Andrew W. Mellon, friend of Finance Minister Volpi, and numerous experts advised Mussolini against the ratio.

The loss through this artificial stabilization was 3,500,000,000 lire according to neutral economists; the stupidity of the gesture has now been recognized even by Rome correspondents.

(This is not true; see text.)

Fascist Senator Ricci, May 30, 1930, announced the increase in deficit from 1926 to 1928 as 50 per cent for the 17 largest communes.

"I do not intend to defend capitalism or capitalists."—Address to first meeting of Fascisti (quoted by Sarfatti).

October, 1926, Mussolini officially announced the successful Littorio bond issue of five billion lire as oversubscribed.

January, 1927, Ex-Finance Minister De Stefani in speech incidentally mentioned the Littorio bond issue as reaching 2,500,000,-000 lire.

Religion

"My deep religious beliefs." (16)
"A Catholic, like myself." (31)
"I asked the assistance of God." (185)

"There is no God."—Mussolini's first published work. "Religion is an absurdity . . . immoral . . . a malady."—Speech in Lausanne.

The Press

"Italian journalism is free."—Signed article in *N. Y. World.*
"You express an error if you suppose that I have suppressed the liberty of the press. All newspapers are free. . . ."—Mass interview with the press, January, 1927.

"All the journals of the Opposition have been suppressed." —Chamber of Deputies declaration, May 26, 1927, referring to events of November, 1926.

General

"To me money is detestable." (38)
"Money has no lure for me." (205)
And four more similar references.

Congratulating Mussolini on being the first to pay the new income taxes, the official Fascist press announced the amount as 200,000 lire, indicating an income of 500,000 lire, or a capital of 10,000,000.

"I have always had against me

In 1922 Freemasonry helped

our Masonry . . . this leprosy."
(158)

"Fiume, most Italian of cities."
(76)

"Fascism will never throw itself at the feet of the king."—
Popolo d'Italia.

"Our formula is this: everything within the State, nothing
outside the State, nothing against
the State."

"It is false that the danger
menacing our country, Bolshevism . . . had disappeared. . . .
Bolshevik activity was most intense (in 1921)."—Signed article, written for the United
Press.

"The death punishment? But
that is a joke, Gentlemen . . .
capital punishment cannot be the
reprisal of a Government." (229)

"An underhand manœuvre by

subsidize Fascism and coöperated
with it until the Matteotti assassination in 1924.

Grossisch, d'Annunzio's president of Fiume, admitted expelling 5,000 before the plebiscite
which Italy won by two hundred
or so.

"From today, intrusted with
the confidence of His Majesty
the King. . . ."—Proclamation
by Mussolini after kissing the
King's hand and taking office.

"Down with the State, the
State of yesterday, today, and tomorrow. . . . There remains for
me nothing but the consoling religion of Anarchism."—*Popolo
d'Italia*, April 6, 1920.

"Bolshevism is conquered."—
Popolo, July 2, 1921.

Over the objection of the King,
Mussolini restored the death penalty following one of the attempts
at assassination.

Ricciotti Garibaldi, grandchild,

some short-weight grandchildren of Garibaldi." (234)

arrested in France, confessed being a Fascist spy in the service of the Duce.

"He [Zaniboni, would-be assassin] . . . having an Austrian rifle with fine sights, the fellow could not miss his aim." (237)

"A Fascist agent worked with Zaniboni for months and chose the day. Being on the wrong side of the building, Zaniboni could not have seen, much less shot, Mussolini."—William Bolitho, *New York World.*

ASSASSINATION OF MATTEOTTI

"I did not have a moment of doubt or discouragement." (223)

"I never lost my calm nor my sense of balance and justice. . . . I ordered the guilty to be arrested. I wanted justice to follow its unwavering course. Now I have fulfilled my task as a just man."

"The Matteotti affair caused him such terrible suffering that for a while his life seemed wrecked."—Sarfatti.

"The sequestration of Matteotti belongs morally to Fascism."—Speech, January, 1925. Most of the murderers were freed and restored to positions in the Fascist party; Filippelli went to jail in 1931 for swindling.

"It has been said that I have founded a Cheka. Where? When? In what way? Nobody is able to say. . . . An Italian Cheka never has had the shadow of existence." (227)

"On September 1, 1922, Cesare Rossi, the political secretary, announced the formation of the Corpo di Polizia Fascisti in Milan to 'purify' the Fascist ranks by eliminating all half-hearted elements."—Beals.

"The mother idea of the Cheka was Mussolini's."—Rossi memorandum.

In 1931 the Fascist government officially announced that its

Cheka—the O.V.R.A.—had been extended for a second period of five years.

THE WORLD WAR

"I had been the most tenacious believer in the war." (A)

For almost three months every editorial signed by Mussolini in *Avanti* denounced the war. One was headlined, "Absolute neutrality."

"Germany began to influence Italian public opinion with methods of propaganda that irritated the sensitiveness of our race. They enraged me." (A)

"The tragic rape of Belgium." (A)

Addressing Milan Socialists in August, 1914, Mussolini asked support for Germany, saying Socialism was strongest there and would triumph after the war. He also said, "Why become excited over the fate of a little nation? It is right that the small go down and that German Imperialism wins."

"I created the Fascisti—a group of daring youths who believed that intervention could be forced. . . . I was their leader." (A)

This is absolutely untrue. The original Fascio of Intervention was founded by enemies of Mussolini and were frequently attacked by him in July to September, 1914. He joined them in October or later that year.

CHRONOLOGY

1883	July 29	Mussolini born at Dovia, commune of Predappio, province of Forli.
1901		Obtains teacher's license; first post at Gualtieri, in Reggio Emilia.
1902	Jan. 3	Went to Switzerland in search of work and to escape military service.
	July	Arrested at Lausanne for vagabondage.
1903	Sept.	Expelled from Berne. Went to Geneva. Called for military service.
1904	March 6	Debate with Tagliatela: "God does not exist."
	April	Declared deserter at Forli.
		Arrested in Geneva for falsifying passport; expelled.
	Dec. 31	Presented himself at Forli for military service in the 10th Bersaglieri regiment.
1906	Nov. 27	Schoolmaster at Tolmezzo.
1908	Feb. 25	Schoolmaster at Oneglia.
	July 22	Sentenced at Predappio to 8 months imprisonment and 200-lire fine for "armed revolt."
	Sept. 10	Sentenced by the municipal judge of Mendola to 100-lire fine for revolutionary expression.
1909	March	Went to Trento, Austria, to work on the *Avvenire*; secretary of the Socialist Party local.
	Sept.	Expelled from Austria for revolutionary writing.
	Oct.	Became leading Socialist at Forli.
	Nov. 10	Arrested and imprisoned ten days for radicalism.
1910	Jan. 2	Published *La Lotta di Classe* (The Class Struggle).
	April 14	Paid secretary of Forli Socialist local.
	Sept. 17	Represented local at Florence Socialist congress.
1911	Sept. 25	Organized armed uprising against Tripoli war.
	Sept. 28	Sentenced to five months' imprisonment.

1912	March 14	Approved the attempted assassination of the King.
	July	Socialist Congress at Reggio Emilia; Mussolini becomes nationally known; becomes director of Socialist Party.
	Dec. 1	Editor of *Avanti*; extreme radical Socialist.
1913		Publishes *John Huss*, with preface attacking Catholic Church.
	Oct.	Defeated candidate for the electoral college.
1914	April	Ancona congress; proposes expulsion of Freemasons from Socialist Party.
	June 7	Mussolini "patron saint" of the Red Week, revolutionary attempt to seize and occupy the factories.
	Aug. 4	Socialist Party declares for Italian neutrality.
	Sept. 9	Mussolini denounces Belgian sentimentality.
	Oct. 13	Prezzolini in *La Voce* notes Mussolini has changed his anti-interventionist policy.
	Oct. 25	Socialist Party accuses Mussolini of treason. Deputy Treves accuses Mussolini of selling out to France.
	Nov. 15	Mussolini issues the *Popolo d'Italia* with funds supplied by the French propaganda department.
	Nov. 23	Mussolini expelled from the Socialist Party "for moral and political betrayal."
1915	April 19	Arrested in Rome for organizing interventionists.
	April 29	Wounded by Treves in duel.
	May 15	Italy declares war on Austro-Hungary.
	Sept. 1	Mussolini called to the colors.
	Dec. 9	Taken to hospital, suffering from gastro-enteritis.
1916	March 10	Fights duel with General Count Spingardi.
1917	Feb. 23	Taken to hospital for removal of shell splinters.
	Aug.	"I took my place as a fighter in my newspaper office."
	Oct.	Italy defeated at Caporetto.
	Nov.	Organization of Fasci di Resistenza.
1918	Oct.	Victory of Vittorio Veneto.

	Nov.	Armistice.
1919	Jan.	Organization of Partito Popolare (Catholic Party).
	March 23	Mussolini, Marinetti, Cesare Rossi and others found the Fascio Italiani di Combattimento in accordance with the suggestions of d'Annunzio.
	March 24	"We are for a Republic; we are absolutely against dictatorship."
	Sept. 12	D'Annunzio occupies Fiume.
		Mussolini defeated for Chamber of Deputies.
	Nov. 10	"We will accept no dictatorship."
1920	April 20	Fascist program includes confiscation of war profits; confiscation of lands, etc.
	Sept. 1-19	Occupation of the factories by workmen; approved by Mussolini.
	Dec. 22-26	Allies bombard d'Annunzio.
	Dec. 29	D'Annunzio quits Fiume.
	Dec. 31	Mussolini writes "Bolshevism has been dyked."
1921	Jan.	Socialist Congress at Livorno expells Communists.
	May 15	Mussolini elected Fascist deputy.
	Aug. 3	Makes peace pact with labor and Socialists.
	Nov.	Partito Nazionale Fascista formed.
1922	Aug. 3	Fascist armed mobilization and violence destroys attempt at general strike protesting Fascist violence.
	Oct. 24	Fascist congress at Naples.
	Oct. 27	Mussolini returns to Milan.
	Oct. 27-29	Mussolini barricades his office while Fascisti "march" on Rome.
	Oct. 29	King calls Mussolini to premiership.
	Oct. 30	Mussolini arrives in Rome via Pullman train; reviews victorious Fascisti with King.
	Nov. 16	Mussolini demands dictatorial powers.
	Nov. 19	Abolishes commission exposing war profiteers (Decree No. 487).
	Dec.	Massacre of workingmen in Turin.

1923	Feb.	Creation of Fascist militia.
	Aug. 23	Murder of Father Minzoni.
	Aug. 27	Five members of Italian delegation assassinated on Albanian side of Albano-Greek border.
	Aug. 31	Mussolini occupies Corfu; massacre of children in American orphanage.
	Sept. 3	Mussolini refuses League of Nations intervention.
1924	Jan.	Treaty with Yugoslavia.
	March	Democrats and Socialists quit government.
	April 4	Fascisti win elections through terrorism; Brianza sacked.
	June 11	Assassination of Matteotti.
	Aug.	Abolition of free press.
1925	June	Augusteo speech: "Violence is profoundly moral."
	Nov. 4	Attempted assassination by Zaniboni; abolition of Freemasonry.
1926	April 7	Attempted assassination by Miss Gibson.
	Aug. 30	Podestá system; municipal elections abolished.
	Sept. 11	Attempted assassination by Lucetti.
	Oct. 31	Bullet fired at Mussolini; Zamboni, Fascist youth in uniform, lynched by Mussolini's entourage.
	Nov. 4	General Ricciotti Garibaldi and Colonel Macia arrested in France; Garibaldi confesses receiving large sums as Fascist agent provocateur.
1927	Jan. 5	Mussolini announces "end of epoch of reprisals, devastations, and violence. Squadrismo must disappear."
	Jan. 24	Pope dissolves Catholic Boy Scouts and protests Fascist monopolization of youth.
	April 21	Fascist Labor Charter abolishes strikes.
	July 2	Mont Blanc christened Monte Mussolini by Fascisti.
	Oct. 22	Manhood suffrage abolished by decree.
	Oct. 27	Decree justifying crimes committed for nationalistic purposes.

	Dec. 21	Stabilization of lira on gold basis announced.
1928	Jan. 23	Fascist arms for Hungary and Hitler found at St. Gothard.
	March 30	Mussolini abolishes Catholic Boy Scouts and other non-Fascist youth organizations.
		Fascism celebrates first anniversary of Corporate State.
	April 14	Mussolini tells peasants price outlay not equaled by crop in "Battle of the Grain."
	June 2	Mussolini expelled from National Press Club, Washington, in resolution charging suppression of the press and denial of personal liberty.
	Sept. 21	Fascism made permanent government; Grand Council, not King, to appoint future premiers.
1929	Feb. 11	Mussolini and Cardinal Gasparri sign Vatican peace treaty.
	March 24	Italy votes Fascist majority; opposition parties not permitted to name candidates.
	April 10	Corporate State announced in force.
	June 7	Pope becomes ruler of Vatican State.
1930	June	Mussolini tours North Italy, making militaristic speeches against France.
	July 23	Writes article favoring revision Versailles Treaty in favor of Germany and Hungary.
	Oct.	New Fascist criminal code abolishes jury system.
	Nov. 20	Military training for youth extended.
	Dec.	In Christmas broadcast Mussolini says, "Italy will never take the initiative of starting a war. Italy needs peace."
1931	Jan. 26	Major-General Butler, U. S. Marines, tells Contemporary Club, Philadelphia, Mussolini ran over child; Ambassador de Martino protests.
	Feb.	International Committee for Political Prisoners, Civil Liberties Union, Ligue des Droits

d'Hommes, Oxford and Cambridge professors protest arrest of intellectuals in Italy.

March 6   Grand Council extends O. V. R. A. (Fascist
            Cheka) for another five years.

April 27   Zamora, President Spanish Republic, cables anti-
            Fascist organizations offering Spain as ref-
            uge.

June 29   To avoid censorship, Pope smuggles encyclical to
            Paris denouncing Fascist "irreverencies, in-
            decencies, destruction, confiscation, and van-
            dalism . . ."; declares Fascism and Catholi-
            cism incompatible.

1932 June 30   Mussolini announces Fascism has support of en-
            tire population; secret tribunal announces re-
            sults February, 1927, to date: 9 sentenced to
            death, 257 to 6,076 years' imprisonment;
            1,391 to 4,040 years; 584 awaiting trial;
            total arrests and tried, 12,000—for political
            offenses.

Aug.   Marriage and birth rate reach lowest point.

Oct.   Domenico Bovone and his mistress charged with
            plotting assassination of Mussolini. Angelo
            Sbardellotto accused of attempting assas-
            sination, admits plot as revenge for execution
            of Michele Schirru, recently executed for
            similar offense. Bovone and Sbardellotto
            executed.

1933 Jan.   Preliminary budget report, 1933-1934, shows defi-
            cit 2,900,000,000 lire; with losses in move-
            ment of capital, deficit of 3,088,000,000 lire
            foreseen, or double deficit current year.

Feb. 11   Italian army planes sold Hungary in violation of
            treaty.

Sept. 19   Mussolini announces for German rearmament.

1934 March   Mussolini announces "a plan, not for five years or
            ten years, but for sixty years . . . at which
            time Italy will have the primacy of the

world. . . . Our future lies in Asia and Africa. . . ."

June   Corporative State voted.

Italians kill ten Greeks in Rhodes uprising.

1935   Encounter at Ual-Ual; Mussolini refuses arbitration by League of Nations, and moves troops to Ethiopia for war of conquest.

BIBLIOGRAPHY

✱ ✱

BIBLIOGRAPHY

Balabanoff, Angelica	*Erinnerungen und Erlebnisse.* *Wesen und Werdegang des Italianischen Fascismus.*
Barnes, Major J. S.	*Fascism.*
Beals, Carleton	*Rome or Death.*
Béraud, Henri	*Ce qui j'ai vu à Rome.*
Bolitho, William	*Italy under Mussolini.*
Bordeux, Jeanne	*Benito Mussolini the Man.*
Borghi, Armando	*Mussolini in camicia.*
Buozzi, Bruno and Nitti, Vincenzo	*Fascisme et Syndicalisme, Paris, 1930.*
Chiesa, Eugene	*The Political, Financial and Economic Situation in Italy, Paris, 1929.*
Child, Richard Washburn	*A Diplomat Looks at Europe.*
Einzig, Paul	*Economic Foundations of Fascism.*
Elwin, William	*Fascism at Work.*
Ferrero, Guglielmo	*Four Years of Fascism.*
Fiori, Vittorio	*Mussolini the Man of Destiny.*
Garibaldi, Ricciotti	*Le Fascisme et l'Italie.*
Gentile, Giovanni	*The Philosophic Basis of Fascism, Foreign Affairs, January, 1928.*
Goad, H. E.	*The Making of the Corporate State.*
Gorgolini, Pietro	*Le Fascisme.*
Haider, Carmen	*Capital and Labor under Fascism.* *Do We Want Fascism?*
Kemechey, L.	*Il Duce.*
King, Bolton	*Fascism in Italy.*
Ludwig, Emil	*Talks with Mussolini.*
Machiavelli	*Le Prince. Preface de Benito Mussolini.*

445

McGuire, Constantine E. — *Italy's International Economic Position (Institute of Economics, 1926).*

Malaparte, Curzio — *L'Art de Coup d'État.*

Matteotti, G. — *The Fascisti Exposed, London, 1924.*

Mowrer, Edgar Ansell — *Immortal Italy.*

Mussolini, Benito — *Campo di Maggio (with G. Forzano).*
Dieu n'existe pas (1904).
John Huss.
Mussolini as revealed in his political speeches.
My Autobiography.
My War Diary.
Socialismo e difesta armata.
The Cardinal's Mistress.

Nenni, P. — *La Lutte des classes en Italie, Paris, 1930.*

Nitti, F. F. — *Nos prisons et notre evasion, Paris, 1930 (translated and published in abridged edition in the United States under the title "Escape").*

Nitti, Francesco — *Bolshevism, Fascism and Democracy.*

Nomad, Max — *Rebels and Renegades.*

Page, Kirby (editor) — *A New Economic Order.*

Phillips, Sir Percival — *The Red Dragon and the Black Shirts.*

Por, Ödön — *Fascism.*

Prezzolini, Giuseppe — *Fascism.*

Roberts, Kenneth L. — *Black Magic.*

Ronin, Paul — *L'Ombre sur Rome.*

Salvemini, Gaetano — *Mussolini Diplomate, Paris, 1932.*
The Fascist Dictatorship, 1927.

Sarfatti, Margherita G. — *The Life of Benito Mussolini.*

Schneider, Herbert W. — *Making the Fascist State.*

Schneider, Herbert W. and Clough, Shepherd B. — *Making Fascists.*

Sforza, Carlo — *Makers of Modern Europe.*
European Dictatorships.

Strachey, John	*The Menace of Fascism.*
Sturzo, Don Luigi	*Italy and Fascismo.*
Suckert (Malaparte), Curzio	*Social, Moral and Economic Conflicts of Fascism.*
Survey, The	*Fascism, a symposium, March 1, 1927.*
Trentin, Sylvio	*L'Aventure Italienne.*
Turati, Augusto	*A Revolution and its Leader.*
Valois, Georges	*Finances Italiennes, Paris, 1930.*
Villari, Luigi	*The Awakening of Italy, London, 1924.*
	The Fascist Experiment, London, 1926.

★ ★

Index

Addis Ababa, 363

Adler, Felix, 367

"Agenzia Stefani, The," 329

Agenelli, Signor, 94

Alba, Santiago, exiled, 266

Albertini, Luigi, 3, 37, 176

Albini, Signor, 61

Alessandro, father of Mussolini, 12-16, 18, 244

Alexander the Great, 370, 372

Alliances, 3, 59

Allies, 3, 5, 12, 50, 52, 57, 70, 83, 272

All Quiet on the Western Front, 345

Alsace-Lorraine, 53

Ambris, Alceste, de, writer, 67, 76, 80, 393

Ambrosiano, 321

Amendola, deputy, 156, 161, 176-179, 180, 195, 206

America, 26, 27, 51, 84, 113

American embassy, 83

American Federation of Labor, 294

American Industrial Workers, 280

American Mercury, 290, 346

American oil deal, 207

American prosperity, 296

American Red Cross, 263

American war crisis, 3, 70

Anarchism, 34, 48, 358

Anatolia, Turkey, 265

Anglo-American budgets, 306

Annuities, list of, 307

Annunziata, 72

Ansoldo enterprise, 147

Anti-Fascists, deported, 239, 292, 293

Anti-Semitism, 340

Aosta, Duke of, 116, 121, 125

Arditi, 74, 75

Aristotle, scientist, 362

Armistice Day in Italy, 225

Arms, sending of, 271

Arpinati, Leandro, 223

Articles on Duce, 53, 64-67, 72, 76, 84, 88, 102, 127, 191, 221, 277, 280, 289, 319

Ashbourne, Baron, 226

Aspettati, Armando, 61

Assassination, Austrian Archduke, 48

Assassinations, 170-174, 209, 262

Assassins, hired, 142, 152, 222

Associated Press, 228, 229, 274, 293, 299, 323, 328, 329, 354

Atheism, 33 to end

Athens, 52

Aulard, Professor, 277

Austria, 3, 18, 35, 37, 38, 43, 50, 58, 72, 155

Austria Commune, 5

Austria, hatred of, 4

Authoritarian State, 356, 360-362

Avanguardista Legions, 320, 340, 378

Avanti, Italy's official organ, 3-7, 11, 20, 23, 24, 43, 45, 48, 54, 60, 103, 114, 125, 142, 143, 157, 227, 394

Aventine, 162, 195

Avignon, 245

Azione Cattolica, 106, 255, 256, 259

Babeuf, 30

Bacci, Giovanni, 23

Badoglio, General, 116, 127

Bakunin, 13

Balabanoff, Dr. Angelica, Mussolini's benefactress, 34, 39, 40, 43-47, 60, 134, 141

Balbo, Gen. Italo, aviator, 206, 216-218, 223, 228, 321, 343

Baldesi, 188, 189

Balilla, 148, 340, 347, 409

Balkans, trouble in, 87

Baltimore Sun, 327

Banca di Roma, 147

Banking houses, 267, 305

Banking interests, 52, 267

449

DATE DUE

GAYLORD — PRINTED IN U.S.A.